ARABIC CULTURE

THROUGH ITS LANGUAGE AND LITERATURE

M.H. BAKALLA
Professor
King Saud University, Riyadh
Kingdom of Saudi Arabia

ARABIC CULTURE
THROUGH ITS LANGUAGE AND LITERATURE

KEGAN PAUL INTERNATIONAL
London, Boston, Melbourne and Henley
1984 (1404 AH)

This edition first published in 1984
by Kegan Paul International Ltd
39 Store Street, London WC1E 7DD,
9 Park Street, Boston,
Mass. 02108, USA,
464 St Kilda Road, Melbourne,
Victoria 3004, Australia, and
Broadway House, Newtown Road,
Henley-on-Thames, Oxon RG9 1EN

Printed in Great Britain by
Unwin Brothers Limited,
Old Woking, Surrey

Library of Congress Cataloging in Publication Data

Bakalla, M. H.
Arabic culture through its language and literature.

Bibliography: p.
Includes index.
1. Arabic philology. 2. Arabic literature—History and criticism. I. Title.
PJ6071.B27 492'.7 82-15328

ISBN 0-7103-0027-1 AACR2

This edition is prepared especially
to celebrate the silver jubilee of
the foundation of
KING SAUD UNIVERSITY, RIYADH,
KINGDOM OF SAUDI ARABIA

بسم الله الرحمن الرحيم

To His Majesty King Fahd Ibn Abd al-Aziz, His Royal Highness, Crown Prince Abd Allah Ibn Abd al-Aziz and His Royal Highness Prince Sultan Ibn Abd al-Aziz for their dedication to, and support of, Arabic and Islamic Studies.

CONTENTS

PART TWO: ABOUT ARABIC LITERATURE

INTRODUCTION

This book aims to present a bird's eye view of its subject. It is intended for the non-specialist student of Arabic, especially those who have not yet mastered the language and are therefore not able to read about Arabic literature in its original sources. The book may also be useful to the general reader who is interested to learn a little about the Arabs and their culture. These introductory notes are meant to be the first step which might eventually lead to a greater interest in the Arabic language and literature. For this reason, some references are given at the end of each chapter for further reading and pursuit of the subject. Footnotes are also appended to some chapters, but their size is kept to a minimum.

The inclusion of more chapters on literature than on the language does not mean that the author considers the former more important. In fact one can add scores of topics on either of the two major parts of this book, namely the Arabic language and literature. On the other hand, I feel that many students, as well as general readers, favour literature and would like to know more about it, as it usually contains lighter and more digestible material than learning about the language. Furthermore, literature is thought to reflect the culture of the people and their way of life and thinking, not to mention history. These factors, among others, have prompted the author to present the material in the way given here, in the hope that the integration of the chapters is maintained.

These introductory notes are based on my readings of books and articles on both the Arabic language and literature. Therefore, I felt free to draw heavily and quite extensively on the works consulted in the preparation of this book. Proper acknowledgements to all of these works and their authors would only add to the size of the book and exceed the limits set by the publisher. However, the notes and references will suffice to make up for this obvious deficiency.

If this work succeeds in stimulating further interest in the Arabic language and its literature, then the main aim of compiling such a book is achieved. The author feels that at present there is still a great need for further and better presentations of the Arabic language and literature to various categories of readers and levels of learners of Arabic, especially non-Arabic speakers. As interest in Arabic is increasingly and steadily growing, such works will find a great welcome in the coming decades.

M.H. Bakalla
London 1981

KEY TO SYMBOLS OF TRANSCRIPTION AND TRANSLITERATION

THE CONSONANTS

Symbols Employed	*Phonetic Equivalent*	*Arabic Counterpart*	*Phonetic Values of the Symbols*
h	h	ه	a voiceless glottal fricative (e.g. English *h* in *H*amburg)
ʔ or ʾ	ʔ	ء	a glottal stop (e.g. Arabic *ʔ*ab= father)
ʾ	ʕ	ع	a voiced pharyngeal fricative (e.g. Arabic ʾarab=Arab)
ḥ	ħ	ح	a voiceless pharyngeal fricative (e.g. Arabic *ḥ*abb = wheat)
ġ, gh	ʁ	غ	a voiced uvular fricative (e.g. Arabic *ġ*arb= west)
q	q	ق	a voiceless uvular stop (e.g. Arabic *q*alam = pen)
x or kh	X	خ	a voiceless uvular fricative (e.g. Arabic *x*amsa = five. Close to Scottish & German *ch*.
g	g	گ	a voiced velar stop
k	k	ک	a voiceless velar stop (similar to English *k* in s*k*y)
j or ǯ	j or ʒ	ج	a voiced palatal stop, affricate or fricative
š or sh	ʃ	ش	a voiceless palatal fricative (similar to English sh in *Sh*ell)
z	z	ز	a voiced alveolar fricative (similar to English *z* in *z*one)
ẓ	ǯ	ظ	a voiced alveolar/interdental emphatic fricative

Symbols Employed	*Phonetic Equivalent*	*Arabic Counterpart*	*Phonetic Values of the Symbols*
s	s	س	a voiceless alveolar non-emphatic fricative (e.g. English *s* in *S*am)
ṣ	ꞩ	ص	a voiceless alveolar emphatic fricative
r	r	ر	a voiced alveolar trill
l	l	ل	a voiced alveolar lateral (e.g. British English *l* in *l*uck)
ḷ	ɫ	ل	a voiced alveolar emphatic lateral (e.g. Arabic A*ll*ah and English *l* in Bi*ll*)
n	n	ن	a voiced alveolar nasal
d	d	د	a voiced dental stop (e.g. English *d* in stu*d*y)
ḍ	đ	ض	a voiced dental emphatic stop
t	t	ت	a voiceless dental stop (e.g. English *t* in s*t*udy)
ṭ	ŧ	ط	a voiceless dental emphatic stop
ḏ or dh	ɤ	ذ	a voiced interdental fricative (e.g. English *th* in *th*is)
ṯ or th	Θ	ث	a voiceless interdental fricative (e.g. English *th* (e.g. English *th* in *th*ick)
č	tʃ or č	چ	a voiceless palatal/alveolar-palatal affricate (e.g. English *ch* in *ch*ur*ch*)
f	f	ف	a voiceless labio-dental fricative (e.g. English *f* in *f*ilm)
b	b	ب	a voiced bilabial stop (e.g. English *b* in *B*ill)
m	m	م	a voiced bilabial nasal
w	w	و	a voiced labio-velar semi-vowel (e.g. English *w* in *w*et)
y	y	ي	a voiced palatal semi-vowel (e.g. English *y* in *y*et)

THE VOWELS

Symbols Employed	*Phonetic Equivalent*	*Arabic Counterpart*	*Phonetic Values of the Symbols*
u	u	ـُ	a short close back rounded (e.g. English *u* in p*u*t)
ū	u:	و	a long close back rounded (e.g. English *u* in J*u*ne)
o	o		a short half-close back rounded
ō	o:		a long half-close back rounded
a	a	ـَ	a short open unrounded
ā	a:	ا	a long open unrounded
ə	ə		a short central (neutral)
i	i	ـِ	a short close front unrounded (e.g. English *i* in s*i*t)
ī	i:	ي	a long close front unrounded (similar to English vowel in s*ee*d)
e	e		a short half-close front unrounded (e.g. English *e* in r*e*d)
ē	e:		a long half-close front unrounded

LIST OF SYMBOLS AND ABBREVIATIONS

A.D.	Anno Domini (Gregorian Calendar)
A.H.	After Hijra (Islamic Calendar)
CA	Classical Arabic
Cf.	Compare
diss.	Dissertation
ed(s.)	Editor (s)
edn (s.)	Edition (s)
f (f)	Following page (s)
fig (s.)	Figure (s)
M.Phil.	Master of Philosophy
p (p)	Page (s)
vol (s)	Volume (s)
/ /	Parallel slashes enclose phonemes
→	Becomes, changes to

LIST OF ILLUSTRATIONS

PLATES

MAPS

FIGURES

PART ONE

ABOUT THE ARABIC LANGUAGE

I

ARABIC AS A SEMITIC LANGUAGE

Linguists, or the scientists of language, divide the languages of the world into a number of families according to their approximate structural relation and interrelation in the history of their evolution. One of the most important amongst these is the Semitic family of languages (which includes languages such as Phonecian, Assyrian, Syriac or Aramaic, Hebrew and Arabic). Through intensive research and comparative studies, linguists have established a theory which assumes the existence of a parent language for all Semitic languages. They call this Proto-Semitic, the mother of all the extinct and extant Semitic languages. No one knows exactly where it started although some linguists suggest Arabia, others suggest the lower Euphrates, Armenia or even Africa. However the majority seem to consider Arabia as the home of Proto-Semitic from where the various Semitic migrations have started.

One of the most important branches of the proto-Semitic languages is that known as South-West Semitic which is composed of North Arabic, South Arabic languages and Ethiopic. North Arabic is also subdivided into Lihyanite, Thamudic, Safaitic and Arabic as we know it today. Although Arabic is considered, as Professor Nicholson (1977:xiv) states:

> "the youngest of the Semitic languages, it is generally allowed to be nearer akin than any of them to the original archetype, the "Ursemitisch" (or Proto-Semitic) from which they all are derived, just as the Arabs by reason of their geographical situation and the monotonous uniformity of desert life, have in some respects preserved the Semitic character more purely and exhibited it more distinctly than any people of the same family."

This statement falls short of saying that the Arabic language is more Semitic than its cognates or sister languages, and that the Arabs are more Semitic than other Semitic nations.

The word "Semitic" is derived from the biblical name Shem or Sam, one of our prophet Noah's sons (Peace be upon them), who is considered the father of the Semitic peoples. It is a German Professor, August Ludwig Schlozer who first used the term "Semitic Languages" around 1781. It is interesting to note that Ibn Hazm, an Andalusian from Muslim Spain, pointed out more than one thousand years ago that Syriac, Hebrew and Arabic stem from one and the same language.

Some linguists also classify Arabic as a Hamito-Semitic language in so far as these two groups of languages show regular structural relationships in phonology (that is the sound structure), in morphology (that is the word structure), in vocabulary, and syntax (that is the sentence structure). Amongst the Hamitic languages are Old Egyptian, Old Libyan, Berber, Hausa, Fula and Cushitic languages such as Somali, Galla, Southern Sudanese languages and so on. A slightly different term is currently in usage which was proposed by the American Professor Greenberg, namely Afro-Asiatic, in which Arabic plays a big role and enjoys the widest distribution of all.

To exemplify the structural affinity in some of the Semitic languages, let us show some regular correspondences in terms of sounds and vocabulary. Note for instance the word for "open"

in	Arabic	*fataḥ*
	Hebrew	*paṯaḥ*
	Aramaic	*pəṯaḥ*
	Ethiopic	*fataḥ*
	Akkadian	*pītū, patū*

The Proto Semitic form for "open" is "*pataḥ-*". Note also in this example and the following ones the triconsonantal root-system which is the main characteristic feature of the Semitic languages.

For another example, note the cognate words which are equivalent of the English numerical number "nine":

in	Arabic	*tis'*
	Hebrew	*teša'*
	Aramaic	*təša'*
	Ethiopic	*teš'ū*
	Akkadian	*tīšu*

The reconstructed Proto Semitic word is *tiš'*-.

Note also the following correspondences in the word which means "tooth" in English:

In	Arabic	*sinn*
	Hebrew	*šen*
	Aramaic	*šennā*
	Ethiopic	*senn*
	Akkadian	*šinnu*

The corresponding reconstructed form in Proto-Semitic is *šinn*-.

Another example is the following set of words meaning "night":

In	Arabic	*laylah*
	Hebrew	*laylax*
	Aramaic	*lelyā*
	Ethiopic	*lēlīt*
	Akkadian	*līlātu*

The equivalent in Proto-Semitic is *layl*- .

The following example is taken from Semitic grammar.
The Perfect tense of the sentence "he wrote":

In	Arabic	*kataba*
	Hebrew	*kāṯav*
	Aramaic	*kəṯav*
	Ethiopic	*kataba*

In Proto-Semitic it is *kataba*.

Another example is the Present tense of the sentence "he writes":

In	Arabic	*yaktubu*
	Hebrew	*yixtōv*
	Aramaic	*yixtuv*
	Ethiopic	*yekteb*

In Proto-Semitic it is *yaktibu*.

Such examples and hundreds more show the affinities between Semitic languages. The same or similar structural affinities also exist amongst Hamito-Semitic, or Afro-Asiatic languages.

In conclusion, Arabic appears to be the youngest of all Semitic languages, yet it can be compared, and it shows resemblance to, some of the oldest Semitic languages such as Akkadian which was a living language about the 3rd millennium before the Prophet Jesus (Peace be upon Him). Amongst the Semitic languages of today, Arabic is the richest in linguistic literature, and is regarded by some as the most primitive Semitic speech extant (Gray 1971:6).

REFERENCES

Gibb, Hamilton A.R. 1974. *Arabic Literature: An Introduction.* Oxford: Oxford University Press. (Especially chapter 2).

Gray, L.H. 1971. *Introduction to Semitic Comparative Linguistics.* Amsterdam: Philo Press.

Greenberg, Joseph H. 1952. *'The Afro-Asiatic (Hamito-Semitic) present",* in *Journal of American Oriental Society* (New Haven, Conn.) 72.1–9.

———. 1955. *Studies in African Linguistic Classification.* New Haven: Compass Publishing Company.

——— . 1963. *The Languages of Africa.* Bloomington: Indiana University Research Center Publication, no. 25.

Nicholson, Reynold A. 1977. *A Literary History of the Arabs.* Cambridge: Cambridge University Press.

Sobeok, Thomas A., Charles Ferguson, C.T. Hodge, et al, eds. 1970. *Current Trends in Linguistics, vol. 6: Linguistics in South West Asia and North Africa.* The Hague & Paris: Mouton. This work also includes:

Hodge, Carleton T. *"Afroasiatic: an overview",* pp. 237–54; Schramm, Gene M. *"The Semitic languages: an overview",* 257–60; and Ullendorff, Edwad *"Comparative Semitics",* 261–73.

Ullendorff, Edward. 1958. *'What is a Semitic language",* in *Orientalia* (Rome) 27.66–75.

II

THE ROLE OF ARABIC IN THE MODERN AGE

There are a number of issues which have to be clarified before this question can be satisfactorily answered. First of all, the question which might be asked: Is there more than one Arabic language? Linguists can easily answer this as they have their own linguistic criteria to group languages together or divide them from each other. According to linguists and Arabists, there are many Arabic languages: Northern Arabic languages and South Arabic languages. Northern Arabic languages include some extinct languages such as Lihyanite and Thamudic. South Arabic languages consist of languages such as Mihri Arabic and Soqotri Arabic which are still spoken, though not widely, in South Arabia.

The Arabic language which I am talking about here is a member of the North Arabic languages, it is the only North Arabic language which is still in existence. This variety of Arabic subsumes a number of dialects and subdialects which are not confined to the Arabian Peninsula but are also prevalent outside Arabia. In other words, Arabic, unqualified as such, is one language in the abstract sense. But it has a number of derivatives or varieties such as Classical Arabic, Modern Standard Arabic, and the spoken Arabic dialects throughout the Arabic speaking countries. This point will be discussed in a later chapter (X).

Another issue to be discussed here is the question of the role of Arabic amongst the languages of the world in general and International languages in particular. Arabic is one of about 3500 languages of the world, and it is also one of the six official International languages (English, French, Russian, Spanish, Chinese and Arabic). The international role has been endowed upon Arabic since 1973, when Arabic was officially announced as one of the languages of the World organizations such as the United Nations and its sister organizations.

Like any language of the world, Arabic is a means of communication, but like only a very few languages of the world it is also a vehicle for a renowned culture and civilization.

Unlike any of the other languages, Arabic has assumed the role of an International language twice.

Admittedly Arabic was confined to Arabia till the beginning of the third decade of the Seventh Century. Since then Arabic has moved from strength to strength, backed by the Holy Qur'ān on the one hand and, on the other, the advancement of the sciences by the Arabs and Muslims of the Golden Age in the East (the Middle or dark ages of the West). Between the eighth and the eleventh centuries Arabic became an International language, the medium of world culture, the widely used language of that age, and the leading language in science and technology for that period. It is through the Arabic language that Ancient and Medieval Greek and Latin philosophy and sciences passed to modern Europe via centres of learning in Spain, Baghdad and Southern Europe. Scores of books were preserved in the Arabic translation whereas the original writings were lost forever.

What makes Arabic an important language in the Twentieth Century? It is not the Petrol question that makes Arabic what it is today as viewed by some romanticists or even economists. Languages cannot be studied or looked at out of their contexts. There are many factors involved in giving Arabic a prestigious place amongst the world languages.

Populationwise, Arabic is spoken by more than 130 million people in the Arabic speaking countries alone. There are more than 5 million speakers outside the Arab Homeland in adjacent Muslim countries, such as Iran, Turkey and some countries in Africa, and in some areas in the Soviet Union. The Arab homeland occupies a strategic geographical position and it is at the crossroads of three continents. It holds a very important cultural position as it was the cradle of many civilizations in the Ancient world. Moreover, it has a very important economic position as it possesses a great percentage of the world power resources, and, agriculturally it possesses a viable land. Furthermore, the Arabic speaking world has begun to exert influence on the world economy and the development plans in developing countries. Economic and technical assistance, through Arab development funds, has been given to countries not only in Asia and Africa but also to some countries in Europe. In addition, Arabic is gaining ground in the Islamic non-Arabic speaking countries. Pakistan has declared Arabic an official language and the use of Arabic in schools, colleges, mass media has been on the increase since 1976. Recently, Iran and the Philippines introduced Arabic as an official second language.

The Arab homeland is entering a period of cultural expansion and literary and scientific renaissance in which the Arabic book is becoming an important source for science, arts and literature. Statistics indicate the growth of Arabic in the last two decades. As it stands now there are about 100 official Arabic newspapers, not less than 120 Arabic periodicals and journals, and an annual publication of about 10,000 Arabic books of which more than 1,000 are translated from other languages. All these features point out the importance of Arabic not only to people who speak it but to the world at large.

To go back to the original question about the role of Arabic in our modern times, it must be said here that Arabic has now become one of the official international languages, it is the sixth language in world organizations, the third in the Organization of African Unity and the first in the Islamic World League.

It is the long-standing history of Arabic as a previous international language of science and arts, and the present state of Arabic as a vehicle of a great culture that have paved the way for Arabic to assume again its role as an international language by a concensus of the official opinion of the world community.

REFERENCES

Chejne, Anwar. 1958. *"The role of Arabic in present-day Arab society"*, in *The Islamic Literature* (Lahore) 35:616–30.

Germanus, Abdul Karim. 1950. *"Linguistic foundation of the unity of the Arabic-speaking peoples"*, in *The Islamic Review* (Woking, England) 38/3:21–24.

Gibb, Hamilton A.R. 1974. *Arabic Literature: An Introduction.* Oxford: Oxford University Press (See Chapter 2).

Al-Kāsimī, Ali Muhammad. 1979. *Modern Trends in Teaching Arabic to Speakers of Other Languages,* (in Arabic). Riyadh: University of Riyadh Press. (Especially pp. 15–48, on *the Place of Arabic Among World Languages).*

Massignon, Louis. 1950. *"The value of Arabic as the custodian of*

culture", in *The Islamic Review* (Woking, England) 38/4: 25–26.
O'Leary, De Lacy. 1980. *How Greek Science Passed to the Arabs.* London & c.: Routledge & Kegan Paul.

III

THE MODERNIZATION OF ARABIC

It goes without saying that Arabic has a long standing history which goes back more than two thousand years. Old Arabic can still be understood even by people with a minimum of education. Modern Arabic is defined as classical, literary Arabic, which has adjusted to the requirements of modern life and, in particular, arts, science and technology. It is not only a written language employed by the press and authors when writing books, but also a spoken language for both the educated and semi-educated people, and is used extensively on the radio and television, as well as in daily talks between scholars and learned people. It is the language of administration, of lectures, and of official correspondance.

It was not until the mid 19th century that Arabic entered a new phase in its development. There were landmarks which helped Arabic to assume its role as a vehicle of modern ideas and technology. The forerunners, whether they were journalists, writers or novelists have paved the way for Arabic to assume its place as a modern language capable of expressing modern thinking and modes of life in the modern age.

Arabic has been under constant influence from other cultures and peoples. As a result of these constant contacts, Arabic has borrowed many words, ideas and concepts from other languages. The Arab Academies in Cairo, Damascus, Baghdad and Amman have been active in the standardization of the Arabic language and in the introduction of new terms and concepts into Arabic. These are a result of translations into Arabic from other languages. This process of rendering new terms into Arabic or constructing a new Arabic vocabulary is known as "coinage", or coining new words.

Building a new vocabulary involves two main linguistic levels, namely semantics and morphology. Semantics concerns itself with the study of the meaning of the words coined, while morphology involves the study of the formation of words or terms. Whereas semantics is the study of the internal content of words; morphology concentrates on the external shape of words.

On the level of semantics, Arabic has absorbed many concepts and ideas by means of literal or free translation from other languages. There are a number of ways in which semantics plays its role in coining a new Arabic vocabulary.

Firstly, rebirth of old, obsolete Arabic words in order to express modern concepts and ideas. For instance, *jawhar* and *'Araḍ* meaning "substance" and "form" respectively. *Sayyāra* used to mean a "caravan of camels," now it means a "motor car". Old words may, however, retain their old meanings, and sometimes they recur with a slightly different meaning in order to express new ideas.

The second semantic process in coining a new vocabulary is metaphor or *majāz*. This involves the use of metaphors or abstractions to render foreign vocabulary into Arabic. For example, such words as *hātif* for "telephone", *hātif* used to mean the "voice of inspiration". *barq* (meaning telegraph) used to mean a "lightening". *Barīd* used to refer to the old way of sending messages when animals were used for transportation. Nowadays *Barīd* means "post", whether by surface or air mail.

A third semantic process for coining a new vocabulary is by rendering cliches from a foreign model. For instance, *wakālat al-Anbā'* "news agency"; *Munaẓẓamat al-Umam al-Muttaḥida* "United Nations Organization"; *kurat al-qadam* "football"; *al-Sūq al-Muštaraka* "Common Market"; *Duwal al-Opec* "OPEC Countries". All these expressions are translated, at times verbatim, from English, French or other languages into Arabic.

Now for the morphological processes involved in coining new Arabic words.

Firstly, derivation. Every Arabic word is normally formed from a root and a pattern or *wazn.* Certain patterns may denote a semantic feature. For example, the pattern *Fi'ālah* denotes a profession, such as *tijārah* "trade", *ḥidādah* "smith", *nijārah* "carpentry", *ṣinā'ah* "manufacture", *zirā'ah* "agriculture", *ḥilāqah* "hair cutting".

Thus *ḥilāqah,* for instance, consists of the triradical root *ḥlq* and the pattern *Fi'ālah.* Derivation involves the formation of nouns, verbs, and other categories.

Secondly, compounding (or *naḥt*) is a process in which two or more words are made into a single word. Abbreviations can be considered to be a kind of compounding. To exemplify, the word ARAMCO is an abbreviation of "Arabian American Oil Company". Compounding was known to early Arabs and there are still a number of compounds in use. *Basmalah* and *ḥamdalah* stand for the expressions *bismillāh irraḥmān irraḥīm* and *al-Ḥamdu lillāh,* respectively. The first means "in the name of God the beneficent, the merciful", the second means "thanks be to God". Compounding is still not used extensively in coining new Arabic words. Because Arabic has a limited number of affixes, one can experience difficulties in translating into Arabic from languages which are rich in prefixes and suffixes. However, Arabic has its own way to handle such cases.

The third morphological device in Arabic is "Arabization", which normally means the adoption of foreign words, with the necessary modification to suit the morphological and phonological patterning of Arabic. This process is not new to Arabic and there were several books written more than a thousand years ago about loan words from Persian and other languages. Many words have entered into Arabic in recent years, such as "telex", "helicopter", "villa", "camera", "radio" and "television", and so on.

Loan words are either adopted without any significant changes, or they may undergo changes according to the rules of Arabic morphology and phonology. Some loan-words gradually disappear as Arabic words are introduced to be used instead. For example, *hātif* is gradually being introduced and may well replace "telephone".

From the above discussion, we can say that Arabic vocabulary is in the process of changing and developing rapidly in order to meet the needs of the modern age. This reflects the fact that Arabic is a flexible language and it has the power of adaptability. Yet not all the resources of such a power have been exploited. No one can deny the role of the Arab Academies in the progress and standardization of Arabic vocabulary, but this influence is still slow in motion and has yet to be manipulated. Technical dictionaries and glossaries in various fields of arts and sciences are abundant in Arabic, but they are not easy to use. There is also the problem of the distribution of the Arabic book both within the

Arab countries and outside.

But all indications show that Arabic can be adopted as a language of science, just as it used to be the language of science and technology in the Middle Ages.

There is nothing lacking in Arabic as a language. What is lacking in the Arab countries are active professional linguists and language planners who can help to participate in the modernization of Arabic.

REFERENCES

Bakalla, M.H. 1981. *Arabic Linguistics: An Introduction and Bibliography*. London: Mansell Publishing Ltd.

Chejne, Anwar. 1969. *The Arabic Language: Its Role in History.* Minneapolis: University of Minnesota Press.

Al–Maghribī, Abdul Qādir. 1947. *Arabic Derivation and Arabization* (in Arabic). 2nd edn. Cairo.

Al–Shihābī, Muṣṭafa. 1965. *Arabic Scientific Terminology in the Past and Present* (in Arabic). Damascus: The Arabic Academy of Damascus.

Stetkevych, Jaroslav. 1970. *The Modern Arabic Literary Language: Lexical and Stylistic Developments.* A publication of the Center for Middle Eastern Studies. Chicago & London: The University of Chicago Press.

Al–Toma (Altoma), Salih J. 1970. *"Language education in Arab countries and the role of the academies"*, in *Current Trends in Linguistics,* vol. 6:690–720, edited by Thomas Sebeok, C.A. Ferguson, C.T. Hodge, et al. The Hague & Paris: Mouton.

IV

THE ROLE OF ARABIC IN AFRICA

It is true to state that the contact between the Arabs and Africa goes back to olden times long before the advent of Islam. Arabic folklore indicates that there were mixed mariages between the Africans and Arabs even during that period.

Since the advent of Islam, the contact between the Arabs and Africa has become even greater. More than one third of the African continent is occupied by an Arabic-speaking population of more than 100 million people. In fact there are more African Arabs living on the west side of the Red Sea than there are Arabs living on the east side.

As a result of this strong contact, the Arabic language has made large strides in Africa and has gained an enormous geographical area, following the Islamic faith wherever it went.

Although Arabic is one of the most widely spoken of the African languages, there are still a number of misconceptions about it especially amongst the modern population of Subsaharan Africa. One of these misconceptions is that Arabic is a foreign language in Africa and that it is only connected with the Qur'ānic teaching and Islamic theology. This view is held, more obviously, by those new generations who were educated in missionary schools or even modern public schools across the continent. It is not easy to dispel this kind of misconception which seems to be a remnant of the colonial past.

A number of factors can be incorporated here to show not only the rights of the existence of Arabic on African soil but also the extent of the Arabic influence on African languages and cultures.

First is the geographical factor. Out of the 11,690,000 square miles of the African continent, the Arab lands in Africa occupy about 5 million square miles, that is more than one third of the continent, as mentioned earlier. Moreover, the Arabic speaking countries extend over the most strategic areas of the continent. These include the waterways of the Red Sea, the Arabian side of the Mediterranean Sea, and the key points of the entrances in the Indian and Atlantic oceans. Thus the Arabic speaking Africans are spread over the Eastern, Northern, Central and Western parts of the continent.

Second is the population factor. Out of the 300 million inhabitants in Africa, more than one third are Arabs or Arabic-speaking Africans. Apart from the Arabic-speaking countries in Africa, there are many Arabic speaking minorities spread all over the continent. Many of such communities live permanently in Subsaharan Africa, such as the Gambia, Senegal, Nigeria and Ghana in West Africa; Tanzania, Uganda and Kenya in East Africa; Zimbabwe and Johannesburg in Southern Africa.

Third is the historical factor. The history of the Arabs in Africa is not well known even to the Africans themselves, and the little that is known has been distorted throughout the ages. In the old Empires of Mali and Ghana, the rulers, who were mainly Muslims, used written Arabic quite extensively. There are a number of books written in Arabic by African historians and learned people, many of these manuscripts are now kept in private collections. A number of Arab travellers in the Middle Ages, like Ibn Baṭṭūṭa, wrote very important accounts about the life and history of some of the Subsaharan countries that they were able to visit during their travels.

Fourth is the political factor. Out of the 50 or so countries in Africa about one fifth are Arab countries. Some of the nine Arab countries in Africa today play an important role in the political scene on both the international and African levels.

Fifth is the linguistic factor. There are more than 1000 languages in Africa, some of them are only used by small groups of people. In the Gambia alone, which is a country of about ½ million people, there exist about 13 languages. Arabic is the only language in Africa which possesses a majority of speakers out of all the other African languages. Even with the introduction, in modern times, of English and French in what are now known as Anglophone and Francophone countries, these two languages compete with each other and neither is spoken as widely as Arabic within the African context. These languages, which admittedly are gaining ground through education and the media, have not as yet reached the majority of the Africans who maintain their own local languages on most occasions.

Another linguistic issue to be mentioned here is the influential role that Arabic has played on most African languages.

Because of its long history in Africa and as a result of the continuous trade with Africa, Arabic as the language of the Qur'ān has had a lasting influence on almost all of the African languages. These have borrowed from Arabic not only words but also expressions and concepts which are reflected in daily expressions, such as greetings and exchanges of cordial or courtesy phrases.

The language situation in Africa is commonly known as multilingualism, that is the co-existence of a number of languages in one and the same country or speech community. Today there is a general tendency towards the use of a common language, for the purpose of speed of communication among people or peoples. Many sociolinguists look at multilingualism as an unhealthy situation which can be a hinderance or a barrier to communication. Language planners have been engaged in finding ways and means to solve this situation in Africa. In some countries like the Republic of the Gambia, English is still the official language even though political independence was granted in 1965. In the last few years some of the local languages have been introduced such as Mandinka, Wolof, Fula and Serkhole as well as English. So on the radio one can listen to the news in five languages one after the other each directed to its respective listeners. To monolingual societies, such as Saudi Arabia, this situation looks rather complicated. However, in Africa multilingualism is the norm or the rule. For more than one decade now, Africa has been looking for an alternative linguistic situation, a single language all Africa can use or understand without recourse to an intermediary language. In East Africa, Swahili has been chosen as the common language of the East African countries such as Tanzania, Kenya, Mozambique and parts of Uganda which have an estimated figure of 10 million speakers. Hausa, on the West Coast of Africa, which has more than 15 million speakers, has been appointed the lingua franca of West Africa. But so far Africa has not been unified linguistically by one language.

Anglophone and Francophone countries of Africa will not give way to each other, and there seems to be no agreement on the use of one language in place of the other. The Organization of African Unity (or O.A.U.) which was founded in 1961 still uses five working languages,

English, French, Arabic, Swahili and Hausa.

Some language planners suggest that Arabic should be the official language of all Africa, or at least the countries belonging to the O.A.U. Some Subsaharan Africans will, of course, disagree. Although these are in a minority, they may have all the power in their hands. Most Muslims who have attended Qur'ānic schools, Dārās or Duksīs will undoubtedly accept such a motion. There is a story of a British Professor of African languages who was visiting the President of a West African country. While they were talking about education and literacy in Africa the President was astonished to hear about the high literacy rate in his country. When he asked the Professor for evidence the Professor asked the President's cook and servants to be brought in. At first they could not write in English or in the Latin script. But when the Professor insisted they should write anything, they started to write their names in the Arabic script. Thus the Professor proved his point to His Excellency who had previously considered his servants illiterate.

Sociolinguistically speaking, Arabic seems to be highly qualified to be the language of all Africa. It is not a foreign language as is the case with English, French, Afrikaans or other non-African languages. It is the language of the Muslim masses in Africa, most of whom can still read the Arabic script, though sometimes without understanding the meanings. Many Subsaharan African languages used to be written in the Arabic script until very recently, before the Latin script was introduced mainly by the missionaries. I remember in my recent visits to West and East Africa, I found that some of the old generation still use the Arabic script in writing their own languages such as Swahili, Mandinka and Wolof. On Radio Gambia I accidentally came across two people, a Mandinkan poet who read to me some of his Arabic poems which were excellent, and another Mandinkan broadcaster who was going to present his programme in Mandinka reading from an Arabic script.

It is interesting to note that languages such as Swahili and Hausa have been greatly influenced by Arabic. Swahili, like Persian, has borrowed more than 30 per cent of its vocabulary from Arabic while Hausa has at least 20 per cent Arabic vocabulary in its lexicon. These words or expressions borrowed from Arabic do not only cover religious words but also words used in daily life, and literature, science and technolgy too.

Another point to be made here is the fact that in recent years there has been a gradual growth in mutual understanding between the Arabs, on both sides of the Red Sea, and the Subsaharan Africans on political, commercial and economic issues. The Arabs are gradually realizing their role in Africa. A special Arab Bank has been established to assist the African States and African projects. African leaders are paying more and more visits to the Arab States, and African students are being accepted by schools, Universities and training centres in the Arabic speaking world.

To conclude, Arabic is the language of communication and culture for more than one third of Africa. It has a role to play in Africa beyond the Sahara, and the Arabs are gradually realizing the importance of Africa which is bound to be the continent of the future. In order for Arabic to make its impact felt in this part of the world, the Arabs must work very hard in order to realise this goal. There are great opportunities now for the Arabs to help Africa and to meet its needs not only economically, commercially and medically, but also culturally and educationally.

REFERENCES

ʿĀbdīn, ʿAbdel-Majīd. 1970. *A Study of the Arabic Language and Culture in Africa* (in Arabic). Cairo: Institute of Arabic Research and Studies of the Arab League.

Bakalla, M.H. 1981. *Arabic Linguistics: An Introduction and Bibliography.* London: Mansell Publishing Ltd. (Also contains many references on the subject).

Blanc, Haim. 1971. *"Arabic"*, in *Current Trends in Linguistics, vol. 7 (Linguistics in Sub-Saharan Africa)* 501–509, edited by T.A. Sebeok, Jack Berry, et al. The Hague: Mouton.

Heine, Bernd. 1970. *Status and Use of African Lingua Francas.* München.

Al-Kāsimī, Ali Muhammad. 1979. *Modern Trends in Teaching Arabic to Speakers of Other Languages* (in Arabic). Riyadh: University of Riyadh Press. (Especially pp. 49–56, on *The Arabic language in Africa*).

V

ARABIC LINGUISTIC SCHOLARSHIP

By Arabic linguistics, I mean the scientific study of the Arabic language, using scientific methodology and approach. Arabic linguistics, like other Arabic disciplines, had its beginnings, a peak of development and a decline and revival.

The beginning of Arabic linguistics is a matter of controversy. Interest in linguistic thinking must have started before the advent of Islam, but our knowledge of this period is still limited. With the revelation of the Holy Qur'ān and its codification, as well as the sayings of the Prophet (Peace Be Upon Him), the codification did not only fix the rules of grammar, but also motivated intensive linguistic studies. Immediately after the revelation of the Holy Qur'ān, interest centred around the *Book* and its interpretation to followers from diverse parts of Arabia and outside Arabia. As a result, a new situation was created in which non-Arab Muslims faced difficulty in learning the Arabic language. Their presence amongst the Arabs led to the adoption of Arabic, but not without a heavy price. This was the gradual loss of the purity of Arabic in form and content. This situation is referred to by early scholars as a corruption or deterioration of the language, manifested in foreign accents, mispronunciation of words, poor enunciation, shifting of vowels and consonants and misuse of certain expressions, among other peculiarities. Some of these peculiarities might well have influenced the Arabs themselves. The beginning of Arabic grammar appears to have been as early as mid seventh century A.D. during the reign of ʻAlī ibn Abī Ṭālib the fourth Caliph in Medina. In his *Biographical Dictionary,* Ibn Khallikān (in the 13th century A.D.) relates the following incident which is considered by many as the starting point in the codification of Arabic grammar.

> "Abu al-Aswad al-Du'alī was one of the eminent among the Tābi'īs, an inhabitant of Basra, and a partisan of ʻAlī ibn Abī Ṭālib, under whom he fought at the battle of Ṣiffīn.

> He was the first who invented grammar. It is said that (the Caliph) 'Alī laid down for him this principle: the parts of speech are three: the noun, the verb, and the particle, telling him to write a complete treatise on it. Others say that he was instructor to the children of Ziyād ibn Abīh, who was then the governor of Arabian and Persian Iraq, and that he went to him one day and said: "Emir, may God direct you! I see that the Arabs have become mingled with these non-Arab nations and that their tongues are altered so that they speak incorrectly; Will you then authorize me to compose for the Arabs something which may enable them to know their language?"

Ibn Khallikān also relates the following:

> "As Abu al-Aswad entered his house on a certain day, one of his daughters said to him: Dad, *mā aḥsanu al-Samā'i*? (What is most beautiful in the sky?) – to which he answered: Its stars," but she replied: "Dad, I do not mean to say what is the most beautiful object in it, I was only expressing my admiration at its beauty." "You must then say, he observed, *"mā aḥsana al-al-Samā'a* (how beautiful is the sky!). He then invented the art of grammar."

Ibn Khallikān continues:

> "Abū Ḥarb, Abu al-Aswad's son, related as follows: "The first section of the art of grammar composed by my father was on the verbs of admiration. Abu al-Aswad having been asked where he had acquired the science of grammar, answered that he had learned the first points of it from 'Alī ibn Abī Ṭālib."

These anecdotes reveal the obscurity of the beginning of Arabic grammar. On the other hand there seemed to be a consistent view that the Caliph 'Alī and Abu al-Aswad shared the credit of being the earliest codifiers of Arabic grammar.

Related to the early writing of Arabic grammar, is the codification of the Qur'ān. Abu al-Aswad also appears to have initiated the vocalization in Arabic script. Ibn Khallikān relates one single story about this case:

> "It is said that Abu al-Aswad never made known any of the principles which he had received from 'Alī, till Ziyād sent to him the order to compose something which might serve as a guide to the public and enable them to understand the *Book of God* (the Qur'ān). He at first asked to be dispensed (from such a task), but on hearing a man recite the following passage out of the Qur'ān: *"Ann allaha barī'un min al-Mushrikīna wa rasūlihi"*, which last word the reader pronounced *rasūlihi*, he exclaimed: "I never thought that things would have come to this." He then returned to Ziyād and said: "I shall do what you ordered; find me an intelligent scribe who will follow my directions. On this a scribe belonging to the tribe of 'Abd al-Qays was brought to him, but did not give him satisfaction; another then came and Abu al-Aswad said to him: When you see me open (*fataḥ*) my mouth in pronouncing a letter, place a point over it; when I close (*ḍamm*) my mouth place a point before (or upon the letter), and when I pucker up (*kasar*) my mouth, place a point under the letter. This the scribe did. The Art of grammar was called *Naḥw* because Abu al-Aswad has said: I asked permission of 'Alī ibn Abī Ṭālib to compose in the same way (*naḥwa*) as he had done."

Whatever the case may be about the origin of Arabic grammar, the fact remains that the first book on complete Arabic grammar which is still extant was compiled by Sībawaihi, a Muslim scholar, of Persian origin born in Shiraz, who died about 793 A.D., more than one century after Abu al-Aswad who died about 688 A.D.

The second century of Islam (8th century) produced scores of very important scholars in Arabic linguistics, one of whom was Sībawaihi, whose work is still an important reference in Arabic grammar up to the present day. Sībawaihi himself was a disciple of al-Khalīl ibn Aḥmad (died 786). Some of the historians considered al-Khalīl to be the originator of formalized Arabic grammar, and also of the vowel signs which are still in current use.

The debate on linguistic issues might have contributed to the establishment of various schools of Arabic grammar, though differing in the details and methodology, rather than the basic, fundamental issues. Sībawaihi and his mentor al-Khalīl were the leaders of the Basrite school of grammar, whereas al-Kisā'ī led the Kufite school. Other schools were also created in Baghdad, Egypt, Syria and Muslim Spain, but the differences among them were still superficial.

Arabic lexicography, which is concerned with the compilation and prepatation of dictionaries, owed its beginning to al-Khalīl ibn Aḥmad. He wrote the first known Arabic dictionary about mid eighth Century A.D., and called it *al–'Ain.* after the sound *'Ain* which he considered as the farthest, genuine gutteral sound in the Arabic language. Thus the items in the dictionary are ordered according to strict phonetic criteria. Some of the later Arabic dictionaries followed al-Khalīl's order, others followed different orders, namely the rhyme order and the alphabetical order. The early Arab lexicographers took great pains in compiling their dictionaries. Some of them had to travel to do field work, from Basra and Baghdad to the heart of the Arabian Peninsula in order to collect, illicit,or verify some points from genuine, pure Arab informants. Arabic dictionaries abound, and each century produced a number of them. Nowadays we still reap the fruits of the work of the early Arabic lexicographers. Many lexicographers also wrote numerous glossaries on a specific subject or topic such as the sword, the horse, the plants, the human body etc. Notable amongst these are al-Aṣma'ī (died 830), Abū 'Ubaidah (died 825) and the Andalusian Arab Ibn Sīdah (died 1065).

The study of Classical Arabic also led to the acknowledgment of some non-Classical Arabic features which were observed in the speech of various dialects or dialectal areas.

Observations on dialectal variations were not made only by grammarians such as Sībawaihi and al-Khalīl, but also by lexicographers, linguists, and rhetoricians, amongst others. Some of these observations are still valid such as the realization of the definite article as *m* in South West of the Peninsula instead of the common equivalent *l*.

Arabic phonetics, which studies the production and perception of the Arabic sounds, was amongst the most advanced subjects in Arabic linguistic scholarship. The Arabs and Muslims excelled in this field and their works were superior to any contemporary phonetic studies. The description of the articulatory movements was precise, the division between consonants and vowels was clear, and the study of the phonotactic features, that is the possible combination of consonants and vowels, was very interesting.

Amongst the early Arab and Muslim phoneticians were al-Khalīl and Sībawaihi (8th century), Ibn Sīna and Ibn Jinnī (10th century). The last two devoted a book each to the study of this subject in greater detail than any of their predecessors. As in other Arabic disciplines, the tenth century A.D. was the golden era in Arabic linguistic scholarship. It marked the climax of scientific research and scholarship. Although scores of scholars have appeared since then, there were no significant changes in the methods of the Arab linguists from the 11th till the end of the 19th century.

Modern Arabic linguistics derives its foundation from both the ancient Arabic linguistic tradition as well as the modern techniques of contemporary development of general linguistics. There has been a growing interest amongst the Arabs and non-Arabs alike in the advancement of the field of Arabic linguistics, both within the Arabic speaking world and outside it.

REFERENCES

Bakalla, M.H. 1981. *Arabic Linguistics: An Introduction and Bibliography.* London: Mansell Publishing Co.

Chejne, Anwar. 1969. *The Arabic Language: Its Role in History.* Minneapolis: University of Minnesota Press.

Ibn Khallikān. 1842–71. *Biographical Dictionary,* 4 vols. Translated from the Arabic by Baron M. de Slane. London. Reprinted, Beirut: Librairie du Liban, 1970.

Semaan, Khalil I.H. 1968. *Linguistics in the Middle Ages.* Leiden: E.J. Brill.

VI

SOME PHONETIC OBSERVATIONS IN SĪBAWAIHI'S BOOK OF ARABIC GRAMMAR

The claim that ancient Arabic phonetics was originally derived from, or influenced by, early Indian writings on phonetics is still unconvincing. All indications show that this Arabic science emerged and developed independently from the Indian one (or other sources, whether Greek or Latin, for that matter) and that both sciences share an important feature. That is, each of them had originated from an intense interest in the study of the religious works. Later this interest extended to non-religious, linguistic material as well. In the case of Arabic phonetics, it grew out of an immense enthusiasm on the part of the Muslims for reading, understanding, and articulating the sounds of the Qur'ān correctly. Later on, the phonetic analysis also involved other areas such as poetry, prose, and the speech of the Arabs. Thus, whereas *'Ilm al-Tajwīd* concerned itself with the recitation of the Qur'ān, *'Ilm al-Aṣwāt wal-Ḥurūf* (as coined by Ibn Jinnī in *Sirr al-Ṣinā'ah*) covered both religious and non-religious material. Sībawaihi's work appears to fall under the latter discipline.

A comparison between *The Kitāb* of Sībawaihi and *al-'Ain* of his professor al-Khalīl Ibn Aḥmad reveals that the former has benefited a great deal from the latter, especially as far as the phonetic material is concerned. This is not surprising since Sībawaihi quite often quotes from al-Khalīl's works. Although Sībawaihi does not mention his professor at all in the chapter on *Idġām,* there are a number of points where the influence of the latter appears quite clearly. We do not assume that Sībawaihi agrees with his professor all the time. To mention some of those points, note the following.

1. Sībawaihi uses many of the phonetic terms employed in *al-'Ain.*
2. Sībawaihi arranges the Arabic sounds in more or less the same way as they are arranged in *al-'Ain.* The arrangement followed

is made according to what can be called the ascending order. That is to say that the sounds which are articulated in the larynx are described first, gradually followed by the sounds whose points of articulation are further forward along the vocal tract until the bilabial sounds are finally reached. Al-Khalīl follows the following arrangement:

Symbol	*Arabic Letter*	*Approximate Phonetic value*
'	ع	Voiced pharyngeal fricative
ḥ	ح	Voiceless pharyngeal fricative
h	ه	Voiceless breathed fricative
x	خ	Voiceless uvular fricative
ġ	غ	Voiced uvular fricative
q	ق	Voiced uvular stop
k	ك	Voiceless velar stop
j	ج	Voiced palatal stop
š	ش	Voiceless palato-alveolar fricative
ḍ	ض	Voiced alveolar lateral fricative emphatic
ṣ	ص	Voiceless alveolar-palatal fricative emphatic
s	س	Voiceless alveolar-palatal fricative non-emphatic
z	ز	Voiced alveolar-palatal fricative non-emphatic
ṭ	ط	Voiced alveolar stop emphatic
t	ت	Voiceless alveolar stop non-emphatic
d	د	Voiced alveolar stop non-emphatic
ẓ	ظ	Voiced interdental fricative emphatic
ṯ	ث	Voiceless interdental fricative non-emphatic
ḏ	ذ	Voiced interdental fricative non-emphatic
r	ر	Voiced dental trill
l	ل	Voiced dental lateral
n	ن	Voiced dental nasal
f	ف	Voiced labio-dental fricative
b	ب	Voiced bilabial stop
m	م	Voiced bilabial nasal
w	و	voiced bilabial semivowel
ū	و	Voiced labiovelar long vowel
ā	ا	Voiced long *a*

Symbol	Arabic Letter	Approximate Phonetic value
y	ي	Voiced palatal semivowel
ī	ي	Voiced palatal long vowel
ʔ	ء	glottal stop

Sībawaihi is more objective in his arrangement than his professor who was influenced by criteria other than the phonetic ones. The following arrangement is given in *al-Kitāb: ʔ , ā, h, ', ḥ, ġ, x, k, q, d, j, š, y / ī, l, r, n, t, d, t, ṣ, z, s, ẓ, d̲, t̲, f, b, m, w / ū.* Sībawaihi's arrangement is more accurate than his professor's: whereas the latter gives this arrangement *', ḥ, h,* the former gives the more accurate arrangement *h, ', ḥ.* On the other hand, Sībawaihi's arrangement of *k* and *q* is not correct.[1] Al-Khalīl and most later Arab phoneticians arrange *q* before *k* as the former is produced further back than *k*.

3. Sībawaihi groups the sounds which are articulated in a given area of the vocal tract into a single group, thus giving:

ḥurūf-ul-ḥalq	the guttural sounds	(laryngeal, pharyngeal and uvular sounds)
ḥurūf-ul-lisān	the tongue sounds	
ḥurūf-ul-famm	the oral sounds	

This method of grouping sounds is frequently followed by al-Khalīl.

4. Sībawaihi treats in his book many of the phonological points which can also be found in *al-'Ain.* For instance, he makes statements regarding initial clusters, phonotactic arrangements. By the latter I mean those statements which deal with the permissible and non-permissible combinations of sounds.

1. *Nūn xafīfah.* This is the *n* which is influenced by the following consonants. E.g. *N* in *ʔ inġalab* ⟶ *ʔ iNġalab* (where ⟶ is an instruction to change the form on the left of the arrow into the form which is on its right; *N* being the

voiced uvular nasal).

2. *hamzat bayna bayna.* This may be interpreted as the glottal stop which is not as strongly articulated as the pure *hamzah.*
3. *ʔalif mumālah.* This may be symbolized as [ē].
4. *šīn kal jīm.* This may be written with the phonetic symbol [c].
5. *ṣād kal zāy.* The nearest sound to this is the one symbolized as [ẓ].
6. *ʔalif tafxīm.* It is pronounced approximately as [ā].

These 35 sound variants, as Sībawaihi tells us, are used in the Standard language, be it in speech, reading poetry, or reciting the Qur'ān (Sībawaihi 1968:404). In addition, he includes another 7 sound variants, chief among which are [p] (*bā' kal fā'*) and [g] (*kāf bayn jīm* and *kāf*). These sounds are used in non standard language and particularly colloquial speech *mušāfahah.* On examination, the first 29 variants are called basic apparently because each of them is represented by a written symbol; the rest of the sounds have no actual symbols of their own in the writing system of Arabic. This point confirms the view that Sībawaihi is interested in the speech of the Arabs, be it standard or colloquial. It seems that he is the first Arab phonetician to tackle this kind of analysis.

Sībawaihi is aware of the articulatory processes involved in the production of the Arabic sounds. He clearly mentions the points of articulation *maxraj* (pl. *maxārij*), and he is also aware of the static and active articulators. In his systematic treatment of the sounds, he divides the vocal tract into 16 points of articulation within each of which one or more sounds can be produced. He gives 18 short and precise statements displaying these points and referring to those sounds which are articulated within each point. Apart from the last statement, he again follows the ascending ordering of sounds as shown earlier. The following are the points stated in *al-Kitāb* (Sībawaihi 1968: 405):

Points of articulation	*The sound symbols*
1. *ʔ aqṣa–l–ḥalq* (larynx)	*ʔ , h, ā*
2. *ʔawsaṭ–ul–ḥalq* (pharynx)	*ʿ, ḥ*

3.	*ʔ adna–l–ḥalq* (uvular)	*ġ, x*
4.	*ʔaqṣa–l–lisān wamā fawqah min ḥanak ʔa ' lā* (uvular or post uvular)	*q*
5.	*min ʔasfal . . . wamā fawqah min ḥanak ʔa'lā* (velar or prevelar).	*k*
6.	*min wasaṭ–il–lisān baynah wabayn wasaṭ–il–ḥanak–il–ʔ a* 'lā (palatal)	*j, š, y / ī*
7.	*ʔawwal ḥāffat–il–lisān wamā yalīh min ʔaḍrās* (the interior side of the tongue against the molars)	*d*
8.	*min ḥāffat–il–lisān min ʔadnāhā ʔilā muntahā ṭaraf–il–lisān mā baynahā wabayna mā yalīhā min ḥanak ʔa'lā wamā fuwayqa–al–ḍāḥik, nāb, rubā'-iyyah, ṯaniyyah* (the front side of the tongue and the tip against the front palate [front ridge, or gum] and the front teeth.)	*l*
9.	*min ṭaraf–il–lisān baynah wabayn mā fuwayq–al–ṯanāyā* (the tip of the tongue against the alveolar)	*n*
10.	*min maxraj–il–nūn ġayr ʔannah ʔadxal fī ẓahr–il–lisān qalīlan* (from the same point except that it is more backed)	*r*
11.	*mimmā bayna ṭaraf–il–lisān wa ʔuṣūl-il–ṯanāyā* (the tip of the tongue is against the roof of the teeth)	
12.	*mimmā bayna ṭaraf–il–lisān wa fuwayq–al–ṯanāyā* (the tip of the tongue is against the area which is a little further back from the teeth)	*ṭ, d, t*
13.	*mimmā bayna ṭaraf–il–lisān wa ʔaṭrāf-il–ṯanāyā* (the tip of the tongue is against the edges of the teeth; inter-dental sounds)	*z, s, ṣ*
14.	*min bāṭin–il–šafat–il–suflā wa ʔ aṭrāf-*	*ẓ, ḏ, ṯ*

	il–tanāyā–al–'ulyā (the inner part of the lower lip is against the edges of the upper teeth; the labio-dentals)	
15.	*mimmā bayn–al–šafatayn maxraj–ul–bā? wal mīm wal wāw* (the bilabials)	*b, m, w* / *ū*
16.	min–al–*xayāšīm maxraj–ul–nūn–il–xafīfah* (from the nostrils)	*N, ŋ, etc.*

The inclusion of 16 as another point of articulation is understandable, since *N* (the uvular nasal), ŋ (the velar nasal), among others, are not articulated from the same point as the alveolar *n*. In other words, it is a variant of *n*.

After discussing the points of articulation, Sībawaihi moves on to divide the sounds according to the phonetic qualities *ṣifāt* (Sībawaihi 1968: 406) they possess; i.e. their manner of articulation. As for the first quality or feature, the *jahr*, he describes certain sounds as *majhūr* and all the rest as *mahmūs* as shown on the following page:

majhūr	*mahmūs*
ʔ	*h*
ā	
ʿ	*ḥ*
ġ	*x*
q	*k*
j	*š*
y / ī	
ḍ	
l	
n	
r	
ṭ	
d	*t*
z	*s*
	ṣ
ẓ	
ḏ	*ṯ*
b	*f*
m	
w / ū	

His definition of *majhūr* and *mahmūs* has puzzled scores of Arab phoneticians and Arabists because of its apparent vagueness. *Majhūr* has been rendered as "voiced, sonorous" and *mahmūs* as "voiceless, muffled, etc." Curiously enough the terms are clearer than their definitions. A large section of Arabic scholars render them as voiced and voiceless, respectively. This can be supported by the text only if it is interpreted in a certain way. Let us translate the relevant text (Sībawaihi 1968: 405):

> "As for the *majhūr,* it is the sound in which the contact (in the larynx) is made and the breath *nafas* is not at all involved during the voicing *ṣawt*. This is the state of the throat and mouth in the articulation of *majhūr* sounds.
> As for *mahmūs,* it is the sound in which the contact (in the larynx) is not made and the breath issues through the mouth during its articulation."

If this interpretation is correct than we can assume that Sībawaihi was aware of the states of the vocal cords during the enunciation of the voiced and non-voiced sounds, or at least the effect of these states. The latter explanation is understood from the terms chosen; namely *majhūr* (derived from *j–h–r* denoting loudness, clarity, sonority) and *mahmūs* (from *h–m–s* denoting voicelessness). If we take the first interpretation that assumes his awareness of the states of the vocal cords, we can then explain why he considers *ʔ* as *majhūr*. That is to say, the vocal cords are close or drawn up together, somehow similar to the state of voicing. Whatever the case may be, the fact remains that almost all the *majhūr* sounds are voiced in modern Arabic and all the *mahmūs* sounds are voiceless.

Another major division of sounds is to *šadīd* and *raxw* (=*rixw*). *šadīd* is rendered as "stop", *raxw* as "fricative or spirant". According to Sībawaihi, *šadīd* is the sound in which the air (*ṣawt,* probably *hawāʔ – ul–ṣawt*) is interrupted, whereas the *raxw* is the sound in which the air issues without complete interruption, as displayed on the following page:

šadīd	*raxw*
ʔ	*h*
	ḥ
q	*ġ, x*
k	
j	*š*
ṭ	
t	
d	
	ṣ
	ḍ
	z
	s
	ẓ
	ṯ
	ḏ
b	*f*

He considers ' as both *šadīd* and *raxw*. In modern analysis it is a fricative consonant. Some modern phoneticians have recognized the fact that ' is produced with a marked, though not complete constriction of the throat and perhaps with some glottalic friction. It is clear from this point that voicing is not the only distinguishing factor between ' and ḥ.

Furthermore, Sībawaihi divides the sounds into *muṭbaq* and *munfatiḥ*. These terms have been rendered in Arabic phonetics as "velarized" and "non-velarized." He is aware of the fact that the raising of the back of the tongue towards the upper palate as a secondary articulation (Sībawaihi 1968: 406). The division may be displayed as follows:

muṭbaq	*munfatiḥ*
ṣ	
ḍ	
ṭ	
ẓ	the rest of the sounds

It is surprising, at this juncture, that he does not mention *ḷ* (*lām mufaxxamah*) among the velarized (emphatic) consonants. Sībawaihi's statement with regard to this division is worth citing here. He says:

> "Sounds are either *muṭbaqah* or *munfatiḥah*. The *muṭbaqah* are: *ṣ*, *ḍ*, *ṭ*, and *ẓ*. The *munfatiḥah* are the rest of the sounds. They are called so because you do not raise your tongue towards the upper palate. When articulating those four consonants, you raise you tongue to the upper palate. In this case the air (*ṣawt*, probably *hawāʔ –ul–ṣawt*) is modified *maḥṣūr* in both the place where the tongue is raised for *ʔiṭbāq*, and the main point of articulation *mawḍi'–ul–ḥurūf*. As for *d* and *z*, etc. the air is modified at the point of articulation only. The aforementioned four consonants have two places of constriction as displayed earlier."

There are also other divisions which will be touched upon shortly.

In retrospect, Sībawaihi appears to study the Arabic sounds from at least two main angles. On the one hand he looks on these sounds as independent units *ḥurūf;* on the other he regards each sound as a complex of phonetic features *ṣifāt.* Concerning the concept of *ḥarf* (pl. *ḥurūf*), Sībawaihi as well as the Arab phoneticians considers that each sound-unit or *ḥarf* has at least three properties:

a. the phonic property, i.e. how the unit is phonetically actualized;
b. the pictorial or visual property, i.e. how this unit is conventionally written or symbolized;
c. and the nomenclature property, i.e. the naming of each unit; e.g. *kāf, hāʔ*, etc.

It is very difficult to know precisely the exact relations among these properties as conceived by Sībawaihi and even later Arab phoneticians. As for the basic units *ʔaṣl ḥurūf–il–'arabiyyah,* which are 29 in number as listed earlier, one can see that each of them possesses the three properties. Thus *k*, for instance, has certain phonetic qualities, certain written shapes, and a certain name *kāf.* Another example is *ā.* It is a vowel *ḥarf madd wa līn,* with certain phonetic characteristics, certain graphic patterns besides the name *ʔalif.* These properties seem to underlie Sībawaihi's analysis of the basic sound-units of Arabic. As for the non-basic units, they may lack one or more of the above-mentioned properties. To exemplify, let us take [*g*] and [*p*], which are not used in Classical or Standard Arabic.

Sībawaihi calls the first *al-jīm allatī kal–kāf,* literally translated as "the *j* which sounds like *k*; i.e. the voiced counterpart of *k.*" On examination, one can see that *j* is voiced and that *j* agrees with *k* in that both are stops. [*g*] has no symbol of its own, and has no accurate name of its own. As for [*p*], it is called *al-bāʔ allatī kal–fāʔ* , literally "the *bāʔ* which is like *fāʔ* "; i.e. "*b* which has the characteristics of *f.*" One can see that the common feature between *p* and *f* is the lacking of voicing in both of them. Sībawaihi does not give any examples for the various non-basic units he mentions in his book. However, it is not impossible to reconstruct the sounds he is referring to from the fairly accurate description he makes in *al–Kitāb.*

We now turn to the second concept which underlies Sībawaihi's analysis of the Arabic sounds. That is, his description on the basis of "Feature" analysis. It seems to me that this is the area which is least understood of Sībawaihi's analysis. Later Arab phoneticians as well as Arabists have overlooked the underlying principles upon which Sībawaihi's description is based. One of the main principles is that he considers each unit as a bundle of phonetic features. In other words, he does not regard the unit as an indivisible whole; it is a whole which consists of various parts. Another important principle underlying Sībawaihi's statements is that Arabic has certain phonetic features, varied combinations of which make up the various units of the language. The third principle is that vowels as well as consonants may share some of the phonetic features. Thus *ā*, the *ʔalif,* is classified amongst the *majhūr* sounds. It is to be noted that *wāw* in Sībawaihi's classification means both the semivowel *w* and the vowel *ū*, and that *yāʔ* refers to both *y* and *ī*. This discrepancy is understandable since *w* and *ū* are normally written with one letter, and *y* and *ī* are represented as a single letter.

Interestingly enough, this technique of analysis has something in common with one of the most recent phonetic theories which is known as "distinctive feature analysis", which is based on some sound scientific grounds drawing from concepts used in disciplines such as information theory, physics, physiology, among others. This theory puts forward the idea that there is a set of universal phonetic features from which each language selects for its own purposes. Thus voicing (entailing the vibration of the vocal cords) exists in all languages as far as we know. The theory also maintains that (Jakobson and Halle 1956:4–8):

> "The phonemes of a language are not sounds but merely sound features lumped together which the speakers have been trained to produce and recognize in the current of speech sounds.
>
> The speaker has learned to make sound producing movements in such a way that the distinctive features are present in the sound waves, and the listener has learned to extract them from these waves.
>
> Each of the distinctive features involves a choice between two terms of an opposition that displays a specific differential property, diverging from the properties of all other opposi-

tions.
If the listener receives a message in a language he knows, he correlates it with the code at hand and this code includes all the distinctive features to be manipulated, all their admissible combinations into bundles of concurrent features termed phonemes."

It follows from this that vowels and consonants are made up of the distinctive features which are used in a given language. Thus in Arabic, voicing is a feature which is found in all vowels and some consonants.

In the following table we shall display the phonetic features recognized in *al–Kitāb,* and their specification with regard to the sounds discussed therein. In my opinion, the main features given in this book are seven: *jahr, ġunnah* (nasality), *madd* (length), *šiddah* (total restriction or stoppage), *ʔ inḥirāf* (laterality), *takrīr* (trilling), and *ʔ iṭbāq* (velarization, emphasis). As for the first feature, the sound which is positively specified with regard to *jahr* is called *majhūr,* the one negatively specified with regard to this feature is called *ġayr majhūr* or *mahmūs.* As regards *ġunnah* the nasal are called *fīhi ġunnah* (*ʔ aġann* is the term used by a later phonetician Ibn Jinnī) the non nasals are described as *laysa fīhi ġunnah* (Sībawaihi 1968:416). As for *madd,* only *ā, ī,* and *ū* are referred to as *ḥurūf madd wa līn* (also specified as *mamdūd*) the rest are *"laysat ḥurūf madd"* (Sībawaihi 1968: 409). Regarding *šiddah* the non continuant sounds are termed as *šadīdah,* the continuant ones are called *ġayr šadīdah* or *raxwah.* The lateral sound is termed *munḥarif,* the rolled one *mukarrar.* Concerning *ʔ iṭbāq* the emphatic sounds are termed *muṭbaqah,* the non emphatic ones *munfatiḥah* or *ġayr muṭbaqah* (Sībawaihi 1968:426). It appears that Sībawaihi uses terms such as *mahmūs, raxw* (or *rixw*), and *munfatiḥ* in a negative way in contrast with the positive specifications. In the table below the sign "+" indicates the presence of the feature (positive), "–" indicates its absence (negative). The phonetic features of Arabic are represented in the form of a two-dimensional matrix in which the columns stand for independent segments; the rows stand for particular features.[2]

	ʔ	ā	h	ʼ	ḥ	ġ	x	q	k	d	j	š	y	ī	l	r	n	ṭ	d	t	ṣ	z	s	ẓ	ḏ	ṯ	f	b	m	w	ū
maj	+	+	−	+	−	+	−	+	−	+	+	−	+	+	+	+	+	+	+	−	−	+	−	+	+	−	−	+	+	+	+
ʔaġ	−	−	−	−	−	−	−	−	−	−	−	−	−	−	−	−	+	−	−	−	−	−	−	−	−	−	−	−	+	−	−
mam	−	+	−	−	−	−	−	−	−	−	−	−	−	+	−	−	−	−	−	−	−	−	−	−	−	−	−	−	−	−	+
šad	+	−	−	−	−	−	−	+	+	−	+	−	−	−	−	+	+	+	+	+	−	−	−	−	−	−	−	+	+	−	−
mun	−	−	−	−	−	−	−	−	−	−	−	−	−	−	+	−	−	−	−	−	−	−	−	−	−	−	−	−	−	−	−
muk	−	−	−	−	−	−	−	−	−	−	−	−	−	−	−	+	−	−	−	−	−	−	−	−	−	−	−	−	−	−	−
muṭ	−	−	−	−	−	−	−	−	−	+	−	−	−	−	−	−	−	+	−	−	+	−	−	+	−	−	−	−	−	−	−

PHONETIC FEATURES COMPOSITION OF ARABIC SEGMENTS

It is to be noted that the information given in the above matrix is reconstructed from the statements made by Sībawaihi. They are numerous, but we can cite some of them for illustrative purposes.

1) "Without *ʔ iṭbāq ṭ* would become *d, ṣ* would become *s*, and *ẓ* would become *ḏ*." (Sībawaihi 1968:406)
2) "d is like *ṭ* in that they both are *majhūr; t* is not *majhūr* (i.e. *mahmūs*)." (Sībawaihi 1968:418)
3) "*d* and *t* differ in terms of *jahr;* they are both lacking *ʔiṭbāq, ʔ istifālah* (continuantness), and *takrīr*." (Sībawaihi 1968:418)
4) "*ṣ* in relation to *z* and *s* is similar to *ṭ* in relation to *d* and *t*. *ṣ* in relation to *s* is like *ṭ* in relation to *d*; because they are both *mahmūs*. What makes them different is the presence of *ʔ iṭbāq* in *ṣ* and its absence in the case of *s*. As for *ṣ* in relation to *z*, it is like *ṭ* in relation to *t*, because *z* is *ġayr mahmūs* (i.e. *majhūr).*" (Sībawaihi 1968: 418)
5) "*ẓ* to *ḏ* is like *ṭ* to *d* because they are all *majhūr*. What distinguishes one from the other is the presence of *ʔ iṭbāq* in the former part of the sets and its absence from the latter. *z* and *t* is like *t* to *t*." (Sībawaihi 1968:418–19)
6) "*z* is like *d* in that they both are *majhūr* and *non-muṭbaq.*" (Sībawaihi 1968:412)
7) "*z* is both *majhūr* and *ġayr muṭbaq*." (Sībawaihi 1968:426)
8) "*s* and *ṣ* are alike in terms of *hams, ṣafīr* (whistling) and *raxāwah* (continuantness)." (Sībawaihi 1968:428)
9) "*s* is near to *t* in terms of point of articulation, and in that they both are *mahmūs*." (Sībawaihi 1968:429)

The implications of the modern use of "distinctive feature analysis" are numerous; some of which are summarized below. The system which uses "feature analysis" uses a small set of features far less in number than the set of sound units employed in the language. Thus whereas one would need more than 29 units for Arabic, one might need 10 or 12 features in order to analyse the Arabic sounds in a more economical way. Moreover, the study of sounds in terms of their feature components would lead to avoiding redundant features; Sībawaihi seems to put emphasis on the distinctive, non-redundant, features. This approach appears to underlie his analysis as can be read between the lines of the above statements and many others.

Furthermore, by using "feature analysis" one can simplify his statement of the "morphophonemic" processes in the language, such as assimilation, dissimilation, etc. It is worth noting that after his major classification of Arabic sounds, Sībawaihi made the following remark (Sībawaihi 1968:406–7):

> "I have described the sound units in terms of the foregoing features in order to show you the cases in which *ʔidġām* is preferable, the cases in which it is permissible, and the cases in which it is neither preferable nor permissible."

ʔidġām here may be regarded as a part of the morphophonemic changes in Arabic. In fact, Sībawaihi's book contains a great number of morphophonemic statements. They are simply and concisely stated. They can easily be recast in mathematical linguistic formulas, or rules. To exemplify, examine Sībawaihi's statements as shown below.

> "*n* is changed into *m* before *b*, because both *b* and *m* have the same point of articulation." (Sībawaihi 1968:414 & 427)

This statement can be formulated as follows:

$$n \longrightarrow [+\text{bilabial}] \quad / \quad \underline{\qquad} \quad b$$

This rule is an instruction to add the feature of Labiality to the features that compose *n* before the Bilabial consonant. The symbol " ⟶ " reads: "rewrite the elements on the left of the arrow as the elements given on its right". the symbol "/" means "in the context of", the symbol "—" indicates the environment in which the change occurs.

Note also the following statement:

"The Arabs say *ʔijdamaʻū* in place of *ʔijtamaʻū*. *t* is approximated to *d* since this is *Maj*. Such an operation applies to the pattern *ʔiFta'aL* forms." (Sībawaihi 1968:427)

This statement can be recast in this form:

$t \longrightarrow [+Maj]$ / $[Maj]$ ___ and / *ʔiFta'aL*

i.e., add the feature *Maj* to the features which constitute *t* after a *Maj* consonant. This operation is restricted to forms of *ʔiFta'aL* pattern; the rule contains two environments symboloized by " / ": the first refers to the segment next to which the operation takes place, the second refers to the general pattern which normally undergoes this kind of morphophonemic alternation.

The phenomenon of Deletion *ḥaḏf* is also one of the morphophonemic operations. In this regard Sībawaihi makes a number of statements one of which reads:

> "In the case of a succession of two *t*'s as in *tatakallamūn,* one has the choice of maintaining it in speech or eliding one of them." (Sībawaihi 1968:425)

This statement can be stated in this formula:

$ta \longrightarrow \phi$ / # ——— ta (Opt)

The symbol " ϕ " indicates Deletion or zeroness; the symbol " # " stands for word-initial position; (Opt) means that this rule is applied optionally in Arabic.

After this long, though not exhaustive, survey of the phonetic conception as revealed in *al-Kitāb* we can make some general remarks rather briefly. *Al-Kitāb* remains a mine of information on Arabic grammar. Only very few, albeit the most important, concepts are discussed in this chapter. There remains a great number of phonetic statements which deserve further consideration and closer examination.

Although Sībawaihi generally gives a good and clear description of the consonants and vowels of Arabic, he does not mention anything which might relate to stress (accent or prominence), pitch and intonation. Later Arab phoneticians add to, and improve upon, Sībawaihi's description; though not in any significant way. In the 4th century A.H. (10th century A.D.) Abū al-Fatḥ 'Uthmān Ibn Jinnī gives a fuller and more systematic description of the Arabic sounds. I have found that he touches upon certain features in Arabic which may be grouped under the phenomenon "stress". In his *Sirr al-Ṣinā'ah,* he presents a more systematic treatment of the short vowels; he also explicitly discusses some phonetic features which are either untouched by Sībawaihi or given a very cursory treatment.[3]

Conclusions

To recapitulate, the following points are noted.

(1) Sībawaihi gives a fairly accurate description of the Arabic sounds, both standard and colloquial. Although he does not mention vocal cords, he seems to be aware of the effect they produce on the ears; hence the division of sounds into *majhūr* and *mahmūs.*

(2) He follows a framework which is based on "feature analysis". By doing so, he seems to have anticipated the most recent technique of feature analysis as proposed by Jakobson, Fant and Halle and their school.

(3) In addition to the valuable phonetic information given in *al-Kitāb,* Sībawaihi keeps closely to a certain methodological plan. He uses the phonetic terminology or vocabulary with a striking degree of consistency and clarity. Further, whenever possible he uses the phonetically ascending order of sounds.

(4) Sībawaihi has laid down the phonetic rules which deal with the sound pattern of Arabic. One can find in his book a number of statements regarding the phonotactic arrangements of Arabic sounds, and the morphophonemic alternations that occur in the language.

(5) Apart from the many advantages and merits which characterize Sībawaihi's analysis of Arabic sounds, little is said about the short vowels in a systematic way. Moreover, he overlooks some of the most important prosodic features such as stress, pitch and intonation.

Sībawaihi's contribution to Arabic phonetics cannot be ignored by any researcher in this field. Nor can it be overlooked by the historians of linguistics who are interested in the development of this science in all parts of the world. Unfortunately, this early Arab phonetician has often been misquoted and his ideas have been misinterpreted by later scholars in the East and the West. In passing I must refer to a work by a German scholar, A. Schaade, who, to my mind, wrote a comprehensive work on Sībawaihi's phonetics. His study is entitled *Sibawaihi's Lautlehre,* published in Leiden in 1911.

It is also unfortunate that Arabic phonetics (not *Tajwīd*) is still in its infancy, and has not changed in a significant way from its traditional form. It is still an academic subject in many Arab countries. Sībawaihi's phonetics is still the main source for modern Arabic phonetics, it feeds it with its rich terminology, its ideas, and its methodology. Arabic phonetics can be applied in various ways in order to make us aware of this social phenomenon, speech. The pronounciation of Arabic, especially Classical or Standard Arabic, can be taught to school children and pupils; it can be taught to non-Arabic speaking people so that they will be able to speak Arabic like the Arabs; and it can be taught to students of speech, theatre, and public speakers in order to train them how to control their breath and articulate sounds properly and more effectively. One of the tasks of modern Arabic phonetics is to devise written symbols for all the possible sounds in Arabic. We have noted that Sībawaihi mentions a number of sounds which have no corresponding written symbols.

This is Sībawaihi, the phonetician. I have tried to give a simple, but comprehensive, picture of this Muslim scholar who for centuries has been the leading figure in the study of Arabic grammar. His work was first published and first translated (into German) in the West. His *Bāb–ul–Idġām* is definitely a chapter on Arabic phonetics, phonology and morphophonemics. His contribution reflects the painstaking effort made through his clever observations, his effort in gathering and arranging the material, and above all his effort to state his ideas clearly and concisely. It is high time to appreciate more fully the achievements of this scholar.

NOTES

1) I am sure that the arrangement given above in Sībawaihi's book is an error on the part of the early scribes. In a later statement, Sībawaihi orders *q* before *k* in terms of point of articulation. Cf. the section on *Points of articulation* in this chapter.

2) Key to abbreviations:

Abbreviation	*Full Term*	*Glosses*
maj	*majhūr*	voiced
ʔaġ	*ʔaġann*	nasal
mam	*mamdūd*	long
šad	*šadīd*	non-continuant
mun	*munḥarif*	lateral
muk	*mukarrar*	rolled
muṭ	*muṭbaq*	emphatic

It is to be noted that according to Sībawaihi's description of the Arabic sounds, it appears that some of these sounds vary slightly from their modern reflexes (e.g., *q*, *ḍ* and *ṭ*). This subject deserves a separate treatment.

3) I made an extensive study of Ibn Jinnī's book and his contribution to Arabic phonetics in my M. Phil thesis (1970).

REFERENCES

Bakalla, M.H. 1970. *The Phonetics and Phonology of Classical Arabic as Described in Ibn Jinnī's Sirr Ṣinā'at al–I'rāb.* M. Phil. thesis, University of London.

——— . 1981. *Arabic Linguistics: An Introduction and Bibliography.* London: Mansell Publishing Ltd.

Chomsky, Noam and Morris Halle. 1968. *The Sound Pattern of English.* New York: Harper and Row Publishers.

Goyvaerts, Didier L. 1978. *Aspects of Post-SPE Phonology.* Ghent-Antwerp-Brussels: E. Story-Scientia P.V.B.A.

Ibn Aḥmad, Al-Khalīl. 1967. *Kitāb al-'Ain,* vol. I. Edited by Abdalla

Abdel–Fattāḥ Darwīsh. Baghdad: al–'Ānī Press.

Ibn Jinnī, Abu al–Fatḥ 'Uthmān. 1954. *Sirr Ṣinā'at al–I'rāb,* vol. I. Edited by Muṣṭafa al–Saqqā, et al. Cairo: Muṣṭafa al–Ḥalabī Press.

Jakobson, Roman, C. Gunnar M. Fant and Morris Halle. 1976. *Preliminaries to Speech Analysis: The Distinctive Features and their Correlates.* 11th printing. Cambridge, Mass.: The M.I.T. Press.

Jakobson, Roman and Morris Halle. 1956. *Fundamental of Language.* The Hague: Mouton.

Omar, Aḥmad Mukhtār. 1972. *The Indian Linguistics and its Influence on Early Arabic Linguistics* (in Arabic). Beirut: Dār al–Thaqāfah.

Semaan, Khalil I.H. 1968. *Linguistics in the Middle Ages: Phonetics in Early Islam.* Leiden: E.J. Brill.

Sībawaihi, Abū Bishr 'Amr. 1968. *Al–Kitāb.* Vol. II. Reprint of Būlaq Edition. Baghdad: al–Muthannā Press.

VII

THE TREATMENT OF NASAL ELEMENTS BY EARLY ARAB AND MUSLIM PHONETICIANS

Introduction. The phonetic observations by early Arab and Muslim grammarians and phoneticians cover a large area of an integral part of Arabic grammar, namely, Arabic phonetics.

The interest in Arabic phonetic studies must have begun prior to al-Khalīl (died 791 A.D.) and his disciple, Sībawaihi (d. 793). By the time these two scholars wrote their works on Arabic phonetics, in terms of the statements and terminology they used, this discipline must have undergone a gradual development to reach such a degree of accuracy and such a stage of progress. Although the main aim then was to help in liturgical interpretation, it was not confined solely to this purpose. Most of the grammatical works written before al-Khalīl and Sībawaihi seem to have been lost. The Arabic lexicon *al–'Ain* by al–Khalīl and the *Book of Grammar, al–Kitāb,* by Sībawaihi had remained the mainstays and models for many of the later grammarians, lexicographers, and orthoepists. Both of them also left an invaluable tradition of phonetic observations which deserve more attention and investigation.

As for the treatment of the nasals, they both recognized this class of phonemes, namely /*n, m*/, except that Sībawaihi's analysis is more detailed and elaborate.[1]

Nasals as a category of sounds

In addition to his analysis of /*n, m*/ as *min al–ʔanf* or nasals (1897: 406), Sībawaihi includes the two nasals in another class, namely *majhūrah* or the voiced sounds (1897: 405). He is also fully aware of the oral articulation of /*n, m*/ as he states (1897: 405):

"Amongst *šadīdah* or the stops during the articulation of

which the air issues through the nose is *n* while (the tip of) the tongue is held against the point of articulation. Similarly is *m*."

In order to prove that these are nasals, Sībawaihi resorts to experimentation. He adds (1897: 405):

"If you hold your nose *ʔanf*, the nasal sounds will not be produced."

Sībawaihi terms the resonant sound which is produced in the nose as *ġunnah* or nasality.

The term *ġunnah* was used to mean a number of things. Firstly, to some scholars it particularly means "nasality" as it appears from the preceding quotations. It simply means the total escape of the air though the nose. In this sense, the Arabic nasal sounds are delimited in a similar way to the modern phonetic description of the nasals. Daniel Jones (1979: 49) defines the nasals as being

"formed by a complete closure in the mouth, the soft palate being, however, lowered so that the air is free to pass through the nose. Examples *m, n*."

The complete closure of the air in the oral cavity in the Arabic nasals *n* and *m* can be deduced from Sībawaihi's statements given earlier. It can also be borne out by his further statements concerning the articulation of these two Arabic consonants (1897:405):

"The place of articulation *maxraj* of *n* is from the tip of the tongue *ṭaraf–ul–lisān* towards that part (of the palate) which is a little above the front incisors *min fawayq–at–ṯanāyā*, i.e. the alveolum. By the two lips *šafatayn* is the articulation of *b (bāʔ). m(mīm)* and *w (wāw).*"

Sībawaihi (1897:405) also describes the nasals /*n,m*/ as *munfatiḥ* or non-velarized. Later on, Ibn Jinnī (10th century) describes them as *munxafiḍ*, or with lowering of the body of the tongue. In addition, Ibn

Jinnī (1954:69) classifies the nasals amongst the sounds which are neither stops *šadīdah* nor fricatives *raxwah* and they include the vowels and semivowels plus *l, r* and ’ .

Sībawaihi follows his mentor’s ordering of the phonemes from the glottis upward to the lips. This is recognized as the phonetic order *bi ḥasab il-maxārij,* or according to points of articulation. They are 16 in number and given in the following order (note here the order of the nasals):

1. the larynx: *ʔ, h, ā*
2. the pharynx: *’ , ḥ*
3. the uvula: *ġ* and *x*
4. the foremost part of uvula: *q*
5. the velum: *k*
6. the middle of the palate: *j, š, y*
7. the front side of the palate towards the molars: *ḍ*
8. the lateral: *l*
9. the alveolum: *n*
10. the alveolum: *r*
11. the post-alveolum: *ṭ, d, t*
12. the foremost of the alveolum: *z, s, ṣ*
13. the interdental: *ẓ , d̲, t̲*
14. the labio-dental: *f*
15. the labial: *b, m, w*
16. the nasal: homorganic: *n*

Ibn Sīnā, or Avicenna (11th century), differs a little from Sībawaihi when he describes the nasals as being produced with both oral and nasal release of the pulmonic air.

> As for *m*, Ibn Sīnā states:
> “The obstruction in (the production of) *m* is complete and is by the bodies of the lips (being pressed) harder and by the outer edges. Not all the (obstructed) air is ejected from the mouth during the expulsion, for a part (of the air) is driven by a forcible thrust into the cavity which lies at the root of the nose, where (the air) swirls around and produces a vibra-

> tion, and the two streams of air, that through the mouth and that through the nasal cavity, are released together."

As regards *n*, he states:

> "The obstruction (of the air in the production of) *n* is (at a point) a little higher than the natural obstruction (for the production of) *t*. (It is affected) by the tip of the tongue, save that the greater part of the (volume of) air is released through the "place which produces the nasal tone" in the nose. Thus the point of obstruction for *n* is a place where the membranes are more flexible, and is further in, while its vibration is greater than *t*, and it has nasal tone."

Still, Sībawaihi's description of the nasals, which is more than two centuries earlier than Ibn Sīnā's, is more accurate and in complete agreement with modern phonetic definition of the nasals.

Secondly, *ġunnah* is also used as a term for the phenomenon of *tanwīn* or nunation, since it involves the alveolar nasal *n*. Abu al–Aswad al–Du'alī (7th century) appears to be one of the first early scholars to use it in this sense. Giving his instructions to the scribe vocalizing the *Holy Qur'ān* for him, (al–Dānī 1960:477), Abu al–Aswad says:

> "If I utter *ġunnah* after any of the short vowels then insert two dots therein."

Abū 'Amr al–Dānī (11th century) commenting on this statement, says in his book *al–Muḥkam* (1960:58):

> "By *ġunnah* here Abu al–Aswad means *tanwīn,* because it is a nasal sound."

Nasality as a distinctive feature

Further, Sībawaihi's analysis of the sounds of Arabic is also based on a kind of Distinctive Features approach. According to this, a sound or a group of sounds may be differentiated from others by means of a phonetic feature, such as nasality, voicing, emphaticness. Later on, Ibn Jinnī puts even more emphasis on this approach (Bakalla 1970: 361 ff.)

Note the following statement in which Sībawaihi (1897:414) differentiates between two Arabic phonemes in terms of nasality:

> "*n* is not changed to *b* because it is far from it in so far as place of articulation is concerned and also because *b* is non–nasal."

He also states that (1897: 414):

> "*n* and *m* are both nasal and voiced, though they are both different in terms of place of articulation."

Similarly, al–Dānī makes the following statement (1960:75):

> "*m* and *n* are sisters in terms of nasality, *m* and *b* are also sisters as both are characterized as labial."

It is also obvious from these descriptions of the Arabic sounds or phonemes that the Arabic phonemes, except *n* and *m* are all non–nasal.

Nasalization

Daniel Jones defines nasalization as follows (1979: 213):

> "When sounds (other than plosive and nasal consonants) are pronounced with simultaneous lowering of the soft palate, so that the air passes through the nose as well as through the mouth, they are said to be nasalized."

The early Arab and Muslim grammarians and phoneticians recognize the effect of nasality on the neighbouring sounds whether consonants or vowels. They also recognize the disappearance of the nasals (especially *n*) in some contexts. This *n* is called *nūn xafiyyah*, or the hidden *n*.

It is interesting to note that the early grammarians, such as Sībawaihi, lay down the rules concerning the nasals. Sībawaihi (1897: 414 ff) discusses at least four cases relating to the phonological behaviour of the nasals.

1. *ʔiẓhār* or *bayān,* i.e. the state when each of the nasals *n* and *m* is fully realized, as in *man* "who". This is when nasals occur before the laryngeal and pharyngeal consonants, namely *ʔ* , *h,* ' and *ḥ.*
2. *ʔidġām bilā ġunnah,* or assimilation without nasality. This is permissible when *n* immediately precedes *l, r, w,* or *y.*

Examples:

man laka	→	*mal laka*
man raʔayta	→	*mar raʔayta*
man waqafa	→	*maw waqafa*
man yaʔkulu	→	*may yaʔkulu*

3. *ʔidġām bi ġunnah,* i.e. assimilation with nasality. This phenomenon can be regarded as a case of the process of nasalization. It applies to the same contexts of *n* as in the examples given in the preceding paragraph. Thus it is possible to pronounce them as follows:

man laka	→	*mal̃ l̃aka*
man raʔayta	→	*mar̃ r̃aʔayta*
man waqafa	→	*maw̃ w̃aqafa*
man yaʔkulu	→	*maỹ ỹaʔkulu*

Here the nasalization undoubtedly affects all the consonants and vowels of the syllables involved.

4. *ʔixfāʔ* of *m* and *n* i.e. the hidden *m* and *n.* This is a case of homorganic assimilation, where *n* is assimilated into the following consonants. In modern analysis such cases are dealt with as variants or members of the phoneme *m* or *n.*

Examples:

man kataba → *maŋ kataba*
man qāla → *maN qāla*
man xaraja → *naN xaraja*
man jāʔ a → *maɲ jāʔ a*
man fataḥa → *maɱ fataḥa*[2]

Measurement of nasality

Attempts were also made to measure the duration of nasality in certain contexts. In fact there were numerous ways by means of which the length of nasality was measured.[3]

Measurement by the palm of the hand

Here the duration of nasality was measured according to the folding and unfolding of the palm in such a way that was neither slow nor fast. Normally, nasality lasts as long as it takes for one folding and one unfolding of the palm.

Counting by the fingers

The duration of nasality was also measured by means of counting by the fingers in such a way that it was neither fast nor slow. Normally, nasality lasts as long as it takes for one folding and one unfolding of the fingers.

By pronouncing a word

The duration of nasality was also measured by means of uttering the word *ʔalif*, i.e. the name of the vowel *ā* in Arabic. It was assumed that the pronunciation of this word lasts as long as nasality normally takes.

By writing a word

The duration of nasality was also measured by means of writing the word *ʔalif*. It was considered that nasality lasts approximately as long as it takes to write down this word.

Of course, all these measurements are approximate but they must have been sufficient for the purpose of analysis in those days when no modern facilities for measuring elements of speech were available.

How is the phenomenon of nasalization marked in writing?

The subject of nasals and nasalization was not dealt with by Arab and Muslim grammarians and phoneticians alone. It was also treated, in fact even more thoroughly, by the Arab and Muslim orthoepists, or the scholars of the Science of *Tajwīd*. This science may be rendered as the phonetics of the *Holy Qur'ān* which deals with the exact and correct pronunciation of its verses. These early scholars studied the phenomenon of nasals and nasalization not only in terms of pronunciation but also laid down a very elaborate system for writing and marking the various properties of this phenomenon. However, their system was mainly devoted to writing down, as well as reading, the *Holy Book* accurately and properly. I shall only touch on this subject, as a thorough treatment of it deserves a separate chapter.

In his book *al–Muḥkam*, al–Dānī (1960) makes statements about *n* both in word–final positions and in *tanwīn* of case–endings of the Arabic nouns. His statements about *n* of *tanwīn* (1960: 57 ff) can be summarized as follows:

(1) When the final *n* of *tanwīn* (i.e. of *–an*, *-un* and *–in*) is followed by *ʔ*, *h*, *ḥ*, *ʽ*, *x*, or *ġ*, the nasality of *n* remains (with no effect on any of the six consonants). In the case of *–an* and *–un*,[4] they can be indicated by placing two *red* dots vertically, one on top of the other (i.e.,:) in front of or above the *nunated* letter (i.e. the letter which is immediately followed by *–an* or *–un*). in the case of *–in*, it can be indicated by placing two *red* dots vertically below the *nunated* letter.[5] Each of the six gutturals (laryngeal, pharyngeal, and uvular consonants) will also have a dot placed above it to indicate that the feature of the nasality of *n* is maintained. If *n* is assimilated to *x* and *ġ*, as it is in the speech of some people, then the two vertical dots will be written horizontally (i.e. . .) to indicate assimilation.

(2) When *n* of *tanwīn* is followed by any of the rest of Arabic letters,

the two dots will invariably be written horizontally.

(a) If the succeeding letter is *r, l, n* or *m,* it will be marked by the sign of doubling *šaddah*[6] to indicate that *n* is totally assimilated to the following letter, either with nasalization or without it.
(b) If the succeeding consonant is *y* or *w*, the sign of *šaddah* will be placed on it in the case of total assimilation, otherwise, a dot will be placed above it to indicate that the nasality is maintained.
(c) If the succeeding letter is *q* or *k, j, š* or any of those remaining letters to which *n* can be assimilated, a dot should be placed above the letter in question.

Al–Dānī (1960: 73 ff) also makes similar statements about the *n* in word–final position. These can be summarized as follows:
(1) When *n* is immediately followed by one of the six guttural consonants, a small dash or a small circle will be placed on it; the guttural letter will have a dot upon it. This indicates that *n* is not assimilated. Example *man ʔāmana.*
(2) When *n* is followed by *r, l, n, m, y* or *w,* it will be unmarked in the case of total assimilation (without nasalization) to any of these six consonants, and the sign of doubling *šaddah* will be placed on each of them to indicate total assimilation. For example: *min rabbihim → mir rabbihim.* In the case of assimilation (with nasalization), a small circle will be placed on *n* and the sign of doubling *šaddah* will be placed on the following guttural letter.
(3) When *n* is followed by any of the other consonants to which it is normally assimilated, then only a dot will be placed on the letter following *n. x* and *ġ* will be marked in the same way, if *n* is assimilated to them.
(4) When *n* is followed by *b*, it will be pronounced as *m*. In this case, a small Arabic letter *m*, written in red, is placed above the letter *n* to indicate this assimilation. Examples: *min ba'di → mim ba'di.*

Especially of interest to us here are the assimilatory processes in which the nasality extends over the next vowel and consonant as it can be deduced from such statements made earlier. In other words, nasality was considered by early Arab and Muslim phoneticians as a prosodic element or suprasegmental feature which can extend beyond the limits of the naturally nasal *n*.

Experimental evidence

Physiologically, nasalization involves lowering of the soft palate so that the air stream passes through the nasal cavity as well as through the oral cavity.[7] Acoustically speaking, nasalization appears as a relatively *dark band* on the sound spectogram. Whereas the nasal *n* loses intensity during the nasal production ranging between 200–300 Hz for a male tract, nasalization shows higher frequency bands ranging between 500–2700 Hz.[8]

The three wide band spectograms (Figs. 1 – 3) shown below represent the first three examples cited earlier. They are *man laka, mal laka,* and *mal̃ l̃aka,* respectively.[9] It seems to me that the early phonetic analysis may be borne out by modern experimental techniques such as speech spectography.[10] Both the relative darkness[11] and the extended length of the formants together as shown in Fig. 3 appear to correspond to the stretch of the prosodic feature of nasality as suggested by the early Arab and Muslim phoneticians. Figs. 2 and 3 visibly show the absence of either the darkness or length of the formant, which clearly indicates the absence of nasalization. It is evident from Fig. 3 that this feature affects adjacent consonants and vowels alike. Here, Formant_1 and Formant_2 clearly demonstrate the spread of nasalization.

Employing another instrumental technique, namely the Electro Aerometer one, in conjunction with the Fundamental Frequency Meter, the Intensity Meter and the Mingograph, the same phrases used in the above experiment were likewise chosen here.[12] Figures 4–6 shown below are the mingograms of these phrases, given in the same order as above. The highest wave form in each mingogram (reading from left to right) indicates the expiratory air flow through the nasal cavity. Nasalization seems to have the longest and most persistent nasal wave form as shown in Fig. 6. This appears to correspond to the prosodic or suprasegmental feature referred to above.

Conclusion

I have attempted here to shed light on an area which is of interest not only to modern Arabic phonetics but also to phonetics in general. It is interesting to note the contributions of the Arab and Muslim grammarians and phoneticians in this field as fore-runners of modern phonetics. So far, their contributions have not been fully acknowledged. There is a very rich mine of information in this area yet to be discovered and introduced to modern phoneticians for consideration and evaluation. I hope that this chapter has succeeded in giving a stimulus to this area of investigation which so far has been partially ignored.

Of course, the phonetic and phonological analysis in early Arabic phonetics can contribute to our knowledge of the past and present state of the Arabic language, both Classical and dialectal. It can also be improved upon in the light of modern experimental phonetics and the new findings of modern phonetics in general, as it has been demonstrated here too.

NOTES

1) The superscript ~ indicates nasalization. ŋ, *N*, ɲ, ɱ are respectively the velar, uvular, palatal, and labio-dental variants of *n*.
2) Similar examples can be found in al-Dānī (1930:45) and (1960: 68–76).
3) The account of the measurement of nasality was outlined in Abū Bakr (1973: 100 ff).
4) In modern Arabic writing, *-an* is rendered as letter *ʔalif* with two strokes above it; *–un* is rendered with two small Arabic letters *wāw* above the nunated consonant. For the origin of these signs, see al-Dānī (1960:7).
5) In modern Arabic writing, *–in* is rendered by two strokes below the nunated letter. For the origin of this usage, see al–Dānī (1960: 7).
6) For the development of the use of this symbol, see al-Dānī (1960: 7).
7) For articulatory definition of nasalization, see Jones (1979: 212), Jakobson et al (1976: 40), and Ladefoged (1975: 81).
8) Very little is known about the perceptual correlates of nasalization. For a quick reference on this aspect, see Borden and Harris (1980: 174 f).

9) For the experimental data, I have used my own voice, strictly following the description given by early Arab and Muslim grammarians and phoneticians. Approximation, and not accuracy, is attempted here. Recording speed is 7½ inches.

10) Set on wide band 300 Hz, linear expand 3000 Hz, Standard bar type, a special new spectograph has been used for this experiment. The spectograph is called VII 1000, which I have been able to develop in collaboration with Voice Identification, Inc. (New Jersey, U.S.A.). This instrument can display right-to-left reading which is very useful for using the Arabic script as shown on figs. 1–3. Set on the English Mode, the same spectograph gives a left-to-right reading. I have got identical results from this mode too, but they have not been included here.

11) Degree of darkness can also mark intensity.

12) These are parts of speech physiology instrumentation manufactured by F–J Electronics, Copenhagen, Denmark.

REFERENCES

Bakalla, M.H. 1970. *The Phonetics and Phonology of Classical Arabic.* M. Phil. thesis, University of London.

------. 1981. *Arabic Linguistics: An Introduction and Bibliography.* London: Mansell.

Borden, G.J. & K.S. Harris, 1980. *Speech Science Primer.* Baltimore & London: Williams & Wilkins.

Al–Dānī, Abū 'Amr 'Uthmān. 1930. *Kitāb al–Taysīr fī al–Qirā'āt al–Sab'. Das Lehrbuch der sieben Koranlesungen.* Edited by Otto Pretzl. Bibliotheca Islamica, Band 2. Istanbul: Staatsdruckerci.

------ . 1960. *Al–Muḥkam fī Naqṭ al–Maṣāḥif.* Edited by 'Izzat Ḥasan. Damascus: Ministry of Culture.

Gairdner, W.H.T. 1935. *"The Arab phoneticians on the consonants and vowels"*, in *The Muslim World* (Hartford, Conn.) 25:242–57.

Ibn Aḥmad, Al–Khalīl. 1967. *Kitāb al–'Ain.* Vol. I. Edited by Abdalla Darwīsh. Baghdad: al–'Ānī Press.

Ibn Jinnī, Abu al–Fatḥ 'Uthmān, 1954. *Sirr Ṣinā'at al–I'rāb.* Vol. I. Edited by Muṣṭafa al–Saqqa, et al. Cairo: Muṣṭafa al–Ḥalabī Press.

Ibn Sīnā. 1963. *Risālah fī Asbāb Ḥudūth al–Ḥurūf. Arabic Phonetics.* Ibn Sīnā's *Risālah on the Points of Articulation of the Speech Sounds.* Translated from Medieval Arabic by Khalil I. Semaan. Arthur Jeffery Memorial Monographs, No. 3. Lahore: Sheikh Muhammad Ashraf.

Jakobson, Roman, C. Gunnar Fant & Morris Halle. 1976. *Preliminaries to Speech Analysis: The Distinctive Features and their Correlates.* Eleventh Printing. Cambridge, Mass.: The M.I.T. Press.

Jones, Daniel. 1979. *An Outline of English Phonetics.* Reprint of 1972 edn. Cambridge & London: Cambridge University Press.

Ladefoged, Peter. 1975. *A Course in Phonetics.* New York: Harcourt Brace Jovanovich, Inc.

Lieberman, Philip. 1977. *Speech Physiology and Acoustic Phonetics.* New York & London: Macmillan Publishing Co. Inc.

Malmberg, Bertil. 1963. *Phonetics.* New York: Dover Publications, Inc.

Semaan, Khalil I.H. 1961. *"Tajwīd as a source in phonetic research"*, in *Weiner Zeitschrift fur die Kunde des Morgenlandes* (Wien) 57:111–19.

------ . 1968. *Linguistics in the Middle Ages: Phonetic Studies in*

Early Islam. Leiden: E.J. Brill.

Sībawaihi. 1897. *Al–Kitāb.* Vol. II. Cairo: Būlaq Press.

Singh, Sadanand & Kala S. Singh. 1977. *Phonetics: Principles and Practices.* Second Printing. Baltimore, London & Tokyo: University Park Press.

Vollers, Karl. 1893. *"The system of Arabic sounds as described by Sībawaihi and Ibn Ya'īsh",* in *Proceedings of the Ninth International Congress of Orientalists* II (London), 130–54.

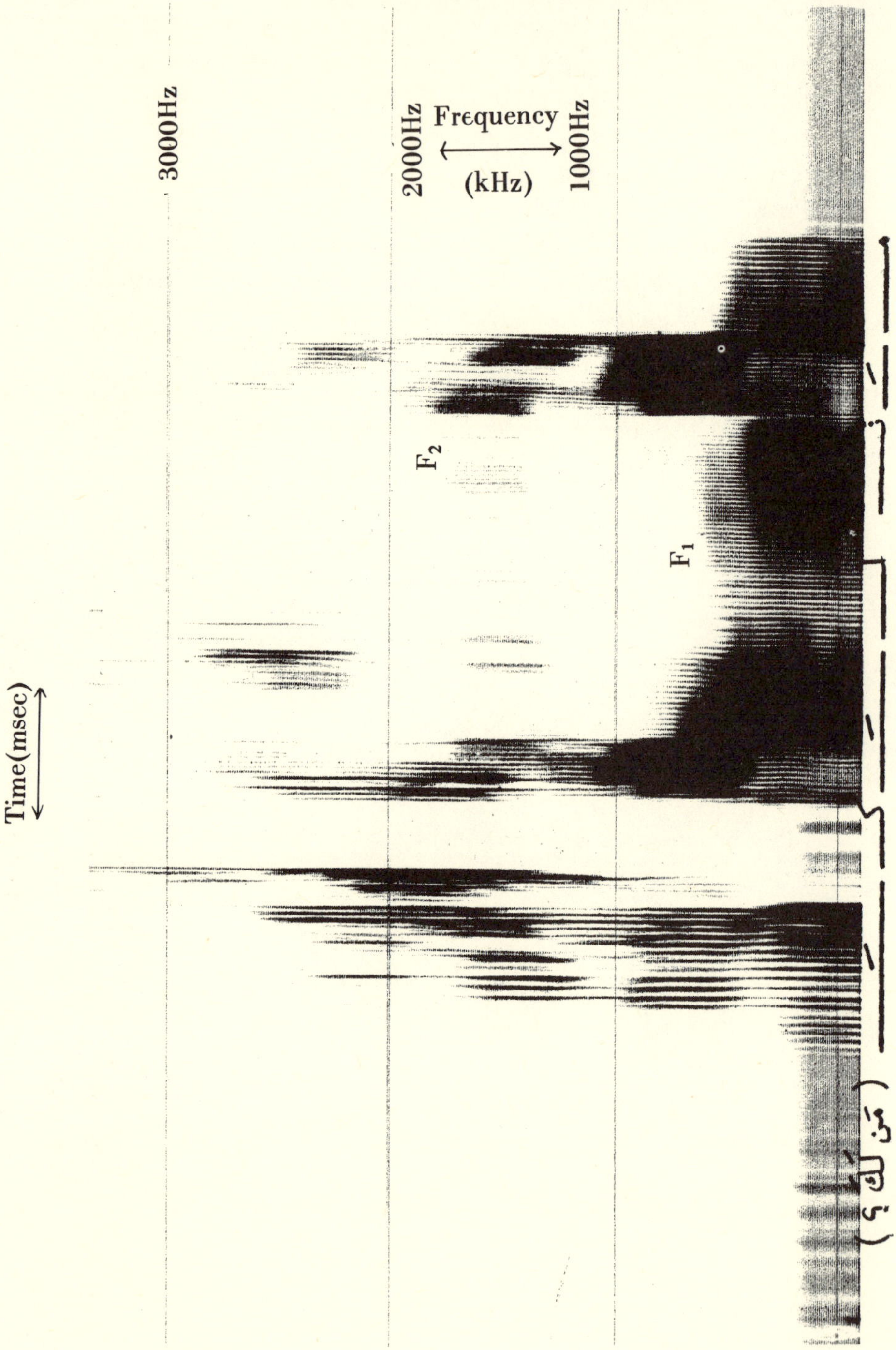

FIG. 1. SPECTOGRAM OF *man laka?*

FIG. 2. A SPECTOGRAM OF *mal laka?* (WITHOUT NASALIZATICN)

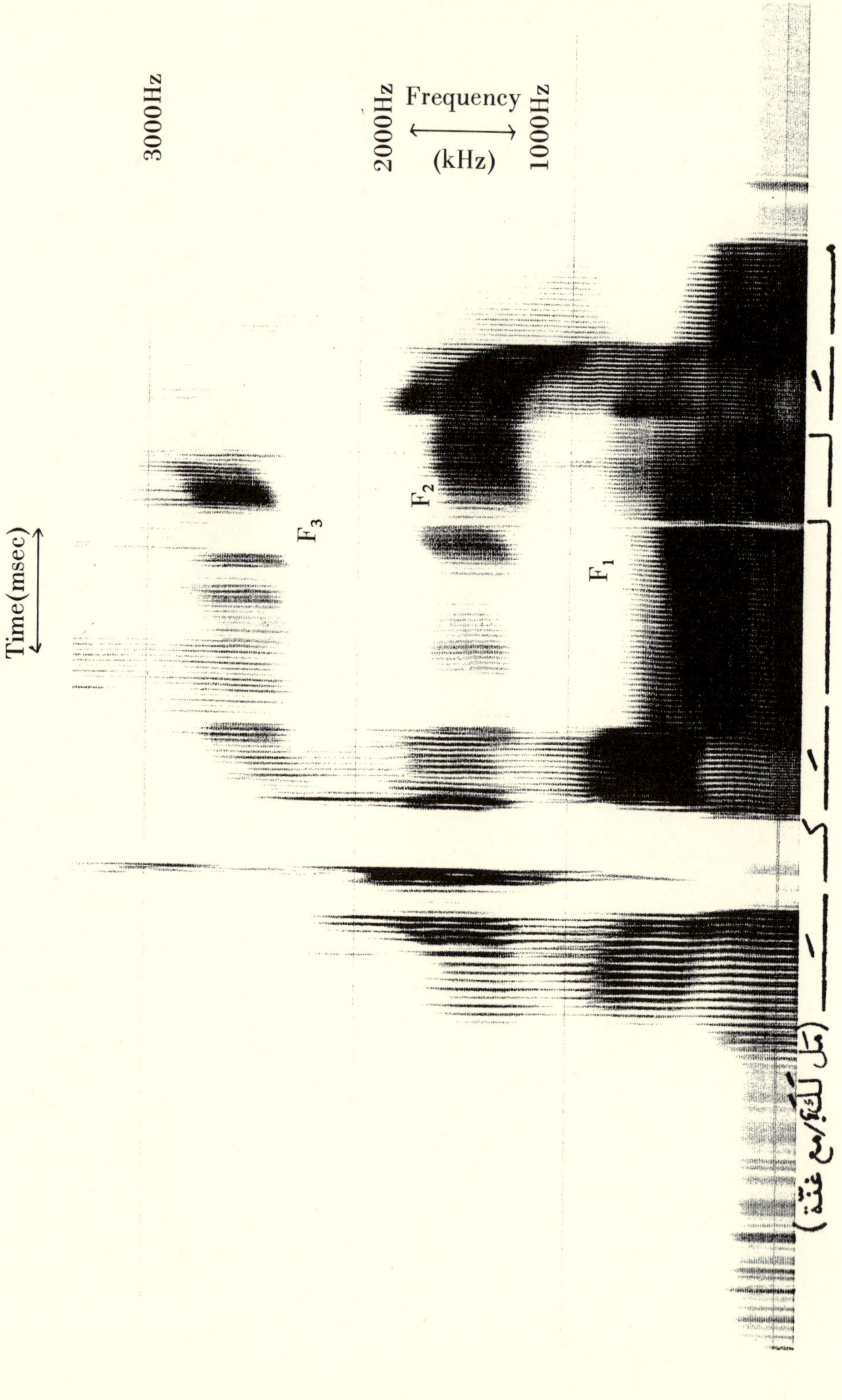

FIG. 3. A SPECTOGRAM OF *mal̃laka?* (WITH NASALIZATION)

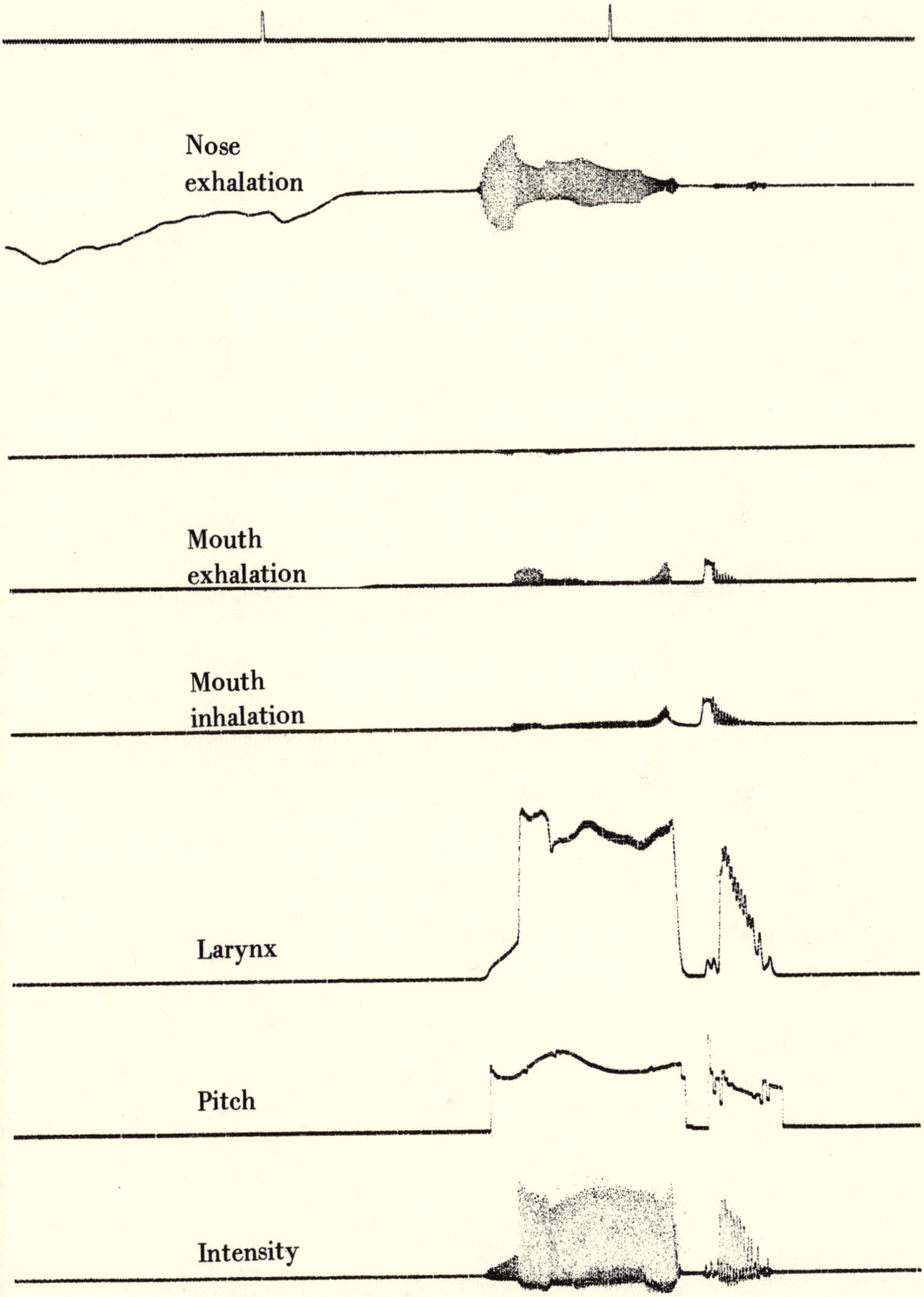

FIG. 4. SOUND MINGOGRAM OF *man laka*?

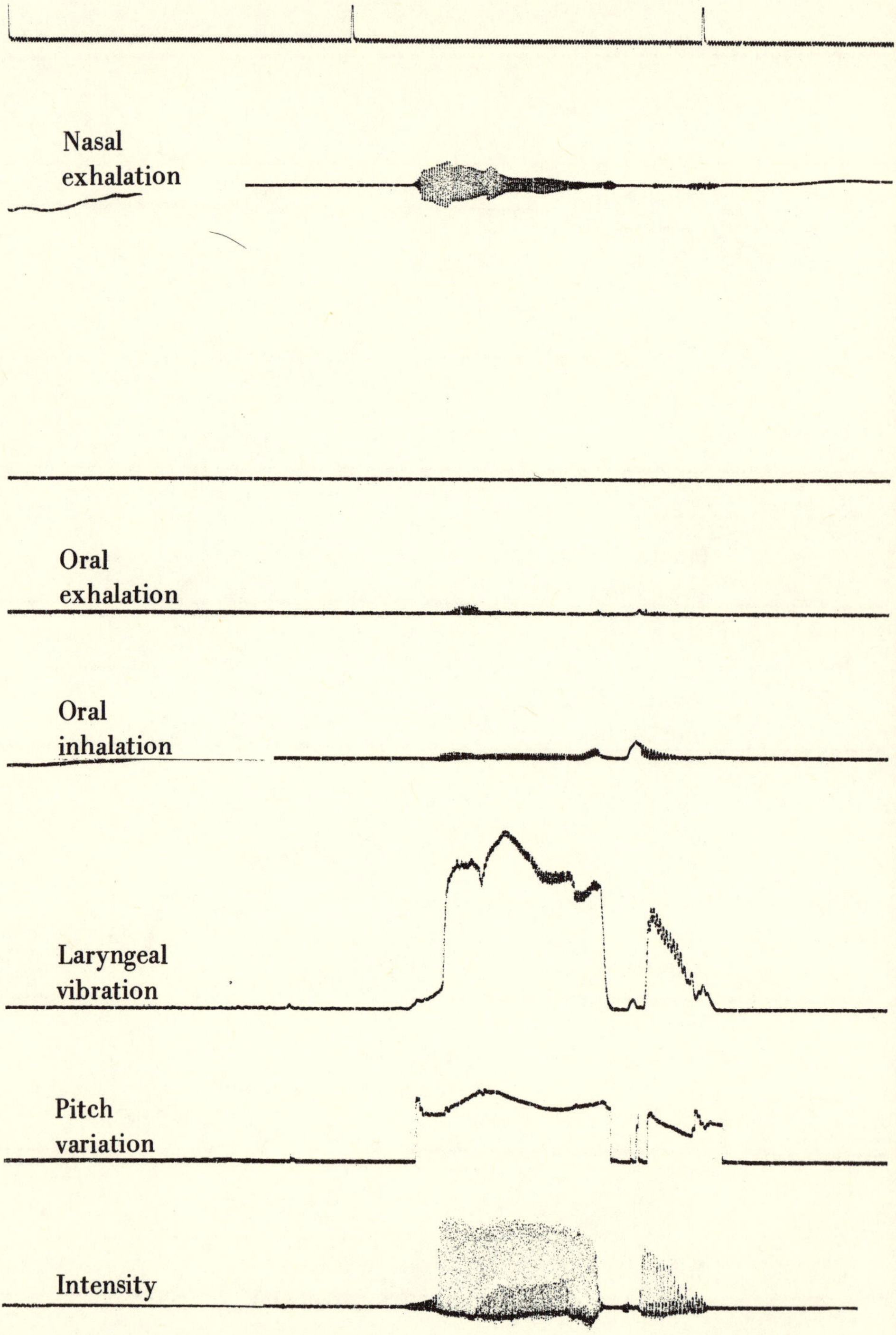

FIG. 5. A MINGOGRAM OF *mal laka*? (WITHOUT NASALIZATION)

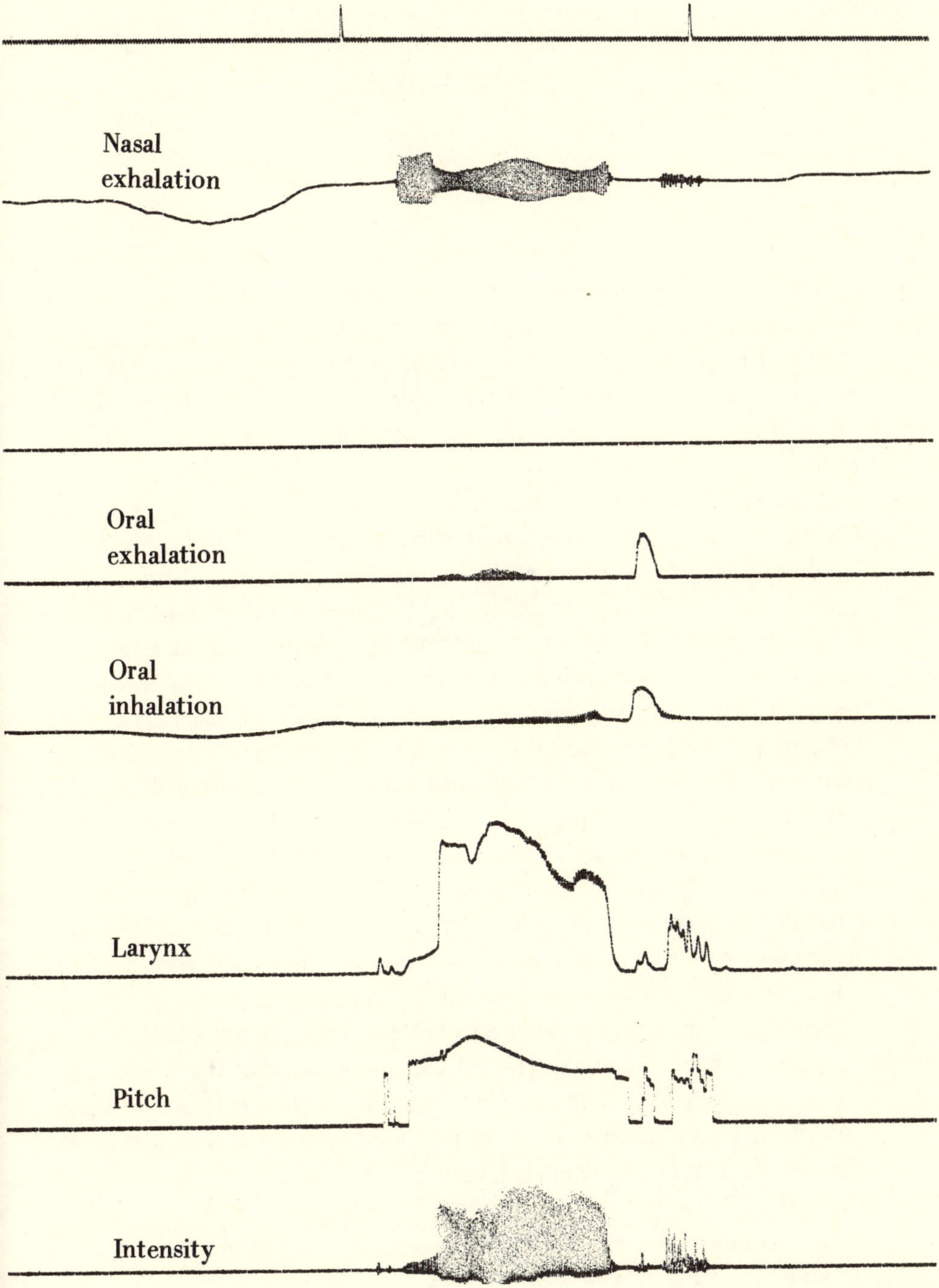

FIG. 6. A MINGOGRAM OF *maī̃laka?* (WITH NASALIZATION)

VIII

THE INFLUENCE OF ARABIC ON OTHER LANGUAGES

There is a hard and fast rule in sociolinguistics which advocates the following principle of language contact. Whenever there is a cultural contact of any form, there must be a linguistic contact as a result. After all language is a system of human communication and the words and ideas of one language can spread through time and space in extremely curious ways.

The influence can be direct as happened during the expansion of the Islamic Empire in many parts of the Ancient World. In Asia we find, for instance, Persia and India coming under the Islamic rule; in Europe, we find Spain and Sicily; in Africa we find the Arabic speaking countries and some countries south of the Sahara such as Kenya and Nigeria. The linguistic influence, on the other hand, can be indirect as is the case with English and some modern European languages which borrowed Arabic vocabulary through another language. As linguists, we can maintain that there are no pure languages in this world. Another linguistic myth which still persists in the minds of many people is that only world languages can influence small languages or even so called "primitive" languages. To linguists, all languages are equal and one language is as important as another in terms of its grammatical and semantic structures. Therefore, languages can influence each other in unidirectional or bidirectional ways.

Borrowing from other languages is not a new phenomenon; it is, in fact, an old process which affected many languages of the world and it is still a strong force which can affect modern languages whenever opportunity or necessity arises. Borrowing can be measured with a high degree of accuracy if a language is studied linguistically in a comprehensive way.

If borrowing is a natural phenomenon, then what are the causes of it and the reasons behind it?

There are a number of reasons for borrowing from or between languages. The following are some of these reasons:

First: Geographical closeness. This means that languages which are close or near to each other influence each other quite readily. One example of this is the situation of multilingualism. It has been found that in multilingual communities the languages spoken there constantly borrow from each other. Borrowing from Arabic by neighbouring non-Arabic speaking countries is also another example which is largely meant to be for ease of coummunication.

Second: is the factor of Domination. For instance, military domination of other countries and expansion in different parts of the world can spread the language or languages of the conquerors as is the case in modern times with some European languages such as Dutch, Spanish and Portuguese which have spread to other countries. Commercial and economic dominance may also be seen as a factor for expanding the territory of a language beyond its original confines. It is not always true that the dominating language gains linguistic expansion. There are some cases when the dominant languages of conquered areas influenced the dominant languages of the conquerors culturally and linguistically. The Moguls (Mongols) who conquered Baghdad embraced Islam and used the Arabic language as well.

The third factor for borrowing is necessity. For instance, nowadays the process of modernization has affected the whole globe in one way or another and as a result some words from Oriental, African or European languages have become internationally recognized. Such words or expressions as tobacco, bye-bye, and encyclopedia are examples of this factor.

The Arabic language is a special case in history. Its survival as a living language for nearly 14 centuries is unparalleled by any other existing language. Arabic loan words and expressions have penetrated many languages in the world. As a vehicle of the Islamic culture, Arabic has affected the languages of Muslims all over the world. The Muslims, Arabic or non-Arabic speakers, quite often use Arabic words and expressions for prayers and greetings as well as in their worldly affairs. Many languages in Asia and Africa have acquired loans from Arabic words and phrases, especially through Islamic sources. In Africa: Hausa, Yoruba, Berber, Somali, Mandinka, Wolof, and Swahili are amongst the languages which have been heavily influenced by Arabic. In Asia too we have Persian, Turkish, Urdu, Bengali, Malay, Maranaw, Tamil, Kurdish and Pashtu.

As a vehicle of a great culture, Arabic has influenced a number of languages in Europe. Spanish and Portuguese still keep hundreds of words and expressions which they inherited from the eight centuries or so of Muslim rule.

It has also been found that there are 2000 Arabic roots in English, two thirds of which have become obsolete and about two thirds of the remaining third are still used in everyday English, such as mosque (for the Arabic *Masjid*), alcohol (for the Arabic *alkuḥūl)* and sugar (for the Arabic *sukkar,* which was originally from the Persian *shakar*). Very few Arabic loans penetrated into English through direct influence. Most of the influence was indirect, through intermediary languages such as Spanish, French and Italian. Recently a book was published entitled "10,000 Arabic Loan Words in English" (Baghdad, 1979).

Two points have to be made here before giving more examples of Arabic loans in other languages.

The first point to be stressed is that the Arabic loan words were not confined to religious terms. They also included some legal and artistic as well as scientific words and expressions, for instance *alchemy* and *alkali* and many words in astrology and astronomy.

The second point to be made here is that many of the Arabic loan words lost part of their phonetic shapes and tones and have become partially or totally unrecognizable by laymen as well as cultivated people, and even by some Arabs.

Let us compare some of the Arabic loan words in Spanish, Portuguese, Italian, French and English.

Arabic	*Spanish*	*Portuguese*	*Italian*	*French*	*English*
maxzan (Plural: *maxāzin* lit. store)	almacen	armazen	magazzino	magazin	magazine
Amīr al–baḥr (lit. Commander of the Sea)	almirante	almirante	ammiraglio	admiral	admiral

dār al–ṣinā'ah (lit. dockyard or factory)	arsenal	arsenal	arsenale	arsenal	arsenal
ṣifr. (lit.	cifra	cifra	cifra	chiffra	
naught or zero)	cero	zero	zero	zero	zero

Also note the Arabic loans in some non-European (Islamic) languages:

Arabic	*Swahili*	*Malay*	*Turkish*	*Persian*
kitāb (book)	kitabu	kitab	kitap	kitāb
xabar (news)	habari	kabar	haber	xabar
'ilm (knowledge)	elimu	ilmu	ilim	'ilm or ilm
ḥisāb (country)	hesabu	hisap or hisab	hesap	hisāb
waqt (time)	wakati	waktu	vakit	vaqt
subḥ (morning)	asabuhi	suboh	sabah	sub
sā'ah (an hour)	saa	saat	saat	saat

To conclude, the influence of Arabic on other languages has been underestimated. There is a definite need for a fresh look at this area plus a thorough investigation. Studies in this area will not only show us more Arabic loan words in other languages but they will display the range and types of the influence and the cultural impact of Arabic on these languages. Moreover, the results of such investigations will be an indication to, or an indicative of, the origin, development and history of Arabic words and expressions in other languages throughout the ages.

REFERENCES

Bakalla, M.H. 1981. *Arabic Linguistics: An Introduction and Bibliography.* London: Mansell Publishing Ltd.

Beg, M.A.J. 1979. *Arabic Loan Words in Malay.* Kuala Lumpur.

Goodman, Morris. 1971. *"Language in contact",* in *Current Trends in Linguistics,* vol. 7 *(Linguistics in Sub-Saharan Africa)* 664–79, edited by T.A. Sebeok, Jack Berry, et al. The Hague: Mouton.

Greenberg, Joseph H. 1947. *"Arabic loan words in Hausa",* in *Word* (New York) 3. 90–91.

Lacroix, P.F. 1967. *"Remarques préliminaires à une étude des emprunts arabe en peul",* in *Africa* (London) 37. 188–202.

Latham, J.D. 1972. *"Arabic into Medieval Latin",* in *Journal of Semitic Studies* (Manchester) 17. 30–67.

Leslau, Wolf. 1956. *"Arabic loan words in Gurage",* in *Arabica* (Leiden) 3. 266–84.

Tolmacheva, Marina. 1978. *'The Arabic influence on Swahili literature: a historian's view",* in *Journal of African Studies* (London) 5/2. 238–9.

Trimingham, J.S. 1968. *The Influence of Islam upon Africa.* London.

------ . 1971. *Islam in East Africa.* London.

Weinreich, Uriel. 1964. *Languages in Contact: Findings and Problems.* The Hague: Mouton.

IX

LOAN-WORDS IN ARABIC

Human cultures are mutually influenced. Language is the vehicle of culture and the medium of culture-transmission. A word is the basic unit of a language. As a result, lexical borrowing from one language to another takes place. This phenomenon seems to be universal. It is almost impossible to find a pure language, that is a language that has not been influenced by another language at a certain point of its history. Arabic is no exception.

Arabic loan-words have influenced hundreds of languages of the world, and in return Arabic has been influenced by many other languages. Classical Arabic was influenced by languages such as Greek, Abyssinian, Latin, Persian, Aramaic and Hebrew long before the advent of Islam. When the Qur'ān was revealed it contained many of these words which appear to have been completely assimilated into the Arabic lexicon. This led some early Arab and Muslim scholars to reject the idea that there were loans in the Qur'ān. Words such as *šayṭān* "Satan", *firdaws* "Paradise", *ṣirāṭ* from the Latin "strata" meaning "way", are thought to be borrowed. Because of its long history, Arabic has borrowed more words and expressions from different languages with which it came into contact. Words such as *falsafa* "philosophy" and *mūsīqa* "music" are from the Greek language.

The cousin of the Prophet, Ibn 'Abbās (7th century) is considered the first Arab philologist to become aware of foreign words in the Arabic language. His primary concern with the Qur'ān led him to inquire into the etymologies of its vocabulary. As a result, there is attributed to him and to his school the singling out of a series of Qur'ānic words as being of foreign origin. Sībawaihi (8th century) held a liberal view which was later rejected by some philologists. The following passage is from Sībawaihi's book *al-Kitāb* (Stetkevych 1970:59–60):

"The Arabs change those foreign words which are absolutely incongruous with their own, sometimes assimilating them into the structure of their words, and sometimes not. As for that which they assimilate into their forms, there is: *dirham* – according to *hijra'; bahraj* – according to *salhab; dīnār* as well as *dībaj* – according to *dimās;* furthermore they say *'Isḥāq* – according to *'i'ṣār; Ya'qūb* - according to *yarbū';* *jawrab* – according to *fa'wal;* and then they say *'ājūr* – according to *'āqūl; šubāriq* – according to *'uḏāqir; rustāq* – according to *qurṭās.*

When they want to Arabize foreign words, they assimilate them into the structure of Arabic words in the same manner that they assimilate their letters to Arabic letters. Often they change the condition of a word from what it was in the foreign language, by assimilating to Arabic letters such as are not Arabic, and replacing a letter, even though it be like Arabic, by another one. Furthermore, they change the vocalization and the position of augmentative letters, without reaching by it the Arabic word structure, for, after all, it is a word of foreign origin whose power to attain the Arabic word structure is in their view not sufficient. To this they are impelled by the fact that the foreign words are changed by their incorporation into Arabic and the alteration of their letters, and this change brings about the substituting and the changing of the vocalization, as the Arabs themselves do in the *nisbah*-construction when they say *hanī* according to *zabānī* and *ṯaqāfī.*

Frequently they shorten, as in the *nisbah*-construction, or they add, whereby they either attain the Arabic structure or not, as in the case of: *'ājurr, 'ibrīsam, Ismā'īl, sarāwīl, fayrūz* and *al-qahramān.*

This they have done with both what was incorporated into their word structure, and what was not incorporated, in the way of change, substitution, addition and elision – all according to the change required.

Often they leave a noun unchanged when its letters are like theirs – be its structure Arabic or not, as the cases of: *Khur-*

asan, Khurram and *al-kurkum.*
Frequently they change a letter which does not exist in Arabic, without changing the original Persian structure of the word, as in *firind, baqqam, 'ājurr* and *jurbuz.*"

A more rigid and discriminating approach to the assimilation of foreign words is that of the famous Muslim lexicographer al-Jawharī, author of the *Siḥāḥ* (10th century). His concern with the purity of the language demands a strict observance of the word-patterns *qawālib,* for these alone can actually Arabize a foreign word. Otherwise it will always remain *a'jamī*. Al-Ḥarīrī maintains a similar point of view too. Professor Stetkevych (1970:61) states:

"In the period of Arabic cultural exhaustion and decadence which became accentuated after the Mongol invasion and continued through the centuries of Ottoman rule, the Arabic language was exposed to strong foreign influences, yet, within its strictly literary form, it was saved from irreversible contamination by its hermetic self-seclusion and inertia. Therefore, most of the vocabulary assimilated during that time without concern for the purity of the *qawālib* should be considered as extraliterary, if not starkly vernacular. The definitive lexicographical codification of the classical language which occurred precisely in those centuries reflects a strictly orthodox movement for preservation of the language."

One of the most important factors which contributed to the rapid modernization of the Arabic language was the assimilation of a great number of words from modern languages. Amongst these languages are: English, French, Italian, Spanish, Turkish and Portuguese. The study of the Arabic spoken or written vocabulary shows that the extent of this influence is enormous. In terms of the linguistic elements, the introduction of modern loan words into Arabic enrich the language, as it provides it with words or concepts which are lacking in the language or its users. Certainly modern technology and the speed of modernization and development require a vocabulary which develops with equal speed and pace. Since the factors relating to its development are external, that is, they are from without and not from within, Arabic has been borrowing hundreds of words. The process of this assimilation into Arabic is called *ta'rīb*, or Arabicization, or Arabization. Arabization as a solution to the urgent need for adequate modern terms in science, literature and everyday life, was not unanimously accepted. Arabization faced a great challenge from another process namely *ištiqāq* , or "derivation", which is meant to replace *ta'rīb* eventually. The total elimination of loan words cannot be achieved by any natural language. It was established later that Arabization neither contaminates nor degrades the language. Some of the modern defenders of Arabization are Muḥammad al-Khuḍarī, Abd al-Qādir al-Maghribī, Ṭāha Husain and Ya'qūb Ṣarrūf. Some of the adversaries of Arabization are Maḥmūd Shukrī al-Alūsī, and Muṣṭafa Ṣādiq al-Rāfi'ī. In his book *al-Ištiqāq* published in 1908 (1st edn.) al-Maghribī writes (Stetkevych 1970:61):

> "Our position with respect to *ta'rīb* is the reverse of that of the Arabs, whereas they seldom let a foreign word retain its original form, we would rarely change it in accordance with the patterns of our language. Thus, we pronounce telegraph, telephone, phonograph, automobile, theatre, program and many similar words, almost as they come down in their pronunciation, yet we term them as Arabized, in accordance with the method of the blessed Sībawaihi."

However, al-Maghribī seems to hold a moderate view. Although he strongly defends *ta'rīb,* as a factor for revitalizing the Arabic language, he does not approve of excessive borrowing from other languages. He expresses his reservation in the following statement (Stetkevych 1970: 62):

> "However much we approve of the point of view of Sībawaihi in not regarding as a condition for the Arabization of a word its assimilation according to the methods and moulds of our language, it is necessary that in our indulgence we should stop at a certain limit. Otherwise, foreign words of different types and forms will multiply in our literary language to the extent that, with the passage of time, it might lose its charac-

ter and become a hybrid language – neither Arabic nor foreign – something like the language of Malta or the remaining dialects of the different regions of Islamdom."

Another approach to *ta'rīb* is observed by Stetkevych (1970:63):

"A conciliatory approach to the problem of *ta'rīb* is that of Maḥmūd Taimūr. Even though he prefers, as most Arab writers do, the method of *ištiqāq*, he would not reject *ta'rīb* completely. Thus, he would rather retain the foreign term *tilifūn* than accept the completely artificial *ištiqāq* form of *'irzīz*. The decisive factor in the configuration of the modern Arabic language, as far as its vocabulary is concerned, is the acceptance the neologisms attain. To Maḥmūd Taimūr this will be determined not by the broad masses of the Arabic-speaking peoples, but by the educated sector of society, which he sees as the true depository of the modern Arabic language."

Loan words in spoken Arabic are more numerous than in written Arabic. Thus the use of the Persian words *darīšah* "window", *dirwāzah* "gate", are used in the spoken dialects of Central and Eastern Provinces of Saudi Arabia, but are replaced by *nāfiḏa* and *bawwāba*, respectively.

Naturally, loan words can go out of use when they are no longer required in the vocabulary of a society or, alternatively, when it is replaced by an old or new equivalent. Thus words like *turumbīl* and *utumbīl* meaning a "motor car" have been replaced by *sayyāra; utubīs* and *bās* could eventually be replaced by the recently coined *ḥāfila*.

Loan words in Arabic cover both specific and general subjects and some of them belong to words of everyday use. I give the following examples from Meccan Arabic.

Food and drink

baṭāṭis	(Italian patata, potato)
sandawitš	(English sandwich)

makarōna	(Italian macaroni)
farāwla	(Italian favola, strawberry)
sijāra	(cigarette).

Clothing and cosmetics

jākitta	(Italian giachetta, coat)
bantalōn	(Italian, pantaloni, pants)
karafitta	(Italian karavatta, tie)
falīna	(Italian flanella, flannel, undershirt)
kulōnya	(French cologne)
manakīr	(French manicure)

Household

batrōl	(English petrol)
banzīn	(English benzine)
baṭṭāriyya	(Italian batteria, battery)
būfēh	(French buffet)
duššš	(French douche, shower)
kanabah	(French canape, sofa)
baranda	(Italian veranda)
filla	(villa)
ṣāla	(Italian sala, living room)
sālūn	(Italian saloon)

Transport and communications

isfilt	(asphalt)
taksi	(taxi)
farāmil	(brake)
rādyu	(radio)
lūri	(English lorry)
karru	(Italian carro, cart)

Music and entertainment

dirāma	(English drama)

kōras	(English chorus)
ḍōmna	(domino)
sinama	(cinema)
nōta	(Italian nota, musical note)
bikab	(Pick up, phonograph, record player)

Diseases and drugs

influwanza	(influenza)
rumatizm	(rheumatism)
kolira	(cholera)
malāriya	(malaria)

Technology

kumbiyūtar	(computer)
tiknulōjiya	(technology)

Apart from object names, loan words are also used as verbs or part of verbal or nominal phrases. Note for instance the word *ta'amrak* "to become American", *talfaz* "to televise" *munāwara ḥarbiyya* "military manoeures", and so on.

REFERENCES

Bakalla, M.H. 1981. *Arabic Linguistics: An Introduction and Bibliography.* London: Mansell Publishing Ltd.

Chejne, A. 1969. *The Arabic Language: Its Role in History.* Minneapolis: University of Minnesota Press.

Drozdík, Ladislav. 1979. *"Lexical innovation through borrowing as presented by Arab scholars",* in *Asian and African Studies* (London) 15.21–29.

Al-Ḥarīrī. 1871. *Kitāb Durrat al-Ghawwāṣ.* Edited by Heinrich Thorbecke. Leipzig.

Al-Jawālīqī. 1969. *Al-Mu'arrab* (the Arabized words). Cairo.

Kopf, Lothar. 1961. *"The treatment of foreign words in medieval Arabic lexicology",* in *Scripta Hierosolmitana* (Jerusalem) 9. 191–205.

Al-Maghribī, Abdul Qādir. 1947. *Derivation and Arabization* (in Arabic), 2nd edn. Cairo.

Sībawaihi. 1968. *Al-Kitāb*, vol. 2. Reprint of Būlaq edn. Baghdad: al-Muthannā Press.

Siddiqi, A. 1919. *Studien über die persischen Fremdwörter in Klassischen Arabisch*. Göttingen.

Stetkevych, J. 1970. *The Modern Arabic Literary Language*. The University of Chicago Press.

X

THE SITUATION OF ARABIC IN THE ARABIC SPEAKING WORLD

Anyone visting, or who has visited any Arab country must have wondered about the linguistic situation in this area of the world. If he or she is lucky enough, as is usually the case, they will pick up some words which they may never use when they go back home. But to some people, these words ring a bell. They are the keys to some aspect of the Arab culture with which they have come in contact during their stay in an Arab country. For visitors to Saudi Arabia, in particular, the picture is even more complex. To them, the Kingdom, or certain parts of it at least, is a melting pot of different Arabic speaking nationals who use different types of Arabic, some of which are not familiar to at least some people of the Kingdom, or other nationals, for that matter.

Dialectologists or linguists call these varieties "dialects". They are dialects, and not languages, because they are mutally intelligible to each other. Mutual intelligibility is a relative matter, but it can linguistically be measured according to a scale which ranges from the highest degree to the lowest degree of intelligibility. A Saudi cannot only understand another Saudi from the same or a different region, but he can also understand other Arabs from various Arab countries.

The degree of intelligibility depends on his familiarity with these dialects. It also depends on the geographical distance between his country and the country where the other dialect is spoken. The greater the distance between the two countries the greater will be the differences between the two dialects.

There are hundreds of Arabic dialects throughout the Arabic speaking countries. In Saudi Arabia alone one can count over 200 dialects scattered all over the Kingdom. The definition of a dialect in this sense is "a set of linguistic features which are characteristics of the speech or utterance used in a geographically defined community." All members of this community share the same speech features. In other words, a dialect is a language variation which occupies a limited geographical area, and it is a part of a language which normally covers a larger area. Dialects can also co-exist in one and the same area. Even a so-called tribe can have as many subdialects as its divisions and subdivisions might allow. Note the following sets of dialectal words representing some Arabic speaking communities. The following are the words used to mean "green pepper".

In Mecca *filfil*
Riyadh *ḥibḥir* or *filfil*
Eastern Province *ḥār*

Now the words for "a clove"

In Mecca *gurunful*
Riyadh *mismār*

Now the words for "water melon"

In Mecca *ḥabḥab*
Cairo *biṭṭīx*
Riyadh *jiḥḥ*

The verb "to begin"

In Mecca *bada? /?abtada*
Jedda *? ibtada*
Casablanca *bada*
Lebanon & Syria *ballaš*

It is interesting to note that *ballaš* has the opposite meaning in the Meccan dialect, that is "finished".

These are lexical variations. The phonological or sound variations among Arabic dialects are even greater. Here are some examples.

Note the consonant and vowel variations in the following words which mean "to have a hair cut"

Cairo *ḥala?*
Mecca *ḥalag*

Note also the change of *j* to *y* in some dialects

Mecca	*dujāja*
Riyaḍh	*dijāja*
Kuwait	*diyāya*

It is to be noted that such variations do not normally hinder communication among the Arabs. In fact, many of such variations are well established and so they are recognised as regional by them.

But this is not the total picture of the position of Arabic as it exists today. Besides these dialects, there also exists Classical Arabic, the language of the Qur'ān and Scriptures, which had its beginnings in the early sixth and seventh centuries. Classical Arabic itself was at one time a dialect (namely *Quraish* dialect) which was chosen as a standard form of the language.

In addition, there is another variety which stems from Classical Arabic and which is also influenced by the regional dialects especially in terms of the lexicon and the sound patterns of these dialects. This variety is called Modern Standard Arabic. Any Arab uses his own dialect informally when he or she speaks with another Arab from his own region or even from a different region. He may also employ a mixture of dialects in the company of Arabs from different regions on informal occasions. But educated Arabs are gradually using more and more Modern Standard Arabic.

Modern Standard Arabic is, in fact, a cover term for the variety of Arabic, both spoken and written, which is utilized in education, mass media (including the press, radio and television) and general lectures, announcements, and advertisements.

It varies little, not only from one Arab country to another, but also from one region to another. It is also influenced quite readily by the speaker's regional background and one can tell without difficulty from which region the speaker of Modern Standard Arabic comes.

Modern Standard Arabic can be seen as an extension of Classical Arabic plus the modern elements which have poured into the main stream of the Classical Arabic.

The Arabic dialects, Classical Arabic and Modern Standard Arabic have so much in common. Note the following examples:

The word for "a back":

In	Classical Arabic	*ẓahr*
	Modern Standard Arabic	*ẓahr*
	Meccan dialect	*ḍahar*
	Riyadh	*ẓahar*
	Baghdad	*ẓahar*

Now the word for "a bird":

Classical Arabic	*ṭayr*
Modern Standard Arabic	*ṭayr*
Meccan dialect	*ṭēr*

The word for "a smoke"

Classical Arabic	*duxān*
Modern Standard Arabic	*duxān*
Meccan dialect	*duxxān*

Now, the word for "rain"

Classical Arabic	*maṭar*
Modern Standard Arabic	*maṭar*
Meccan dialect	*maṭar*
Baghdad	*muṭar*

Now, the word for "water"

Classical Arabic	*mā'*
Modern Standard Arabic	*mā'*
Meccan dialect	*mōya*
Baghdad	*māy*

Now the verb "he drank":

Classical Arabic	*šariba*
Modern Standard Arabic	*šariba*
Meccan dialect	*širib*
Baghdad	*širab*

Note the following word *sayyārah*. In Classical Arabic it meant "camel caravan", in Modern Standard Arabic and most modern dialects it refers to "a motor car".

Quite a few Classical Arabic words have been replaced by modern words. For instance the wide use of the word *luġah* meaning "language" instead of the Classical Arabic word *lisān*. *Luġah* itself in Classical Arabic meant "dialect" but has now been replaced by the new term *lahjah*.

These are some features of the development which Arabic has undergone in the course of its long history.

The co-existence of various types of the same language is technically termed "diglossia". Professor Charles Ferguson, an Arabist and sociolinguist, introduced this term in English around 1959 and defined it as follows:

> "Diglossia is a relatively stable language situation in which, in addition to the primary dialects of the language (which may include a standard or regional standards), there is a very divergent highly codified (often grammatically more complex) superposed variety, the vehicle of a large and respected body of written literature, either of an earlier period or in another speech community, which is learned largely by formal education and is used for most written and formal spoken purposes but is not used by any sector of the community for ordinary conversation."

REFERENCES

Al–Ani, Salman, H., ed. 1978. *Readings in Arabic Linguistics*. Bloomington, Indiana: Indiana University Linguistics Club.

Bakalla, M.H. 1981. *Arabic Linguistics: An Introduction and Bibliography*. London.

Sebeok, Thomas A., C.A. Ferguson, C.T. Hodge, et al, eds. 1970. *Current Trends in Linguistics*, vol. 6: *Linguistics in South West Asia and North Africa*. The Hague: Mouton. Also includes: C.G. Killean's *"Classical Arabic"*, pp. 413–38, and Peter F. Abboud's *"Spoken Arabic"*, 439–66.

XI

DIGLOSSIA IN ARABIC

Diglossia is a sociolinguistic term used to denote a state of language situation in a specific speech community. This word consists of two elements, the prefix *di* – meaning two, and *glossia* which means "language" or "tongue". It indicates a situation in a speech community in which two types or variations of the same language co-exist side by side, each of which performs a specific function. The situation where two different languages exist side by side in a speech community is usually described as bilingualism, or even multilingualism.

Diglossia can be observed in Greek, Swiss German and Arabic. In an Arab context, it refers to the co-existence of both a standard form of the language and a colloquial form of the same language. On the one hand, there is Classical Arabic, referred to also as "literary", "standard", and "written", which maintains a high degree of uniformity, and functions as the official standard language in all the Arabic speaking countries. In other words, it is the official language which is used in formal situations including: sermons, lectures in education and the mass media. On the other hand, Colloquial Arabic is the actual language of everyday activities, mainly spoken, and it varies not only from one country to another but also from one area to another within each country.

Arabic diglossia is not a new phenomenon. It goes back to the pre-Islamic era and it was observed by Arab and Muslim grammarians and philologists for centuries. Classical or Standard Arabic or *al-'Arabiyya al-al-Fuṣḥā* always co-existed with the local dialects and there was no controversy such as that which began around the nineteenth century. Although Colloquial Arabic has always been viewed as being below the standard required for literary, religious and political expression, it was not considered as a threat to Classical Arabic. It was not until the nineteenth century that the question of partial or total adoption of Colloquial Arabic as the language of culture and literature was raised. Some scholars, Arabs and non-Arabs alike, promoted this idea on the grounds that written Arabic and spoken or colloquial Arabic are so different, to the extent that written Arabic sounded strange to the present generation. Some of them went so far as to suggest that the gains which could be attained from the use of the colloquials, far outnumber the losses which would result from the abandonment of Classical Arabic.

This challenge of pitting colloquialism against classicism or rather standardization, brought home an awareness of the language situation. Traditionalists and most of the literary men opposed this idea which proposed the abandonment of Classical Arabic completely or even partially and the controversy went on for more than one hundred years.

Nowadays this issue is almost dead. It is no longer a burning question and cannot engender talks, lectures and discussions in books, newspapers and other branches of the mass media as was previously the case.

Amongst the difficulties which faced those colloquialists or proponents of the colloquials, were the following factors:

Firstly: The traditional heritage which is mainly a classical, living heritage, represented by books on literature, arts and sciences. The Qur'ān preserved Arabic throughout the ages. Without the *Holy Book,* Arabic would have probably been divided into many languages, just like Maltese, which was once a pure Arabic dialect but which later on developed independently as a separate language due to certain circumstances.

Secondly: The religious attitude. The Muslim Arabs have always advocated Classical Arabic as a unifying factor not only for the Arabs but also for non-Arab Muslims who share this language and its heritage with the Arabs.

Thirdly: The question of which variety of Arabic should be adopted. If all dialects are to be written it would mean the loss of the standardization which Classical Arabic has always maintained. An Indian or Indonesian scholar who uses any form of Classical Arabic can be understood all over the Arabic speaking world, which does not tend to adopt a particular dialect as a standard language. Which dialect amongst hundreds of Arabic dialects could be chosen as a standard language was a question which could not be answered satisfactorily.

Fourthly: If we are to use all the dialects of Arabic in written as well as spoken expression then which one should be used in teaching Arabic as a first, second or even as a foreign language? No doubt that a standard, widely accepted form of a language is needed for Arabic.

Fifthly: As there are many regional dialects in each Arab country there are also social dialects within each region. These include the dialectal varieties used by various classes of people, and the dialectal varieties employed by various vernaculars and jargons and secret languages of a particular society or a small professional group of it.

Against this background, diglossia does not seem to express the situation of Arabic accurately. Diglossia normally involves a two poles system, in which each pole stands on its own and does not contribute to the other in any significant way. But this is not the exact linguistic picture of the Arabic-speaking world. It is true that Classical Arabic, in the sense of living standard Arabic, has the most prestigious place, and dialect is looked down upon by the educated Arabs who use it in day to day affairs and non-official situations. But throughout the ages, there has been another variety of Arabic which comes between these two varieties. In modern times, it is mainly known as common, or middle Arabic. This variety is based mainly on Classical Arabic but it is influenced by the dialectal environment to a lesser or greater degree.

To me it seems better to view the situation of Arabic not as a mere diglossic or triglossic situation, but as a spectrum or better still a continuum which has at one extreme the purest Classical Arabic and at the other the purest type of colloquial Arabic. In between these two extremes lie the varieties of Arabic which are either relatively closer to classical or colloquial Arabic. Also criss-crossing this continuum are the various social and professional jargons or sub-dialects. I term this state as the spectroglossia of Arabic.

The study of spectroglossia, like diglossia, is a sociolinguistic study which concerns itself with the study of language and society and the interrelation between them. The scope of this study is unlimited and the objectives of such an investigation are manifold. So far the dialects and subdialects and other varieties of Arabic have not been given proper consideration and unless such studies are given proper emphasis, our knowledge of the Arabic speaking societies will not be complete or even accurate. Language is considered a mirror which reflects the various facets of a society, and without a thorough investigation of these facets our understanding of this society will be incomplete.

REFERENCES

Bakalla, M.H. 1981. *Arabic Linguistics: An Introduction and Bibliography*. London.

Ferguson, Charles A. 1959. *"Diglossia"*, in *Word* (New York) 15. 325–40.

Kaye, Alan Stewart. 1972. *"Remarks on diglossia in Arabic well-defined vs. ill-defined"*, in *Linguistics* (The Hague) 81. 32–48.

Al-Toma(Altoma), Salih J. 1969. *The Problem of Diglossia in Arabic: A Comparative Study of Classical Arabic and Iraqi Arabic.* Cambridge, Mass.: Harvard University Press.

XII

THE ARABIC DIALECTS OF THE MAGHRIB

By "dialect" I mean the linguistic variety spoken in non-formal situations in a certain community or region. Unlike the Modern Standard Arabic, many of the dialects do not possess any form of official script. Maghrib is a cover term which includes several North African and West African countries such as: Libya, Tunisia, Algeria, Morocco and Mauritania and at one time it also included Malta, Sicily, Spain, and Pantelleria and the Balearic Islands in the Mediterranean. The dialects and subdialects of the Maghrib form a unified, homogenous group which has lost its Maghrib proto-language without any trace.

The unity of the dialects spoken west of the Nile (hence the word Maghrib meaning the West) has long been acknowledged by Arab and Muslim geographers and historians. They have also recognized the differences and dissimilarities between the Eastern and Western dialects of Arabic. In his book *Aḥsan al-Taqāsīm* written in the 10th Century A.D., the Arab Muslim geographer al-Muqaddasī observed that the varieties of Arabic spoken in the Maghrib were not easy to understand since they differed from the Arabic dialects of other regions such as those of Arabia, Syria, Iraq and Egypt. His contemporary Abū 'Alī al-Qālī, a linguist from Baghdad who had travelled through North Africa on his way to Andalusia or Muslim Spain, observed that "the farther one departs from the East, the worse is the Arabic spoken by Muslims." At one point, he thought he might have to employ an interpreter before he reached his destination. In his *Muqaddimah* written in the 15th century, Ibn Khaldūn (1978: 249–95) also noted the Maghrib dialects were corrupted and that they differed from the Arabic dialects of the Arabian Peninsula. Ibn Khaldūn also noted that Bedouin dialects also varied from the dialects of urban regions, town dwellers and villagers.

The modern Arabic dialects of Maghrib are mostly confined to North Africa, where they are spoken by some 40 million people. Their habitat stretches from the borders of Egypt in the East until it reaches the Atlantic ocean in the West, the rivers Senegal and Niger in the South-west and Lake Chad in the South-east. Modern Maltese is not included as it is considered by some scholars to be a separate language, since its writing system is based on the Latin script and because its literature has developed outside the realm of Arabic and Islamic culture.

It is interesting to note that the Bedouin subdialects exhibit far greater affinity to Classical Arabic than the urban subdialects of the Modern Maghrib. The Bedouin subdialects still retain the Classical Arabic pronunciation of the interdentals ṯ and ḏ and such archaic characteristics of Classical Arabic morphology as the patterns of the verbs, the dual number in nouns, and the grammatical gender in pronouns, while the sedentary subdialects have already lost some of these Classical features. In terms of vocabulary, sedentary and rural subdialects contain far more Berber elements, and foreign loan-words than the Bedouin subdialects. There has been an increasing interest in the dialects of the Maghrib both at the academic and non-academic levels since the mid 19th century. So far about 30 subdialects have been studied in the area, though not all of them in sufficient depth. Traditionally the German and French linguists are famous in contributing to the studies of Algerian, Tunisian and Mauritanian dialects, the Italians to Libyan dialects and the Spanish, French and Germans to Moroccan dialectology. In the last two decades or so, this interest has spread to the U.S.A, U.S.S.R., Great Britain and other European countries. About 40 modern Maghribi dialects have been investigated, but there are many more which are still waiting to be studied linguistically as well as sociolinguistically.

Amongst the subdialects studied in Morocco are Rabat, Tangier, Casablanca, Tetuan, Fez, Larache, Marrakesh, Sale; in Tunisia they are Tunis, Sfax, Sousse; in Mauritania it is Hassaniya; in Algeria: they are Algiers, Tlemsen and Constantine; and in Libya they are Benghazi, Tripoli and Cyrenaica.

In Morocco, which has a population of about 19 million, about 55% speak Arabic as a mother tongue; 40% use Berber and most of them are bilingual, Arabic being the language of education, religion, culture and commerce. The remaining 5% are Europeans from France, Spain and other European countries. The Urban dialects of Morocco include Tangier in the northern region, with about 250,000 speakers, Fez in the

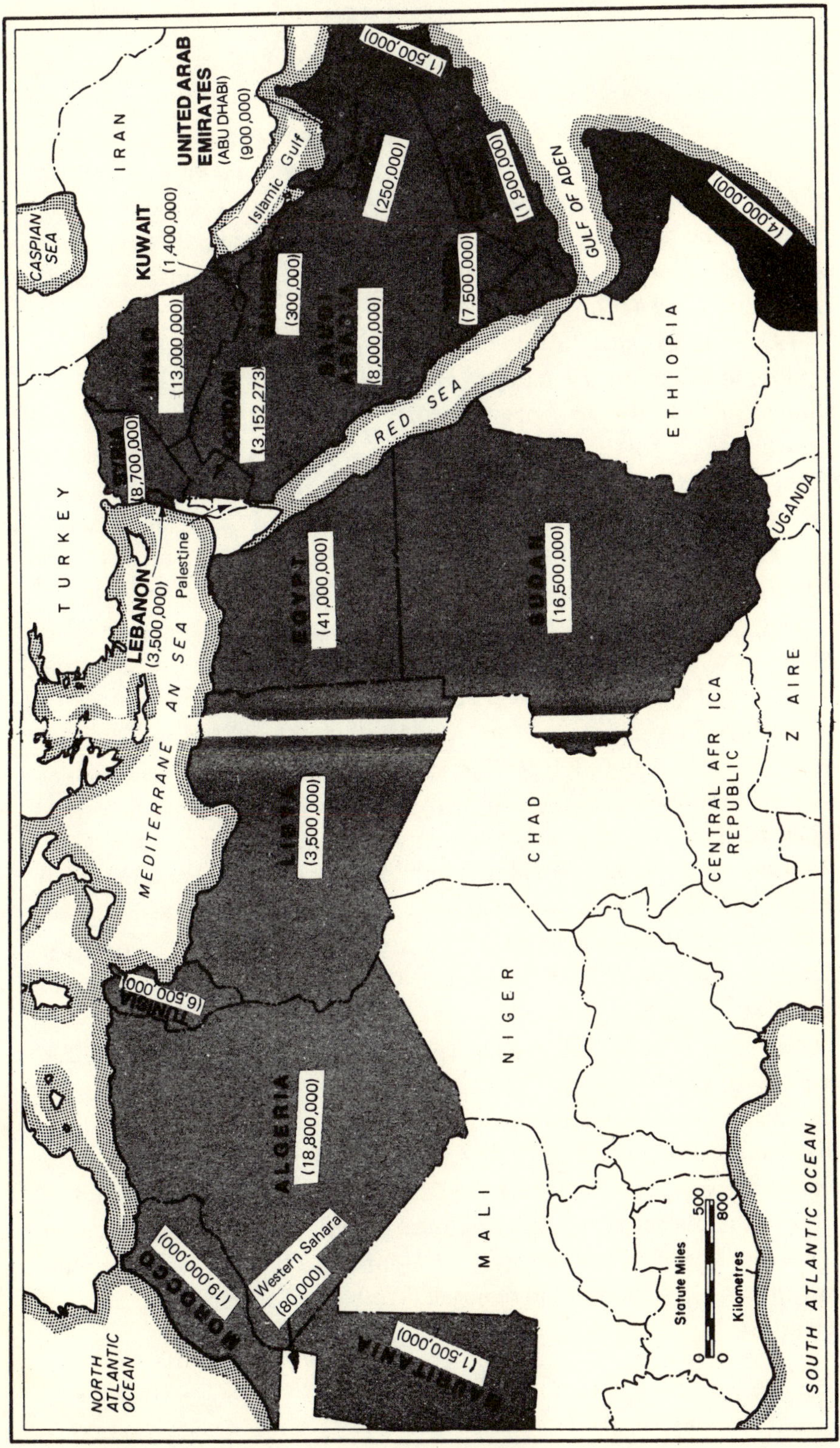

MAP 1. Approximate Population of the Arab Countries.

Central Region with about 240,000 speakers; Meknes with about 200, 000. The standard dialect in Morocco is the dialect of the modern capital Rabat. Rural Moroccan dialects are found largely in northern Morocco as in The Rif whose dialect is known as Jabli. Moroccan Bedouin dialects are widely scattered and they are used by nomadic and semi-nomadic tribesmen as well as by the population of the valleys. Casablanca accounts for more than half a million Bedouins; Marrakesh with about a quarter of a million.

Algeria has native Arabic speakers of about 12 million out of a population of about 19 million. Berber is used by about 20% of the population. The Berber language clusters near Constantine; along the Jurjura Range; in the Atlas mountains, Saharan oasis. The Algerian urban dialects are found in Constantine with an estimated 200,000 speakers, Algiers with more than half a million, and Oran, and Tlemsen with about 150,000. Rural dialects include the Jijelli dialect. The Bedouin dialects are found in Ulad Brahim, Oran.

Descending the ladder, Tunisia has a population of more than six million and more than 90% speak the Arabic language, apart from about 70% of the 70,000 Berber speaking Tunisians.

Urban Tunisian dialects are widely scattered and the capital Tunis has more than 1,000,000 Arabic speakers. Rural dialects are spoken along eastern Tunisian coast, known as Sāḥel. Bedouin dialects include Gabes, Gasfa with about 30,000 speakers each.

Libya has about 3½ million inhabitants, about 90% are speakers of Arabic. Berber speakers are generally bilingual, and there are about 80, 000 of them. The dialects of Libya are said to be derived from the dialect of the Beni-Sulaim tribe. The Cyrenaican dialects account for more than 350,000 speakers who live in Benghazi, Barkee, Derna, and Tobruk. The Tripolitanian dialect accounts for more than 450,000 speakers of Arabic in Tripoli, Misurata and Homs.

In Mauritania which has a population of about 1½ million inhabitants, Hassaniya dialect of Arabic is spoken. The word Hassaniya is derived from the name of a tribe Dhawī Hassān which conquered this region. This dialect structurally belongs to the Moroccan dialects and it is now the *lingua franca* not only of Mauritania but also of other West African regions such as Mali, Senegal, Gambia and the so-called Spanish Sahara.

Although the dialects of Maghrib share common features which distinguish them from the Eastern Arabic dialects, they differ among themselves in certain areas of vocabulary and grammar. Lexically speaking, the Urban dialects display greater differences amongst themselves than the rural or Bedouin dialects which are relatively homogenous. The lexical differences between Maghrib dialects in Morocco, Algeria, Tunisia and Libya are not confined only to variations in words referring to the human body, family relations, taboos, clothes, household utensils and official vocabulary. They also involve a very wide range of widely used words such as catch-words, affirmative, negative, and interrogative expressions; pronouns, verbs and adverbs too.

The following list displays the lexical differences between some Western Arabic dialects compared to my Meccan dialect.

	Moroccan	*Algerian*	*Libyan*	*Tunisian*	*Hassaniya*	*Meccan*
now	*dāba*	*delwóq* *druk*	*alān*	*táwwa*	*ḍark*	*dahḥīn*
well	*mazyan* *waxxa*	*mlīeḥ*	*bāhi*	*ṭayyab*	*zeyn*	*ṭayyib*
there is	*kāyn*	*kan*	*fīh*	*famma*	*Xalag*	*fī*
there is no	*makānš*	*makānš*	*mafīš*	*mafammaš*	*maxalagši*	*māfiš*
how much	*ašḥāl/* *šḥāl*	*gaddaš*	*kam*	*qaddaš*	*kamm*	*kam*
much	*bazzaf/* *bal'a*	*bazzaf*	*yāsar*	*barša*	*ḥatta*	*katīr*
to do	*dar/idir* *qā*	*yalqi* *xdam*	*sawa*	*'āmal*	*wāsa*	*sawwa*
eggs	*awlād žaž*	*biḍ*	*deḥi*	*'aḍām*	*béẓ*	*bēḍ*
rain	*naw/nu*	*sḥab /* *naw*	*mṭār*	*štā*	*sḥāb*	*maṭara*
nothing	*wālu*	*ši*	*kān-l-* *barka*	*šay*	*ši*	*walašay*

It is interesting to note the variations between these dialects which can be traced back to early Arabic dialectal forms, Classical Arabic or even idiosyncracy or neologism that developed at a certain stage of the evolution of a dialect.

As the Coptic language substratum played an important role in the evolution of Egyptian Arabic dialects, and Aramaic substratum in the evolution of Lebanese Arabic dialects, so did the Berber substratum in the evolution of the Maghrib dialects. The influence of Berber stratum is not only in terms of the vocabulary but also in the phonological, morphological and syntactic components of the Western Arabic dialects. Berber loan words in Moroccan dialects are estimated to be between 10–15 per cent, in Tunisian and Algerian dialects between 8–10 per cent, in the Libyan dialect between 2–4 per cent. Some of these words are totally assimilated into the vocabularies of these dialects. Words such as *agwāl* "kind of a drum", *bakkūš* meaning "deaf" and *fakrūn* meaning "turtle" are borrowed from Berber.

Since the Western Arabic dialects came into constant contact with other cultures, a large number of foreign words found their way into one or more of these dialects. Thus, we find lexical borrowings in the Western Arabic dialects from languages such as Turkish, Greek, Latin, Spanish, Portuguese, Italian and French. The influence of the Spanish loans on the Maghrib vocabulary was the greatest, especially in Algeria and Morocco. The influence of Italian on the Libyan dialect is also very great. French borrowings are by far the largest influence on Maghribi dialects and specifically Algerian dialects.

REFERENCES

Bakalla, M.H. 1981. *Arabic Linguistics: An Introduction and Bibliography*. London.

Heine, Bernd. 1970. *Status and Use of African Lingua Francas*. München.

Ibn Khaldūn. 1978. *Al-Muqaddimah. An Introduction to History*. Translated from the Arabic by Franz Rosenthal, abridged and edited by N.J. Dawood. London & Henley: Routledge & Kegan Paul in association with Secker & Warburg.

XIII

EASTERN ARABIAN DIALECTS

By Eastern Arabian dialects I mean the dialects of the areas lying at the East and Northeast of the Arabian Peninsula. They include the dialects spoken in the Eastern Province of Saudi Arabia, Bahrain, Qatar, United Arab Emirates and Kuwait. Another appelation for this group of dialects is Gulf Arabic, sometimes this term excludes Saudi Arabia. It must not, however, be confused with the Eastern Arabic group of dialects, which is more generic and also includes all those Arabic dialects lying to the east of the Nile.

There are more than 4 million inhabitants in the Gulf area, about 85 per cent of whom use Arabic as a first language. The Eastern Province of Saudi Arabia accounts for approximately one fifth of the total Eastern Arabian dialect speakers. About 20 per cent of the population of Eastern Arabia are bilinguals, whose mother tongues are Persian, Urdu, and Indian or African languages, Arabic being a second language to them. Many of the Gulf Arab population came from Central or Northern Arabia. A number of 'Anaza sub-tribes have moved to the Gulf area since the 18th century. The ruling families in Kuwait and Bahrain are descendents of the 'Anaza tribe. The dialects of Kuwait include Rashāyda, 'Awāzim and Muṭair. Before the discovery of oil, most of the population of the Gulf were mainly occupied in fishing, trading, pearling, farming and handicrafts. Some of these professions have been badly affected since the 1930's. The population of the Gulf countries has also increased. As a result of modern development in the area, hundreds of people from neighbouring Arab and Muslim countries, including Egypt and the Fertile Crescent, have settled in the area. These do not include the vast numbers of workers who are on temporary employment in this area.

Eastern Arabian dialects constitute a unified group which share some general distinctive features which bind them together. Morphologically, the dialects of this group are closely related to the 'Anazi type dialects. However they can be clearly distinguished from them in terms

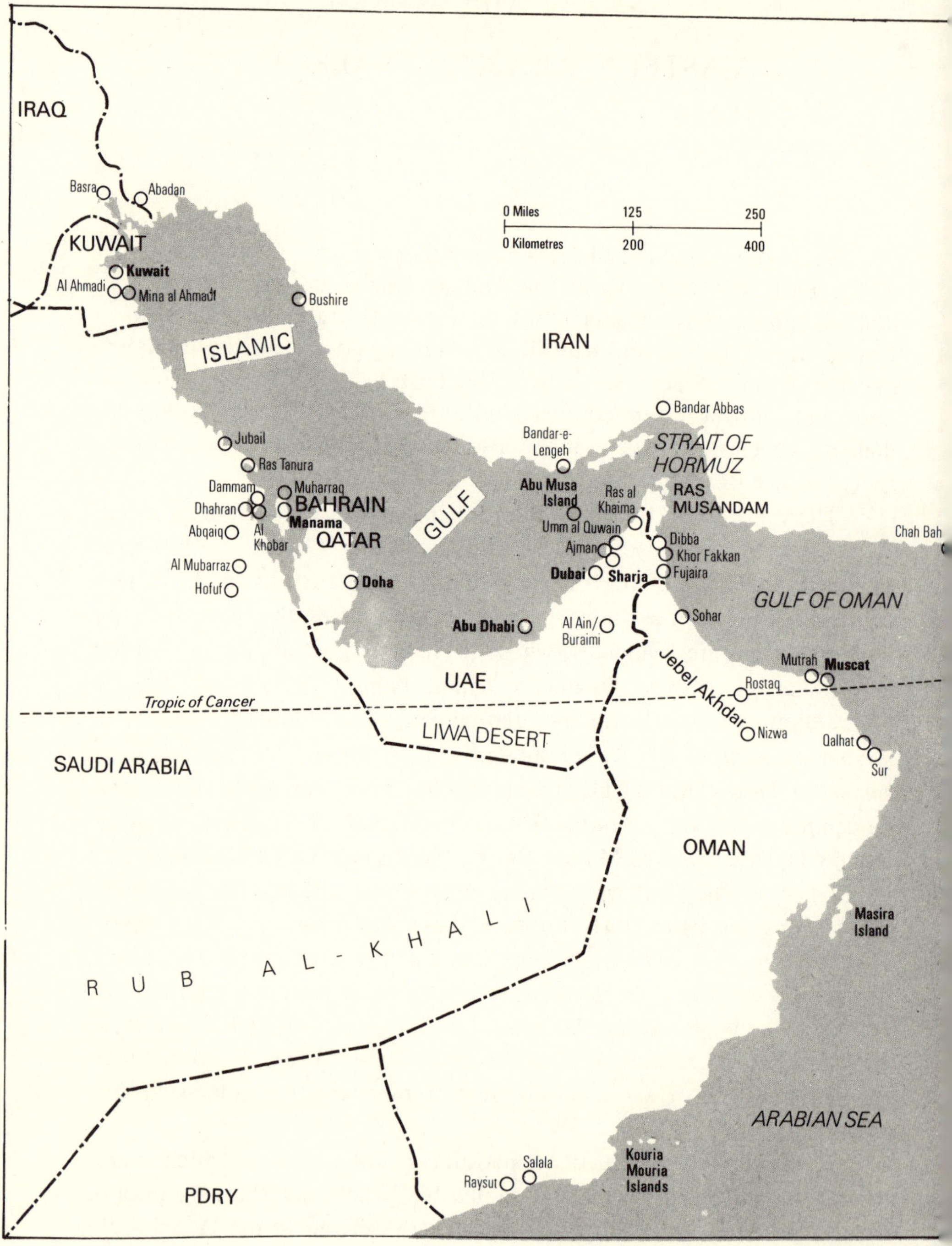

MAP 2. The Gulf States.

of the phonology and vocabulary as the result of developments over the last two centuries or so.

The dialects of Eastern Arabia also share a common oral literature and folklore, such as proverbs, fairy tales, riddles, songs and dances which portray life on the farms, and by the sea.

As for the phonology or sound system of the dialects of Eastern Arabia, the dialects possess the affricate consonants *č* and *j*, as in Kuwaitī Arabic *čan* "if", *hači* "talk", *jāsim* for a man's name Qāsim.

The Eastern Arabic dialects, differ from the Central Arabian dialects in the pronunciation of *k* and *g*. In Central Arabian dialects *k* and *g* are pronounced as affricates *ts* and *dz*, respectively.
Thus:

	Shammarī dialect	Kuwaitī dialect	Meccan dialect
kaff "palm of hand"	*ćaf*	*čaf*	*kaff*
ibrīq "jug"	*brīdz*	*brīj*	*ibrīg*

Central and Western Arabian dialects do not possess the affricates *c* and *j*. Instead, they possess the affricates *ć* / *ts* / and *dz*.

Compare the following examples from a number of dialects including my own Meccan dialect.

	Qaṭarī dialect	Kuwaitī	Meccan dialect
fish	*simač*		*samak*
large	*čibīr*		*kabīr*
to divide		*jassam*	*gassam*

Here *k* is realized in Qaṭarī as *č*, *g* as *j* with or without affrication.

Eastern Arabian dialects share with Central Arabian dialects the following phonological features:

1. When a non-final closed syllable whose vowel is *a* in which the closing consonant is a gutteral, it becomes an open syllable of the structure *cca-*. Thus if *G* is any of the guttural consonants *ġ, x, h,* or *ḥ* then *CaG* – *CGa*. Thus for example:

ṣaxla	→	*ṣxala*	"kid"
gahwa	→	*ghawa*	"coffee"

2. *af'al* → *fa'al*
for example:

aḥmar	→	*ḥamar*	"red"
axḍar	→	*xaḍar*	"green"

3. *maf'ūl* → *mfa'ūl*
for example:

ma'rūf	→	*m'arūf*	"known"
maḥzūm	→	*mḥazūm*	"tied"

4. In the dialects of Central and Northern Arabia in general a series of short syllables cannot stand, and forms of the syllable structure *f'ala(t), f'ila(t)* and *f'alaw, f'ilaw* correspond to forms of the type فَعَلَة ، فَعَلَت and فَعَلوا in Modern Standard Arabic.
Thus:

	Eastern & Central Arabic	Meccan Arabic
raqabah "neck"	*rguba*	*ragaba*
baqarah "cow"	*bgara*	*bagara*
katabat "she wrote"	*ktibat*	*katabat*

5. Both Eastern and Central Arabian dialects share the fact that the masculine singular imperatives of the verbs with final *y* lose their final vowel. For example:

	Eastern and Central Arabic	Meccan Arabic
imši "go/walk"	*imši*	*amši*
ištari "buy"	*ištir*	*aštari*
xalli "allow"	*xaḹḹ*	*xalli*

The pronunciation of "j"

Eastern Arabian dialects, South, and South West Arabian dialects share the fact that they all pronounce the *j* as *y*.
For example:

	Ḥaḍramī	Kuwaitī	Meccan
yaxruj "he goes out"	*yixroy*		*yixruj*
rajul "man"	*rayyāl*	*rayyāl*	*rijjāl*
ji't "I came"	*yīt*	*yīt*	*jīt*

The distribution of the *y* variant of *j* shows that this is a feature which does not occur in Central Arabic. It is, therefore, possible to conclude that this feature was acquired by Eastern Arabian dialects at one point of their development.

The following are some characteristic features of the Eastern Arabian dialects.

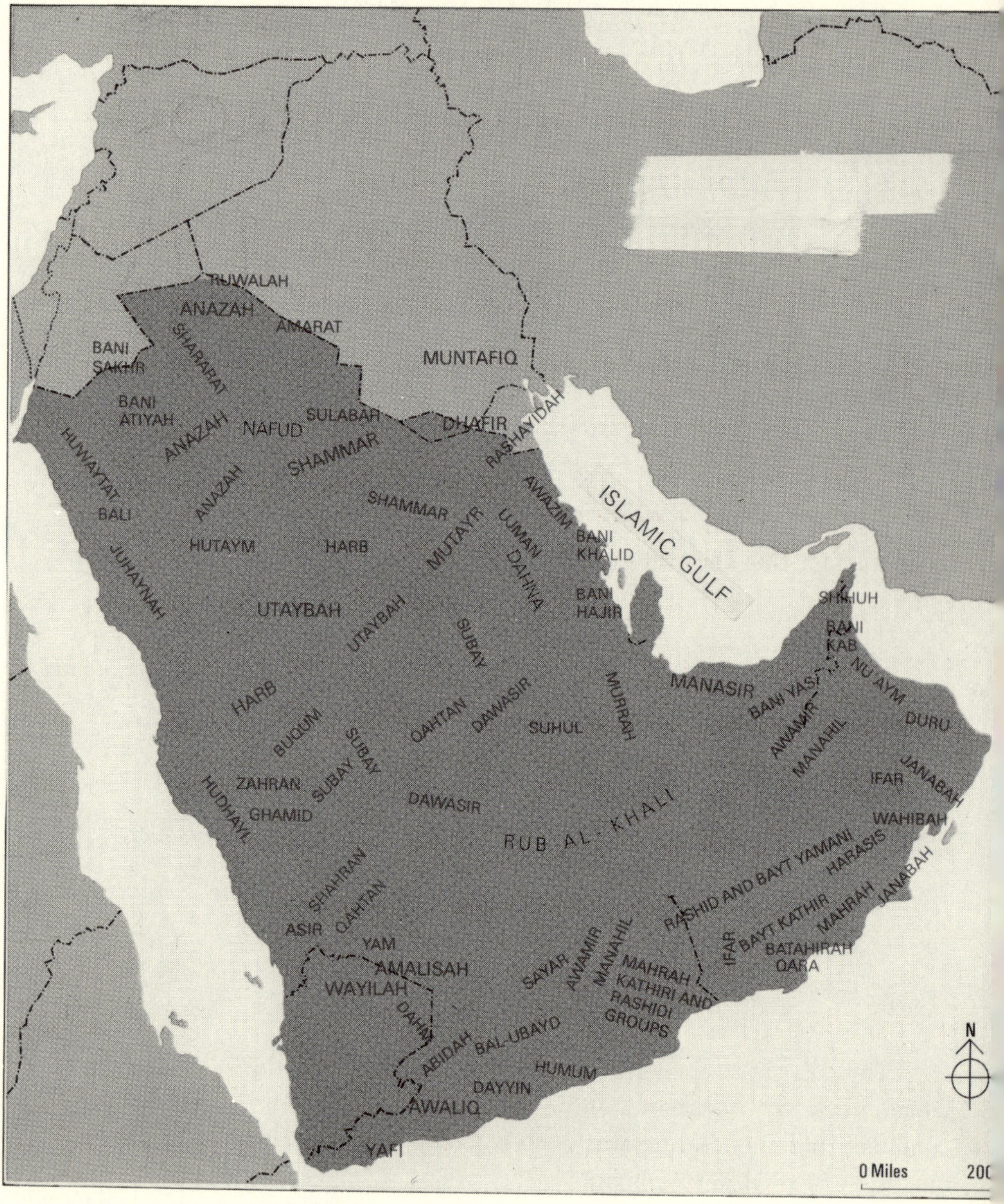

MAP 3. Principal Tribes of the Arabian Peninsula.

1. *The strong verb.*
The perfect of the simple strong verb in the Eastern Arabian dialects corresponding to the Modern Standard Arabic *fa'al* is of the same structure *fa'al* where the first or second radical is a guttéral consonant, or where the medial radical is *l, n,* or *r,* as in *ḥabas* to detain", *ẓarab* "to beat". Otherwise, the pattern is *fi'al* as in *kitab* "to write", *niṭar* "to wait" or *fu'al* as in *kufar "to deny".*

2. *The weak verb.*
In the Eastern Arabian dialects verbs corresponding to Modern Standard Arabic initially *hamzated* are often assimilated in pattern to the verbs final *y,* as in *kala* "to eat", *xaḏa* "to take". The imperative of such verbs in these dialects has an initial hamza. Thus *'ixiḏ, 'uxuḏ* and *'ukul.*
The verbs with initial *w* in these dialects retain the *w* in the imperfect and imperative. For example:

	Eastern Arabian dialects	Meccan Arabic
yaṣil "to arrive"	*yōṣal*	*yiwṣal*
yaqif "to stand"	*yōgaf*	*yiwgaf*

3. *Personal Pronouns*
Except for the Bahraini dialect, the rest of the East Arabian dialects possess the third person singular pronouns *hū* "he" and *hī* "she". Their equivalents in Meccan Arabic are *huwwa* and *hiyya; huwa* and *hiya* in Modern Standard Arabic.

4. *Demonstratives*
In the Eastern Arabian dialects the plural demonstratives are compounds with a *-ḏōl* element. For instance:

	Kuwaitī	Meccan
these	*haḏōl*	*hadōl*
those	*haḏōlāk*	*hadōla/hadōlāk*

5. *Particles*
The conditional and demonstrative particle *iḏā* in Modern Standard Arabic is realized as *ilā* (or its variants *wilā, lē*) in all of the Eastern

Arabian dialects. In Meccan Arabic it is realized as *izā*.

6. *Vocabulary*

The Eastern Arabian dialects share a high percentage of their vocabulary. The following are examples from the common vocabulary compared with my Meccan dialect.

	Kuwaitī dialect	Baḥrainī dialect	Qaṭarī dialect	Meccan dialect
"to become"	*ṣār*	*ṣār*	*ṣār*	*sār*
"get up"	*gūm*	*gūm*	*gum*	*gūm*
"he wants"	*yabi*	*yabi*	*yabi*	*ibġa*
"to go"	*rāḥ*	*rāḥ*	*rāḥ*	*rāḥ*
"camels"	*ibil*	*ibil*	*ibil*	*jumāl*
"fan"	*mirwaḥa/ panka*	*mrūḥa/ panka*		*marūḥa* or *marwaḥa*
"flies"	*d̠ibbān*	*d̠ibbān*	*d̠ibbān*	*dubbān*
"tea"	*čāy*	*čāy*	*čāy*	*šāhi*
"water"	*māy*	*māy*	*māy*	*mōya*
"tobacco leaf"		*titin*		*tumbāk*
"here"	*hnī/hani*		*hnī/hanī*	*hina*
"how"	*čēf*	*čēf*	*čēf*	*kef*
"much"	*wāyid*	*wāyid*	*wāyid*	*katīr*
"so"	*čid̠i*	*čid̠i*	*čid̠i*	*kida*
"there is"	*aku*	*hast*	*hast*	*fī*
"there is not"	*māku*	*ma-hast ma-mīš*	*ma-hast ma-mīš*	*māfi/ māfiš*
"take!"	*ixid̠*	*xid̠*	*ixid̠*	*xud*

In conclusion, the Eastern Arabian dialects appear to belong essentially to the 'Anazi dialect group. Naturally, each dialect has undergone different changes and developed in its own right. This has led to differences and idiosyncracies. Hence, we find differences amongst these dialects, and particularly in terms of phonology, morphology and vocabulary. Some of these differences may also have resulted from external linguistic influences from neighbouring countries. Thus Kuwaitī has been influenced by the Iraqī dialect, and the dialects of the United

Arab Emirates have also been influenced by the Omani dialect. Some coastal dialects possess a rich and well-developed nautical and commercial terminology, as well as a large number of words borrowed from Persian, Urdu, Portuguese and recently from English.

REFERENCES

Bakalla, M.H. 1981. *Arabic Linguistics: An Introduction and Bibliography*. London.

Ingham, B. 1979. *"Notes on the dialect of the Muṭair of Eastern Arabia"*, in *Zeitschrift für arabische Linguistik* (Wiesbaden) 2. 23–35.

Johnstone, T.M. 1967. *Eastern Arabian Dialects.* London: Oxford University Press. Translated into Arabic by Ahmad al-Dhubaib, Riyadh: Publication of the University of Riyadh, no. 7, 1975.

Smeaton, B. Hunter. 1973. *Lexical Expansion due to Technical Change, as Illustrated by the Arabic of al-Hasa, Saudi Arabia.* Bloomington, Indiana: Indiana University Press.

XIV

THE ORIGIN AND DEVELOPMENT OF THE ARABIC SCRIPT

To some people who are not familiar with it, Arabic writing seems to be nothing less than a scribble. To others of more artistic taste, Arabic writing appears to be an ornamental type of script. But to a beginner, just introduced to Arabic and Islamic culture, Arabic writing looks difficult, being cursive as well as being written from right to left. There is nothing new about such subjective impressions or views, as they apply to any person or community with little or no information about other people's cultures.

One has to differentiate between Arabic writing and Arabic calligraphy. Although both are variations of the Arabic script, the former is more formal, communicative and straightforward. Calligraphy, on the other hand, is a creative art which only the gifted or talented can achieve. Arabic writing is a form of alphabetical writing. This form took several centuries before Islam and Christianity to evolve.

Writing started as fully pictorial drawings of the objects talked about, as in the case of certain forms of ancient Egyptian writing. It became less pictorial later, as is the case in the Old Chinese form of writing. Modern Chinese uses the so-called idiographs, a form in which a picture of the idea or object or parts of it, is used to symbolize the idea expressed. This form is still employed in European and other countries where stars are used to refer to the grade of hotel, knives and forks for restaurants, and spanners for garages. Another stage in the development of writing is the syllabic stage, in which a given symbol is used to denote a syllable of the word. Egyptian hieroglyphics display this form, in which a written word is symbolized by several pictograms, one pictogram for each syllable of the word. The syllable of the pictogram forms the first syllable of the name of the object shown.

It was not till the 16th century B.C. that the alphabetical writing started to emerge. Then, the Phonecians in the East of the Mediterranean, particularly Lebanon, developed a script which was the basis for all

PLATE 1. *The Kalima* Written in Slightly Floriated Script.

modern scripts. Thus the Indian Davingari script, the Aramaic, Hebrew, Greek, Latin and Arabic scripts among others, were all off-shoots of the Phonecian alphabet. Like the modern western scripts which evolved either from the Greek script as Cyrallic, or the Latin script as French and English, the Arabic writing developed in its own way. We still find similarities between Arabic letters and western letters. They appear as mirror images of each other. Thus Arabic *lām* and *nūn* and English or French *l* and *n* display striking similarities. The direction of the writing has largely determined the shape and quality of the letters in each script which has eminated from the Phonecian alphabet.

Like most of the scripts which branched off from the Phonecian alphabet, the Arabic script kept some of the characteristic features of the mother alphabet. Therefore the sister-scripts and their off-shoots share the fact that they have all kept some of the Phonecian names for the letters and their order and arrangement. Note for instance, the Greek *alpha, beta, gama,* and *delta;* the Hebrew *aleph, beth,* gamel, *dalet;* English *a, b, c, d* and the Arabic letters in the word *abjad.* Also note the names and order of the following letters: Arabic *kāf, lām, mīm,* and *nūn* abbreviated in the word *kalamun,* and the English equivalents *k, l, m, n.*

There are a number of theories regarding the exact birthplace of the Arabic script. Some early Arab scholars, like Ibn Khaldūn, took the view that the Arabic writing had evolved from the South Arabian Sabaen and Himiarite scripts which travelled North East to Iraq and then west to Hijaz. The popular modern theory is that the Northern and Southern Arabian scripts were derived independently from the Phonecian alphabet, and hence the similarities which exist between the two types of script and which led the Arab and Muslim scholars to advance such an idea as that held by Ibn Khaldūn.

In modern times it has been held that the Arabic script was developed by the Nabataeans who were Arabs reputed for their successful trade in North West Arabia and Greater Syria. They founded a powerful Kingdom towards the end of the last century B.C. and established their capital in Petra (now in Jordan) and also had other settlements in Northern Arabia. The earliest discovered Nabataean inscriptions were found in Northern Arabia, and they are known as *Namāra* (dating 328 A.D), *Umm al-Jimāl* (dating 250 A.D.) and *Zabad* (dating 512 A.D.),

PLATE 2. A View of the Kaaba's (Ka'ba) Door and Cover Embroidered with Verses from the *Qur'ān*. Arabic Calligraphy is Frequently Used for Decorative Purposes.

and they bear resemblance to those inscriptions found in 'Ulā and Madā'in Ṣāliḥ in Saudi Arabia.

This suggests that the Arabic script developed around this region in Northern Arabia. However, the future might reveal a new and better understanding of the development.

The Nabataeans who kept in touch with the Syrians were influenced by the Syriac or Aramaic script. This influence was passed on to the Arabs in Hijaz through the Nabataeans. *Namāra* inscriptions show the extent of the Syriac influence upon the Nabataeans as the Arabic text is heavily influenced by Syriac. It is interesting to note that the Nabataeans had two distinct variants of the Arabic script, one is old and "angular" and is used in writing on rocks or coins and the other is of more recent origin and "cursive" which is used for commercial and day-to-day purposes.

It is possible that the Arabic Naskhi and Kufi scripts correspond to the Nabataean cursive and angular scripts, respectively. It is also possible that the use of the angular, floriated, decorative style in writing Qur'ānic manuscripts was an influence from Syriac as the Holy Bible originally used to be written in a floriated, decorative form. It is to be noted that the Qur'ānic manuscripts were written in Naskhi style for a short while before the Kufic style was given preference. The Kufi script is so-called because it was undertaken and developed in Kufa, Iraq.

Thus Arabic writing is a development of the Nabataean script which itself developed from the Aramaic script. The development continued, adding more subtleties and refinements to the system of writing Arabic. With the advent of Islam, writing was greatly encouraged and literacy became almost synonymous with the word "Islam". During the first year in the Islamic calendar, dots above or below letters were systematically used to differentiate between letters which were identical without the dots. Thus the letters, *b, t, ṯ,* which hold resemblances in their shapes, were marked with one dot below *b,* two dots above *t,* three dots above *ṯ*. The process of inserting the dots was called *i'jām.* Although dotting was used by the Aramaens, it was used systematically in the writing of Arabic. Towards the middle of the first century of the Islamic calendar the process of vocalization was introduced by Abu al-Aswad. Red dots were employed above or below the Arabic letters to indicate the short vowels following them. As there are three short vowels in Classical Arabic, three symbols were devised. Again this process might have been an Aramaic influence, but it was consistently used in Arabic. Later on the dots were replaced by other marks which are still in current use. This invention is attributed to Al-Khalīl ibn Aḥmad in the second century A.H./8th century A.D. Invention of other diacritical marks followed, such as the *šaddah,* and *tanwīn,* which helped to reduce Arabic writing to a kind of shorthand script.

Another point to be made here is that before the introduction of the Indian numerals into Arabic, later on given the name Arabic numerals, the letters of the alphabet were used for numbering. Thus *alif* or *ā* is 1, *bā* or *b* equals 2, *qāf* or *q* equals 100, and so on. The letters are still used as serial numbers. The modern order of the Arabic letters differs from the old one. The old one is usually called *Abjadi order,* which was inherited from the Phonecians. The modern order is called alphabetical, which was of a later origin. A third type of ordering used since the eighth century A.D. is called the phonetic order. Al-Khalīl ibn Aḥmad is known to have ordered the letters according to the places of their articulation. Thus the laryngeal letters are ordered before the pharyngeal letters and so forth, the labial and labiodental letters were ordered last in the series.

To sum up, the story of the Arabic script is a long one. Like all Western scripts, it branched off from the Phonecian alphabet and developed in its own right. Arabic possesses an enormous bulk of material which has accumulated without interruption for the past 17 centuries or so. At times more than a hundred languages of the world have used the Arabic script, with modifications, as a medium of writing non-Arabic languages. These include Senegalese in West Africa, Urdu and Sindhi in the Indian Subcontinent, and Spanish in Europe.

Arabic still has the potential for writing modern languages in an efficient way. However, it can only do so if the specialists make the effort to tailor the Arabic script according to the needs of its users, or would-be users.

REFERENCES

Abbott, Nabia. 1939. *The Rise of the North Arabic Script*. Chicago.

Bakalla. M.H. 1981. *Arabic Linguistics: An Introduction and Bibliography*. London.

Dringer, David. 1949. *The Alphabet*. New York.

Gelb, I.J. 1952. *A Study of Writing*. London.

Mitchell, T.F. 1970. *Writing Arabic: A Practical Introduction to Ruq'ah Script*. London: Oxford University Press.

Morag, Shelomo. 1961. *The Vocalization of Arabic, Hebrew and Aramaic: Their Phonetic and Phonemic Principles*. The Hague: Mouton.

Naim, C. Mohammed. 1971. *"Arabic orthography and some non-Semitic languages"*, in *Islam and its Divergence* (Studies in honour of Gustave E. von Grunebaum), edited by Girdhari L. Tikku. Urbana: University of Illinois Press, pp. 113–44.

Revell, E. 1975. *'The diacritical dots and the development of the Arabic alphabet"*, in *Journal of Semitic Studies* (Manchester) 20. 178–90.

Segal, J.B. 1953. *The Diacritical Point and the Accents in Syriac*. London: Oxford University Press.

Semaan, Khalil I.H. 1967. *"A linguistic view of the development of the Arabic writing system"*, in *Wiener Zeitschrift für die Kunde des Morgenlandes* (Wien) 61. 22–45.

Al-Toma (Altoma), Salih J. 1961. *'The Arabic writing system and proposals for its reform"*, in *The Middle East Journal* (Washington, D.C.) 15. 403–14.

PART TWO

ABOUT ARABIC LITERATURE

XV

AN OVERVIEW OF ARABIC LITERATURE

Arabic possesses one of the richest literatures in the world. Its history goes back more than fifteen hundred years and has made substantial contributions to other literatures throughout the world at various periods in its history.

The Arabic word for literature is *Adab* which originally meant good manners and behaviour. In early Arabic literature, a kind of secretarial literature was employed to lay down the rules of conduct and behaviour for different classes of people such as administrators, princes and the like. These rules were written in various literary styles and introduced in the shape of poems, anecdotes, and manuals. Such works were then subsumed under the word *Adab*. Later on, the word was given a more specialized meaning, that is "literature" or the various styles of writing prose or verse creatively.

Arabic literature is generally divided into six periods:

1. The Pre-Islamic period
2. The Early Islamic period
3. The Umayyad period
4. The Abbasid period
5. The Mamlūk period.
6. The Modern period.

The pre-Islamic period is also known as *Jāhiliyya* or Age of Darkness or Ignorance, because it expresses a non-Islamic spirit. It covers a period of two centuries at least. Professor Gibb calls it the *Heroic Age* as it is famous for its courageous heroes and deeds. There are four main sources of information for this period:

Firstly: Poetry which came down in abundance.

Secondly: Sermons and epistles.

Thirdly: Proverbs.

Fourthly: Legends and traditions.

Some of the literature was written down during this period but most of it was handed down orally. It was not until the Eighth Century that the *Jāhiliyya* literature was committed to writing by early Muslim scholars.

Professor Gibb (1974:13) vividly describes the beginnings of Arabic literature in the following statement:

> "The most striking feature in Arabic literature is its unexpectedness. Over and over again, with scarcely a hint to give warning of what is coming, a new literary art emerges fully-fledged, often with a perfection never equalled by later exponents of the same art. Nowhere is this element of surprise more striking than in the first appearance of Arabic as a vehicle of literature. At one moment Arabic seems, in a literary sense, empty and dumb except for some votive or businesslike inscriptions in a variety of dialects. At the next, companies of poets spring up all over northern Arabia, reciting complex odes, *qaṣīdas*, in which a series of themes are elaborated with unsurpassed vigour, vividness of imagination, and precision of imagery, in an infinitely rich and highly articulated language, showing little or no traces of dialect, and cast into complex and flexible metrical schemes that rhyme throughout the poem."

We now progress to the second phase of Arabic literature, that is the Early Islamic age. This covers the period in which the Prophet Muḥammad (Peace Be Upon Him) and the four Caliphs lived. Literature was then centred in Medina, Mecca, Taif and Najd. It is during this period that the Qur'ān was revealed and Muslim poets and writers started to produce what was later recognized as the beginnings of Islamic literature.

Gibb (1974:36) states:

> "As a literary monument the Qur'ān stands thus by itself, a production unique in Arabic literature having neither forerunners nor successors in its own idiom. Muslims of all ages are united in proclaiming the inimitability not only of its contents but of its style."

He continues:

> "The influence of the Qur'ān on the development of Arabic literature has been incalculable and exerted in many directions. Its ideas, its language, its rhythms pervade all subsequent literary works in greater or lesser measure. Its specific linguistic features were not emulated, either in the chancery prose of the next century or in later prose writings, but it was at least partly due to the flexibility imparted by the Qur'ān to the High Arabic idiom that the former could be so rapidly developed and adjusted to the new needs of imperial government and an expanding society. Even greater was its indirect influence, in that it was to the studies connected with the Qur'ān that the majority of branches of Arabic literature owe their origin."

The Umayyad literature flourished in Syria, Arabia, Iraq and wherever Islam reached during the first half of the eighth century.

This was followed by the Abbasid period in which literature reached an even higher standard and complexity. It is normally subdivided into two periods, the Golden Age, which extends between the years 750–1055, and the Silver Age, between 1055–1258. Gibb states again:

> "What most sharply distinguishes the new production, in both poetry and prose, is that it was, with few exceptions, produced by and for an urban society, concentrated mainly in Iraq, and that the majority of its producers were half Arabs or non-Arabs, converts or descendants of converts from the original Aramaean and Persian population. Of the charges and developments that resulted from these new conditions the most significant is the emergence of an Arabic literary prose, clear, precise and well articulated. This was the final product of a confluence of literary activities, which, during this first Abbasid period, were pursued separately by the secretaries, the philologists, and the lawyers and Traditionalists."

The Mamlūk literature extends from 1258, the year which witnessed the end of the Abbasid Caliphate in Baghdad, until 1800, the year which marks the beginning of Modern Arabic literature.

In conclusion, Arabic literature has had a long history, each period of which has reflected the lives and social conditions of the people living then.

REFERENCES

Gibb, H.A.R. 1974. *Arabic Literature: An Introduction.* Oxford: Oxford University Press.

Nicholson, R.A. 1977. *A Literary History of the Arabs.* Cambridge: Cambridge University Press.

XVI

THE LITERATURE OF THE HEROIC AGE

This name is given to the pre-Islamic period in which literature flourished, and poetry apparently was the main tool of expression of intricate thoughts, and the poets were the great journalists or spokesmen of that particular age. It was recognized a long time ago that poetry is the public register or records of the Arabs; thereby genealogies are kept in mind and famous actions and events are made familiar.

Professor Nicholson (1977: 72) states:

> "By the Ancient Arabs the poet (*šā'ir*, plural *šu'arā'*), as his name implies, was held to be a person endowed with supernatural knowledge, a wizard in league with spirits (*jinn*) or satans (*šayāṭīn*) and dependent on them for the magical powers which he displayed. This view of his personality, as well as the influential position which he occupied, are curiously indicated by the story of a certain youth who was refused the hand of his beloved on the ground that he was neither a poet nor a soothsayer nor a water diviner. The idea of poetry as an art was developed afterwards; the pagan *šā'ir* is the oracle of his tribe, their guide in peace and their champion in war."

Pre-Islamic Classical Arabic poetry had been produced and transmitted through "oral tradition". It was not committed to writing until the eighth century. Scholars could then call for help from the "fantastic memories" so "well attested" of illiterate people. Although doubt has been cast upon the authenticity and originality of their poetry, at least in part, it does not really shake the solid foundations which were laid down by early Arab oral transmitters, literary critics, and philologists.

Once the pre-Islamic poetry was written down, its formal characteristics became the model for later poets. Even in modern times we find those who are adherents and proponents of such models.

The most ancient of the Arabian poetry was that known as *Rajaz*. *Rajaz* is an irregular iambic metre usually consisting of two or three feet to the line. All the lines of *Rajaz* rhyme with each other. Another characteristic of *Rajaz* is the fact that it should be uttered extempore to express some personal feelings, emotion, or experience, like those of the aged warrior Duraid Ibn Zaid Ibn Nahd when he lay dying. (Nicholson 1977: 75):

> "The house of death is builded for Durayd to-day.
> Could Time be worn out, sure had I worn Time away.
> No single foe but I had faced and brought to bay.
> The spoils I gathered in, how excellent were they!
> The women that I loved, how fine was their array."

Later, *Rajaz* was chosen as the metre most suitable for outlining the Arabic sciences designed for memorization and easy reference. Another type of the Classical Arabic poetry is *Qaṣīda* or ode. The early Arabic lexicographers mention that *Qaṣīda* means a poem with an artistic purpose, though they differed as to the precise sense in which "purpose" is to be understood. Nicholson (1977: 76) states:

> "Ahlwardt connects it with *Qaṣada,* to break, because it consists of verses, every one of which is divided into two halves, with a common end-rhyme: thus the whole poem is broken, as it were, into two halves; while in the *Rajaz* verses there is no such break."

The Arabic term for verse is *bayt* and its plural *abyāt*.

An Arabic ode seldom consists of less than 25 verses or more than a hundred. The arrangement of the rhymes is such that, while the two halves of the first verse rhyme together, the same rhyme is repeated once in the second, third, and every following verse to the end of the poem. It is a monorhyme poem that demands great technical skill and experience.

The most renowned odes of the Classical poetry are the *mu'allaqāt* or the long poems. They are ten in number. *Mu'allaqat* means the "hanged odes". It is believed that these ten odes or at least seven of them were chosen by the Ancient Arab literary critics, written in gold and displayed on the Kaaba in Mecca. Hence the name the Golden Odes which is also given to them.

The Thematic properties of an ode can be depicted as follows:

(1) reminiscence at the deserted campsite *nasīb*.
(2) journey by camel or horse
(3) and concluding eulogy *madīḥ*

An ode also contains minor thematic units which bind the verses of a poem together.

The classical poetry appears to express more freely and honestly the pre-Islamic way of life and thought. Nicholson (1977: 79) states again:

> "Here the Arab has drawn himself at full length without embellishment or extenuation. It is not mere chance that Abū Tammām's famous Anthologies called the *Ḥamāsa,* meaning "fortitude" from the title of its first chapter, which occupies nearly a half of the book. "*Ḥamāsa*" denotes the virtues most highly prized by the Arabs – bravery in battle, patience in misfortune, persistence in revenge, protection of the weak and defiance of the strong, the will, as Tennyson has said:
>
> "To strive, to seek, to find, and to yield"."

Thousands of poems, a few of them incomplete, have survived. The list of names of the poets is a long one. Some of the poets who are reputed for their bravery, courage, romance, wisdom and generosity are 'Antarah, Shanfara, Imru' al-Qays, and Zuhair who lived around the fifth and sixth centuries.

'Antarah's golden ode is famous for its stirring battle-scenes, one of which is translated here:

"Learn, Mālik's daughter, how
I rush into the fray,
And how I draw back only
At sharing of the prey.

I never quit the saddle,
My strong steed nimbly bounds;
Warrior after warrior
Have covered him with wounds.

Full-armed against me stood
One feared of fighting men:
He fled not oversoon
Nor let himself be ta'en.

With straight hard-shafted spear
I dealt him in his side
A sudden thrust which opened
Two streaming gashes wide,

Two gashes whence outgurgled
His life-blood; at the sound
Night-roaming ravenous wolves
Flock eagerly around.

So with my doughty spear
I trussed his coat of mail.
For truly, when the spear strikes,
The noblest man is frail.

And left him low to banquet
The wild beasts gathering there;
They have torn off his fingers,
His wrist and fingers fair!"

Another famous poet is Zuhair who is reputed for his wisdom and professional composition of poetry. His ode, which apparently was composed at the age of eighty, contains a number of lines expressing this attitude (Nicholson 1977: 118):

> "I am weary of life's burden: well a man may weary be
> After eighty years, and this much now is manifest to me:
> Death is like a night-blind camel stumbling on: – the smitten die
> But the others age and wax in weakness whom he passes by.
> He that often deals with folk in unkind fashion, underneath
> They will trample him and make him feel the sharpness of their teeth.
> He that hath enough and over and is niggard with his pelf
> Will be hated of his people and left free to praise himself.
> He alone who with fair actions ever fortifies his fame
> Wins it fully: blame will find him out unless he shrinks from blame.
> He that for his cistern's guarding trusts not in his own stout arm
> Sees it ruined: he must harm his foe or he must suffer harm.
> He that fears the bridge of Death across it finally is driven,
> Though he span as with a ladder all the space 'twixt earth and heaven.
> He that will not take the lance's butt-end while he has the chance
> Must thereafter be contented with the spike-end of the lance.
> He that keeps his word is blamed not; he whose heart repaireth straight
> To the sanctuary of duty never needs to hesitate.
> He that hies abroad to strangers doth account his friends his foes;
> He that honours not himself lacks honour wheresoe'er he goes.
> Be a man's true nature what it will, that nature is revealed
> To his neighbours, let him fancy as he may that 'tis concealed."

In conclusion, Classical Arabic poetry is a mine of information about the life of the pre-Islamic era. Thanks to the early Muslim anthologists and philologists who have preserved this poetry from complete extinction. It is also due to their efforts that the formal characteristic features of the odes have influenced all later poets up till the present day.

The Classical Arabic ode was not only an artistic piece of work, but it also functioned as a skilful tool which could play upon the emotions of his hearers. "The poet was not merely lauded as an artist but venerated as the protector and guarantor of the honour of the tribe and a potent weapon against its enemies."

It is because of its heroes, many of whom were also famous poets, that this period was called the Heroic Age.

REFERENCES

Bateson, Mary Catherine. 1970. *Structural Continuity in Poetry: A Linguistic Study in Five Pre-Islamic Arabic Odes*. The Hague: Mouton.

Gibb, H.A.R. 1974. *Arabic Literature: An Introduction.* Oxford.

Nicholson, R.A. 1977. *A Literary History of the Arabs.* Cambridge.

XVII

THE THEMES OF PRE-ISLAMIC POETRY

Misconceived ideas about Arabic poetry in general abound, and about pre-Islamic poetry they are even greater! Some people might have the idea that the pre-Islamic Arabic poem consists of one theme which is recurrent throughout the poem. To them this theme is confined to descriptions of the desert and its life in a more concrete form. This is not true of the pre-Islamic poem. There are tens of pre-Islamic poets who have left hundreds of poems which deserve more than just a glance at them. They are really worth a thorough study, a better understanding, and deserve an objective investigation.

The pre-Islamic poem displays a wide range of themes. It was described by a scholar as "a string of beads on which images are accumulated and juxtaposed one after the other without any seeming connection beyond that of a strict quantitative meter."

Some pre-Islamic poets are well reputed for expressing specific themes. For instance, 'Antarah is well known for his poems expressing heroism and his courage in battlefields. Imru' al-Qays is well-renowned for his love poetry and his adventures in the desert.

Al-Khansā' was chiefly renowned for her poignant elegies. We shall now give some examples of a number of the themes treated in the pre-Islamic poem.

The following lines are attributed to al-Samaw'al Ibn Gharīḍ ibn 'Ādiyā'. He became well known around the middle of the sixth century. As a member of a Jewish Arab tribe, he lived in a fortress known as al-'Ablaq near Taimā'. His name was proverbial for fidelity.

This poem expresses the generosity and courage of the poet and his tribe. (Arberry 1965: 30f):

إذا المَرءُ لَم يَدنَس مِنَ اللُؤمِ عِرضُهُ
فَكُلُّ رِداءٍ يَرتَديهِ جَميلُ

وإن هُوَ لَم يَحمِل عَلى النَفسِ ضَيمَها
فَلَيسَ إلى حُسنِ الثَناءِ سَبيلُ

"When a man's honour is not defiled by baseness, then every cloak he cloaks himself in is comely;
And if he has never constrained himself to endure despite, then there is no way for him to attain goodly praise.
She was reproaching us, that we were few in numbers; so I said to her, "Indeed, noble men are few."
Not few are they whose remains are like to us – youths who have climbed to the heights, and old men too.
It harms us not that we are few, seeing that our kinsman is mighty, whereas the kinsman of the most part of men is abased.
We have a mountain where those we protect come to dwell, impregnable, turning back the eye and it a-weary;
Its trunk is anchored beneath the soil, and a branch of it soars with it to the stars, unattainable, tall.
We indeed are a folk who deem not being killed a disgrace, though 'Āmir and Salūl may so consider it.
The love of death brings our term of life near to us, but their term hates death, and is therefore prolonged.
Not one sayyid of ours ever died a natural death, nor was any slain of ours ever left where he lay unavenged.
Our souls flow out along the edge of the swordblades, and do not flow out along other than the swordblades.
We have remained pure and unsullied, and females and stallions who bore us in goodly fame kept intact our stock.
We climbed on to the best of backs, and a descending brought us down in due time to the best of bellies.
So we are as the water of the rain-shower – in our metal is no bluntness, neither is any miser numbered amongst us.
We disapprove if we will of what other men say, but they disavow never words spoken by us.
Whenever a sayyid of ours disappears, another sayyid arises, one eloquent to speak as noble men speak, and strong to act moreover.
No fire of ours was ever doused against a night-visitor, neither has any casual guest alighting found fault with us.
Our 'days' are famous amongst our foes; they have well-

marked blazes and white pasterns;
And our swords – in all west and east they have been blunted from smiting against armoured warriers;
Their blades are accustomed not to be drawn and then sheathed until the blood of a host is spilled.
If you are ignorant, ask the people concerning us and them – and he who knows and he who is ignorant are assuredly not equal."
Surely the Banū al-Dayyān are as a pole for their people, their mills turn and rotate around them."

Another pre-Islamic poet is Ziyād ibn Mu'āwiya known as al–Nābighah. A member of the Dhubyān tribe, he died about 604. He attended the court of the Lakhmīds of al-Ḥīra in Iraq. He was reputed for his great praise of the Lakhmīds and later on the Ghassānīds in Syria. The following lines are extracted from a poem addressed to al–Nu'mān ibn al–Mundhir, last of the Lakhmīd kings who reigned between 580–602 (Arberry 1965:32f):

أَتاني أَبَيتَ اللَعنَ أَنَّكَ لُمتَني
وَتِلكَ الَّتي أَهتَمُّ مِنها وَأَنصَبُ

"News came to me – may you spurn the curse! – that you had blamed me, and those things at which I am full of care and trouble.
So I passed the night as if the recurrent thoughts had spread for me a thornbush, wherewith my bed was raised high and disturbed.
I swore – and I left no doubt to your mind – and a man has no recourse beyond God –
Surely, if you had been informed of treachery on my part, then your embroidering informant was indeed false and lying.
But I was a man who had an ample part of the earth where I might roam at will and betake myself,
Kings and brothers – whenever I came to them I would be given control of their wealth and advanced in favour –

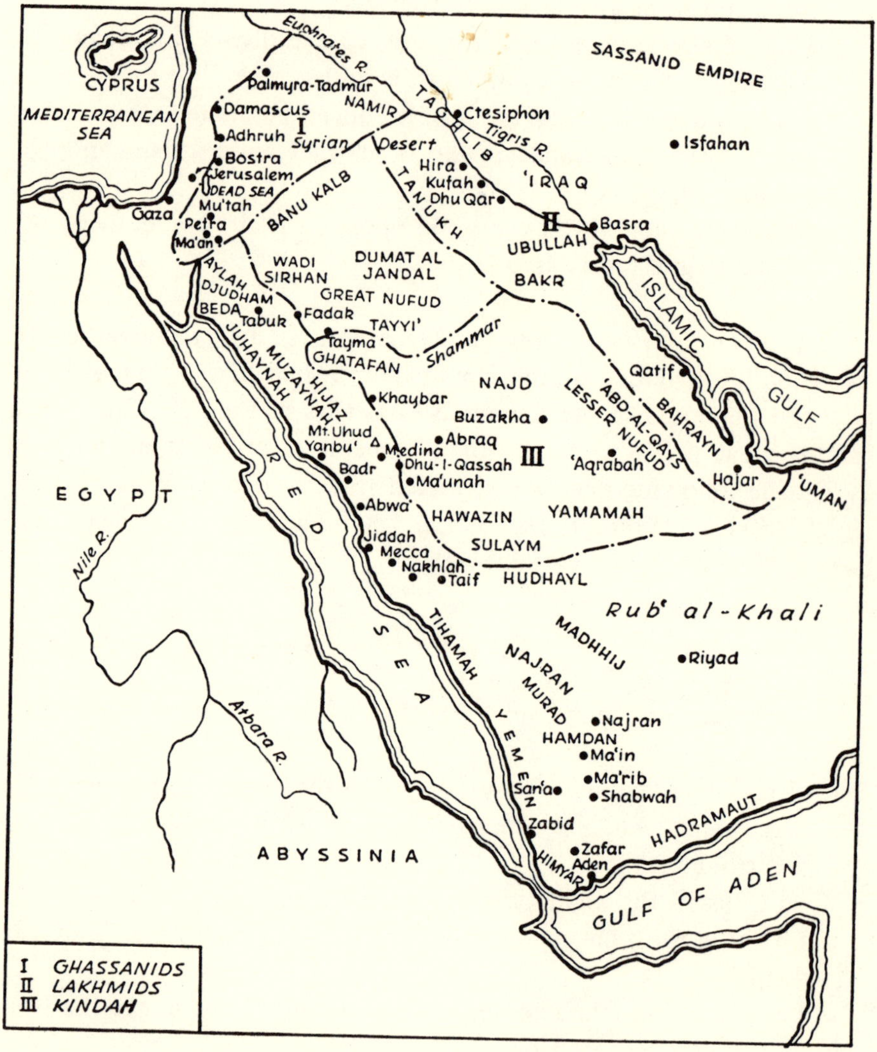

MAP 4. Arabia Before the Advent of Islam.

Just as you do with regard to a people I have seen you take as your intimates, not considering them to have sinned in the matter of gratitude.
For you are as a sun, and the other kings are stars; when your sun rises, not one star appears from amongst them.
So do not leave me with a threat, as though I were to other men (as) one smeared with pitch, a scabby (camel).
Do you not see that God has given you great might, (so that) you see every king quivering before it?
You are not one to spare a brother whose disordered state you have not repaired. Who is the (truly) polished man?
So if I am wronged, yet I am a slave whom you have wronged; and if you are a complacent man, then the like of you is apt to be complacent."

'Antarah ibn Shaddād, the "black Knight" was a member of the 'Abs tribe. He was the son of an Arab father and an Abyssinian mother, and considered one of the greatest hero-poets of the sixth century. His Mu'allaqa or "golden ode" became, in medieval Islam, the basis of an extensive popular romance. His bravery and courage is expressed in the following lines (Arberry 1965:34f):

حارِبيني يا نائِباتِ اللَيالي
عَن يَميني وَتارَةً عَن شِمالي

وَٱجهَدي في عَداوَتي وَعِنادي
أنتِ وَاللهِ لَم تُلِمّي بِبالي

"Make war on me, O vicissitudes of the nights, now on my right hand and now on my left,
And labour to be hostile to me and to thwart me; by God! you have never occupied my mind.
I have a high purpose firmer than a rock and stronger than immovable mountains,
And a sword which, when I strike with it ever, the useless spearheads give way before it,
And a lance-point which, whenever I lose my way in the night, guides me and restores me from straying,

And a mettlesome steed that never sped, but that the lightning trailed behind it from the striking of his hooves.
Dark of hue it is, splitting the starless night with a blackness, between its eyes a blaze like the crescent moon,
Ransoming me with its own life, and I ransom it with my life, on the day of battle, and with my wealth.
And whenever the market of the war of the tall lances is afoot, and it blazes with the polished, whetted blades,
I am the broker thereof, and my spear-point is a merchant purchasing precious souls.
Wild beasts of the wilderness, when war breaks into flame, follow me from the empty wastes;
Follow me, and you will see the blood of the foremen streaming between the hillocks and the sands.
Then return thereafter, and thank me, and remember what you have seen of my deeds,
And take sustenance of the skulls of the people for your little children and your whelps."

'Antarah, despite his pride in his tribe and his people, was outcast in his youth by his father and later on by his uncle Mālik, whose daughter, 'Abla, he loved passionately but was forbidden to marry. He became the hero of the celebrated popular epic entitled *Sīrat 'Antara ibn Shaddād al-'Absī.* Note the following lines addressing his cousin 'Abla, and vaunting his prowess on the battlefield:

Those who were present at the engagement will acquaint you
how I plunge into battle, but abstain at the booty-sharing.
Many's the bristling knight the warriors have shunned to take on,
those not in a hurry to flee or capitulate,
to them my hands have been right generous with the hasty thrust
of a well-tempered, strong-jointed, straightened spear
giving him a broad, double-sided gash, the hiss of which
guides in the night-season the prowling, famished wolves;
I split through his shielding armor with my solid lance
for even the noblest is not sacrosanct to the spear
and left him carrion for the wild beasts to pounce on,
all of him, from the crown of his head to his limp wrists."

Tumādir bint 'Amr ibn al-Sharīd known as al-Khansā', of the Sulaim tribe, is considered one of the greatest of Arab poetesses. Lamenting the slaying of her brother, Şakhr, she tells of her sorrow in the following lines (Arberry 1965: 38f):

إِنِّي أَرِقتُ فَبِتُّ اللَّيلَ ساهِرَةً
كَأَنَّما كُحِلَت عَيني بِعُوّارِ

"I was sleepless, and I passed the night keeping vigil, as if my eyes had been anointed with pus,
Watching the stars — and I had not been charged to watch them — and anon wrapping myself in the ends of ragged robes.
For I had heard — and it was not news to rejoice me — one making report, who had come repeating intelligence,
Saying, "Sakhr is dwelling there in a tomb, struck to the ground beside the grave, between certain stones".
So I shall weep for you, so long as ringdove laments and the night stars shine for the night-traveller."

Zuhair ibn Abī Sulmā, a member of the Muzayna tribe, was well reputed for his epigrams, wise sayings and his teaching of morality and conduct. Note the following lines from his golden ode(Nicholson: 1977:118):

"I am weary of life's burden: well a man may weary be
After eighty years, and this much now is manifest to me:
Death is like a night-blind camel stumbling on: — the smitten die
But the others age and wax in weakness whom he passes by.
He that often deals with folk in unkind fashion, underneath
They will trample him and make him feel the sharpness of their teeth.
He that hath enough and over and is niggard with his pelf
Will be hated of his people and left free to praise himself.
He alone who with fair actions ever fortifies his fame
Wins it fully: blame will find him out unless he shrinks from blame.

He that for his cistern's guarding trusts not in his own stout arm
Sees it ruined: he must harm his foe or he must suffer harm.
He that fears the bridge of Death across it finally is driven,
Though he span as with a ladder all the space 'twixt earth and heaven.
He that will not take the lance's butt-end while he has the chance
Must thereafter be contented with the spike-end of the lance.
He that keeps his word is blamed not; he whose heart repaireth straight
To the sanctuary of duty never needs to hesitate.
He that hies abroad to strangers doth account his friends his foes;
He that honours not himself lacks honour wheresoe'er he goes.
Be a man's true nature what it will, that nature is revealed
To his neighbours, let him fancy as he may that 'tis concealed."

The above examples show the wide range of themes employed by pre-Islamic poets. The exposition here is in no way exhaustive or even complete.

REFERENCES

Arberry, A.J. 1965. *Arabic Poetry. A Primer for Students.* London & New York: Cambridge University Press.

Bateson, M.C. 1970. *Structural Continuity in Poetry: A Linguistic Study in Five Pre-Islamic Arabic Odes.* The Hague.

Gibb, H.A.R. 1974. *Arabic Literature: An Introduction.* Oxford. (See chapter 3, on the *Heroic Age*).

Nicholson, R.A. 1977. *A Literary History of the Arabs.* Cambridge. (See chapters 2 & 3).

XVIII

THE PRE-ISLAMIC ODE

The most outstanding type of Arabic poetry before Islam is that which is known as the "long poems" or *mu'allaqāt* which were believed to have been hung on the wall of the Kaaba in Mecca. There are seven to ten of them which are still extant. Each of these long poems consist of about 100 lines or "*abyāt*".

A *qaṣīda* or an ode usually begins with *nasīb,* a section designed to evoke nostalgia and sympathy on the part of the listener.

Ibn Qutaiba writing in the ninth century states (Nicholson 1977: 77f):

> "The composer of odes began by mentioning the deserted dwelling-places and the relics and traces of habitation. Then he wept and complained and addressed the desolate encampment, and begged his companion to make a halt, in order that he might have occasion to speak of those who had once lived there and afterwards departed, for the dwellers in tents were different from townsmen or villagers in respect of coming and going, because they moved from one water-spring to another, seeking pasture and searching out the places where rain had fallen.
>
> Then to this he linked the erotic prelude *nasīb,* and bewailed the violence of his love and the anguish of separation from his woman and the extremity of his passion and desire, so as to win the hearts of his hearers and direct their eyes towards him and invite their ears to listen to him, since the song of love touches men's souls and takes hold of their hearts."

Imru' al-Qays, a grandson of King Ḥārith of Kinda, is famous for his "Golden Ode", and he is reckoned to be the greatest of the pre-Islamic poets. He is much praised for his exquisite diction and splended images. His ode begins with *nasīb,* the opening described above by Ibn Qutaiba (Gibb 1974: 16):

> "Stay! let us weep, while memory tries to trace
> The long-lost fair one's sand-girt dwelling-place;
> Though the rude winds have swept the sandy plain,
> Still some faint traces of that spot remain.
> My comrades reined their coursers by my side
> And 'Yield not, yield not to despair' they cried.
> Tears were my sole reply; yet what avail
> Tears shed on sands, or sighs upon the gale?."

He then tells us about his love (Nicholson 1977: 105 f):

> "Once, on the hill, she mocked at me and swore,
> 'This hour I leave thee to return no more'
> Soft! if farewell is planted in thy mind,
> Yet spare me, Fatima, disdain unkind.
> Because my passion slays me, wilt thou part?
> Because thy wish is law unto mine heart?
> Nay, if thou so mislikest aught in me,
> Shake loose my robe and let if fall down free.
> But ah, the deadly pair, thy streaming eyes!
> They pierce a heart that all in ruin lies.
>
> How many a noble tent hath opened its treasure
> To me, and I have ta'en my fill of pleasure,
> Passing the warders who with eager speed
> Had slain me, if they might but hush the deed,
> What time in heaven the Pleiades unfold
> A belt of orient gems distinct with gold.
> I entered. By the curtain there stood she,
> Clad lightly as for sleep, and looked on me.
> 'By God,' she cried, 'what recks thee of the cost?

I see thine ancient madness is not lost.'
I led her forth – she trailing as we go
Her broidered skirt, lest any footprint show –
Until beyond the tents the valley sank
With curving dunes and many a piled bank.

Then with both hands I drew her head to mine,
And lovingly the damsel did incline
Her slender waist and legs more plump than fine; –
A graceful figure, a complexion bright,
A bosom like a mirror in the light;
A white pale virgin pearl such lustre keeps,
Fed with clear water in untrodden deeps.
Now she bends half away: two cheeks appear,
And such an eye as marks the frighted deer
Beside her fawn; and lo, the shapely neck
Not bare of ornament, else without a fleck;
While from her shoulders in profusion fair,
Like clusters on the palm, hangs down her coal-dark hair."

The second major theme which is a characteristic of the pre-Islamic ode is the description of the poet's journey by horse or by camel. This is usually termed the "travel theme". In this section the poet gives an account of his adventures in the wild life of the desert, the hunting scenes, the difficulties he might have experienced and the danger he may have come across.

Labīd's ode portrays this theme quite efficiently (Gibb 1974: 17):

"She, the white cow, shone there through the dark night luminous, like a pearl of deep-seas, freed from the string of it,
Thus till morn, till day-dawn folded back night's canopy; then she fled bewildered, sliding the feet of her . . .
Voices now she hears near, human tones, they startle her, though to her eye naught is: Man! he, the bane of her!
Seeketh a safe issue, the forenoon through listening, now in front, behind now, fearing her enemy.
And they failed, the archers, Loosed they then to deal with

her fine-trained hounds, the lop-eared, slender the sides of them.
They outran her lightly. Turned she swift her horns on them,
like twin spears of *Samhar,* sharp-set the points of them.
Well she knew her danger, knew if her fence failed with them
hers must be the red death. Hence her wrath's strategy.
And she slew *Kasābi,* foremost hound of all them, stretched
the brach in blood there, ay, and *Sukhām* of them."

The closing theme in the ode is usually the praise of his tribe and a proclamation of its glorious deeds and the disgrace of its rivals or enemies.

It also includes the poet's praises of his patron and his generosity.

The following lines are from an ode by 'Amr ibn Kulthūm, the spokesman of the tribe of Taghlib (Gibb 1974: 23):

"With what intent, o 'Amr son of Hind, do you scorn us.
And follow the whim of those who embroider against us?
With what intent, 0 'Amr son of Hind, are we to be made
Domestics under the thumb of your little kinglet?
Be sparing in menace, go gently with threats against us—
When, pray, did we come to be your mother's minions?
Our spearshafts, 0 'Amr, are tough, and have foiled the efforts
Of enemies ere your time to cause them to bend."

The ode ends with an extravagant climax of boasts (Gibb 1974: 23):

"To us belongs the earth, and all who dwell thereon;
When we despoil, resistless is our swoop . . . .
The mainland grows too narrow for our swelling hosts,
The sea is ours, we fill it with our ships."

In conclusion, the pre-Islamic ode represents the culmination of a period of poetical creativity and experimentation during which the new metres were apparently discovered and standardized. The most important formal characteristic of pre-Islamic poetry is the use of Classical

Arabic as a standard medium of literary expression and for formal communications between tribes which used divergent colloquial dialects. The lengthy size and polished form of the ode, together with its true reflection of the pre-Islamic life and society, helped in the making of the odes of the pre-Islamic era.

REFERENCES

Bateson, M.C. 1970. *Structural Continuity in Poetry: A Linguistic Study in Five Pre-Islamic Odes.* The Hague.

Gibb, H.A.R. 1974. *Arabic Literature: An Introduction.* Oxford. (See chapter 3).

Nicholson, R.A. 1977. *A Literary History of the Arabs.* Cambridge. (See chapter 3).

XIX

ISLAMIC LITERATURE

By Islamic literature I mean the literary output which appeared with, and after the advent of Islam. It stretches for a relatively short period of time, namely between 622–750. This period witnessed the greatest expansion in the ancient world, that of Islam. With the appearance of the Prophet Muḥammad (Peace Be Upon Him), a new era started which revolutionized the life and ideology of the Arabs. In Mecca, and later in Medina, the Prophet received the message of God and the *Holy Qur'ān* was revealed, laying the foundations for a new society.

Although the Prophet and the four Caliphs in Medina were preoccupied by the building up of the Islamic state and defending it from various attacks within Arabia and also outside Arabia, literature did not cease to exist. In fact, the Qur'ān and the Prophet's sayings and traditions have exerted a lasting influence on Arabic literature since that time. There was a time when poetry was given a lesser emphasis than in the pre-Islamic era. There are at least two reasons for this attitude. Firstly the preoccupation of the Muslim minority with the study of the Qur'ān and its interpretation. Secondly, it took time to absorb the new concepts and spirit of Islam and to incorporate them into a mature literary output. However, the Prophet himself had a poet, Ḥassān ibn Thābit, who was considered his spokesman. Ḥassān himself, like many of the Prophet Muḥammad's followers, lived partly in the pre-Islamic period. During the life of the Prophet, and afterwards, he composed a number of poems which defend the Islamic faith and expound the Islamic belief and ideology.

The Qur'ān, apart from being the word of God, is also considered a great literary monument, as described by Professor Gibb (1974: 36):

> "The Qur'ān is a unique production in Arabic literature, having neither forerunners nor successors in its own idiom.

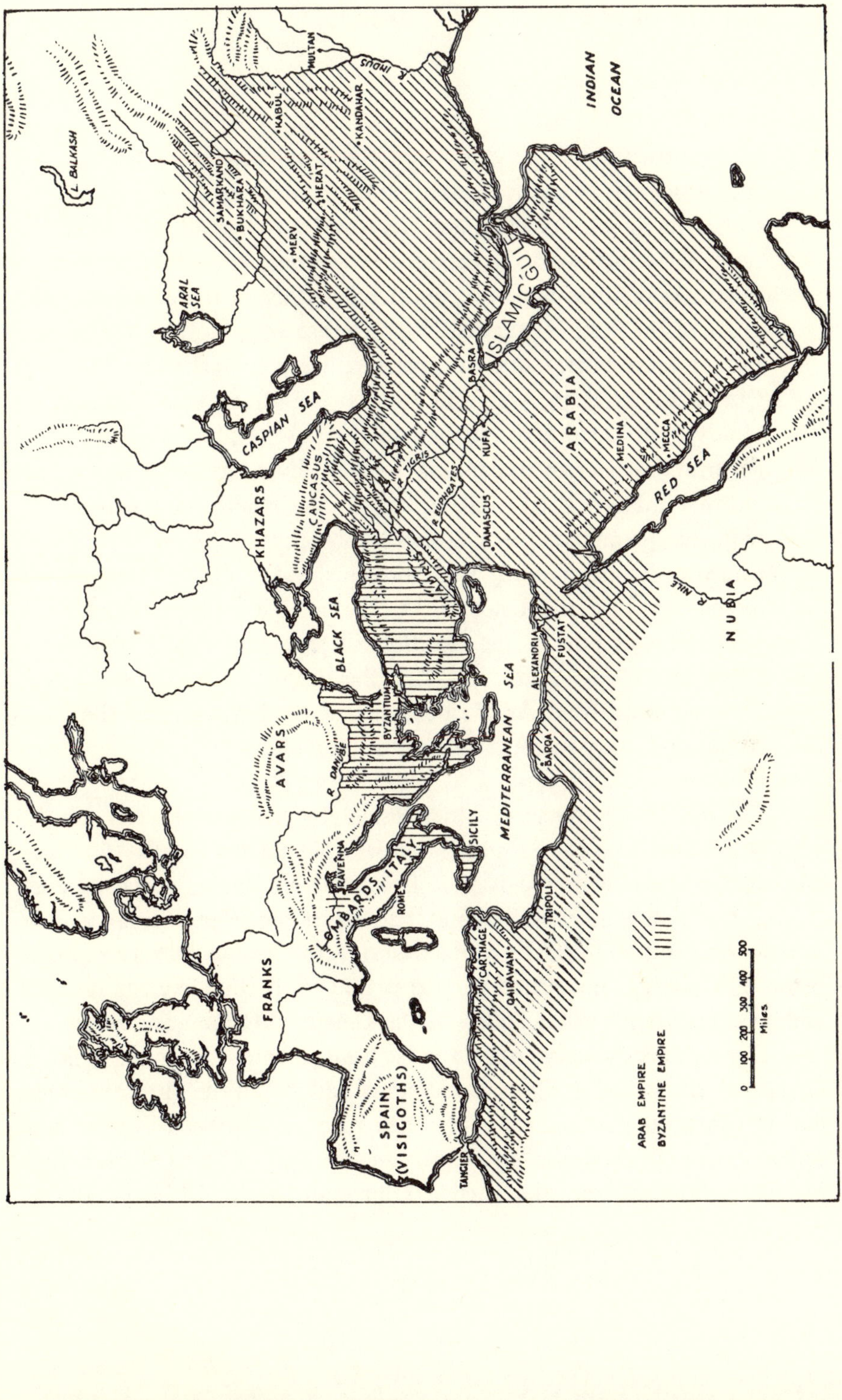

MAP 5. The Arab Islamic Empire in 680 A.D.

> Muslims of all ages are united in proclaiming the inimitability not only of its contents but of its style."

He goes on to say (1974: 36f):

> "The influence of the Qur'ān on the development of Arabic literature has been incalculable, and exerted in many directions. Its ideas, its language, its rhythms pervade all subsequent literary works in greater or lesser measure. Its specific linguistic features were not emulated, either in the chancery prose of the next century or in later prose writings, but it was not at least partly due to the flexibility imparted by the Qur'ān to the High Arabic idiom that the former could be so rapidly developed and adjusted to the new needs of imperial government and an expanding society. Even greater was its indirect influence, in that it was to the studies connected with the Qur'ān that the majority of branches of Arabic literature owe its origin. Moreover, though the standard of literary Arabic was in fact set not by the Qur'ān but by the heathen poets, it was due to the position of the Qur'ān as "Bible, prayer-book, delectus, and first law-book to Muslims of whatever sect" that Arabic became a world-language and the common literary medium of all Muslim peoples."

The Umayyad dynasty, which originated from a Meccan family who were related to the Prophet, followed the fourth Caliph 'Alī's rule, and shifted the seat of the Islamic Empire from Medina to Damascus. During the Umayyad period the expansion of the Islamic Empire into Africa, Asia and Europe took its fullest turn. Arabic literature, both prose and poetry, flourished in this period, as it found fertile ground and was encouraged at the courts of the Umayyad Caliphs and rulers.

During this dynasty, Arabia must have suffered the most striking change of all. Its most vigorous elements had joined the Muslim armies and left Arabia, perhaps for ever. They reached Southern Europe and Spain in the West, India and China in the East. The expansion had brought influences from the outside. Gibb states again (1974: 38f):

"The most vital results of the Arab conquests was the gradual absorption of the conquered peoples into the Islamic community. With them they brought the experience and habits of their distinctive civilizations and thus carried Arabic literature and thought to a stage of development beyond the unaided powers of the Arabs. It was not, however, until the close of our present period that their influence began to be felt. With few exceptions the studies which were carried on during the first century of the Muslim era were carried on by Arabs, though it was partly the influx of such numbers of non-Arabic speaking peoples into the Muslim community that led to the first steps in the development of the "Muslim sciences". "

The Umayyad literature reflected the various aspects of life in that period. The poetry reflected the political sciences, the battles, the courts and the great expansion of the Islamic world. An Umayyad poet expressing his courage and love of heroism went as far as to say these lines:

"I fear that I might die in bed, and hope for a death under the points of full spears."

The Umayyad period also witnessed the rise of a kind of pure love poetry which is called *'Udrī ġazal.* This poetry flourished in rural areas of Hijaz. Here we meet a number of love poets who express their sincere feelings towards their beloveds. One of these great poets is Jamīl who loved Buthayna and composed tens of poems to attract her.
Jamīl says (Nicholson 1977: 238):

"Oh, might it flower anew, that youthful prime
And restore to us, Buthayna, the bygone time!
And might we again be blest as we wont to be
When thy folk were nigh and grudged what thou gavest me'

Shall I ever meet Buthayna alone again
Each of us full of love as a cloud of rain?

Fast in her net was I when a lad, and till
This day my love is growing and waxing still.

I have spent my lifetime, waiting for her to speak,
And the bloom of youth is faded from off my cheek;
But I will not suffer that she my suit deny,
My love remains undying, though all things die!"

In another poem he says:

"They say: "Take part in the Holy War *jihād*, Jamīl, go on a raid!" But what *jihād* do I want besides the one that has to do with women? Conversation in their company brings joy; but each man who dies in their midst is a martyr."

Away from the Umayyad's courts, also flourished the sensational *ġazal* poetry in Urban cities. 'Umar ibn Abī Rabī'ah from Mecca is reputed for this kind of literary genre. Note the following poem expressing his feelings towards women (Arberry 1965: 40f):

"Would that Hind had fulfilled to us her promise, and healed our souls of their suffering!
Would that she had acted independently for once! It is the weakling who does not act independently.
They asserted that she asked our lady-neighbours, when she stripped herself one day to bathe,
"Do you see me to be as he describes me – in God's name answer me truly! – or does he not observe moderation?"
Then they laughed together, saying to her, "Fair in every eye is the one you love!"
So they spoke out of an envy with which they were charged because of her; and of old envy has existed amongst men.
A young maiden is she who, when she discloses her cool lips, there is revealed from them teeth white as camomile-blossoms or hailstones.
She has two eyes whose lids contain an intense whiteness and blackness, and in her neck is a slender softness.

Tender is she, cool in the season of heat when the vehemence of the summer has burst into flame,
Warm in wintertime, a coverlet for a lad under the night when the bitter cold wraps him around.
Well I remember when I spoke to her, the tears running down over my cheek,
I said, "Who are you?" She answered, "I am one emaciated by passion, worn out by sorrow.
We are the people of al-Khaif, of the people of Mina; for any slain by us there is no retaliation."
I said, "Welcome! You are the goal of our desire. Name yourselves now!" She said, "I am Hind.
My heart is destroyed by grief, and it yet comprehends a youth slim as a straight, true lance, clad in fine raiment.
Your people are indeed neighbours of ours; we and they are but a single thing!"
They told me that she bewitched me – how excellent is that bewitchment!
Whenever I said, "When shall be our tryst?" Hind would laugh and say, "After tomorrow!"

The Umayyad period also produced the poets of *Naqā'iḍ* like Jarīr and Farazdaq who for years fought a cold war between them which is recorded in their poems, some of which are still extant till today.

Homesickness was also a feature of the poems of the Arabian poets who left Arabia for good. Here is Maysūn, the wife of Mu'āwya the first Umayyad Caliph, who expresses her discontent with the luxurious life in Damascus (Nicholson 1977: 195):

"A tent with rustling breezes cool
Delights me more than palace high
And more the cloak of simple wool
Than robes in which I learned to sigh.

And more than purr of friendly cat
I love the watch-dog's bark to hear;
And more than any lubbard fat
I love a Bedouin cavalier."

The Umayyad Period has produced a number of semi-Sufi poets like Rābi'a al-'Adawiyyah, a native lady from Basra who died in Jerusalem. Her poems stress her love and devotion to Almighty God. In one of these poems she says (Nicholson 1977: 234):

"Two ways I love Thee: selfishly,
And next, as worthy is of Thee.
'Tis selfish love that I do naught
Save think on Thee with every thought;
'Tis purest love when Thou dost raise
The veil to my adoring gaze.

To sum up, this Islamic period, which lasted for about 130 years, witnessed the rise of Islam and the expansion of the Islamic Empire. It witnessed the advent of Islam and the appearance of the Prophet, and the four Caliphs in Medina, and then the rise of the Umayyad dynasty in Damascus. During this period literature took a new turn away from the pre-Islamic way of life, beliefs, and thinking. Although the Islamic poetry then started to express a new life, spirit, and content, pre-Islamic influence in the poetical shapes took a long time to loose its effect on Islamic poetry.

REFERENCES

Arberry, A.J. 1965. *Arabic Poetry: A Primer for Students.* London & New York: Cambridge University Press.
Gibb, H.A.R. 1974. *Arabic Literature: An Introduction.* Oxford.
Nicholson, R.A. 1977. *A Literary History of the Arabs.* Cambridge.

XX

THE CHARACTERISTICS OF ARABIC LITERATURE IN THE GOLDEN AGE

By the Golden Age, I refer to the period between the years 749–1055 A.D. The year 749 marked the rise of a new dynasty, that of the Abbasids who came to power after the Umayyad Dynasty of Damascus. The Abbasids established their seat of Government in Baghdad, which also used to be called Madīnat al-Salām or the City of Peace. Then the Arab Caliphate became more settled and Islamic culture flourished for more than three centuries. Baghdad became the melting pot of the Muslim world where Persians, Aramaeans, Greeks, Indians as well as the Arabs were intermixed and the Persians had by far the most influential role in the Abbasid Islamic Empire. This situation allowed the different cultures to meet and influence each other and eventually produce a new form of life and culture which has been looked at with respect until the present time.

The new capital became the centre of literature, science and arts. An Arab historian described it as "the market to which the wares of the sciences and arts were brought, where wisdom was sought as a man seeks after his stray camels, and whose judgement of values was accepted by the whole world." (Gibb 1974: 46).

Literary activities, like other subjects, continued to develop away from the standards set by the previous periods of Arabic literature which we have discussed earlier. This is a natural development both in terms of quality and quantity. The new Abbasid Caliphs encouraged their subjects, Arabs and non-Arabs, Muslims and non-Muslims alike, to contribute towards the advancement of their own disciplines. In fact the courts of the Caliphs started to attract all kinds of learned people such as men of letters, scientists and philosophers. The Caliphs and rulers became the patrons of many of these people. It is important to mention that the Abbasid literature was influenced by the Persian, Hellenized and Aramaic peoples and cultures and these indirect influences came from the older centres of culture in Iraq and Persia.

One of the characteristics of the literature of this period is the emergence of an Arabic literary prose which is different from the epistles composed by 'Abd al-Ḥamīd al-Kātib, died in 750, who was the secretary of the last Umayyad Caliph Marwān II. The Abbasid prose is distinguished by being clear, precise and well-articulated. One of the first literary writers of this age was 'Abdullah ibn al-Muqaffa' a disciple of 'Abd al-Ḥamīd al-Kātib. Ibn al-Muqaffa' translated into Arabic the Persian court literature, including a version of the hero-saga and "Book of Kings". He also adapted and translated into Arabic the well known Indian fables of Bidpai, best known in Arabic as *Kalīla wa Dimna.* The use of this style of prose and other types of secretarial literature was to lay down the rules of conduct for princes and administrators at all levels, by means of manuals, and anecdotes among other types of prose writing (cf. chapters XXXV).

Secular literature developed rapidly in this Age as a result of the influence from various sciences and philosphy and also as a result of a growing interest in bringing together or at least bridging the gap between the ivory tower, in which many scientists as well as men of letters lived, and the life of the ordinary people or the public with all the social issues of the day.

'Amr ibn Baḥr known as al–Jāḥiẓ, was the most genial writer of the age. He was a prolific author who wrote more than 40 literary works some of which run into several volumes. Later on, Ibn Qutaibah and Ibn al–Nadīm compiled in a literary Arabic prose the first encyclopedias known to us today.

Along these lines the study of Arabic linguistics and philology also flourished. Al–Khalīl had written the first comprehensive lexicon of Arabic before the year 791. The Persian scholar Sībawaihi, a student of al–Khalīl, had written the first comprehensive Arabic grammar before the year 793 (cf. chapters V–VII).

This period also witnessed the development of other areas such as the compilation of works on the tradition of the Prophet, and historical writing of events.

It is during this period that the splendour of the Abbasid Caliphate reached its zenith. The courts of the Caliphs of Baghdad and the life in the new city were well described by the well-known stories of the

Thousand and One Nights. Hārūn al-Rashīd, who died in the year 809, and his son Ma'mūn were reputed for their interest in the development of Arabic sciences and literature. It is during the reign of the latter, Ma'mūn, that a great deal of translation from Greek, Persian, and Syriac took place. His famous Academy, called *Bayt al–Ḥikmah* or the "House of Wisdom," was the most advanced centre of learning during his reign. Other centres of the Islamic Empire stretching from Samarqand to Spain had also contributed to the advancement of Arabic science and literature.

Poetry also flourished in this period, but it became more sophisticated as a result of a continued cultivation of the poem. The poem started to acquire a ceremonial function. Language of Arabic poetry became simpler and smoother, without losing any of the precision and quality of the high Arabic idiom.

The Abbasid poets took more care of the artistic shape of the poem, adding to Arabic literature various new styles. Hundreds of new poets appeared in the Golden Age. A number of these were either of half Arab or of non-Arab origin. Amongst the greatest poets of the Abbasid Caliphate of this period were Abū Nuwās, Abū al-'Atāhiyah, al-al-Mutanabbī and Abū al-'Alā'.

Al-Ḥasan ibn Hānī known as Abū Nuwās who died in the year 803, is one of the figures of the Thousand and One Nights. He was renowned for his versatility, elegance and command of the Arabic language. His Anthology, which contains his poems, features both secular and religious poetry. His poems about love and wine, the two motives by which his genius was most brilliantly inspired, are generally considered to be unparalleled. To cite one of the shortest poems (Nicholson 1977:294):

"Thou scolder of the grape and me,
I ne'er shall win thy smile!
Because against thee I rebel,
'Tis churlish to revile.

Ah, breathe no more the name of wine
Until thou cease to blame,
For fear that thy foul tongue should smirch
Its fair and lovely name!

Come, pour it out, ye gentle boys,
A vintage ten years old,
That seems as though 'twere in the cup
A lake of liquid gold.

And when the water mingles there,
To fancy's eye are set
Pearls over shining pearls close strung
As in a carcanet."

Note also these lines of his (Nicholson 1977:295):

"Ho! a cup, and fill it up, and tell me it is wine,
For I will never drink in shade if I can drink in shine!
Curst and poor is every hour that sober I must go,
But rich am I whene'er well drunk I stagger to and fro.
Speak, for shame, the loved one's name, let vain disguise alone:
No good there is in pleasures o'er which a veil is thrown."

If Abū Nuwās portrayed an appalling picture of a corrupt high society devoted to pleasure, his contemporary Abū al-'Atāhiyah presented the bright picture of the religious beliefs which characterized the middle and lower classes of that age. Abū al-'Atāhiyah is well known in the Arabic literature as the father of religious poetry.

Note the following lines expressing his dismay at this world (Nicholson 1977:299 f):

"What ails me, World, that every place perforce
I lodge thee in, it galleth me to stay?
And, O Time, how do I behold thee run
To spoil me? Thine own gift thou tak'st away!
O Time! inconstant, mutable art thou,
And o'er the realm of ruin is thy sway.
What ails me that no glad result it brings
Whene'er, O World, to milk thee I essay?
And then I court thee, why dost thou raise up

On all sides only trouble and dismay?
Men seek thee every wise, but thou art like
A dream; the shadow of a cloud; the day
Which hath but now departed, nevermore
To dawn again; a glittering vapour gay."

Like many other provincial courts, the Ḥamdānīds' court in Aleppo also attracted scientists and literary men who were patronized by the rulers. The poet al-Mutanabbī stayed at Prince Saif al-Dawlah's court for nine years. Al-Mutanabbī's Anthology contains many poems in which he addresses his master as if he was addressing a friend. Here the poet rebukes his Prince in an extraordinarily bold manner. (Nicholson 1977: 306):

"How glows mine heart for him whose heart to me is cold,
Who liketh ill my case and me in fault doth hold!
Why should I hide a love that hath worn thin my frame?
To Sayfu'l-Dawla all the world avows the same.
Tho' love of his high star unites us, would that we
According to our love might so divide the fee!
Him have I visited when sword in sheath was laid,
And I have seen him when in blood swam every blade:
Him, both in peace and war the best of all mankind,
Whose crown of excellence was still his noble mind.

O justest of the just save in thy deeds to me!
Thou art accused and thou, O sire, must judge the plea.
Look, I implore thee, well! Let not thine eye cajoled
See fat in empty froth, in all that glisters gold!
What use and profit reaps a mortal of his sight,
If darkness unto him be indistinct from light?

My deep poetic art the blind have eyes to see,
My verses ring in ears as deaf as deaf can be.

The desert knows me well, the night, the mounted men,
The battle and the sword, the paper and the pen!"

The fourth great poet who lived in the latter part of this period is the blind philosopher Abū al–'Alā' of Ma'arra, about 20 miles south of Aleppo. His poetry expressed, among other things, the sceptical and pessimistic tendancies of an age of social decay and political anarchy. He lived a life of relative seclusion. He said (Nicholson 1977: 315):

"Methinks, I am thrice imprisoned – ask not me
Of news that need no telling –
By loss of sight, confinement to my house
And this vile body for my spirit's dwelling."

The following lines also show the negative side of his philosophy (Nicholson 1977: 321):

"Falsehood hath so corrupted all the world
That wrangling sects each other's gospel chide;
But were not hate Man's natural element,
Churches and mosques had risen side by side."

He was said to have the following verse inscribed on his grave (Nicholson 1977: 317):

"This wrong was by my father done
To me, but ne'er by me to one."

To conclude, the Golden Age witnessed the growth of Arabic literature both religious and secular and the Caliph's courts and the other provincial centres encouraged the natural sciences and literary sciences to flourish under their patronage. Literary criticism also developed in this age which set the standard for a number of generations to follow (see chapter XXXVI).

REFERENCES

Gibb, H.A.R. 1974. *Arabic Literature: An Introduction.* Oxford. (See chapter 5 on *'The Golden Age*").

Nicholson, R.A. 1977. *A Literary History of the Arabs.* Cambridge. (See chapter 7, on *'Poetry, literature and science in the Abbasid period*").

XXI

AL-MUTANABBĪ IN ARABIC LITERATURE

Al-Mutanabbī is the surname of one of the very celebrated Arab poets of the fourth century A.H. (10th century A.D.). His name is Aḥmad Ibn al–Ḥusain, and he is a descendant of a Yemeni sub-tribe called Jo'fa, which is a branch of the famous Kinda tribe. He was born in al-Kūfah, an old city of learning in Iraq, in the year 303 A.H. (915 A.D.). The famous biographer Ibn Khallikān in his "Biographical Dictionary" gives a good description of al–Mutanabbī. He relates:

> "Al-Mutanabbī came of a family which inhabited Kuūfa, but he went to Syria in his youth, and, travelling over its provinces, studied and attained proficiency in various branches of literature. He had acquired an extensive knowledge of classical Arabic, drawn from the best sources and which he has handed down in his political compositions and he possessed so great information on the subject of its idiomatic and obsolete expressions that, when a question was proposed to him, he never failed to prove his opinion citing analogous examples in prose and verse composed by the Arabs of the desert. It is related that the learned Abū 'Alī al-Fārisī, author of (the philological and grammatical books) of *al–Īḍāḥ* and *al–Takmilah,* once asked him how many plural nouns there were of the form *fi'la,* and received immediately for answer *Ḥijla* and *Zirba:* and Abū 'Alī says that he passed three nights in consulting philological works to find a third plural noun of a similar form, but without success."

Ibn Khallikān goes on to say:

> "Such a remark, coming from Abū 'Alī, is quite sufficient to establish al-Mutanabbī's proficiency in philology. *Ḥijla* is the

plural of *Ḥajal* a cock-partridge, and *Zirba* is the plural of *Zaribān,* a word which serves to designate a small quadruped emitting a fetid smell."

Some sources relate that as a young man al-Mutanabbī was involved with one or other of the Shi'ite conspiracies which were a perennial feature of those disturbed times, when the authority of the Abbasid Caliphate in Baghdad was declining. It has also been related that he claimed 'Alīd descent, and that he joined the notorious Carmathian movement, a revolutionary group which, during those years, was terrorising southern Iraq and Arabia and which attacked Mecca at one point in time. There is also a story relating to the acquisition of his surname, al-Mutanabbī which means the man who set himself up as a prophet. The story claims that in his youth al-Mutanabbī pretended to be a prophet with a new Qur'ān, and that he led a revolt in al-Samāwah, in Iraq. He was imprisoned in the year 322 A.H. (933 A.D.). When the revolt failed, he became politically minded and began to attend the courts of the provincial rulers in Iraq, Persia, Egypt and Syria.

The first court which welcomed al-Mutanabbī was the court of Prince Saif al-Dawla in Aleppo in 337 A.H. (948 A.D.) Saif al-Dawla is well known for his victorious campaigns against the Byzantine Empire. Al-Mutanabbī was patronized in his court and he participated in Saif al-al-Dawla's campaigns for nine years. It is here in the company of Saif al-al–Dawla that al-Mutanabbī reached full maturity. The odes which he composed in praise of Saif al-Dawla rank amongst the masterpieces of Arabic literature. After nine years of patronage in Aleppo, al-Mutanabbī moved to Damascus for a short while, then he went to Egypt. There he attended Kāfūr's court. Kāfūr was then the ruler of Egypt. He was a Nubian slave who had come to power as guardian of the young successor to Muḥammad al-Ikhshīd, an original ruler of Egypt. Al-Mutanabbī stayed for about 5 years under the patronage of Kāfūr, that is, between 346/350 A.H. (957–960 A.D.). Then after a misunderstanding between him and Kāfūr he left for Baghdad where he lectured on Arabic literature and in particular, poetry, including his own. After a while he attended the Buwaihīd's court in Shiraz, Persia, where he was welcomed by its ruler Sultan 'Aḍud al-Dawla. After a short while he left for Baghdad. On his way back to Baghdad, and on the Ahwaz road near

Dair al—'Āqūl, he was attacked by some assassins and was slain fighting together with his son. He died in Ramadan 354 A.H. (August 965).

Al-Mutanabbī is well renowned for his anthology or collection of poems which were even studied during his lifetime, by himself or other famous contemporary scholars such as Ibn Jinnī and later philologists. Al-Mutanabbī enjoyed a reputation which very few Arab poets achieved. He was proud of his odes and his styles of expression. He is to Arabic literature what Milton is to English literature or Dante to Italian literature. Al-Mutanabbī was a controversial figure. Some of his critics were contemporaries with whom he exchanged opinions and scholarly arguments. Commentaries on his poetry are abundant and his 10th century poems are still recited with great joy and zeal.

One of his opponents wrote the following lines about al-Mutanabbī:

> "What merit is there in a poet who from morning to night seeks for reward? At one time he lived by selling water in Kūfah; at another, by selling his prostituted talent."

By this remark the opponent refers to al-Mutanabbī's father al-Ḥusain who was a water carrier in Kūfah.

It is also related by Ibn Khallikān that "al-Motamid ibn 'Abbād, Prince of Cordoba and Seville in Muslim Spain, recited one day the following lines from a celebrated poem of al-Mutanabbī's:

> "Our camels, broken with fatigue, receive fresh strength when their eyes obtain a sight of thee."

Ibn Khallikān continues:

> "In his admiration, the Prince continued repeating this verse, when Ibn Wahbūn who was one of the company, improvised the two following:
>
> If the son of al-Ḥusain was skilled in making generous gifts! 'tis gifts which open the lips of grateful poets. Proud of his poetic talent, al-Mutanabbī declared himself a prophet; had he known that you would recite his poems, he had thought himself a God."

The following poem is one of al-Mutanabbī's famous odes. It was composed to rebuke his patron Prince Saif al-Dawla, and in which he threatens to leave the Prince's service (Arberry 1967:70–4; cf. the same poem translated by Nicholson, chapter XX):

"Alas for a heart feverish on account of one whose heart is cold, and with whom there is a sickness in my body and estate.
Why do I conceal a love that has wasted my frame, when all the nations make claim to love Saif al-Dawla?
If we are indeed united by the love for his shining brow, would that we might take shares according to the degree of our love.
I have visited him when the Indian swords were sheathed, and I have gazed on him when the swords were bloody, and he was the fairest of all God's creatures, and the fairest thing in the fairest was his character.
The missing of the foe whom you sought was a victory in whose folds was regret, in whose fold were blessings;
Mighty fear deputised for you, and awe for you wrought more than the heroes achieved.
You required of yourself a thing that was by no means incumbent, namely that neither earth nor broad mountain should hide them.
What, whenever you seek out an army and it recoils in flight, do lofty aspirations take charge of you in following their tracks?
It is your duty to rout them in every engagement, but you are not obliged to disgrace them when they are routed.
Do you not regard a victory as sweet, except it be a victory in which the white Indian swords shake hands with the dusky locks?
O justest of mortals, save in your treatment of me, the quarrel is regarding yourself, and you are at once the adversary and the arbiter.
I take refuge with your glances, true and just that they are, lest they should suppose fatness to be in one whose fatness is

a mere swelling;
And what benefit does a mortal man derive from his eyes, when all alike in his sight are lights and darknesses?
I am he whose accomplishments even the blind can see, and whose words have made even the deaf to hear;
I sleep in sublime unconcern for the words which wander abroad, whilst other men are sleepless on their account, contending mightily.
Many an ignoramus there is whom I have indulged in his ignorance with my smile, until suddenly he has been surprised by a pouncing hand and devouring mouth.
When you see the fangs of lions exposed, do not suppose that the lion is smiling.
And many a heart there is, whose owner has purposed my heart's destruction, I have overtaken riding a noble steed whose back was inviolable,
His feet in the gallop as one foot, his hands one hand, and his action all that the hand and foot desire.
And many a slender blade I have advanced with between the two hosts until I smote, what time death's waves were dashing together;
For the horsemen know me, and the night, and the desert, and the sword and lance, and the paper and pen.
I have companioned the wild beasts in the wastes, alone, so that the stony slopes and the hills have marvelled at me.
O you, to be parted from whom is grievous to us, after you, our attaining every thing is utter want,
How worthy we were to receive consideration from you, if only your concern corresponded with our concern.
If what our envious rival said delighted you, a wound does not hurt so long as it pleases you.
Between us—if only you were mindful of that—is an acquaintanceship, and acquaintanceships are binding convenants for men of prudent minds.
However much you may seek a fault in us to reproach us with, you will not find it, and God detests what you are doing, and nobility too.

How far removed is fault and defect from my honour! I am the Pleiades, and those are white hairs and old age.
Would that the raincloud whose thunderbolts are falling on me would cause them to pass away to him who is receiving the gentle shower!
I perceive that the distance requires of me to travel every stage which not even the wide-striding, heavily-pacing camels would master.
If they leave Ḍumair on our right hand, repining will surely come upon those we have bidden farewell.
When you depart from a people who were well able not to let you part from them, it is they who really set forth.
The worst of lands is a place where there is no friend, and the worst thing a man can acquire is what dishonours him;
And the worst quarry my hand has taken is a quarry in which the gray falcon is equal with the vulture.
With what manner of utterance do certain vile ones, neither Arab nor even Persian, speak poetry that they should pass muster with you?
This is a reproach against you, but it is an expression of love, inlaid with pearls, only they are words."

It is believed that this poem was the last to be composed for the Prince who seemed to have got tired of the poet's conceit, self-praise and political ambitions which had become intolerable. The Prince's court was always full of learned people and scholars some of whom could not wait to see the departure of al-Mutanabbī from the court. One can read between the lines al-Mutanabbī's growing distaste of what was going on in the Prince's court and his support of al-Mutanabbī's rivals.

The following is part of a poem which was composed by al-Mutanabbī in which he abuses the Prince openly. The poem was translated by Herbert Howarth and Ibrahim Shakrullah. Al-Mutanabbī says:

"Promiscuous tags and liberal lip I hate,
The gutter currency that swamps the state
Where slaves who knock their master down and clear
The till, are certain of a great career.
I went there as the guest of liars, who

Would neither entertain nor let me go,
Liars for whose putrid frames death would not function
Unless equipped with a carbolic truncheon.

I saw the land an orchard, the foxes creeping
Between the crumbling walls and watchmen sleeping;
On grapes perennial the foxes thrive.
I saw what I hoped never to see alive,
The dog that fouled me pampered and well-fed,
The nigger king in plumes, the good men dead.

I saw the cult of slaves, the rites imposed
On jailbirds by a eunuch in priest's clothes,
From which peeped out his servile origin: –
The best-dressed leper cannot change his skin.
A local proverb: when you buy your slave
Buy a stick too, and teach him how to behave.

I saw the hole in the black lip that rules
The poltroons and the gluttons and the fools.
The nation governed by a pregnant pathic
Is either lunatic or astigmatic.
He picked my brain, forbade me to depart,
Postured abroad as patron of the arts.
I shouted death to escort me from pain
And would have relished it like sugar-cane,
But found a simpler way, this camel crupper,
And ride, damming his midwife and his mother.

What howling sires, what genteel baboon set
Taught the tawny eunuch etiquette?
Did he learn manners from his auctioneer
When sold for twopence (discount for the tattered ear)?
Supremely sordid sir, in your defence
I'll be an advocate, and plead that since
The great white bulls at moments fail to rise
To the occasion, eunuchs can't do otherwise."

REFERENCES

Arberry, A.J. 1967. *Poems of al-Mutanabbī. A Selection with Introduction, Translations and Notes.* Cambridge: The University Press.

Howarth, Herbert and Ibrahim Shakrullah. 1944. *Images from the Arab World.* London: Pilot Press.

Ibn Khallikān. 1842–71. *Biographical Dictionary,* 4 vols. London.

XXII

AL-MUTANABBĪ IN PERSIA

The tenth century poet, al-Mutanabbī spent the last two years of his life in Persia where he attended the Buwaihīds Court. He was welcomed by the Buwaihīd ruler, Prince 'Aḍud al-Dawla whose court attracted scores of scholars, scientists, artists and men of letters. Al-Mutanabbī spent some time travelling in Southern Persia, in Arrajān and in Shiraz.

The following two poems were composed by al-Mutanabbī while he was at the Buwaihīds court. They were translated into English by the late Professor Arberry (1967).

The first of these poems is in praise of 'Aḍud al-Dawla and his sons the Crown Prince Abū'l Fawāris and Prince Abū Dulaf. Al-Mutanabbī begins this poem by describing his journey in the Bawwān Valley, a famous beauty spot near Shiraz (Arberry 1967: 134):

> "The abodes of the Valley in respect of delightfulness are, in relation to all other abodes, as spring among all other times. But the Arab lad amidst them is a stranger in face, hand and tongue."

By the Arab lad he probably refers to himself as being of a dark complexion and a foreign tongue.

He goes on to give details of his observations in this valley in daylight; and depicts his tiresome journey before his arrival at the court of Prince 'Aḍud al-Dawla, whose original Persian name was Fannakusru and who was also known as Abū Shujā': –

> "They are places of jinns to play in – if Solomon had journeyed in them, he would have journeyed with an interpreter. They invited our horsemen and steeds, until I feared, for all their nobility, that they would be refractory.

We set out in the morning, the branches scattering over their manes the like of pearls,
And I proceeded, the branches veiling the sun from me and yet bringing me sufficient radiance,
And the orient sun cast from them upon my garments dinars that fled from my fingers.
On the branches were fruits, pointing to you sweet potions standing without vessels;
And there were waters in which the pebbles chinked like the chink of ornaments on the hands of young girls."

The poet pauses to remember his hometown, Damascus, and the Arab generosity, thus he mentions *t̲arīd* which was a popular Arab broth. He says (Arberry 1967: 136):

"If they had been Damascus, my reins would have been turned back by a man skilled in respect of his *t̲arīd,* having Chinese bowls,
Aloes-wood being heaped up on his fires of hospitality, its smoke fragrant as *nadd;*
You alight with him with a heroic heart, and depart from him out of a cowardly heart –
Dwelling-places, the phantom of which has not ceased to accompany me to al-Naubandhajān;
When the grey doves chanted therein, the songs of the minstrel-girls responded to them."

Al-Mutanabbī does not forget his horse. He personalizes him and makes him talk and ask questions and listen to the answers. Al-Mutanabbī says:

"My steed says at the Valley of Bawwān, "Must we proceed from this place to thrusting at the foe?
Your father Adam laid down for you disobedience and taught you to depart from Paradise".
I replied, "When I saw Abū Shujā' I forgot the rest of mankind, and this place;

For men, and this world, are a road leading to him who has no second amongst men".
I had taught myself to speak concerning them as jousting is learned without spear-points."

Then al-Mutanabbī begins to praise his host, Prince 'Aḍud al-Dawla and attributes to him generosity, courage and other virtues:

"Through 'Aḍud al-Dawla the State is impregnable and mighty and none has hands who lacks a fore-arm
Nor any grip on the cutting swords, nor any enjoyment of the supple lances.
The State calls him the refuge of its members on a day of war, whether virgin or oft repeated,
And none names any like Fannākhusru, and none nicknames any like Fannākhusru.
His virtues are not comprehended by supposition, or report, or eyewitnessing.
The earths of other men are of dust and fear, but the earth of Abū Shujā' is of security
Protecting against robbers every merchant, and guaranteeing to swords every wrongdoer.
When their deposits demand trustees, they are committed to the valley windings and the mountaintops
And thereon pass the night uncompanioned, calling to all who passes by, "Do you not see me?"
His magic charm is every *Mashrafī* blade against every deaf basilisk and viper,
Yet his bounties are not charmed against his munificence, neither his noble wealth against contempt."

Al-Mutanabbī then depicts the battles in which Prince Abū Shujā' was victorious (Arberry 1967: 138):

"A man of vigour protects the boundaries of Fars, inciting to survival by means of annihilation
With a blow that arouses the emotions of the fates, not the

> striking of the lutes' second and third strings.
> It is as though the blood of the crania among the scattered locks had dotted the lands with the feathers of francolins;
> So that if the hearts of lovers were flung down there, they would not fear the eyeballs of lovely women."

He then moves on to praise the two young Princes of 'Aḍud al-Dawla. He mentions their politeness and obedience to their father as well their courageous manner and nobility:

> "I had not seen, before him, two lion-cubs the like of his cubs, nor two racing colts
> More vigorously contesting nobility of stock, or more like in appearance to a pure-blooded sire,
> Or listening in his assemblies more eagerly to "So-and-so shattered a spear in So-and-so".
> The first object they beheld was the heights, and they were passionate for them before the due season;
> And the first utterance they understood, or spoke, was to succour the suppliant, or to free the captive."

Al-Mutanabbī describes 'Aḍud al-Dawla's pride in his two sons, and prays for the Prince and his family to live for ever (Arberry 1967:140):

> "You were the sun dazzling every eye; so how now, seeing that two others have appeared along with it.
> May they live the life of the sun and moon, giving life by their light, not envious of each other,
> And may they not rule save the kingdom of their enemies, neither inherit save from those they kill,
> And may the two sons of any foe with whom they vie in numbers be to him as the two *yās* in the letters of the word *unaisiyān*.
> This prayer is as praise without hypocrisy, conveyed from heart to heart;
> You have become in respect of it arrayed in the water of a blade, and it has become in respect of you upon a Yemeni

sword. or your being amongst mankind, mankind would have
a babble, like words without meanings."

The second poem is also in praise of 'Aḍud al-Dawla and it was a farewell poem written before al-Mutanabbī left Persia. It was composed in August 965, two weeks before his death on his way home. Many critics think that al-Mutanabbī predicted his fate shortly after his departure from 'Aḍud al-Dawla's court.

He begins the poem by praising the Prince and showing his genuine nobility (Arberry 1967: 140):

"May every king who falls short of your extent be a ransom for you: then there will be no king who is not your ransom.
Had we said, "Let him who is equal to you be your ransom", we would have prayed for the survival of him who hates you,
And we would have secured from being your ransom every soul, even if it were the mainstay of a kingdom,
And whoever supposes the scattering of grain an act of generosity, whilst setting up a snare under what he has scattered,
And whoever has reached the dust, there sleeping, whilst his situation had brought him to the skies.
For if their hearts had indeed been friendly, their characters would have been your foe,
Because you hate any lean nobility when you perceive his worldly goods to be stout."

Al-Mutanabbī goes on to bid farewell to the Prince and shows his worry and suffering as a result of this impending separation (Arberry 1967: 142).

"I set forth, you having sealed my heart with your love, lest any but you should alight in it,
And you have loaded me with gratitude both long and with which I can scarcely move;
I fear that it will be painful for the riding beasts, so that they will only bear us along totteringly.

> Haply God will make it a departure assisting us to abide in your protection.
> If I could, I would lower my eyes so as not to see them, until I behold you;
> And how can I endure to lose you, seeing that your overflowing bounty has sufficed me, but not sufficed you?
> Will you leave me, with the eye of the sun for my shoe, so that my walking in it cuts the throngs?
> I see how I grieve whilst yet we have not travelled far; how will it be, then, when the pace quickens?
> This yearning before separation is a sword – behold, I had not been struck yet, and it had left its mark.
> When the time for goodbye came, my heart said, "See you keep silent, and may you not keep company with your mouth".
> And but that the thing it desired was a return, I would have said, "And may you not attain your desire.
> You have sought healing from a sickness in a sickness, and what has healed you is its most fatal draught."
> So I was veiling from you our secret converse, and concealing anxieties with which I have battled long;
> When I disobeyed them, they were strong, and if I obeyed them, they would be weak."

Al-Mutanabbī then describes his sadness and mentions Thawiyya the place he was going to (Arberry 1967: 144):

> "And to how many a grief-stricken one this side of *al-Thawiyya* will my approach say, "This for that!"
> And how many a one sweet of saliva, when we halt the camels, will kiss the saddle and saddle-cloth of *Turwak,*
> Forbidding himself to touch perfume after I was gone, though the sweet scent diffused and clung to him,
> And refusing his mouth to every lover, but bestowing it on *bashāma* and *arāk.*
> Sleep was conversing with his eyes about me – would that sleep would have told him of your bounty,

And that the Bactrian camels will not reach Iraq without your bounty has emaciated the solid beasts.
I would not have his eyes visited by a dream which, when they awake, he imagines was a lie;
Neither but that he should listen, whilst I relate – and would that passion for you may not enslave him.
And how many a hearer will rejoice, not knowing whether to marvel at my praise or your sublimity.
That sweet odour, your reputation, is musk, and that poetry my pestle and pounding-stone;
So do not praise them, but praise a hero who, even when his praiser does not name him, he means you.
Very noble he is, and he has characteristics from his father by means of which your sons tomorrow will meet your father.
Among friends some are specially marked by passionate grief, which others claim to share with them;
When tears resemble one another on cheeks, the true weeper is distinct from him who feigns to weep."

Finally al-Mutanabbī prays the journey may be speedy and his anguish short and shows that he is indifferent to fate whatever it may be (Arberry 1967: 146):

"The noble deeds of Abū Shujā' have secured from my remoteness safety for my eyes from the latter;
So distance, depart from the hands of riding-beasts which pierce your bowels like spear-points,
And O ways, be whatever you wish, whether suffering, or escape, or destruction.
If we set forth whilst Tashrin had yet five days, they will see me before they see Arcturus,
The luck of Fannākhusru scaring away the enemy's lances and repeated thrusts,
And on my way I shall wear – of his good pleasure – bristling armour that will frighten off even champions.
In whom shall I find compensation for you when we part, seeing that all men are false but you?

I am naught but a shaft in the air that returns, not finding there anything to hold to,
Ashamed that my God should behold me having left your house, whilst He has chosen you."

REFERENCES

Arberry, A.J. 1967. *Poems of al-Mutanabbī.* Cambridge.
Gibb, H.A.R. 1974. *Arabic Literature: An Introduction.* Oxford.
Nicholson, R.A. 1977. *A Literary History of the Arabs.* Cambridge.

XXIII

THE PLACE OF BASHSHĀR AND AL-MA'ARRĪ IN ARABIC LITERATURE

Bashshār and al-Ma'arrī are two of the greatest personalities in Arabic literature. The common denominator between the two is that they are both distinguished poets, eminent thinkers and both completely blind.

The full name of the first is Bashshār Ibn Burd, a descendent of a noble Iranian family and a member by adoption of the famous 'Oqail tribe. His father Burd was a slave. He was born blind in Basra and lived between the years 96–167 A.H. (about 720–783 A.D.) during the Abbasid rule in Baghdad.

In his "Biographical Dictionary" Ibn Khallikān designates a chapter to Bashshār's biography. In this chapter he relates the following:

> "Bashshār held the highest rank among the eminent poets in the first period of Islam, and the following verses, composed by him on good counsel, are among the best made on the subject:
> When your projects are so far advanced that counsel becomes necessary, have recourse to the decision of a sincere counsellor, or to the counsel of a determined man. Let not good advice be irksome to you, for the short feathers of a wing are close to and sustain the long. Of what use is one hand when the other is confined in a pillory? Of what use is the sword, if it have no handle to give it power?
>
> He is also author of this verse, which is so current:
>
> I have attained the furthest bounds of love; is there, beyond that, a station which I must reach in order to be nearer to thee?

He also composed the following verse, which is the most gallant of any made by the poets of that epoch:

> Yes, by Allah! I love the magic of your eyes, and yet I dread the weapons by which so many lovers fell.

By the same:

> Yes, my friends! my ear is charmed by a person in that tribe; for the ear is sometimes enamoured sooner than the eye. You say that I am led by one whom I never saw; know that the ear, as well as the eye, can inform the mind of facts."

Bashshār composed many poems and he has an anthology *Dīwān* which contains hundreds of his poems. He composed for various reasons, political praise of the Caliphs and eminent people as well as morals and love.

In the following poem Bashshār expresses his love for his dearest 'Abdah:

> "O my night, you grow ever more hateful, because of the love I bear towards a maiden with whom I have become enamoured.
> A sparkling-eyed maiden is she; if she glances towards you, she makes you drunk by those two eyes.
> The pattern of her discourse seems like meadow plots garbed in flowers, and as though beneath her tongue Harut sat breathing spells therein.
> You might well imagine the body on which she gathers her garments to be all gold and scent.
> It is as though she were the very coolness of drink itself – drink pure and suited to your breaking fast.
> Be she a maiden of the jinn, a human girl, or somewhat between, she is a most splendid thing.
> It is enough to say that I never heard tell of any complaint about the one I love,
> Save the cry of one who would visit her: She has scattered

sorrows all around for me,
Victim of passion for a ten-days space, and of very death for ten."

The following poem expresses Bashshār's deepest concern about morals and true friendship. He says:

"If your brother is an oft-taster of passion, the steeds of his inclinations being turned in every direction,
Then leave open for him the way of parting, and do not be the mount of a rider whose goings are all too frequent.
Your true friend is he who, when you give him cause for suspicion, says, 'It was I that did so'; and when you upbraid him, receives it mildly.
If you are inclined to reproach your friend over every matter, you will not find anyone whom you never have cause to reproach.
So live in solitude, or be in amity with your brother; sometimes he may avoid a fault, but sometimes cling to it.
If you do not at times drink a bitter cup and endure it, you must go thirsty; what man is there whose drink is always limpid?"

He also composed the following poem on the same subject:

"The best of your two friends is he in whose society there is comfort and in whom, when he is far away, there is still advantage.
Intimacy belongs only to him who endears himself to you, even though a man may be born of Jurhum or Sudā'.
There is no good in a man who affects qualities he does not possess; true friendship is sincerity.
I will be reconciled with my friends, and pardon my close companion for any hasty deed he has incautiously committed;
How should I not pardon, even if he has vexed me, when my own soul is vexed by the deeds of my hands?
To reproach a man every day is a wretched business, and to

set right the spites of women is a distress.
I can endure the greatest misfortune, but I cannot endure a company that disparages me.
I preserve my friendship by mildness, and *in mildness* have a cure for him possessed of the inveterate ill of *rancour*."

One of his most famous similes runs as follows (Gibb 1974: 61):

"Meseemed that upon their heads the dust of battle lay,
And swords a night of flaming stars that cleave the abyss."

Bashshār also composed a number of poems which boast about his Persian descent. The following is an extract from one of these poems:

"Is there a messenger, who will carry my message to all the Arabs, to him among them who is alive and to him who lies hid in the dust?
To say, that I am a man of lineage, lofty above any other one of lineage:
The grandfather in whom I glory was Chosroes, and Sasān was my father, Caesar was my uncle, if you ever reckon my ancestry.
How many, how many a forebear I have, whose brow was encircled by his diadem,
Haughty in his court, to whom knees were bowed,
Coming in the morning to his court, clothed in blazing gems, one splendidly attired in ermine, standing within the curtains."

He was accused by his enemies of being an atheist. The Abbasid Caliph al-Mahdī ordered Bashshār to receive seventy strokes of a whip which caused his death.

Ibn Khallikān gives the following account after he relates the cause of Bashshār's death:

"It is related that he considered the element of fire superior to that of earth, and that he justified Satan for refusing to fall prostrate before Adam. The following verse, on the

superiority of fire to earth, is attributed to him:
Earth is dark and fire is bright;
Fire has been worshipped ever since it was fire."

Al-Ma'arrī is a surname of Abū al-'Alā' Aḥmad ibn Abdalla. He was born in al-Ma'arra in Syria and lived between 363–449 A.H./973–1057 A.D.

Al-Ma'arrī was not only a poet, he was also a critic and author of a number of books on literature and philosophy and philology. Amongst his works enumerated by Ibn Khallikān are:

The Luzūm: or poetical pieces composed by al-Ma'arrī on a more strict principle than is required by the usual rules of prosody.

The Siqṭ al-Zind (Falling Spark of Tinder). Al-Ma'arrī also wrote a commentary himself on this book of his entitled. *Ḍaw' al-Siqṭ* (Light of the Spark which falls). He also wrote a commentary on the poems of al-Mutanabbī. With regard to this, Ibn Khallikān relates the following anecdote:

> "When Abū al-'Alā' had finished his *al-Lāmī al-'Azīzī,* which is a commentary on the poems of al-Mutanabbī, one of the company happened to read to him some of the descriptive passages composed by that poet, on which Abū al-'Alā' said: "one would think that al-Mutanabbī had looked into futurity and seen me when he pronounced this verse:
> "I am he whose learning is seen by the blind, and whose word causeth the deaf to hear". "

He travelled to Syria and Iraq and lectured on Arabic literature in general and Arabic poetry in particular. Ibn Khallikān tells us more about al-Ma'arrī's life:

> "Numbers then frequented his lessons; pupils came to him from every region; and learned men, vizirs, and persons of rank became his correspondents. He called himself the doubly imprisoned captive, in allusion to his voluntary confinement, and the loss of his sight. During forty-five years he abstained from flesh through a religious motive, as he followed the

opinion of those ancient philosophers who refused to eat flesh so as to avoid causing the death of any animal; for in killing it, pain is inflicted; and they held it as a positive principle, that no hurt should be done to any living creature."

Abū al-'Alā' refers to this seclusion in a poem by him (Nicholson 1977: 315):

"Methinks I am thrice imprisoned – ask not me
Of news that need no telling –
By loss of sight, confinement to my house
And this vile body for my spirit's dwelling."

Professor Nicholson wrote the following account about Abū al-'Alā' (1977: 324):

"After Mutanabbī, he must appear strangely modern to the European reader. It is astonishing to reflect that a spirit so unconventional, so free from dogmatic prejudice, so rational in spite of his pessimism and deeply religious notwithstanding his attacks on revealed religion, should have ended his life in a Syrian country-town some years before the battle of Senlac. Although he did not meddle with politics and held aloof from every sect, he could truly say of himself "I am the son of my time."
His poems leave no aspect of the age untouched, and present a vivid picture of degeneracy and corruption, in which tyrannous rulers, venal judges, hypocritical and unscrupulous theologians, swindling astrologers, roving swarms of dervishes and godless Carmathians occupy a prominent place."

The following verses by Abū al-'Ala' portray some of these characteristics of al-Ma'arrī (Nicholson 1977: 322f):

"How have I provoked your enmity?
Christ or Muḥammad, 'tis one to me,
No rays of dawn our path illume,

We are sunk together in ceaseless gloom.
Can blind perceptions lead aright,
Or blear eyes ever have clear sight?
Well may a body racked with pain
Envy mouldering bones in vain;
Yet comes a day when the weary sword
Reposes, to its sheath restored.
Ah, who to me a frame will give
As clod or stone insensitive?–
For when spirit is joined to flesh, the pair
Anguish of mortal sickness share,
O Wind, be still, if wind thy name,
O Flame, die out, if thou art flame!"

He also says (Nicholson 1977: 323):

"Take Reason for thy guide and do what she
Approves, the best of counsellors in sooth.
Accept no law the Pentateuch lays down:
Not there is what thou seekest – the plain truth."

Al-Ma'arrī's influence on European philosophy and literature cannot be underestimated, especially during the Middle Ages. It has been undeniably accepted that Dante's Divine Comedy could not have been written without the influence of al-Ma'arrī's *"The Message of Forgiveness"*, written a few centuries earlier.

REFERENCES

Asin, Miguel. 1925. *Islam and the Divine Comedy*. Translated from the Spanish and abridged by Harold Sunderland. Madrid. Reprinted, Lahore, 1977.

Beeston, A.F.L. 1977. *Selections from the Poetry of Bashshār*. Cambridge: Cambridge University Press.

Cerulli. E. 1949. *Il "Libro della Scala" e la questione delle fonti arabo-spangnole della Divina Comedia*. Vatican City.

Ibn Khallikān. 1842–71. *Biographical Dictionary*, 4 vols. Paris.

Nicholson, R.A. 1977. *A Literary History of the Arabs*. Cambridge.

XXIV

THE SILVER AGE IN ARABIC LITERATURE

The Silver Age is a cover term for the period between 1055–1258 A.D. The year 1055 marked the rise of the Turks in Asia Minor and Central Asia which resulted in the establishment of a new dynasty, namely the Seljukīd dynasty. It stretched through northern and eastern Iran, Adharbaijan, Anatolia and northern Syria. During this period the Caliphate in Baghdad started to weaken politically as many of the Islamic provinces began to gradually separate themselves from the direct rule of the Caliphs.

Although the political scene was not stable, Arabic literature maintained its growth, especially in terms of quantity. The quality of Arabic literature started to deteriorate. During this period Persian literature re-established its pre-dominance. It is sufficient to mention in passing the well-renowned poet and scientist Omar Khayyam who lived between 1050–1122 and who wrote both in Persian and Arabic in addition to his famous quartets.

As for the quality of the literature of this period, Professor Gibb states (1974: 119):

> "As the literary circle narrowed down to a highly educated minority, its mind and literary standards narrowed in keeping and, as always happens, sought to compensate for loss of range and vitality by pedantry and affectation. Independence of thought gave place to reliance on authority; original works were superseded by the popular compendium, or the encyclopaedia. The elegance and artistry that clothed the inventive productions of bygone writers with grace and wit were now cultivated for themselves and smothered the matter as if to hide the essential dullness of mind of the age."

He goes on to say (1974: 119 f):

> "It must be remembered, too, how the richest growth of Arabic literature resulted from the contact of the native sciences with Greek thought. By now the Greek input was almost worked out, while the studies in which it was still the chief dynamic were discouraged and confined to a rapidly decreasing circle."

One characteristic feature of this period was the increasing interest in scholastic tradition. This resulted from the establishment of some schools and universities like the Niẓāmiyya University in Baghdad. Here stress was put on memorization or memory-training. The Qur'ān, the prophetic tradition, poetry and the *Maqāmāt* were amongst the most important subjects which were memorized by young boys between the ages of seven and ten.

Literary works were affected by the increasing interest in theological subjects. Amongst the great writers and philosophers of this period were al-Ghazālī who lived between 1059–1111, al-Zamakhsharī between 1075–1143, and al–Rāzī between 1149–1209. Al-Ghazālī's literary work began to take shape in Baghdad. His books in which he questioned philosophy and dogma included *"The Incoherence of the Philosophers"*, *"The Rescuer from Error,"* and *"The Revivication of the Religious Sciences"*. His literary style was, and is, still interesting to theologians and men of letters. Al-Zamakhsharī contributed to philology and Qur'ānic studies in his grammar book *al-Mufaṣṣal* and also the *"Unveiler"* on the interpretation of the Qur'ān.

Al-Rāzī's book *"The Golden Necklaces"* is an interesting literary work in which he also discussed various sciences varying from philosophy and theology to alchemy and astrology.

One of the most important personalities of this age was al-Ḥarīrī of Basra who lived between 1054–1122. He is reputed for his book *al–Maqāmāt* which contains 50 stories or assemblies written in an extremely elaborate style of rhymed prose. The Assemblies can also be a very good source of information on the customs, manners and social aspects of life in the Muslim world of that period. One must not forget to mention here another prolific author of this period. His name is Yāqūt whose most interesting literary work is his Dictionary of Men of Letters which is, in fact, an Encyclopedia of Arabic Literature of the Islamic world of that period.

Assemblies were highly prized by many people of this age and later. Al-Zamakhsharī who was a contemporary of al-Ḥarīrī wrote these lines (Nicholson 1977: 336):

"I swear by God and His marvels,
By the pilgrims' rite and their shrine:
Ḥarīrī's Assemblies are worthy
To be written in gold each line."

Professor Thomas Chenery who translated 26 assemblies into English wrote (Gibb 1974: 125):

"For more than seven centuries his work has been esteemed as, next to the Qur'ān, the chief treasure of the Arabic tongue. Contemporaries and posterity have vied in praise of him. His assemblies have been commented on with infinite learning and labour in Andalusia, and on the banks of the Oxus. To appreciate his marvellous eloquence, to fathom his profound learning, to understand his varied and endless allusions, have always been the highest object of the literary, not only among the Arabic-speaking peoples, but wherever the Arabic language has been scientifically studied."

In Egypt and Syria we meet many writers and authors such as the autobiographer Usāma ibn Munqidh who lived between 1095–1188, whose autobiography is considered "a gallery of brilliant and revealing vignettes of the age." At this point of time Egypt and Syria were united by Saladin and his successors. Here mystical poetry flourished, and came under the influence of the great Andalusian poet Ibn 'Arabī of Murcia who lived between 1165–1240. He once said the following lines which are based on mystical thinking (Nicholson 1977:403):

"My heart is capable of every form,
A cloister for the monk, a fane for idols,

A pasture for gazelles, the pilgrim's Ka'ba,
The Tables of the Torah, the Koran.
Love is the faith I hold: wherever turn
His camels, still the one true faith is mine."

One of the most important Arabic mystic poets then was Omar ibn al-Fāriḍ of Cairo who lived between 1181–1235. His anthology or Diwān contains tens of mystical odes. Note these lines "On a blind girl" (Gibb 1974: 131):

"They called my love a poor blind maid:
I love her more for that, I said;
I love her, for she cannot see
These gray hairs which disfigure me.
We wonder not that wounds are made
By an unsheathed and naked blade;
The marvel is that swords should slay,
While yet within their sheaths they stay.
She is a garden fair, where I
Need fear no guardian's prying eye;
Where, though in beauty blooms the rose,
Narcissuses their eyelids close."

During this age, Sicily and Spain produced many men of letters. In Spain where the Almoravid dynasty and the Almohades dynasty were now in power we meet the great poet Ibn Quzmān who died in 1159, and Ibn Ṭufail whose novel *Ḥayy ibn Yaqẓān* portrays the development of the mind of a boy isolated on an island and enabled, through his own innate and uncorrupted powers, to reach the highest philosophical level and the vision of the divine (Nicholson 1977: 433).

We cannot forget to mention here Ibn Jubair of Valencia who lived between 1145–1217 and whose famous book on his travels in the Ancient world is still of value as a literary work.

Sicily came under the influence of Spain and produced during this period a number of philologists and poets. Ibn Ḥamdīs who lived between 1055–1132 was so reputed for his love of nature that he is given the name "The Arabic Wordsworth". The following is a poem about nature by Ibn Sahl of Seville who died in 1260 (Arberry 1965: 134):

> "The earth had put on a green robe, whilst the dew was scattering pearls on its slopes;
> It stirred in the breeze, and I supposed the flowers were camphor there, and I thought the soil there was pungent musk,
> And it was as though earth's lilies were embracing her roses – mouth kissing red cheek.
> And the river between the meadows – you would suppose it to be a sword suspended in a green harness;
> And the slopes ran along their side, so that I supposed them to be a hand tracing lines on the page.
> And it was as though, when the pure silver (of the river) gleamed, the hand of the sun turned it into yellow gold.
> And the birds – the preachers of them were standing there, having taken for a pulpit naught other than the arāk–tree."

Two new forms of Arabic folk poetry were developed in Muslim Spain: *Muwaššaḥ* and *Zajal.* Both types, used for folk songs and ballads, had a very similar structure "consisting of several stanzas in which the rhymes are so arranged that the master-rhyme ending each stanza and running through the whole poem like a refrain is continually interrupted by a various succession of subordinate rhymes" (Nicholson 1977: 416). Here is an example of *muwaššaḥ* given by Nicholson (1977:417):

> "Come, hand the precious cup to me,
> And brim it high with a golden sea!
> Let the old wine circle from guest to guest,
> While the bubbles gleam like pearls on its breast,
> So that night is of darkness dispossessed.
> How it foams and twinkles in fiery glee!
> 'Tis drawn from the Pleiads' cluster, perdie.
>
> Pass it, to music's melting sound,
> Here on this flowery carpet round,
> Where gentle dews refresh the ground
> And bathe my limbs deliciously
> In their cool and balmy fragrancy.

Alone with me in the garden green
A singing-girl enchants the scene:
Her smile diffuses a radiant sheen.
I cast off shame, for no spy can see,
And 'Hola,' I cry, 'let us merry be!'."

Here is another stanza of *muwaššah̬* by an Arab poet from Seville in Andalusia, Abū Bakr Muḥammad Ibn Zuhr who lived between 1110–1200 (Arberry 1965:120):

"Resign the affair to destiny – that is more profitable to the soul –
And make the most of it when there advances the shining face of a full moon. Do not talk of cares, do not! –
Whatever is past and has come to an end cannot be brought back by sorrow –
And greet the morning with a cup of wine from the hand of a soft gazelle; when he parts (his lips) to disclose an ordered row (of pearly teeth)
Therein a lightning has flashed, and wine a-glitter.
I will be the ransom for the fawn that he is, slender of stature and waist; he has been given beauty to drink, and has become intoxicated.
When he turns his back and goes away, then my heart is torn to pieces.
Who will succour a lover who was excited with desire, and was drowned in his tears when they set forth in the direction of the enclosure of al-'Aqīq
And they mounted at the place of the tamarisks? I cry alas for the day they said farewell.
What do you think? When the cavalcade set forth and rode at midnight, and the night was garmented in radiance,
Was it their light that shone forth, or was Joshua with the riders?"

Let us conclude by citing a poem which expresses homesickness and a longing to return to the homeland. The poem is by the exiled

Umayyad Caliph 'Abd al-Raḥmān I, known as the Falcon of Quraish who was also a ruler in Spain between 756–88, in which he expresses his longing to a palm tree which he brought with him to Cordoba from Damascus. He exclaims (Nicholson 1977: 418):

> "O Palm, thou art a stranger in the West,
> Far from thy Orient home, like me unblest.
> Weep! But thou canst not. Dumb, dejected tree,
> Thou art not made to sympathise with me
> Ah, thou wouldst weep, if thou hadst tears to pour,
> For thy companions on Euphrates' shore;
> But yonder tall groves thou rememberest not,
> As I, in hating foes, have my old friends forgot."

REFERENCES

Arberry, A.J. 1965. *Arabic Poetry. A Primer for Students.* London and New York.

Gibb, H.A.R. 1974. *Arabic Literature: An Introduction.* Oxford. (See chapter 6 entitled *'The Silver Age'*).

Nicholson, R.A. 1977. *A Literary History of the Arabs.* Cambridge.

O'Leary, De Lacy. 1949. *How Greek Science Passed to the Arabs.* London & c.: Routledge & Kegan Paul Ltd.

XXV

ARABIC LITERATURE DURING THE MAMLŪKS PERIOD

The Mamlūk dynasty covers the period between 1258–1800 A.D. of the Islamic history. The name Mamlūks refers to the Turkish and Circassian military caste, who were independent rulers of Egypt and its dependency Syria. The year 1258 marks the end of an independent Abbasid Caliphate in Baghdad as a result of the Mongol invasion which sacked the capital and destroyed its political and cultural heritage. One of the poets of this period recorded the state of the devastated city in the following lines (Nicholson 1977: 446):

"The pulpits and the thrones are empty of them;
I bid them, till the hour of death, farewell!"

Thousands of books were destroyed and thrown into the great rivers of Iraq. By then the Muslim world was divided into separate states, and Arabic literature was greatly weakened in the Eastern part of it, especially in Persia, Anatolia and northern India.

The age of the Mamlūks can be divided into two periods. The first is between 1258–1517 when the Mamlūks were independent and relatively prosperous. The second is from 1517 onwards. During this year the Ottoman Empire started to expand and historians of literature consider this time as a period of stagnation and decay. During the first period Arabic literature was steadily losing its qualities of originality, creativeness, imagination and vitality, while during the second period Arabic literature was completely stagnant.

The Age of the Mamlūks is normally known as the Age of Decadence in Arabic Literature and Sciences, because during this period Arabic studies apparently reached their lowest ebb. The great Arab Muslim traveller Ibn Baṭṭūṭa was shocked when he arrived in the land of the early Arabic grammarians, Basra, in 1327 to find that even learned people committed mistakes in Arabic. Here is his account of this experience (Ibn Baṭṭūṭa 1929: 87):

> "I was present once at the Friday prayers in the Mosque, and when the preacher rose to deliver his sermon, he committed many serious grammatical errors. I was astonished at this and spoke of it to the *qāḍī*, who answered, 'In this town there is not one left who knows anything about grammar'. Here indeed is a warning for men to reflect on – Magnified be He who changes all things and overturns all human affairs! This Basra, in whose people the mastery of grammar reached its height, whence it had its origin and where it developed, which was the home of its leader Sībawaihi whose preeminence is undisputed, has no preacher who can deliver a sermon without breaking its rules!"

However there are exceptions to every rule, and the Age of the Mamlūks produced a few literary men and authors who may be considered as a beam of light in this age of darkness in the Muslim World.

Al–Būṣīrī was one of the most important poets who lived between 1212–1296. He was, and still is, well known for his poem, the *Burda* or the Mantle Ode in which he praises the Prophet and he has always been considered as presenting the medieval view of the Prophet.

In geographical literature we also meet al-Dimishqī who died in 1327; Abū al-Fidā who lived between 1273–1331; Ibn Mājid of Najd who lived in the second half of the 15th century and who claimed that it was he who piloted Vasco da Gama from Africa to the Indian Coast. Al–Qalqashandī who died in 1418 wrote an Encyclopedic work which was addressed to writers and secretaries to show them the technicalities and manners which must be observed in writing. Literary styles and precis-writing were among other subjects which were also treated in this invaluable piece of work of the 14th century which is still extant until the present. A number of important historians and biographers emerged during this age. To mention some: al-Dhahabī who died in 1314 wrote his book *"History of Islam"* the biographer al-Ṣafadī who died in 1363 whose biography covered the first seven centuries in Islamic history in which the biographees were arranged in alphabetical order. One cannot forget to mention here the historian and biographer Ibn Ḥajar who died in 1449; al-Sakhāwī who died in 1497 and who produced a twelve volume biographical work, the twelfth volume of which is devoted to women; al–Damīrī's Zoological Dictionary compiled in the late fourteenth century is as much a literary work as it is a work on natural science; al-Maqrīzī who lived between 1346–1442 wrote his famous topographical work on the description of Egypt; Ibn 'Arabshāh of Damascus who lived between 1392–1450 wrote his biography of the Tīmūr (Tamerlane) entitled *"Marvels of Destiny"*; Ibn Taghrībirdī who died in 1469 wrote the *"Annals of Egypt"*; and al–Maqqarī of Tilimsan who died in 1632 wrote his monumental work on the political and literary history of Muslim Spain.

Ibn Taimīya of Damascus who died in 1328 was one of the great religious thinkers of this age. The encyclopedist Jalāl al–Dīn al–Suyūṭī of Usyūṭ in Egypt who lived between 1445–1505 wrote 561 works, about 450 of which are still extant. Although many of these works are short treatises, a few of them run into several volumes. Amongst his famous works are: "*Itqān*" on the sciences of the Qur'ān, a number of books on Arabic grammar, an autobiography, a dictionary of grammarians and literary men, and a book entitled *History of the Caliph.*

In Muslim Spain we meet the politician Ibn al–Khaṭīb who lived between 1313–1374. He was one of the last Andalusian poets and writers of folksongs or *muwaššaḥas* which seem to have died out in Spain by the end of the 14th century (see chapter XXIV).

In North Africa we meet the great Arab historian and sociologist Ibn Khaldūn of Tunis who lived between 1332–1406. His volumninous work on history is still invaluable to us in modern times. More interesting still is the book which was originally an introduction to his history, and it bears the title "the Introduction". Here Ibn Khaldūn summed up the principles of sociological thought, and the first account ever of a philosophic conception of history.

One must also mention here the great Muslim traveller, al-Wazzān of Fez who died about 1526. He was captured by Christian corsairs and taken to Italy where he was converted and named John Leo or Leo Africanus. Later he returned to Africa. His work on the history of Africa was translated recently from Italian and French by Professor Ḥamīdullah (Riyadh 1978). Al–Wazzān's book remained the chief reference for European works on Africa until the end of the 18th century.

Amongst the later writers of this period were: the biographer Aḥmad Bābā of Timbuktu who died in 1627; the Egyptian Sufi poet al–Sha'rānī who died in 1565; and the prolific Syrian writer 'Abd al–Ghanī of Nablus who died in 1731. In Ottoman Turkey we meet a number of great authors of this age amongst whom are: the Turkish biographer Tashköprüzāda who died in 1560; the great bibliographer Ḥajji Khalīfa who was a secretary in the War Department at Constantinople and who died in 1658.

In Africa South of the Sahara, one can mention a number of great authors from this age. Amongst these were: the Somali 'Arabfaqīh who wrote about the struggle between Muslims and Christians in Abyssinia; al–Sa'dī of Timbuktu who wrote an invaluable political and ethnographical account of the Songhay Kingdom.

One of the characteristic features of this age is the interest in popular literature, both popular poetry and popular romances. It is during this period that *alf layla wa layla* or Thousand and One Nights was given its final shape. The legends and romances such as that of *'Antara and 'Abla* were also given a special emphasis. Here the writers of this age were accomplished artists whose works displayed technical skill with which the old themes were varied and revived. Moreover, the literary styles used brilliantly the colloquial idiom and played with words and phrases.

Ṣafiyy al–Dīn al–Ḥillī of Ḥilla in Iraq who died in 1350 was one of the most popular poets. He wrote a special treatise on the *"Arabian Folk Songs."*

Let us end here with the following lines composed by Ṣafiyy al–Dīn al–Ḥillī (Nicholson 1977: 449):

> "How can I have patience, and thou, mine eye's delight,
> All the livelong year not one moment in my sight?
> And with what can I rejoice my heart, when thou that art a joy
> Unto every human heart, from me hast taken flight?
> I swear by Him who made thy form the envy of the sun
> (So graciously He clad thee with lovely beams of light):

The day when I behold thy beauty doth appear to me
As tho's it gleamed on Time's dull brow a constellation bright.
O thou scorner of my passion, for whose sake I count as naught
All the woe that I endure, all the injury and despite,
Come, regard the ways of God! for never He at life's last gasp
Suffereth the weight to perish even of one mite!"

REFERENCES

Gibb, H.A.R. 1974. *Arabic Literature: An Introduction.* Oxford.
Ibn Baṭṭūṭa. 1929. *Ibn Baṭṭūṭa's Travels in Asia and Africa, 1325–54.* London: George Routledge & Sons Ltd.
Nicholson, R.A. 1977. *A Literary History of the Arabs.* Cambridge.

XXVI

THE RENAISSANCE OF ARABIC LITERATURE

The period between 1798 and 1920 is usually referred to as the Age of the Renaissance or *Nahḍa* of Arabic Literature. Some literary historians include this period within the so-called Modern Arabic Literature which stretches until the present time.

The beginning of the Renaissance of Arabic literature is usually attributed to the first wide-scale contact between the Arab World and modern Europe when Napoleon Bonaparte set foot on Arab soil in 1798. Napoleon's Egyptian Expedition appears to have shaken the foundations of the Arabic-speaking world culturally as well as politically. It exposed the Egyptians, and later on the Arabs, to French culture and western sciences. Another factor of the Renaissance was the introduction of the first official Press which was brought to Egypt by Napoleon. The first year of the French occupation a newspaper entitled *Courier de l'Egypte* and a literary magazine entitled *La Décade Egyptienne* were issued. Later on, Muḥammad 'Alī, the ruler of Egypt, started the Boulaq Press which produced the newspaper *al–Waqā'i' al–Miṣriyyah* in 1828. The Egyptian historian al–Jabartī here gives his point of view of the invasion that he witnessed:

> "The year 1898 was the beginning of a period of great battles, terrible events, disastrous occurrences, ghastly calamities, ever-increasing misfortunes, successive trials and tribulations, persecutions, disorders, upsetting of the order of things, continual terrors, revolutions, administrative disorders, catastrophes and general devastation. In a word, it was the beginning of a whole series of misfortunes."

Without these radical changes one would not expect the resultant revival of Egypt and the rest of the Arab countries.

Other factors which played their roles in the Renaissance were:

First, the active role played by the Christian missionaries, especially those of the Roman Catholic Church. The Maronite Christian Arabs and Armenians of Greater Syria were among the main revivalists of this period. Here we find an increasing interest in literary activities and the revival of Classical literary works.

Second is Muḥammad 'Alī's revival of culture in Egypt reflected in his interest in education and translations of western sciences into Arabic. He also sent several missions to Europe, especially to France in order to study at the Universities.

Third is the existence of a number of Institutions, like al–Azhar of Cairo, which had already been involved in the preservation of the Classical Arabic language and literature. These institutions paved the way for the Renaissance not only of the political systems but also the cultural and literary contributions of this period. These last two factors made Egypt one of the great centres of the literary Renaissance.

The literary renaissance can be characterized by the following features:

Firstly: the great interest in the revival of Classical Arabic works of the preceding centuries, in literature as well as philosophy and other disciplines. This also led to the emergence of writers who were too faithful to their classical heritage. The classical forms and styles were followed by a number of literary men of the early Renaissance period.

For instance, in Egypt we enounter Sayyid 'Alī al–Darwīsh who composed poetry and wrote *maqāmāt* or Assemblies on the Ḥarīrī's model of the 12th Century A.D., besides editing al–Mutanabbī's poetry of the 10th century. In Lebanon, we find Nāṣif al–Yāzijī who lived between 1800–71. He came from a literary and learned family and was a poet. He once said about his cold beloved (Haywood 1971: 45):

"My eyes ever entice,
Setting the heart on fire.
I am as white as ice,
But ice can set hearts on fire."

He was also a famous writer of rhymed prose. In his book *Majma' al–Baḥrain* (the conjunction of the two seas), published in 1855, he composed 60 Assemblies on the pattern of al–Ḥarīrī and al–Hamadhānī's Assemblies.

In Iraq, we find Shihāb al–Dīn al–Alūsī who lived between 1802–54 and wrote his Five Assemblies published in Kerbala in 1856. He is also renowned for his ode in celebration of Queen Victoria's reign in 1850.

Secondly, the recurrent disputes between the traditionalists, the modernists and those in between. There were also clashes between the traditional Islamic culture and the modern European culture.

Thirdly, the introduction of new trends in Arabic literature and the emergence of followers of various schools of literary movements. This change came through reading books as well as through direct contact through travel or university education abroad.

Fourthly, a number of literary *fūnūn* "genres" or "styles" emerged during the Renaissance, as a result of the new development and in particular the contact with western literature. Some of these were: the novel, short story, essay, drama, theatre, travel, autobiography, criticism, narrative and romantic poetry, political and scientific writing and journalism. It must be noted here that the increase in the number of Presses in different Arab countries helped the progress of Arabic literature, both in kind and degree, as well as in quantity and quality.

One of the most important figures of the Arabic literary Renaissance was Rifā'a Rāfi' al–Ṭahṭāwī who was born in Upper Egypt and lived between 1801–73. He was one of the 44 people whom Muḥammad 'Alī Pasha sent to France and other European countries. He stayed in Paris from 1826 to 1831. He learnt French and was later able to translate accurately from French into Arabic. He became conversant with works by French men of letters and philosophers such as Voltaire, Rousseau and Montesquieu. When he returned to Cairo he became a teacher of French in the Medical School and later in a Military Academy. In 1836 he became the director of a new School of Languages for training translators. He himself translated various books on history, engineering and geography and these books constitute most of his 27 published works. His students translated more than 2000 books into Arabic. He was also one of the editors of the official newspaper *al–Waqā'i' al–Miṣriyyah* which was founded by Muḥammad 'Alī in 1828. By translating from the French *Fenelon's Telemaque* he is considered one of the pioneers of the novel in Arabic. He was also renowned for his insistence on girls' education and a year before his death he founded the first girls' school in Egypt. He is well known for his travel book on Paris, entitled *"The refinement of gold in the resumé of Paris"* published in Cairo in 1905.

In the chapter which deals with how the people of Paris are normally housed and allied matters, he states:

> "It is acknowledged that a country or city is civilized to the extent of its knowledge and its remoteness from a state of crudeness and wilderness. European countries abound in various sorts of knowledge and arts which, as no man can deny, induce sociability and adorn civilization. It is recognized that the French people are outstanding among the European nations in their great attachment to arts and sciences. They are the greatest in literature and civilization."

The poetry of the Renaissance was also gradually affected by the new European influences. Although the changes faced difficulties from traditionalists who wanted to keep the classical conventions of monorhyme in the Arabic poem.

It should be noted here that like all other literary genres, poetry began to express the political, social and cultural issues of the age.

Amongst the renowned poets of this period were Maḥmoud Sāmī al–Bārūdī who lived between 1838–1904. He was a soldier and statesman, in fact a prime minister in Aḥmad 'Arābī's government in Egypt, he was exiled to Ceylon for 17 years, living in Colombo. Then he returned to Egypt four years before his death. He was described as al–Mutanabbī of the Renaissance.

Other important poets of this period are the Egyptian triad: Aḥmad Shawqī who lived between 1868–1932; Ḥāfiẓ Ibrāhīm who lived between 1871–1932 and Khalīl Maṭrān who lived between 1872–1949.

They all composed poems on political as well as social and cultural issues. Shawqī was also reputed as one of the greatest exponents of verse drama. He wrote seven plays among them were *"Cleopatra"*, *"Carnbyses"* and *"Ali Bey al–Kabīr"*, three typical Egyptian historical subjects. Ḥāfiẓ was a nationalistic poet who defied the Turkish and British rule. He wrote about the Dinshawai incident using bitter language:

"I wish I knew, was that the inquisition
Returned, or Nero's reign in repetition?"

On the same theme his contemporary Shawqī wrote:

"Had Nero known Lord Cromer's regime, without a doubt,
He would have known how sentences should be carried out."

Ḥāfiẓ was well-reputed for translating into Arabic Victor Hugo's *Les Miserables*.

Maṭrān was born in Baalabaak in the Lebanon. He had to flee his country at the age of twenty and he went first to France and then on to Cairo. He was politically minded and his lyrical poetry covered many nationalistic themes. He translated into Arabic several plays from French and English: *Corneille's Cina, Poly ceute, Le Cid* and Hugo's *Hernani;* Shakespeare's *The Merchant of Venice* and *Othello*.

Note here his ode "The Arab's Awakening" (Arberry 1975: 15f):

"O noble company of Arabs! Ye
My pride and boast, o'er every company,
Long have I chid your carelessness and sloth,
Yet not as one that might despise, or loathe,
But candidly, as if to wake a friend,
Unconscious of vast perils that impend.
Long nights of intercession and of pleas,
Your slumber kept me wakeful with unease,
Till I would cry, "Had ever nation kept
Its bed such centuries, as ye have slept?
Do ye not know, 'tis loss for those that drowse
Till noon, the spoils to them who early rouse?
Already ye outsleep, in countryside
As in built town, all men that ever died!
Ye are folk whose chronicles abound

With noble deeds, since valour was renowned.
Yea, from when Qaḥṭān found a hero's grave
Even to Shaibān's Qais, and 'Antar brave,
To that Quraishite orphan, who was lord
Of wisdom marvellous, and mighty sword,
Vessel of God's revealing, battling down
Kisrā, and spoiling Caesar of his crown;
And then that hero of the Arab host,
His wisdom mightiest, his experience most,
And next the incomparable ruler, he
Who spreads the bounds in peerless equity;
And Affān's glorious son, who as he read
The scriptures, o'er the script his blood was shed;
And 'Alī, his bright sword to battle bared,
His voice from pulpit rapturously heard;
Those flashing stars innumerable that be,
Great generals, and dauntless soldiery;
Wise governors, that with accomplished skill
Revolved the world's affairs upon their will;
Scholars profound, who shed true learning's light
On human hearts, to guide mankind aright."
All this I whispered in my people's ear,
Softly persuasive, or cried loud and clear;
And all the while reverted, with the grief
Of one who would, but cannot, bring relief,
Unslumbering, yet through the nighttime drear
My faith and hope still gave my spirit cheer,
Like the pole-star immovable, a light
That lit my thoughts, and shone upon my sight.
In vain I chid; until the terror struck,
A ghost of malice, dusty locks that shook
Upon the wind, in armour helmeted
And terribly arrayed, with treacherous tread,
Able to soar in air, to march, to ride,
To see in murk, to traverse ocean wide.
"Now is the hour of peril come!" I said,
"That shall awake them! O my soul, be glad!

Danger's the thing to stir a frozen soul,
A people's screwed-up virtue to unroll!"

REFERENCES

Arberry, A.J. 1975. *Modern Arabic Poetry: An Anthology with English Verse Translations.* London & New York: Cambridge University Press.

Gibb, H.A.R. 1974. *Arabic Literature: An Introduction.* Oxford.

Haywood, John A. 1971. *Modern Arabic Literature 1800–1970: An Introduction With Extracts in Translation.* London: Lund Humphries.

XXVII

THE CHARACTERISTICS OF MODERN ARABIC LITERATURE

By Modern Arabic Literature I mean the literature which has been produced since the end of the First World War, and in particular since 1920. This year marks the beginning of a new era of independence from colonial rule. In 1921 Iraq became an independent kingdom; in 1923 Egypt proclaimed a new constitution after British rule was terminated in 1922; in 1926 Lebanon was declared an independent Republic. Other Arab countries later followed this pattern.

It is not easy to draw the line between the literature of the Renaissance and that of the modern period. However, there are certain differences which can help to distinguish between the two independent eras. Modern Arabic literature is no doubt richer in quantity and quality than the preceding periods. The themes are more varied, and, now, the Arabs are more open to external influences from both East and West. Translations of literary works by great classical and contemporary writers and poets are accessible to the Arabs in hardback and paperback editions. Many European and American universities as well as Arab universities take great interest in classical and modern Arabic literature. Chairs have been established in Universities to give courses and encourage research in Arabic as well as world literatures. There are more Arabic newspapers and magazines and books which discuss the literary movements both on a national and international basis. The Arab and non-Arab students of literature nowadays have a wider choice of places in which to study Arabic literature and comparative literature in institutes and universities all over the world. Men of letters are no longer confined to the upper classes, nowadays they come from all walks of life. Women of letters have been increasing in number due to the expansion of women's education.

Therefore one cannot deny the fact that Modern Arabic literature is in a state of flux, a state of experimentation and is reaping the benefits of the Renaissance.

Modern Arabic literature mirrors the contemporary scenes of life in all their aspects and diverse manifestations. These have been expressed in various genres and styles. The literary classical flavour continues to appear though in a gradually decreasing manner. The conflict between the conservatives and the modernists still exists especially in the more conservative environments.

The prose literature has succeeded in expressing contemporary feeling and issues relating to the individual, family and society. Children's literature, novels, plays, drama, short stories and detective stories abound. The literary essay as well as other literary styles have played an important role in the gradual reshaping of modern society through the mass media, and in particular, the press, radio, television and nowadays the video.

The Modern Literary Arabic language has also changed. It has come a little nearer the colloquial, but without the regional idiosyncrasies of syntax and vocabulary, and without offending against classical grammatical rules except in dialogue. Arabs can read in this form of language Arabic literature as well as world literatures which have increasingly been translated into Arabic. Conversely, a few Arabic plays, novels, and poems can now be read in French, English, and Russian among other languages.

Some of the great modern literary men include Ṭāha Ḥusain who lived between 1889–1975, Tawfīq al–Ḥakīm, Maḥmūd Taimūr, Najīb Maḥfūẓ, Anīs Manṣour, Yousif al–Sibā'ī in Egypt; the late Ḥāmid Damanhourī in Saudi Arabia; Mikhail Naima in Lebanon; al–Ṭayyib Ṣāliḥ in the Sudan; Muḥammad al–'Arūsī al–Maṭwī in Tunisia and scores of other writers throughout the Arab world.

The late professor Ṭāha Ḥusain was known as the leader of the modernists in the 1920's and the "Dean of Arabic literature" in the 1930's. Born in Upper Egypt, he became blind at the age of two. He attended school in his village and went to al–Azhar in Cairo at the age of 13. Ten years later he was accepted by the Egyptian University where he studied Arabic literature under the Orientalists Nallino and Littmann and wrote his Ph.D. thesis on the 4th century blind poet Abū al–'Alā' al–Ma'arrī of Aleppo. Then he was sent to the Sorbonne in Paris and wrote a second Ph.D. thesis on Ibn Khaldūn, between 1915 and 1919.

On his return to Cairo, he was appointed to a new Chair of Ancient History in the Egyptian University and later to the Chair of Ancient Arabic literature. Later on, he was appointed Rector of Alexandria University in 1936 and in 1950 he became Minister of Education. He was a leading figure who started a number of controversies such as his early view of pre-Islamic literature, which he claimed to be a forgery. He wrote more than 20 literary books amongst which are novels and an autobiography in three volumes. Some of his books have been translated into European languages. His autobiography has been translated into at least 15 languages including Chinese, Hebrew, Malay and Persian. His ideas have had a lasting effect on the Arabs and Arabic literature.

In 1948 a new state was set up in the heart of the Arab and Muslim world in Palestine, that is the Zionist State of Israel. The theme of the struggle between the Arabs and the Israelis has occupied a great portion of modern Arabic literature, both prose and poetry. Even before the occupation the literary expression, on a Pan Arab scale, illustrated the injustice, pain and suffering experienced by the Palestinians, Christians and Muslims alike.

One of the most important Palestinian poets is Fadwā Tūqān. She was born in Nablus in 1917. She wrote several books and hundreds of poems marking the stuggle for the self-determination of the Palestinian nation in diaspora. Here are some lines of her poem entitled "Gone are those we love", written after the slaughter of three Palestinian leaders of the PLO by an Israeli raid into Beirut on 10th April 1973 (cf. chapter XXIX).

"One eagle after another
vanished into darkness.
One by one they were
slain
for having towered above the clouds.
Motherland
for your sake
their blood was spilled
like rosary beads of rubies slip.
Gone are those we love.

Palestine
in the seasons of your irremediable mourning
you drank cups of absinthe we drank
Your thirst was unquenched
ours eternal.
Waterless we shall remain
here at the mouth of the fountain
till the day of their return
with the ocean of dawns that they embraced;
A vision that knows no death
A love that has no end."

Western influence on Modern Arabic literature cannot be underestimated. Different movements such as Romanticism, Realism, Surrealism, Symbolism, Lyrical Analysis, Existentialism, Expressionism, and Regionalism have affected Modern Arabic literature in various degrees. The influence has not only been in subject and content but also in form and style. Modern Arabic poetry shows this influence very clearly. The introduction of Strophic verse, blank verse and free verse and the wide extent of their uses in Arabic literature is undeniably modern. Romanticism, blank and free verses influenced to a certain extent the three important literary movements or schools in the Arab world, one in America and the other two in Egypt.

The first is the school of the three pre-Romanticist poets: Abbās al—'Aqqād, Ibrāhīm al—Māzinī, and 'Abd al—Raḥmān Shukrī, who used Strophic poetry and constituted what was known in the 1920's and 30's as the Dīwān group.

The second movement was the Romanticist school founded by Aḥmad Zakī Abū Shādī who lived between 1892–1955. Born and educated in Cairo, he qualified as a doctor and bacteriologist in England between 1912–1922. He developed a keen interest in English literature, especially the romanticists Shelley, Wordsworth and Keats, as well as Dickens and George Bernard Shaw. On his return to Egypt he formed a group of Romanticist poets known as the "Apollo Group," named after his literary journal "Apollo" which appeared between 1932–1934 and which encouraged strophic verse, English sonnets, blank verse and free verse.

The third movement is the *Mahjarī* or emigrant literature, or the Arabic poetry in the Americas. The Arab émigres of 1860 fled to the Americas from insurrections in Syria and Lebanon. This group founded a school and published their own Arabic newspapers and magazines. Many of its members were influenced by American literature, especially Edgar Alan Poe, Walt Whitman and Longfellow. Amongst the emigrant poets were Ilia Abū Māḍī, who lived between 1889–1958, and Gibrān Khalīl Gibrān, who lived between 1883–1931.

In the following lines Abū Māḍi expresses his doubts about life:

"I came, I know not whence, yet came this way;
I saw a path – along it made my way;
I must go on – or say I yea or nay!
How have I come? How did I find the way?
I do not know."

One must not forget the great modern poets such as Badr Shākir al–Sayyāb and Professor Nāzik al–Malaika from Iraq; Nizār Qabbānī in Lebanon; Omar Abū Rīshah in Syria; Muḥammad Ḥasan 'Awwād and Muḥammad Ḥasan Faqīh in Saudi Arabia.

We now choose two poems written by Saudi poets. The first is by Dr. Ghazi Al-Gosaibi, the current Minister of Industry and Electricity. This poem, entitled "When Yara Smiles", is extracted from his Dīwān *"From the Orient and the Desert"*.

"When Yara smiles
a rainbow dances
in her eyes,
and dawn escapes her lips,
and even objects
seem to smile.

When Yara laughs
the pigeons coo
and Fairooz sings:
it is a wedding day.

But when she frowns
the breezes cease,
and spring is gone
and joy is lost."

The second poem is by the contemporary Saudi poetess, Fawziyya Abū Khālid, and it is called "Mother's inheritance".

"Mother,
You did not leave me an inheritance of necklaces for a wedding
but a neck
that towers above the guillotine.
Not an embroidered veil for my face
but the eyes of a falcon
that glitters like the daggers
in the belts of our men.
Not a piece of land large enough
to plant a single date palm
but the primal fruit of The Fertile Crescent.

In the bundle of your will
I thought I could find
a seed from The Garden of Eden
that I may plant in my heart
forsaken by the seasons.
Instead
You left me with a sheathless sword
the name of an obscure child carved on its blade.
Every pore in me
every crack
opened up:
A sheath.

I plunged the sword into my heart
but the wall could not contain it.
I thrust it into my lungs
but the window could not box it.

I dipped it into my waist
but the house was too small for it.
It lengthened into the streets
defoliating the decorations
of official holidays
Tilling asphalt
Announcing the season of
The Coming Feast.

REFERENCES

Boullata, I.J. 1976. *Modern Arab Poets.* London: Heinemann.

Boullata, Kamal, ed. 1978. *Women of the Fertile Crescent: Modern Poetry by Arab Women.* Washington.

Al–Gosaibi (Algosaibi), Ghazi. 1977. *From the Orient and the Desert.* London.

Haywood, J.A. 1971. *Modern Arabic Literature 1800–1970.* London.

XXVIII

WOMEN'S POETRY IN ARABIC LITERATURE

The contribution of women to Arabic literature is both prolific and varied. It can be traced from the early beginnings of Arabic literature and it continues through its different periods until the present time. Even in the few literary books which are preserved we still find information about the participation of women in various literary activities. In these works we meet poetesses, women of letters, and pioneers in Arabic literature and since the advent of the Arab Renaissance we also encounter an increasing number of novelists, short story authoresses, journalists and leaders of literary movements, both in rural and urban areas, across the Arabic speaking world.

In its totality, women's poetry expresses various spheres and situations, personal as well as the social aspects of life, and in modern times it has even gone so far as to deal with political as well as international and more humane subjects. Anthologies have been compiled for the last 13 centuries and many of them include odes and poems by various poetesses. Two anthologies have appeared quite recently, one is by a Saudi compiler, Abdallah Bin Raddās entitled *Bedouin Poetesses* (in Arabic), in two volumes, published in Riyadh, 1975; the other is called *Women of the Fertile Crescent: Modern Poetry by Arab Women,* edited by Kamal Boullata, Washington 1978.

There also exist anthologies by specific poetesses. For instance al-Khansā's Anthology which contains more than 50 of her poems.

Al-Khansā' is a surname of Tamāḍir bint 'Amr ibn al-Sharīd, of the Banū Sulaim in West Central Arabia. She is considered one of the greatest poetesses in Arabic literature. She was born towards the end of the sixth century, and was renowned for her elegies which she composed on the slaying of her brothers Mu'āwiyah and Sakhr. Sakhr was killed in battle about 615 A.D., i.e. before the advent of Islam. Literary records also show the participation of al-Khansā' in poetic tournaments at Ukāẓ, near Taif, in the company of other famous poets and men of letters. Here we choose one of the poems composed by al-Khansā' on the death of her brother Sakhr. Here the poetess expresses her sorrow and grief with vivid emotion and promises a revenge against the enemies who killed her courageous brother (Arberry 1976: 38):

> "I was sleepless, and I passed the night keeping vigil, as if my eyes had been anointed with pus,
> Watching the stars – and I had not been charged to watch them – and anon wrapping myself in the ends of ragged robes.
> For I had heard – and it was not news to rejoice me – one making report, who had come repeating intelligence,
> Saying "Sakhr is dwelling there in a tomb, struck to the ground beside the grave, between certain stones".
> Depart then, and may God not keep you far from Him, being a man who eschewed injustice, and ever sought after blood-wit.
> You used to carry a heart that brooked no wrong, compounded in a nature that was never cowardly,
> Like a spear-point whose bright shape lights up the night, a man bitter in resolution, free and the son of free-men.
> So I shall weep for you, so long as ringdove laments and the night stars shine for the night-traveller,
> And I shall never make my peace with a people with whom you were at war, not till the black cooking-pot of the good host becomes white!"

One of the women critics in Arabic literature is Sukaina bint al-Ḥusain, the grand daughter of the Prophet Muḥammad (Peace Be Upon Him). In his Biographical Dictionary Ibn Khallikān describes her as:

> "the first among the women of her time by birth, beauty, wit and virtue."

She was well known for her *Parlour* or Saloon in which many men and women of letters, poets and poetesses used to gather. Ibn Khallikān relates the following about her:

"Many amusing anecdotes are related of her witty sallies and repartees to poets and other persons: meeting one day with 'Orwa ibn Ozaina, a man eminent for his learning and piety, and author of some pretty poetry, she said to him: "Was it you who made these verses?"
"When I feel in my heart the flames of love, I try to cool its ardour by draughts of water. Could I ever succeed in cooling with water the exterior of my heart, how should I extinguish the fire which rages in its interior?"
On his answer that they were composed by him, she asked him if he was the author of the following piece:
When I revealed to her the secret of my love, she replied, "You used to desire secrecy and concealment when with me, be veiled then as to your passion: see you not how many are around us?"
To this I answered "The love I bear you and the pains I feel have already cast a veil over my sight."
He admitted that these were also his, on which she said to the slave-girls who were standing around her:
"You are free if such verses ever came "from a heart wounded by love!"

Sukaina died in her hometown Medina in 117 A.H. (April 735A.D.).

Another interesting Arab poetess is Rābi'a al-'Adawiyyah (from the tribe of 'Adī), a native of Basra in Iraq, who died in Jerusalem about 135 A.H. (753 A.D.) and is buried on the Mount of Tor, on the eastern side of Jerusalem. She was renowned for her devotion to God. Sufi writers include her amongst the greatest Muslim Sufis of early Islam. She is believed to have composed several poems. Here is one of them (Nicholson 1977: 234):

"Two ways I love thee: selfishly,
And next, as worthy is of thee.
'Tis selfish love that I do naught
Save think on Thee with every thought.

'Tis purest love when Thou dost raise
The veil to my adoring gaze.
Not mine the praise in that or this,
Thine is the praise in both, I wis."

Another poem is mentioned by Ibn Khallikān of which he cites the following lines:

"I reserve my heart for thy
converse, O Lord! and leave
my body to keep company with
those who desire my society.
My body is thus the companion
of the visitor, but my
dearly beloved is the companion
of my heart."

Ibn Khallikān also mentions the following anecdote which he attributes to Ibn al-Jawzī:

"'Abda bint Abī Shawwāl, one of the God's excellent handmaids and the servant of Rābi'a relates as follows: Rābi'a used to pass the whole night in prayer, and at morning dawn she took a slight sleep in her oratory till daylight; and I have heard her say, when she sprang in dread from her couch: O my soul! how long wilt thou sleep? When wilt thou awake? Soon thou shalt sleep to rise no more, till the call shall summon thee on the day of resurrection! – This was her constant custom till the time of her death. On its approach she called me and said: O 'Abda! inform none of my death and shroud me in this gown. This was a gown of hair-cloth which she wore when praying, at the time in which the eyes of others were closed in sleep. I shrouded her in that gown, and in a woollen veil which she used to wear; and about a year afterwards, I saw her in a dream clothed in a gown of green satin and a veil of green silk, the like of which for beauty I never beheld. And I said: "O Rābi'a! what has become of the gown in which I shrouded thee, and of the woollen veil?"

> To which she answered: "By Allah! it was taken off me and I received in exchange what thou seest on me; my shroud was folded up, a seal was put upon it, and it was taken up to the highest heaven, that by it my reward might be complete on the day of resurrection." "It was for this," I observed, "that thou didst work when in the world." "And what is this," she rejoined, "compared with what I saw of Almighty God's bounty to his saints!" I then asked her in what state was 'Obaida, the daughter of Abū Kallab, and she replied: "It cannot be described! By Allah, she has surpassed us, and reached the highest place in paradise." "And how so?" said I, "when the people considered thee far, far above her." To which she answered: "Because, when in the world she cared not what her state might be on the next morning or the next night." "And what doeth Abū Mālik Daigham?" "He visiteth Almighty God when he pleaseth". "And Bishr Ibn Manṣūr?" "Admirable! admirable! he hath received a recompense far beyond his hopes." I then said to her: "Tell me a means by which I may approach nearer to Almighty God." And she answered: "Think on him often, and by that thou wilt, after a little while, be happy in thy tomb"."

Last but not least, one must not overlook the Bedouin poetess Maysūn, the mother of Yazīd ibn Mu'āwiyah the Second Umayyad Caliph in Damascus who reigned between 680–683 A.D. Maysūn composed an interesting poem to express her feeling of homesickness for the desert and her desire to go back to it instead of living a luxurious life in Damascus. She recited this poem in front of Mu'āwiyah the first Umayyad Caliph (Nicholson 1977: 195):

> "A tent with rustling breezes cool
> Delights me more than Palace high,
> And more the cloak of simple wool
> Than robes in which I learned to sigh.

The crust I ate beside my tent
Was more than this fine bread to me;
The wind's voice where the hill path went
Was more than tambourine can be.

And more than purr of friendly cat
I love the watch-dog's bark to hear;
And more than any lubbard fat
I love a Bedouin cavalier."

Mu'āwiyah was annoyed by these contemptuous remarks and sent Maysūn to her family, where she raised her son Yazīd.

REFERENCES

Arberry, A.J. 1967. *Arabic Poetry: A Primer for Students.* Cambridge.
Ibn Khallikān. 1842–71. *Biographical Dictionary,* 4 vols. Paris.
Nicholson, R.A. 1977. *A Literary History of the Arabs.* Cambridge.

XXIX

MODERN ARAB POETESSES I

It is very difficult to assess the quality and quantity of Modern Arabic poetry, in particular that produced by women. It is largely due to the mass media that we now know more about modern Arab women's poetry and all the indications are that their number is on the increase.

There are more collections of poems or *Dīwāns* written and published by Arab women than ever before. Poetry is a creative and expressive art, and Arab women try to express their feelings, emotions, and desires in a creative way. Modern Arab poetesses follow different schools of literature, amongst them are the Classicists, Romanticists, Realists and leaders or followers of other trends and movements. By comparison, Arab poets are still in the lead both in terms of number and volume of production and publication. Yet, there are a number of poetesses who have engaged in various literary movements for the last four decades or so. The following selection reflects the diverse aspects of the Arab woman's contribution to literature.

We start with Nāzik al-Malaika, who was born in Baghdad in 1923. Coming from a literary background where her mother was a poetess, Nāzik, a poetess and literary critic, became a lecturer on Arabic literature at the University of Musol, Iraq and now she is a Professor of Arabic literature at the University of Kuwait. She is considered by many critics as the first Arab to break away from the traditional, classical Arabic *Qaṣīda* and is also considered as the first to lead the movement of Modern Arabic Free Verse.

Her first collection of free verse appeared in Baghdad in 1947 under the title *'Āshiqat al-Layl* "the Woman Lover of the Night". Later it was followed by *Shaẓāyā wa Ramād* "Splinters and Ashes", published in Baghdad in 1949, *Qarārat al-Mawj* "The Bottom of the Wave", Beirut 1957, *Shajarat al-Qamar* "The Moontree", Beirut 1968, and *Ma'sāt al-Ḥayāt wa Ughniya lil-Insān* "The Tragedy of Being and a Song to Man". One of her interesting studies is *Qaḍāyā al-Shi'r al-'Arabī al-*

Mu'āṣir "Some Issues of Contemporary Arabic Poetry", Beirut 1962.

The following poem is entitled "I am" published in 1949 (Boullata 1978):

"The night asks me who I am
Its impenetrable black, its unquiet secret I am
Its lull rebellious
I veil myself with silence
Wrapping my heart with doubt
Solemnly, I gaze
While ages ask me
Who I am.

The wind asks me who I am
Its bedevilled spirit I am
Denied by Time, going nowhere
I journey on and on
Passing without a pause
And when reaching an edge
I think it may be the end
Of suffering, but then:
The void.

Time asks me who I am
A giant unfolding centuries I am
Later to give new births
I have created the dim past
From the bliss of unbound hope
I push it back into its grave
To make a new yesterday, its tomorrow
Is ice.

The self asks me who I am
Baffled, I stare into the dark
Nothing brings me peace
I ask, but the answer
Remains hooded in mirage
I keep thinking it is near
Upon reaching it, it dissolves."

The second poem by Nāzik is entitled *Jamīla*, published in 1968. Jamila Būḥaired was an Algerian woman commando who fought with the Front for the National Liberation of Algeria against the French occupation and was condemed to death on 15th July 1957. Here Nāzik portrays her deep feeling about Jamīla (Boullata 1978):

"Yonder you weep
Your hair is loose, your hands are weak
Jamīla
But men sang extravagant songs
for you they offered their best
Aren't you drowned in their praise?
Why weep?
We melted with her smile
her face and the dimple,
her braids;
Our passions were kindled
with her beauty
in chains.

We sighed: they made her quench her thirst
with human blood
and flames,
We were convinced they nailed a heroine to the cross
and we sang to the glories of martyrdom.
We will save her, we gasped
and then drowned amidst our drunken words
We shouted: Long live *Jamīla*.
They have wounded her with knives
we with words
and the wounds afflicted by one's kin
are deeper than those afflicted by the French.
Shame on us
for the doubled wounds of
Jamīla."

Another celebrated poetess is Fadwā Ṭūqān. She was born in Nablus, Palestine in 1917, and was educated at home under her older brother Ibrāhīm who was also a renowned Palestinian nationalist poet. By the mid sixties her poetry became involved with the political struggle for the self-determination of the Palestinian nationhood and motherland. Amongst her collections or *Dīwāns* are:

Waḥdī ma'a al-Ayyām "Alone with the Days", Beirut 1955;
Wajadtuhā "I Found It", Beirut 1962;
A'ṭinā Ḥubban "Give Us Love", Beirut 1965;
Amām al-Bāb al-Mughlaq "Before Closed Door", Beirut 1967;
Fidā'ī wal-Arḍ "The Freedom Fighter and the Land," Beirut, 1968;
al-Layl wal Fursān "Night and the Knights", Beirut 1969;
'Alā Qimmat al-Dunyā Waḥīdan "Alone, on the Top of the World", Beirut 1973; and
Kābūs al-Layl wal-Nahār "Nightmare in Daylight," Beirut 1974.

Here is a poem entitled "Gone are Those We Love" (an elegy for slaying the three martyrs of the PLO movement, Kamāl Naṣer, Kamāl 'Adwān and Yusef Najjār who were slaughtered by an Israeli raid into Beirut on 10th April 1973). Fadwā says (Boullata 1978):

"One eagle after another
vanished into darkness.
One by one they were
slain
for having towered above the clouds.
Motherland
for your sake
their blood was spilled
like rosary beads of rubies slip.
Gone are those we love.

Sorrow had no voice, behold
Sorrow flowers silence to my lips
and words
fall
much the same as their bodies fell
corpses

distorted.
what else could I say?
their blood is smearing
my vision.
Gone are those we love.

Before their vessel ever anchored
before their eyes ever caught sight of
the distant port.
Palestine
in the seasons of your irremediable mourning
you drank cups of absinthe we drank
your thirst was unquenched
ours eternal.
Waterless we shall remain
here at the mouth of this fountain
till the day of their return
with the ocean of dawns that they embraced:
A vision that knows no death.
A love that has no end."

Fadwā also wrote the following poem which was published in Beirut in 1973. Its title is "To Etan, an Israeli Child from the Kibbutz Ma'oz Hayim": (Boullata 1978):

"He falls
under the star that branches
a wild tree in his hands
a web woven with the threads of steel stretching
walls of blood
around The Dream.
He is caught.
Opening his eyes
Etan, the child, asks,
"How long do we have to watch over this land?"
And time deformed
dragged in khaki, bypasses him

through flames and smoke
sorrows and death.

If only the Star would foretell the truth.

Etan, my child
Like the harbor that is drowning
I can see you drown
through the lie
The bloated dream is a sinking load.
I am afraid for you, my child
to have to grow up in this web of things
to be gradually stripped of
your human heart and face
you could fall again, my child
and fall
and fall
fading into a fathomless end."

The following poem "The Visitor" is composed by the poetess Dr. Samar Attar who was born in Damascus in 1945. She received her B.A. in Arabic and English Literature from the University of Damascus and her Ph.D. in comparative literature from the University of New York at Binghampton. Samar says (Boullata 1978):

"And if he knocked again,
The man with the frosty smile
And hooded cloak,
Where should we go
And how could we pretend
We heard no sound?

You don't seem to care
But he was there
By the gate.
Was it the owl that shrieked?
Why can't you speak?
Or isn't he there?

To know my place
To say what I haven't said
To put the lilacs in a bowl
To comb my hair
Now that the porter
Is over there.
I have heard his key
Turn in the door
I have seen
His forehead bare.

The ferry he sat in
Yawned
Like an open grave.
How can't you see
Those dreadful sails?
Fool me not, my friend!
Half-past two
Is it so late?

And the dog
Still wags its tail?
Could it have dug out
All our friends
With its dirty nails?

Fetch me a mirror
(But thy eternal summer shall not fade.)
Beguile me not.
I was never born and never dead.
I took no sides
No.

Nor from the Devil fled.

Naked, naked my soul
And in November fog

No crowd to see?
No sorrow to bear?

Knock, knock, knock
Who is there?
Porter wait!
My shoes at the door
Let the curtains fall
And I shall descend.

REFERENCES

Boullata, Kamal. 1978. *Women of the Fertile Crescent: Modern Poetry by Arab Women.* Washington.

Jayyūsī, Salma Khadra. 1978. *Trends and Movements in Modern Arabic Poetry,* 2 vols. Leiden: E.J. Brill.

XXX

MODERN ARAB POETESSES II

The following are selections from literary works by Mona Sa'ūdī, Saniyya Ṣāleh, Aisha Arna'out, Nādia Tueni, and Fawziyya Abū Khālid.

Mona Sa'ūdī was born in Amman, Jordan in 1945, and studied sculpture in Paris. She held exhibitions of her work in Jordan, Lebanon and France. As a writer and poetess, she started to publish her work in Arab literary journals such as *Mawāqif* and *Shi'r* in the Lebanon as well as journals in other parts of the Arab World. She was on the Editorial Board of the literary magazine *Mawāqif.* Amongst her books are *Ru'ya 'Ūla* (First Visions), published in Beirut in 1972 which contains a collection of her poems as well as drawings done in Paris between 1965–67. Another book of hers is *Shihādat al-Aṭfāl fi Zaman al-Ḥarb* (In Times of War Children Testify), published in Beirut in 1970 which contains drawings of Palestinian children from the Baqa'a Refugee Camp, and also dialogue and conversation with the children from the Camp. She once expressed herself in the following words:

> "At times I feel I have not matured at the same level with my dreams. I find myself rootless and abandoned like a stone. Without love, there is no meaning to life nor to art. Why can't man love a woman without having to choke her, shut her up, controlling her mind, her dreams . . .how can we love in freedom, not in oppression, only the woman is capable of that!
>
> I refuse to fall. For months now, I have been feeling a tremendous longing for death, or rather to put an end to this continuity, but the lucid presence of the great woman that is my mother forbids me to do anything about it, her love is the only authority to judge my action. I cannot cause her any sorrow, her immense capacity for love and for giving is my guide for survival.

I know I have lived over a thousand years and I am yet to be born."

The following is a selection of her poems written between 1969–1974 translated by Kamal Ballouta (1978):

(1) "Blind city,
In its streets my visions multiply
In the chaos of objects
In the labyrinths of insomnia
I hear voices of silence
The stillness of time and sea
The death of night.
I warm myself with weeping pavements
There, life glows in an instant
Born in a puddle of light."

(2) "I left my home to its walls
Opened myself to expanses of rebellion.
The light of my colors dies.

I draw away
I change to something folding the sea into soft prayer
And madness.
Earth mute
Sky a desert

Death, When shall I be?"

(3) "In her heart she planted a tree
and said to sorrow:
Come forth.
Together we shall cross a distance
immeasurable but
by the heartbeat;
Stretching over a thread of light
we shall penetrate desolation.

Overwhelm me
she said
to the dream
that I may be reborn
without a road
save the shivering of the heart."

(4) "I shall sculpt for you both two
always two
lovers, male –
female, mother –
earth, son –
flesh, form
embracing another
dialogue-silence.

For what is found in the dream
as on earth,
man is the seedling of his own dream."

The poetess Saniyya Ṣāleh is a Syrian who was born in Misyaf in 1935, and who is married to the Syrian poet and playwright, Muḥammad al-Māghūt. She has published two works, the first is entitled *al-Zamān al-Ḍayyiq* (The Pressed Time), Beirut 1964 which is a collection of her early poems. She dedicated it to her sister Khalida al-Sa'īd, one of the leading literary critics in the Arabic speaking countries. The other book by Saniyya Ṣāleh is entitled *Ḥibr al-I'dām* (The Ink of Execution), published in Damascus in 1970 which was awarded the first prize for women's poetry by the famous woman's magazine *al-Ḥasnā'*. The following is a poem of hers entitled 'Exile" (Boullata 1978):

"For grief
he wore those colorful bells,
a mask of joy.
He bound his stories
to his tongue's tip
so they would not betray him
at the crucial moment.

And he walked
lightly
in jewel-studded shoes –
alone as the night
with no stars waiting
but my eyes.

Bird, hovering over the horizon
remember
bullets are everywhere –
Remember
me
the perpetual traveler –
All my life
I have willed to go forward and have not
advanced beyond
the borders of my grave."

The following poem is also by Saniyya Ṣāleh, entitled "Tears" (Boullata 1978):

"There is a scream that binds my heart to
the throat of the Earth
And that foam is
my lost voice.

My robe illusion
My necklace of counterfeit stone
All that is the world may be
deceit
but my tears.

I am the woman bleeding the sharpened years
I come and go behind
Tall windows.
a woman in veils about to flee
My childhood smashed by this
nightmare."

Another Syrian poetess and writer is Aisha Arna'out who was born in Damascus in 1946. As a teacher, she has been working in schools on projects and programmes involved with the creative talents and hobbies of children. Besides her talent as a poetess she is a writer of short stories. We select two of her poems. The first is entitled "Ever in Consciousness" published in *Mawāqif,* Beirut, 1974 (Boullata 1978):

"Ever in consciousness
I am and am not
not always, in the dream
I either am or am
not.

Behind curtains
I see him
There, waiting
for the piece of bread
I own
but refuse to give him.
Each one of us
standing on a bank.
Some sleeping god seeking revenge
stirred up
carried me over
absent waves
and like a fish
placed me in his mouth."

Arna'out also wrote this poem entitled "They Will Say I Imitate Poets", published in Beirut 1974 (Boullata 1978):

"They will say I imitate the poets
As a matter of fact, nothing of the sort,
no preconceived intentions.

For I have read books that remained closed
I have slept through daylight hours
in reception halls.

I scribbled stuff with the mere tip of a pencil

Their judgment was passed
It erased everything
To rectify it
They later said,
She imitated
No one
She did not write
At all."

We now come to the Lebanese writer and poetess Nādia Tueni, who was born in Beirut in 1935, and who holds a degree in law from St. Joseph's University in Beirut, and writes in both Arabic and French. Nādia is also the author of four books in French published between 1966 and 1977. The following are two poems composed by Nādia Tueni and translated by Elaine Gardiner. The first is entitled "You Depart Like a Winter Sky", published in Paris, 1972 (Boullata 1978):

"You depart like a winter sky
your eyes blue with cold;
take care, the night walks,
moons hollow our faces
in search of sleeping water,
blue like madness.

The autumn bird has flown
thus kites fly
over gardens and dreams
Who has resolved to leave
when sleep is warm with childhood
and the season wounds deeper than a sword?

The girl with her medal look
with her tongue of look
with her tongue of sun,
has grown twenty years in the shade of trees.
Remember the country where evenings have no age,
where the earth opens like a window,
where first love is a white town.
Who has resolved to leave?
You depart in sadness like a sage."

The second poem is entitled "Le Soir", also published in Paris, 1975 (Boullata 1978):

"Tonight
the dark my protector is lost in the town
the moon is an image
Tonight
a memory persistent as a nettle
as daily bread
is again a bird of passage on the walls
Tonight makes way for all the moves
colored boats line up in my eyes
it rains on a resonant universe
your rainbow body arrives before the dawn
my voice rotates around death
Tonight
a passion walks the desert led by a wise man
your arms are sweet water
the dark my protector embraces you!"

The last of our poetesses is the Saudi Fawziyya Abū Khālid. Born in Riyadh in 1955 she holds a degree in sociology. She is a writer and a critic. She wrote the following words expressing her womanhood:

> "Before the ghost of the veil started haunting my life the June War broke out. June 1967 was the blade over which I walked barefoot from childhood into womanhood. Since then I was realizing at every step that the chains of my people are heavier than the chastity belt."

The following poem is entitled "Tattoo Writing" taken from her first collection, published in Beirut 1973, and translated by Kamal Boullata (1978):

"Not with your tribe's spears I write
for they are dull
but with my nails
Words without walls.
Sister,
For you I have inscribed
Love-songs
weaving the sun's rays
to your latticed window.

To tell me you accept
The Tribe's traditions and prescriptions
is a concession
to being buried alive.
The noble inch or two
of tattoo
over your skin
Shall carve a bottomless night
into
your flesh.

It pains me
to see The Tribe dwell
in you sprawling
in your college seat not unlike
your grandmother
who thought she was
a lottery ticket won
at home. A woman
in her twenties
sitting before some tent

shrouded with robes and veils
carrying the spindle
but does not spin.
To hear you talk
about a cloak
the clan's men bought
for you;
to hear your boast
about blue-blood
the heirs
and chip off the old oak tree.
The Sheikh's voice in your voice
cancels
you.

Sister
My kingdom does not claim
doweries of cows and cattle
thus The Tribe rejects me
for you are their legitimate child
I am the one disavowed
You belong to lords of virgin
lands
I to seasons bleeding flames.

Should The Tribe's drums and barking dogs
Shut off your hearing
the rippling
of women's
blood

It doesn't mean –
you are without a wound
as being captive of your tent
doesn't remove
the sky above.

You may cross deserts
on camel back
It won't hinder a satellite from
reaching the moon.

Sister If you wish to reject me now
Say "no" with your own nails
I only tried
to comb
nocturnal grief
out of your crownless hair."

REFERENCES

Boullata, I.J. 1976. *Modern Arab Poets.* London.
Boullata, Kamal. 1978. *Women of the Fertile Crescent: Modern Poetry by Arab Women.* Washington.
Haywood, J.A. 1971. *Modern Arabic Literature 1800–1970.* London.

XXXI

ARABIC SHORT STORIES

Arabic literature has contributed to world literature in various ways, and it has many different aspects and manifestations. Poetry in its various forms and contexts, literary criticism, legends, tales, anecdotes and mythical stories go back for several centuries. Novels and short stories in their new forms and principles are fairly modern. This is attributed to the modern European influence on Arabic literature, since the mid nineteenth century. Short stories in particular in their modern manifestation found a fertile ground in which to flourish. Arabic literature had already come close to the creation of this type of literary genre. Arabic literary writings for several centuries produced stories, such as those in *Kalīla wa Dimna, Thousand and One Nights, al-Bukhalā'* by al-Jāḥiẓ and *al-Maqāmāt* by al-Ḥarīrī and others. In modern times, Arabic literature has been under the constant influence of Western literature and its various schools and movements. The nineteenth century has been designated as the age of the novel. Maupassant, and Daudet in France, Oscar Wilde in England, Edgar Allan Poe in America, Anton Tchekov and Nicolai Gogol in Russia and Ernst Hoffmann in Germany are amongst the most distinguished pioneers of novels and short stories. Many of these have had a tremendous influence on the beginnings of Arabic short stories. All the pioneers of Arabic short stories have come in one way or another under this influence. Muḥammad Taimūr who was born in Egypt and lived between 1892–1921 published a short story in 1917 which is considered the first published short story in modern Arabic literature. He studied medicine in Berlin and law in Paris. The Russian Arabist Kratchofski considers him the founder of the modern Arabic short story and the creator of real scenes of modern social life and who writes in a style similar to that of Maupassant and Tchekov. Haywood (1971: 126) regards Salim Butrus al-Bustani as the pioneer of the Arabic short story. One of his short stories published in 1870 was entitled *Ramya min ġayr rāmī.* The short story in Arabic literature is flourishing and it occupies an important place in the literature. It has been encouraged by journals, magazines, and newspapers as well as collective works of short stories.

It is very difficult to give any statistical information about the number of modern short story writers in the Arabic speaking world, as the number is on the increase all the time. But there are a number of distinguished and established writers of novels and short stories. Amongst them are Maḥmūd Taimūr, the brothers Shiḥātah 'Īsa 'Ubaid, Ṭāhir Lāshīn, Najīb Maḥfouz, Jādhibiyya Ṣidqī, Iḥsān 'Abd al-Qaddūs, Ṣūfi Abdallah, Yousuf Idris in Egypt; Mikha'il Na'ima, Mārūn 'Abbūd, Laila Ba'labakki, Hind Salāmah in the Lebanon; Dr. Abdul Salām al-'Ujailī, Ghādah al-Sammān, Zakariyya Tāmir in Syria; Ghassān Kanafānī, Ibrahim Abū Nāb in Palestine: Shākir al-Sukkarī, Luṭfiyyah al-Dulaimī in Iraq; al-Ṭayyib Abū Ṣāliḥ in the Sudan; Abdul Karīm Ghallāb in Morocco; Ali al-Misrātī in Libya; Abū al-'Īd Dūdu in Algeria, and Samīra Khāshuqjī, Abdalla Abd al-Raḥmān Jifrī in Saudi Arabia, to mention just a few.

The modern Arabic short story reflects the contemporary scene, both on the personal and social levels, as well as political, cultural and other aspects of life.

To exemplify, here is a short story entitled "The Dead Afternoon" by the Syrian Walid Ikhlassi, and translated by Denys Johnson-Davies (1978: 19ff).

The Dead Afternoon

The wall-clock struck five, filling the house with its ringing. I was watching the swallows from my window as they crossed the city sky; thousands of swallows, black moving specks.

The evening, meanwhile, prepared to occupy its place in a new day.

'May they find favour with God,' I said to my grandmother, who had finished her prayers.

'I was late performing the afternoon prayer,' she answered sadly.

'Never mind, there will be other afternoons.'

My grandmother did not hear me.

I looked at an enormous fly squatting on the outside of the window-pane: it seemed to be defying me, sitting there so close to my nose.

'This fly has annoyed me all day,' I said, 'and I haven't been able to kill it.'

My grandmother did not reply: she had started on a new prayer.

I was not conscious of the passage of time: the fly had taken up so much of it. I had threatened it by tapping on the glass, but it had not stirred. Looking at my finger-nails and seeing that they were long, I produced a pair of scissors and began to pare them.

The sky was being engulfed in soft darkness, and the only sound to cut across my grandmother's voice as she recited her prayers, seated in her gazelle-skin chair, was the clock striking six.

My young sister came in from the other room.

'Today we'll be eating *kunāfa* with walnuts,' she announced.

'I don't like it.'

My sister laughed. 'This morning you said you wanted *kunāfa.'*

"I just don't like it.'

Turning again to the window, I was surprised to find that the fly was still asleep.

My grandmother, caressing my young sister, said to her:

'Turn on the radio so we can listen to Feiruz.'

'We listened to her at midday,' I said firmly. The darkness outside prevented me from seeing the swallows. Even so, though, I liked Feiruz's voice.

'We'll listen to her again,' said my grandmother.

I did not reply: I was contemplating the sleeping fly.

A frightening thought occurred to me: what if one of them should watch me as I lay sound asleep?

I heard my sister asking my grandmother to tell us the story of *The Singing Nightingale* this evening and my grandmother saying, 'Didn't we finish it yesterday?'

The little girl cried out petulantly:

'Yesterday! Yesterday's over.'

'You won't hear the story of the singing nightingale any more,' I whispered to myself and I was filled with sadness.

'I'll tell you a new one today,' said my grandmother.

'We don't want a new story,' exclaimed my sister.

'But the old one's finished.'

'It's *not* finished,' shouted my sister.

I tried to excuse my sister, as she jumped off my grandmother's lap and hurried out of the room, but I too felt annoyed; I too wanted the old story.

After a while I complied with my grandmother's request to switch on the radio, and searched round for a station. I found one as the clock struck seven.

'This is Aleppo.'

I drew a veil of silence over the voice.

'Let's hear the news,' protested my grandmother.

Flicking through the pages of the morning paper, I said:

'It's stale news.'

'New things may happen, my son,' exclaimed the old lady, suddenly conscious of her age.

I began reading the headlines: having already done so at midday, they did not affect me.

All at once I wanted to get out of that room, but I had nowhere particular to go, so I changed my mind and stayed where I was.

The little girl returned with her large doll.

'Will you tell Suzanne a story?' she asked, looking at her grandmother with a challenge in her eyes.

The old lady laughed.

I went back to the window: the darkness had settled down completely in the vastness of the sky.

I felt a great desire to tease the sleeping fly coming over me. I no longer felt any resentment against it and had forgotten its impudence.

'Won't you tell Suzanne a new story?' asked my sister.

The fact was that I did not know any story. Then I remembered one I had heard on the radio at noon.

'I'll tell you the story of *The Bear and the Honey,'* I replied.

'But it's an old one,' cried my sister.

Confused, I returned to observing the fly.

'What is it?' asked the little girl, coming towards me as I sat by the window.

'A sleeping fly.'

'A sleeping fly?' my sister asked, knitting her brows. 'Is that a new story?'

'It's asleep, it's tired.'

'Will you tell it to Suzanne?' she said.

'All right, I'll tell it.'

My sister drew close to me.

'What are you looking at?' she demanded.

'I'm looking at the fly.'

She climbed on to a chair and stared at it. Then she proclaimed triumphantly in her shrill voice:

'But it's dead!'

I felt uneasy as I looked at the girl who was suddenly as tall as I was.

'It's asleep.'

'It's dead!' said my sister, amazed at my ignorance.

I opened the window cautiously and blew softly on the fly: it fell off like a wisp of paper.

I remembered it flying around me, remembered that I had hated it and then loved it.

'Won't you tell Suzanne the story of *The Sleeping Fly*?'

I didn't answer her: I was listening to the striking of the clock which reverberated through the house.

Here is another short story entitled "A Stranger", by the Moroccan poet Abd al-Majīd Ben Jallūn, published in Cairo 1947 and translated by Haywood (1971: 269ff).

A Stranger

One intensely dark winter's night, a stranger knocked at the door, having been buffeted the whole night by a violent storm. When the door was opened, the man collapsed on the ground, and they carried him into the house.

The people living in the house looked at each other. This was a strange man, the like of whom they had not seen before in these settlements. But their perplexity did not last long. They hastened to warm the stranger, feed him, and change his muddy, soaking clothes for others, ample and pure-white. A book dropped from the stranger's clothes, without any one noticing.

The humble room was warm and calm, like a haven of rest, a

refuge from the howling wind which could be heard outside, violent and continual . . . as if it were the shouts of heaven, as it looked down from on high on the impending future. The wind was shouting: 'Read that book! Read that book!' But nobody heard.

The stranger went out into the settlements. The sun was up, and the sky was clear. The earth breathed, the herbage could be smelled, and beauty was burgeoning all around. The man said to himself: 'This is the land we Frenchmen have promised ourselves.' His eyes shone, as he looked with delight at the vegetation, herbage and cultivation.

The landowner was a kind man, so he said to him: 'I am out of work.' And he was clever at simulating humility and misery.

Henceforward, then, the stranger would live on this farm, his Arabic improving day by day, taking in all around him, examining, learning, mastering all he saw. In time he was to attract attention by his energy and intelligence. He ingratiated himself with the landowner by his zeal for work. He would advise him, and explain to him various modern agricultural methods. In the end, the landowner became very fond of him, and began to treat him as a friend and relation.

So he took his place among the sons of Uncle 'Abd al-Salām in his household and in his heart. And the latter was an old man, who had spent his life on this farm, feeding the people on it: for they lived under a sort of socialism which was common among Moroccan tribes. He had two sons and a daughter: Muḥammad was twenty, Aḥmad ten, and Fatima fourteen. Uncle 'Abd al-Salām was having a good look at his men, 'feeling their pulses', to choose a strong and reliable man from among them to succeed him when he died.

The stranger, whose name was André, realized this, so he used all his skill and intelligence to gain the ascendancy over the hearts of this man and his children, and the farm workers. He prayed with them in the mosque, and dressed and ate like them. So he was able to obliterate the signs of his former life, and became a different person.

He was like them in everything. But he was cleverer and more perspicacious than they. So he stood out among them, and the people praised his intelligence. In course of time, Uncle 'Abd al-Salām's life began to ebb away little by little. The inevitable day came, and all the farm people wept, following the funeral-procession of the man who had lived for them with heart, mind and body; the man who had brought them a life of sunshine and laughter; under whose kind protection had lived orphans, waifs and strays. They followed his bier, weeping for him as their grandfather, father, brother or friend, as if they felt that they were following the bier of the past.

The people of the farm were filled with anxiety when news reached them from the towns of the war and the occupation. But they were less upset than they might have been at this news because of their belief in their new chief.

André – let us not mention his assumed name, since we know his real one – succeeded Uncle 'Abd al-Salām in the farm and the house, and the people did not notice any change. They thanked God for having sent them this stranger to preserve their living standards.

At the same time, they noticed a minor and absolutely unimportant matter: which was that he used to be absent from the farm from time to time, only for a few days at a time – never more than four. They would ask themselves about the reason for his absence, and where he had gone. And why not, as their former chief had never once left the farm?

At first they just wondered. But then they began to notice a series of things which were new to them. The people's shares began to change. He would favour some, without actually wronging the rest. Then he began to wear strange shoes. Again, his indoor clothes changed, and he sometimes missed going to the mosque.

The cultivators realized what was at the bottom of it, when a group of Frenchmen visited their fields, and they grumbled audibly. That evening, André talked with Muḥammad, Fatima and Aḥmad, and told them that from these men he was learning how to improve the state of the farm.

When this had sunk in with the people, one of them came up to him one morning, when he was outside the house, and said to him: 'The farm people do not want to see the likes of these men on the farm again. These are the ones who have brought destruction to the cities, and they must not be allowed to get at the farms as well.'

The blood rushed to André's head, and he determined to nip ideas like this in the bud, before they got out of hand. Had he not boasted to his masters in Rabat that he could prevent such ideas from gaining ground on his farm? So he shouted at the man:

'Go back and tell the men that this is the wish of their chief, Uncle 'Abd al-Salām's successor and heir.'

'But Uncle 'Abd al–Salām would have had no dealings with such scum!'

At this point, André lost his temper, and his hot French blood rushed to his head. He attacked the man, seized him by the chest, shaking him, saying: 'Don't you ever talk like that again, or I'll break your head in, you filthy fellow! Do you understand?' Then he let him go.

The news spread everywhere, and people reproached him during working hours as one friend to another. For they could not conceive of chiefdom without friendship. The children of Uncle 'Abd al-Salām chided him at home, too, and André began to feel that this chiding was alienating him everywhere. He became tired of the act he had been putting on for over five years. So he resolved to exercise his authority in fact, seeing that he must inevitably lose their esteem.

There was a detachment of fully-armed mounted soldiers approaching the farm, with Andre at their head. When they reached it, the cultivators gathered round them, their eyes nearly popping out of their heads. André dismounted and walked among them, saying: 'Get back to your work! From now onwards, I'll teach you how to do your work, and to obey me as you obeyed Uncle 'Abd al-Salām. What has happened, fellows, is that you have gone to the bad, so you need to be treated differently. Now off you go to your work!'

It was not long before an imposing building stood on the farm – the office of the dictator André – the trickster André, who, with the aid of his superiors, had become the possessor of this wide territory: it belonged to him, with everything and everybody on it.

Each family had a small herd of cattle and sheep, and André determined that these, too, should be his property alone.

The beauty of life was gone from the farm – that life which had been full of kindness, mercy and love. That beautiful fertile land also was no more, that land which used to feed their bodies and souls at one and the same time. And those cattle and sheep, too, were lost, which had been members of the households. Alas! The days revealed the terrible truth that they had become slaves . . .

Now Muḥammad had a beautiful cow he wanted to keep, but

André would not let him; and when he defied him, he had him arrested. He did the same to his brother, when he tried to retain some attractive personal possession. And if this was how the sons of Uncle 'Abd al-Salām were treated, you can imagine what happened to the others!

André had left his poor village in the south of France, poor and destitute. He had left it to secure a worthwhile life for himself. And now he had secured a life of wealth, position and authority. But this was not everything. He had satisfied all his natural urges but one: and when Fatima, daughter of Uncle 'Abd al-Salām, hurried to the 'palace' to beg for her two brothers' release, there was aroused in him that most hungry and covetous of urges.

The innocent girl fell at his feet, entreating him to forgive her brothers, apologizing to him for their rashness. For she had always defended André to them, considering his defence the defence of her father, who had trusted him. She felt him embracing her, 'making a pass at her', exciting her desire, though his speech was confused. Then he lost control, and pressed her to him with mad strength. She pulled herself free, and stood at a distance from him. Then, in a sudden nervous movement, he pulled out a pistol, and shot at the lamp, shattering it and scattering it in the air. He then threw the pistol on the desk, and rushed at her.

'Get this straight! I will just as surely kill you and your brothers, if you go on behaving like this, you bitch!'

Her eyes flashed: 'Send for them to come here, for I have no alternative but to be a bitch while my two brothers are imprisoned.'

He looked at her for a moment, as if trying to read her thoughts. Then he scoffingly shrugged his shoulders, and made for the door, leaving the girl behind him, foaming with wrath and rage.

Her brothers came in, followed by André, who said: 'Take your brothers, and teach them how to obey the law!'

Boiling with anger, Fatima glanced carelessly around the room. Suddenly her flashing eyes fell on the pistol on the desk. As quick as lightning in mind and movement, she leapt at it, and aimed it straight at André's chest, saying:

'Stay where you are, villain! Close the door, Aḥmad; and you, Muḥammad, tie him up! . . . Vengeance for the cultivators and the shepherds! Do you remember how you first came to us, a mere nobody, shabbily clothed, covered in mud, trembling in the storm from weakness and exhaustion? Today, we see you in your true light, a dastardly devil! You hold power over this farm and others around it, near and far. But you can never have power over our hearts. And so long as you are powerless to take away the contempt I feel, you are still as you were when you arrived, weak and exhausted! You are now in my hands – I, the simple farm-girl. And you are trembling with terror and fear, despite your knowledge and your authority – because it is I who hold the weapon today. I have snatched it from you, you coward, to reveal you as a weak man cringing before a weak girl. Because the weak girl has a piece of steel in her hand. Stand back, or I'll mangle you!'

He thought better of the step forward he was going to take, saying between his teeth: 'Steady on, you wretch!'

One of the brothers, seized with fear, shouted: 'Don't kill him! Don't kill him!'

She turned to him, without turning the muzzle of the pistol from its aim at André's chest: 'What? Not kill him? He snatched from us our land and liberty, our cattle and contentment. He seized this land which our forefathers owned for thousands of years. And only a moment ago, he came at me, with the intention of raping me!'

These last words were inaudible, as they were accompanied by a pistol shot. It was followed by a cry from André, the stranger, writhing in his blood.

REFERENCES

Haywood, J.A. 1971. *Modern Arabic Literature 1800–1970.* London.
Johnson-Davies, Denys. 1978. *Modern Arabic Short Stories.* London: Heinemann.

XXXII

ARABIC FOLKTALES

Arabic popular literature has a long traditional standing as it goes back to pre-Islamic times. It was completely oral before the advent of Islam, but later some of the oral material was committed to writing. Arabic folktales have been amongst the most popular oral art which played, and still plays, a significant role in some societies as a means of learning about morals, richer experiences in life, and as a guide to good behaviour and way of life. It is to be noted that Arabic popular literature in general and folktales in particular are still considered beyond the bounds of Arabic literature proper, although folktales evidently formed the basic part of early Arabic literature. To mention just a few of these, there are the fairy stories in Thousand and One Nights, and the Story of Prince Ḥamzah al-Bahlawān among others. We still encounter many oral folktales, some are old and some are of more recent origin. There are many of them across the Arabic speaking countries. They deserve to be collected and studied very closely. Nowadays there is a growing interest in this field of Arabic popular literature in particular and Arab folklore in general.

Folktales can still be heard in various Arab countries, though with degrees of variation due to the nature of oral tradition. As usual with many of the oral traditional popular tales, a folktale normally has no author or even a boundary. It travels with people all over the place. The following folktale, translated by Helen Mitchnik, is entitled the Fisherman and the Prince.

The Fisherman and the Prince

There was once a fisherman, and early one morning he caught a very big fish. So big, in fact, that he took it to his hut, intending to return for it when he had finished him morning's fishing, and take it to market where he felt sure it would fetch a record price.

To his great surprise, however, when he did return for it he found neither fish nor hut. Instead, he found a palatial mansion whose mistress, he was told, was a very beautiful lady.

The fisherman asked to see her, and when he was ushered into her presence, he asked her if she knew what had happened to his hut and the fish he had left therein.

'I was the fish,' said the lady, 'and this was my home before I was transformed by a wicked ogre and thrown into the river; but in fishing me out you have broken the spell and thus restored me to my human form.'

The fisherman expressed his delight at having been the unconscious agent of such a miraculous restoration, and whilst invoking Allah's blessings on the lady and her palatial home, he couldn't help deploring the loss of his own humble abode, for he had now nowhere else to go.

As he talked, the beautiful lady couldn't take her eyes off him, for he was young and virile and easy on the eye. Neither did she once stop to consider his lowly state. She simply fell in love with him, and asked him to marry her. And who was the fisherman to refuse?

So they got married, and were it not for an unforeseen development, I would have now ended my tale with the traditional saying, 'and they lived happily together forever after'. But . . . .

Early one spring morning, the beautiful lady went for a swim, and as she stepped out of the river, straight and slender as a carnation stalk, her shining black tresses rippling over her shoulders like a costly silken mantle, the ruling Prince of the land espied her and fell hopelessly in love with her.

He immediately ordered his courtiers to find out who she was, and when they told him that she was the wife of the local fisherman, he was sick with envy and secretly resolved to eliminate the man by every means in his princely powers.

Accordingly, the fisherman was summoned to the Palace the next morning, and stood before the Prince deeply apprehensive.

The Prince looked him haughtily up and down, then said: 'It is my wish that you come and see me tomorrow laughing and crying at the same time. Else, I'll have you thrown in jail.'

The fisherman panicked. For how can one laugh and cry at the same time?

'Not to worry!' said his wife. 'Put an onion in your pocket, and before you step into the Prince's presence, bash the onion with your fist and inhale it good and proper. *That* should take care of your crying. At the same time, throw back your head and laugh long and loud and you will have fulfilled the Prince's wish.'

The fisherman did exactly as his wife told him, and as he stepped into the great hall where the Prince and his courtiers were assembled, he emitted great guffaws of laughter whilst his eyes and nose smarted and streamed like two waterworks combined.

The courtiers loudly applauded the fisherman's performance, and complimented him on the admirable manner in which he had carried out the Prince's orders. So the Prince could find no excuse for jailing the fisherman. But his determination to eliminate him was as firm as ever.

So, before many days had passed, he again sent for the fisherman, and said to him: 'it is my wish that you come and see me tomorrow dressed and naked at the same time. Else, I'll have you impaled on the Palace walls.'

The fisherman trembled with fear. For how can one be dressed and naked at the same time?

'Not to worry!' again said his wife. 'Wear your fishing net right over your naked body, and the Prince will find no cause for complaint.'

The fisherman did exactly that. And, sure enough, when he stood before the Prince and his courtiers with nothing on save his fishing net, not one of them could deny that he was, in fact, dressed and naked at the same time.

So once again the Prince was foiled in his evil designs; but he wasn't going to give up so easily. He let a few days pass, then once again he sent for the fisherman and said to him: 'It is my wish that you come and see me tomorrow with a newborn babe that can tell me a story. Else, I'll cut off your head.' And this time, he thought gloatingly to himself, I have you where I want you, my man!

The fisherman left the Palace in a state of black despair. For whoever heard of a newborn babe that can talk, much less tell a story?

But here again his beautiful wife came to the rescue. 'Go to the river,' she said to him, 'and strike the water with your fishing-rod at the same spot where you fished me out. My half-sister will then appear to you. Ask her to let you have the babe which was born to her yesterday, and take him to the Palace. He will tell the Prince a story.'

The fisherman was too depressed to argue. He did exactly as he was told. And when his wife's half-sister appeared to him, he asked her to let him have the babe which was born to her the day before. She gave it him. He then took it to the Palace and stood before the Prince, cradling it in his arms.

The Prince looked at him mockingly, and said: 'Is *that* there going to tell me a story?'

'Yes, it is!' answered the babe, suddenly wriggling out of the fisherman's arms, and walking up to the Prince. 'Now step off that throne, and let me sit on it.'

The Prince was startled out of his wits, for he had never in his life heard a newborn babe talk. Meekly he stepped off his throne, and stood, as one mesmerized, before the babe who sat fair and square upon it, and began to tell this story.

'Once upon a time, there was a very rich man and he possessed acres and acres of land which yielded him, every year, a magnificent crop of wheat and barley and rice and maize. Then, one year, this rich man decided to sow all his land with sesame seeds only. The crop he reaped was a bumper one; giving him hundreds and hundreds of sacks of sesame, each sack of which was meticulously checked and weighed and then stored away. In the final count, however, it was discovered that one sack lacked one sesame seed. But instead of letting this go, the rich man insisted on having this particular sesame seed, and set all his farmhands looking for it. They did their best, but were unable to procure it for him. Nonetheless, he kept plaguing them about it, and...'

'Rubbish!' here interrupted the Prince who had now got over his fright. 'Why should such a rich man insist on having that particular sesame seed when he had hundreds and hundreds of sacks of sesame at his disposal?'

'For the same reason that a Prince who has an entire Principality of beautiful ladies at his disposal, insists on having a particular one, therefore employing every unprincely means in his power to usurp her from her lawful husband,' retorted the babe.

The rebuke struck home. And this time the Prince, who was not a bad man at heart, dismissed the fisherman with full pardon, and never again attempted to separate him from his wife.

And so, as you well see, it is only now that I can conclude this tale by saying, 'and they lived happily together for ever after'.

REFERENCES

Al-Jawharī, Muḥammad. 1975. *The Sources of the Study of Arabic Folklore* (in Arabic). Cairo.

Al-Marzūqī, Muḥammad. 1967. *Folk Literature in Tunisia* (in Arabic). Tunis: The National Press.

Mitchnik, Helen. 1978. *Egyptian and Sudanese Folktales*. London.

XXXIII

THE ARABIAN NIGHTS

Alf Layla wa Layla or the Thousand and One Nights, better known in the West as the Arabian Nights, is an Arabic literary work which contains fabulous tales and anecdotes. It is a part of Arabic folk literature. To many ordinary Arabs this work is merely a collection of folktales which are easy to read for enjoyment. In their eyes, the work is regarded as a piece of the forgotten past. To the Western audience, it is regarded – at least by some, as one of the masterpieces of literature and an epoch-making work reaching the peak of romance, glamour and fantasy of the Orient. Some of the stories in the Arabian Nights, like those of the *Ebony Horse, Ali Baba and the Forty Thieves, Aladdin and the Magic Lamp, Sinbad the Sailor* and *The Trader and the Genie,* have almost become an integral part of English Folk literature. This is probably largely due to the English Pantomimes, which have also contributed to the international reputation of the Arabian Nights.

The Arabic version of this work dates back to Medieval times. Although the exact date is uncertain, it might well have originated about the eighth century A.D.[1] The names of the Caliph Hārūn al-Rashīd, his companions and court attendants figure prominently in this work (cf. chapters XX and XXV). It is apparent that the stories and tales of the Arabian Nights are of diverse and mixed origins: Persian, Indian, Greek and African besides their Arabian and Semitic character. For centuries, the stories were the source of many Arabic oral folktales as well as Arabic folk literature and Arts.

The basic form or technique of the Arabian Nights is that of the primary story which in its turn contains shorter stories, well incorporated and interwoven into the total work. Its style is direct, its language and dialogue is natural and simple, and it is free from padding. It is also full of the elements of surprise and mystery which are intended to capture the readers and listeners' attention and interest. The entire Arabic work reveals and mirrors certain aspects and sections of the Arab societies in the Middle Ages, though some of the scenes must not be taken seriously as absolute facts, or *fait accompli.* In many instances it portrays the richness of the cultural environment of that age. The significance of the Arabian Nights can only be fully interpreted, expounded, and appreciated if it is viewed in its own cultural environment and social context.

It is fair to say that it is due to the Western influence that the Arabian Nights gained the international reputation it holds now. The first known European translation, by the French scholar Antoine Galland, appeared in Paris/Hague between 1704–1717 entitled: *Les Mille et Une Nuits.* Later on, other translations into many languages of the Occident and the Orient followed. The best known English translations are those by Payne, Lane and Burton.[2]

The following is one of the most outstanding stories of the Arabian Nights, entitled "Aladdin & the Magic Lamp", excellently translated and edited by Sheila Schwartz (1979: 80ff):[3]

Aladdin and the Magic Lamp

There lived in a city of the East a poor tailor who had a son, Aladdin by name. Alas, the boy was a lazy idler and try as he might the tailor could not teach him a trade. When Aladdin was ten years old, his father died and his mother took up spinning to feed them, for Aladdin became lazier than ever. For five years Aladdin's mother toiled on, her heart sick over his idleness.

Then one day an African magician came to town and upon seeing Aladdin said to himself, "This is the lad I need and for whom I left my native land."

Approaching Aladdin, the magician announced, "I am your uncle, the brother of your father. My brother and I parted when we were still young and now I have travelled across the world to be reunited with him."

When Aladdin told him that his father was dead, the magician embraced Aladdin and cried out, "O my boy, you are then my only kin, my comfort and joy! I shall live with you and regard you as a son. Tell me, what trade do you practice to support yourself and your mother?" Now Aladdin was puzzled at the magician's claim, since he had never heard his father speak of a brother, and he was wary as well of yet another man who wanted him to work for a living. Still, the magician was dressed in fine garments, obviously a man of means, and Aladdin decided he would do well to please him. So when the magician offered to open a merchant's shop for him, filled with the costliest goods, Aladdin eagerly agreed and took the magician home to his mother.

The next day, the magician said to Aladdin, "Before you become a merchant, you must journey with me to another city and see how the merchants in that place conduct their affairs." So they set off and walked for a whole day. When evening came, the magician asked Aladdin to kindle a fire. This done, the magician sprinkled some incense on the fire and muttered strange words the boy could not understand. All of a sudden the earth trembled, and a deep cleft opened in the ground beneath them. The frightened Aladdin tried to run away, but the magician stopped him, saying, "Know that there is a great treasure stored below that is waiting for you alone. Fear not. Do what I tell you and the riches shall be yours!"

Thus it was that Aladdin forgot his fear and listened to the magician's instructions. "Descend into the pit. At the bottom you will find four halls. Go into the fourth hall only. It is the entrance to the Enchanted Treasury. There you will find a door. Pronounce the names of your father and mother and the door will open into a garden filled with fruit trees. At the end of the garden is a domed terrace, within which is a ladder. You will see a lamp hanging from the ceiling. Climb the ladder and retrieve the lamp, placing it in your pocket. On the way back, you may pick whatever you wish from the trees, for so long as the lamp is in your possession everything in the garden is yours." Then the magician placed a signet ring on Aladdin's finger and said, "If you obey my instructions this ring will protect you from evil."

Aladdin did as he was told. Arriving at last on the terrace, he took down the lamp and put it in his pocket. Passing again through the garden, he looked closely at the trees and suddenly noticed that they were hung not with fruits but with precious gems—diamonds, rubies, and sapphires, the size of which he had never seen. Gleefully, he filled all of his pockets with the jewels, even the one that held the lamp.

Aladdin then hastened back to the bottom of the pit, where he asked the magician to help him ascend. "Give me the lamp first," said the man, "it will lighten the load." But Aladdin could not get at the lamp, for it had fallen low in his pocket, buried under the precious gems. "Just help me out and I will give you the lamp," Aladdin answered innocently. But the magician, who was of course no uncle to Aladdin, thought that the boy was trying to deceive him and lost all hope of ever getting the lamp. He raged because the lamp was the most marvellous thing in the Enchanted Treasury. Whoever possessed it would have unsurpassed riches and power.

In a fury at now being deprived of the lamp, he conjured and swore and cast more incense into the fire. Whereupon the earth closed over Aladdin and the magician returned to Africa.

Aladdin shouted out in the dark but no one answered. When he realized that he could not escape, he sat down and wept bitterly, wringing his hands in grief. In this way, his fingers chanced to rub the signet ring and behold! a genie appeared before him. "I am the Genie of the Ring," he told Aladdin. "Whoever rubs it is my lord and master. Ask what you will of me." The astonished Aladdin said, "I beg you, kind spirit, place me upon the face of the earth!" Hardly had he spoken when he found himself outside again.

He went in joy to his mother and told her all that had happened. But when she saw the jewels, she said, "My son, we must bury these gems, for we are paupers and if anyone found them in our hands, they would think us thieves. It is better for us to be hungry than to languish in prison." The treasure buried, they wanted to have dinner, but could find nothing in the pantry to eat. So they decided to sell the lamp in the marketplace. Aladdin began to polish it, thinking it would fetch a better price if it were clean and shining. He had no sooner rubbed the lamp than a gigantic genie came forth from it. "I am the Genie of the Lamp," he boomed, "and whoever rubs it is my lord and master." So Aladdin commanded the genie to provide a sumptuous dinner. The genie disappeared and returned in a twinkle with platters of sweet meats and delicacies.

After this, whenever Aladdin and his mother were hungry, Aladdin rubbed the magic lamp and bade the genie provide them with nourishment. But they ate in secret, telling no one of their good fortune lest they be accused of sorcery. And the jewels remained buried in the garden.

But with wealth so near at hand, Aladdin repented of the idle ways of his youth and began to frequent the merchants' quarter, conversing with the shopkeepers and tradesman and becoming skilled in all manner of business.

One day, while Aladdin was visiting a jeweller's shop, the sultan's daughter rode by and Aladdin was struck by her beauty. From the moment he saw the princess his heart was filled with love. Aladdin went to his mother and said, "I cannot live without the princess and must have her for my wife. Go to the sultan on my behalf and ask for her hand."

"It is true, dear mother," Aladdin said, "that we come from pauper folk. But thanks to the Genie of the Lamp immense riches are ours for the asking. And do not forget the treasure buried in the garden. Now that we know the genie can protect us, we need not fear to use the jewels. You shall dress in fine clothes and go before the sultan with a magnificent gift as a sign of our wealth."

So Aladdin unearthed the jewels and set them within a porcelain bowl. The next day, his mother presented herself to the sultan, saying, "Honoured master, my son desires to have the hand of your daughter in marriage and he has sent me with this gift as a token of his esteem for you and the beautiful lady." Now the sultan had already promised his daughter to the son of his vizier, but upon seeing the bowl of jewels, he began to regret his decision.

"Never has I seen such marvels," he exclaimed. "Surely the man who gives them away is more worthy than any other to be my son-in-law!" When the vizier heard the sultan's words, he grew anxious. Said he to the sultan, "It is only right and proper that you declare a three-month delay in the ceremony. Since you once gave your daughter to my son, you should allow him time in which to obtain a gift even costlier than the one now before you." The sultan agreed, but the vizier's son could not match Aladdin's gift, and Aladdin and the beautiful princess were married.

After the wedding, Aladdin went to pay his respects to the sultan, "My tongue is helpless to thank you for the great favour you have bestowed upon me," he told his new father-in-law. "Pray grant me one more kindness. Give me a parcel of land on which I shall build a magnificent palace to honour my wife, your daughter." The sultan was touched by these words and the more he spoke with Aladdin, the more his affection for him grew. The sultan then walked to the window and pointed to an empty tract of land across the way. "There you may build your palace for my daughter," the sultan said, "for I love her dearly and want to keep her in my sight."

Aladdin returned home, where he took out the magic lamp and summoned the genie. "It is my wish that you build me a palace across the way from the sultan as speedily as you can. And it must be a marvel for all to behold, with royal furnishings and rich decorations." Said the genie, "Your wish is my command," and he vanished. When the sultan arose the next morning and looked out his window, he rubbed his eyes in disbelief. Before him was an extraordinary palace where only yesterday there had been nothing but weeds. And not even the mightiest monarch on earth could have built such a palace! The walls gleamed with alabaster, marble, and mosaic. The furniture was made of gold and silver, and the decorative work fashioned with precious gems. And all in one night!

Then the sultan turned to his vizier and said, "Do you see now that Aladdin is worthy to be the husband of my daughter?" But the vizier, highly envious of Aladdin's good fortune, replied, "I fear that such opulence and such speedy construction could not be save by means of magic." However, the sultan attributed the vizier's warning to envy and would not believe that all the splendour he saw before him was the work of magic rather than man.

Aladdin and his bride moved into the palace and lived in contentment. And when the sultan saw how happy his daughter was, he rejoiced at his choice of a son-in-law. Every day Aladdin would walk through the streets of the city, scattering gold pieces (supplied by the Genie of the Lamp) wherever he went. In this way, Aladdin endeared himself to the people of the city and won great renown throughout the realm.

Meanwhile, the African magician—he who had pretended to be Aladdin's uncle in order to steal the lamp—never ceased to bemoan the cruel trick of fate that had robbed him of the lamp when it was almost within his grasp. He cursed Aladdin and was glad to think of the boy rotting away in the Enchanted Treasury. One day, after several years had gone by, the magician chanced to look into his crystal ball to make sure the lamp still hung safely from the ceiling of the domed terrace. He searched deeply into the ball, but to his great surprise could not find the lamp in the Enchanted Treasury. Nor could he see Aladdin anywhere in the underground cavern. The magician raged when he realized that Aladdin had escaped and had become the owner of the lamp. And then he saw in the crystal ball a vision of Aladdin, rich beyond measure and married to the sultan's daughter. "I will destroy him!" the magician swore.

So once more the African magician journeyed across the world to the land of the East. When he arrived in the sultan's capital, he quickly found the grand palace Aladdin had built and understood at once that it was the work of the Genie of the Lamp. At this, the magician's anger and hatred increased tenfold. "With the help of the fates, I will do away with this cursed fellow and send his mother back to spinning at her wheel. And I see now that getting the lamp back will be an easy task." Then the magician went to a coppersmith and ordered a few dozen copper lamps. Presently, he began wandering about the streets, crying, "Who will exchange old lamps for new lamps?" The people thought him mad, but flocked around him anyway, thrusting their old lamps into his hands and receiving new ones in return.

The magician's strange behaviour caused such a commotion that it came to the ears of the princess, Aladdin's wife. Now the lady knew nothing of the magic lamp, only that her husband kept an old lamp in a chest in their chambers. One day, when Aladdin was out hunting with the sultan, she decided to surprise him with the gift of a new lamp. The lady therefore sent her servant girl to fetch the old one and bring it to the madman. This the girl did. But when the magician saw he had the magic lamp in his hands, he dropped the others and ran gleefully away. He ran until he was out of the city and there he stopped and rubbed the lamp. "Your wish is my command," said the genie. "It is my desire," the magician responded, "that Aladdin's palace and all those who dwell within be lifted into the air and spirited back to Africa with me, there to be set down in my own gardens." In a flash it was done.

When Aladdin and the sultan returned from the hunt, accompanied by the vizier, they were startled to see the palace gone and the site as smooth as highway. "Such a thing could not be!" cried the sultan. At which the vizier said wryly, "My lord, I warned you that Aladdin's palace and treasures were the work of magic. Now you may perceive the truth of my words!" And indeed the sultan did. He turned angrily upon Aladdin and called for the soldiers to take him to the dungeon and cut off his head. But Aladdin, who saw the African magician's hand in this, pleaded for a stay of execution. "O great sultan, I beg you give me forty days to find your daughter, my wife. If I do not rescue her in that time, I will return and you may proceed with the execution." The sultan agreed, willing to try anything to get his daughter back.

Thus it happened that Aladdin left the city and walked aimlessly about, not knowing where to turn. He stopped at a stream to refresh himself, and while washing his hands in its cool waters, happened to rub his finger upon that very signet ring which the magician had long ago given him. Out came the Genie of the Ring, and Aladdin rejoiced. "O genie," he cried, "I order you to return my palace and all within it to its place in our city!" But the genie said, "Alas, you ask for something beyond my power. Only the Genie of the Lamp can perform such a feat. I can, however, take you to the place where the palace now stands and set you down beside your wife." Aladdin said, "So be it," and soon found himself in Africa, sitting next to the princess.

When the princess related her tale, Aladdin understood how the magician had got the lamp. "Where does he keep this lamp?" Aladdin asked his wife. "He carries it with him always," answered the princess, "under his robe." So Aladdin plotted to retrieve the lamp. He purchased a vial of poison in the marketplace and gave it to his wife. "Tonight," he instructed her, "when you are dining with the magician, feign good will and drink a toast to his health. He will then drink one to yours. Do the same again and again until he is so drowsy that you can slip up unnoticed and pour this vial into his wine. Then drink one more toast together. It will be his last."

And it was. No sooner had the magician swallowed the poisoned wine than he fell over dead and Aladdin rushed in and took the lamp. He quickly rubbed it and ordered the genie to carry them to the land of the East.

Upon awakening in the morning and discovering the palace and his daughter returned, the sultan was overjoyed and forgave Aladdin. Aladdin, in his turn, felt secure in the knowledge that the evil magician was dead and thought no more of danger. But it happened that the magician had a brother, even more villanous than he and equally skilled in the magic arts, who resolved to kill Aladdin in revenge for his brother's death. He travelled to the land of the East and wandered about Aladdin's city, searching for a means to exact vengeance. Presently, he entered a coffeehouse, where he heard the patrons talking about a saintly lady named Fatima, a devout woman, ancient of years, who performed miraculous cures on the sick. "When I have found this woman." the magician thought, "I will be able to destroy Aladdin."

The next night, the magician waylaid the holy lady as she was walking home, slew her and donned her garments. Then he stained his face so that the colour matched Fatima's own. In this disguise, he walked through the city curing all who came to him—not by faith, as Fatima had done, but by black magic.

So it was that the magician in the guise of Fatima came to the attention of the princess, who invited the saintly woman to abide with her in the palace. The princess asked Fatima what she thought of her new home. "O lady," the magician replied in a creaky voice, "it is truly wondrous. But if you had the egg of a roc to place in the middle of the dome, it would enhance the beauty of the place!" Now the princess did not know where to obtain such a thing, so she went to Aladdin and asked him to summon the Genie of the Lamp. After his wife had gone to bed, Aladdin rubbed the lamp. But to his astonishment the genie refused to do his bidding. "It is not your own wish," he explained to Aladdin. "Nor is it really your wife's. It is the wish of the evil magician who at this very moment is living under your own roof, pretending to be the devout Fatima." Then the genie vanished.

Hearning these words, Aladdin trembled in fear. But he soon regained his courage and resolved to deal with this magician as he had with the other. So Aladdin went to his wife and affected a severe headache. "Worry not," she said, "I will call upon Fatima, who can heal all pain." When the magician received the princess's summons, he could hardly believe his good luck and hastened to Aladdin. He placed his hand upon Aladdin's head, but slipped the other hand under his gown and slowly drew out a dagger. Aladdin watched him patiently until the weapon was fully unsheathed. Then he seized the magician with a forceful grip, wrenched the dagger from his grasp, and plunged it deep into the villain's heart. Whereupon he tore off the magician's disguise and revealed to his wife the true face of evil.

With both magicians dead and their ashes scattered to the winds, Aladdin and his wife lived happily on. For the rest of his days, Aladdin the pauper's son knew only wealth and prosperity.

NOTES

1) Nicholson (1977: 456 ff).
2) J. Payne translated the complete work of the Arabian nights in 13 vols., published in London 1839–41. E.W. Lane's abridged translation in 3 vols. appeared in London 1839–41. Richard Burton's voluminous work was published by Burton Club, London 1880 & c.
3) Thanks are due to Octopus Books Ltd, London for the citation from their publication.

REFERENCES

Gibb, H.A.R. 1974. *Arabic Literature: An Introduction.* Oxford (See pp. 148–9).

Nicholson, R.A. 1977. *A Literary History of the Arabs.* Cambridge. (see pp. 456–59).

Said, Edward W. 1978. *Orientalism.* London & Henley, England: Routledge & Kegan Paul Ltd. See pp. 63–4, 196.

Schwartz, Sheila. 1979. *The Arabian Nights: Stories of the Fabulous and Fantastic World of Kings and Princes, Monsters and Genies.* Edited by S. Schwartz. London: Octupus Books Ltd.

XXXIV

ARABIC PROVERBS, THEIR CULTURAL IMPLICATIONS

A proverb is called *mathal* in Arabic. It is commonly defined as "a brief epigramic saying presenting a well known truth that is popular and familiar to all. It is often used colloquially and set forth in the guise of a metaphor and in the form of a rhyme, and is sometimes alliterative." A proverb must bear the sign of antiquity and in most cases they have no authors and their origins are not normally known. Proverbs are not necessarily borrowed from another culture but different cultures may well have proverbs which are similar or identical without being borrowed. For instance the old Meccan Arabic proverb *yi'mal min al-ḥabba gubba* literally means "he makes a dome out of a grain" is said to describe exaggeration, and has an English equivalent which says: "he makes a mountain out of a molehill", to express the same idea. Proverbs nearly always say something more than that which is expressed in ordinary language.

Arabic dialects share some of the general proverbs or proverbial phrases, but each dialect may possess some localized proverbs which are not used or understood by users of another dialect or dialects. Arabic proverbs fall into two categories: those which belong to the colloquial lore and those which are borrowed from the standard language, and usually used by the educated speakers of a dialect.

On the whole proverbs constitute a rich mine or source for Arabic literature. Linguistically speaking, they are interesting as they retain certain features of the early stages of the language. One can expect lexical differences as well as syntactic and semantic changes which might affect the proverbs in the course of transmission from one generation to the next, or from one culture to another.

Proverbs constituted an important segment in the literary output of the Arabs. The Arab and Muslim philologists, linguists, literary historians and proverb collectors and compilers are numerous in Arabic literature. This interest goes back to a period as early as the eighth century A.D. Amongst the reputed philologists who wrote about Arabic proberbs are Abū 'Ubaidah, al-Maidānī, Ibn Qutaiba, ibn al-Anbārī, al-Zamakhsharī, and al-Bakrī.

Al-Maidānī wrote his book *Majma' al-Amthāl* in which he collected more than 5000 proverbs or proverbial phrases. He differentiated between the ancient Arab proverbs and the proverbs of non-Arab origin, in some cases a story or an anecdote was related and used as the context in which a proverb had evolved. The traditional studies of Arabic proverbs are still of interest in modern times. It is interesting to note that some of the ancient proverbs are still in current, modern, use. Early Arabic proverbs reflect the ancient life of the Arabs, their way of life, habitat, social relations, moral values, manners and customs. In addition, it reflects their sharp ideas and wit, their powerful expressions and eloquence, and their mastery of the Arabic language.

Arabic proverbs are interesting in terms of their stylistic characteristics, that is, the relations which hold between the elements represented in a proverb. In terms of the phrase structure, a proverb may consist of two or more equal or almost equal number of elements, such as syllables, stresses, and words. Note the following proverb:

sakata dahran wa naṭaqa kufran

meaning "he was silent for a long time, when he spoke blasphemy."

Here both *sakata* and *naṭaqa* are verbs in the past tense and each consists of three short syllables of CV type. The two nouns *dahran* and *kufran,* each contains two syllables. The place of the main stresses are also the same. The rhythm is also equally maintained by the harmonious arrangement of the syllables.

Arabic proverbs make good use of alliteration. In some instances, the initial consonants of all or some of the words in the proverb are identical. For instance:

al-ḥurr min ġamzah, wal-ḥumār min rafzah

meaning "A good person learns from a wink, a bad one learns from a kick." Here *ḥurr* and *ḥumār* both begin with the consonant *ḥā'* followed by the vowel *u*.

Note another example of alliteration:

tiji tṣīdu yiṣīdak

meaning "you try to ensnare him but he ensnares you". Here alliteration is based on the repetition of the bound prefix *ti* in the first two imperfect verbs.

Arabic proverbs make extensive use of rhyme. That is the appearance of identical or phonetically similar consonants or vowels at the end of the words in the proverb. For instance:

min ḥabbak dabbak

meaning "He who loves you, beats you". Here the words *ḥabbak* and *dabbak* have five identical elements, two vowels and three consonants. Another example:

Kamā yadīn ul-fatā yudān

meaning "with the same judgment the person judges, he will be judged."

Proverbs also manipulate other formal devices such as those involving repetition of certain words, affixes or grammatical categories in the same proverb. For instance,

lā nāqata lī fīhā walā jamal

meaning "I have no interest in this matter". Literally," I have neither a she-camel nor a he-camel in this matter." Here the negative particle *lā* is repeated twice. Note also the use of the opposite meanings such as she- or he-camel. There are also other stylistic devices such as deletion of certain elements, pattern symmetry, inversion of word order and metaphor among others.

Like other proverbs, the Arabic proverbs have their cultural implications in the sense that they can reveal the hidden character of the society and show its genuine characteristics, and attitudes. Because of their brevity, proverbs have been used quite often either as evidence to support one's viewpoint or give advice to people. It is interesting to note that in modern urban Arab societies the use of proverbs is limited or minimized whereas in rural societies the opposite seems to be the case. Another point of interest here is the fact that older Arab generations use proverbs more often than the younger generations.

Each proverb has a life of its own. It is born, and it can live and die, and it can be reborn or revived when a society decides to do so.

Because of their long history and richness, Arabic proverbs can express all kinds of situations and attitudes. Here are some situations and examples.

Consolation

min šāf muṣībat ġēru tihūn 'alē muṣībatu

meaning "he who observes the calamity of other people finds his own calamity is lighter."

Warning

It is said about the sea:

ad-dāxil mafgūd wal-xārij mawlūd

meaning "avoid the sea, as he who enters into it is lost and he who comes out of it is like a newborn."

Advice

To encourage silence one can say:

ʔiḏā kāna al-kalām min fiḍḍah fas-sukūtu min ḏahab

meaning "if speech is silver, silence is golden."

Weather News

One can tell about the degree of coldness of winter, as in:

"al-'Agrab taḥt as-sama lā-tigrab"

meaning, now it's the sign of Scorpio, one must sleep indoors and not on the roof.

Excuses

One can excuse absentees by saying:

al–ġāyib 'uḏru ma'āh

meaning "the absentee has a good excuse."

Threatening

One can threaten those who do not listen to their elder's advice saying:

Illi mā yisma' kalām al-kabīr yiṭīḥ fil bīr

meaning "he who does not listen to the older people, he will fall in the well."

Arabic proverbs also express attitudes of people towards one another and towards life. For instance, the real attitude of relatives to marriage. Thus the proverb:

al-agārib 'agārib

meaning "relatives are scorpions," warns from marrying relatives.

Attitudes also refer to human qualities by praising the good ones and condemning the bad ones. Thus calmness, patience, modesty, and good manners are encouraged whereas greediness, lying and selfishness are discouraged. The proverb:

al-ṣabur muftāḥ al-faraj

meaning "Patience is the key to success," praises patience and stresses that it is rewarded.

The Meccan proverb:

al-kidib ḥarām wal gabur ḍalām

meaning "lying is a taboo, and the tomb is pitch dark", suggests the strong feeling against lying and reminds the liar of the after death punishment.

To sum up, Arabic proverbs constitute an important part of Arabic literature, and particularly popular literature.

They are still used as an effective weapon for convincing people, advising them, warning them, and winning them too. People, whether individuals or groups, vary in the frequency of using proverbs, as well as in the choice of the right proverb in the right context, and above all the number of proverbs used at a given time. Arabic proverbs may be considered as one of the best sources for the study of Arabian society and culture.

REFERENCES

Bakalla, M.H. 1981. *Arabic Linguistics: An Introduction and Bibliography*. London. (useful for further references on the subject).

Burckhardt, J.L. 1980 *Arabic Proverbs*. Reprint. London: Curzon Press.

Al-Dhubaib, Ahmad M. 1966. *A Critical and Comparative Study of the Ancient Arabic Proverbs Contained in al-Maidānī's Collection*. Ph.D. diss., University of Leeds.

Mahgoub, Fatma M. 1968. *A Linguistic Study of Cairene Proverbs*. Bloomington: Indiana University, Research Center for the Language Science. The Hague: Mouton.

XXXV

STYLISTIC INNOVATIONS IN ARABIC

In this chapter I shall treat the modes of expression in Modern Standard Arabic and attempt to relate some of the innovations to their possible sources of origin. Many of these expressions have been so assimilated into Arabic usage that it is at times difficult to pinpoint whether they are of pure Arabic or foreign extraction. It is to be noted that borrowing words from other languages is more frequent in language than borrowing phrases, idiomatic phrases, and various stylistic expressions. Because of its long and constant contact with other cultures, the Arabic language has been influenced by loan words (for this, see Chapter IX) and expressions. In the past they were loans from the ancient world; at the present time they are mainly from the modern world, particularly the Western World.

Looking back into the history of Arabic stylistic development, which is still a greatly neglected area of scholarship, we find a number of points where innovations can be clearly observed. One can cite Abū Nuwās in Arabic poetry and Ibn al-Muqaffa' in Arabic prose. Both were Arabs by adoption as they partially belonged to Persian stock. Abū Nuwās, who lived in Baghdad in the 8th century A.D. was reputed in Arabic poetry for his genius, versatility, elegance and command of the Arabic language. He exemplified a new development which had a strong effect on various forms of Arabic poetry. Stylistically, he introduced a number of new ideas, forms and poetic styles into Arabic literature, some of which can be traced to Persian origin. The Anthology of Abū Nuwās which is still extant, provides us with an interesting account of life in eighth century Baghdad, the time and epoch when the Tales of Thousand and One Nights were, in some respects, a reality (see Chapter XX).

Ibn al-Muqaffa' also lived during the Abbasid period and died in the year 757 A.D. He translated a number of books from Persian into Arabic, including the "Book of Kings" and the Fables of the Indian

Philosopher Bidpai, known in Arabic literature as *Kalīla wa Dimna.* He also founded the secretarial school of letters and translated into Arabic the Secretarial tradition of Sasanid court-literature, reputed not only for its scientific and philosophical contribution, but also for its artistic temperament and literary styles which were fairly new in Arabic. Ibn al-al-Muqaffa' 's contributions to Arabic prose cannot be underestimated. His works were considered ideal models for imitation, as they met the needs and standards of Arabic prose: clarity, purity and moderation. Both Abū Nuwās and Ibn al-Muqaffa' had introduced or made use of Persian words, idiomatic phrases and some literary styles, which later on were totally assimilated and became integral parts and elements of the Arabic language and literature.

The Renaissance of the Arabic language and literature which started in the early 19th century, gives a clear example of the modern influences on both Arabic poetry and prose. Stylistic innovations and mode of expressions abound in modern Arabic and the process of borrowing still continues. The influence can be observed not only in literary works and journalism but also in scientific works which are translations from languages such as English, French and Russian. Since many of the translations are made in a hurry, probably under pressure from the publisher, and since some translators do not have a good command of the Arabic language proper, one would expect literal translations and at times even loan terms and expressions which are partially Arabized. Thus, besides words such as *kumbyūtar* for "computer", *talfōn* for "telephone", we find compound nouns such as *kīlūmitr* for "kilometer" and *kīlū jirām* or *kīlūġrām* for "kilogram" as well as full phrases mainly translated into Arabic.

A number of studies have been made about modern stylistic peculiarities and innovations in Arabic. Amongst the early treatments are Ibrāhīm al-Yāzijī's *Lughat al-Jarā'id* "The Language of the Newspaper" (Published in 1901), Jurjī Zaidān's *al-Lughat al-'Arabiyyah Kā'in Ḥayy* "Arabic as a Living Being" (1904), and Abd al-Qādir al-Maghribī's *Kitāb al-Ishtiqāq wal-Ta'rīb* "On Coining New Words and Arabization" (published in 1908 and later in 1947).

Ibrāhīm al-Yāzijī who lived between 1856–89 wrote his monograph on "The language of the Newspaper" in which he listed hundreds of words with diverse semantic and stylistic irregularities employed by journals and newspapers. He was more concerned about the errors of Arabs and non-Arabs in the language used in the Press, than with the faithful recording and description of the language of his time. He once described Arabic language as "a mirror of the conditions of a community and the image of its civilization."

Jurjī Zaidān (who died in 1914) wrote his book on Arabic as a living "language". It includes a chapter on the foreign modes of expression, in which he discusses some of the non-Arabic stylistic peculiarities and innovations. To exemplify: First, he points out the excessive use of the relative pronoun as being a modern tendency in the Arabic language. Thus the modern Arabic expression *ra'aytu ṣadīqī alladī a'ṭānī al-kitāba* uses the relative pronoun *alladī* instead of the particle *fa*. The more correct sentence would be *ra'aytu ṣadīqī fa a'ṭānī al-kitāba*, "I saw my friend who gave me the book."

Secondly he observes the frequent use of *yūjad* for "there is", and considers it a new development in Modern Standard Arabic. For instance, *yūjad fī bilādi al-Hijaz 'iddatu jibālin*, "There are many mountains in the region of Hijaz."

Al-Maghribī who lived between 1867–1956 is considered one of the modern Arab linguistic leaders and an important reformer of the Arabic language. Right from the turn of the century, he showed a special interest in the problem of coining new terminology through derivation and Arabization, with a proviso that they conform to certain rules which are consistent with the spirit of the Arabic language. By doing so, al-Maghribī follows in the steps of the early Arabs who made extensive use of loan words and expressions. To him, an Arabized word or expression is as good as any other word or expression of Arabic origin (cf. Chapter IX). He states (Chejne 1969: 152f):

> "Arabization is not an innovation in the Arabic language: nor does the existence of Arabized words and expressions constitute a foreign element in the language like a strange particle in the human body in the sense that it hurts and, therefore, ought to be removed. Arabization is a natural development or a gradual change that occurs in the language and follows its general characteristics. Throughout the development of the language, Arabization remained consistent with the language and in the same manner can do so now and in the future."

Al-Maghribī classifies the modern Arabic modes of expression into three types.

Type 1 includes Arabic expressions which display close similarities to, or parallelisms with, expressions in other languages without being influenced by them. For example:

fulān axaḏa naṣīb al-asad (to take the lion's share)

ramā āxir sahmin fi kinānatih (to fire one's last cartridge).

Type 2 contains Arabic expressions which are authentically Arabic but at one point of history they became abandoned only to be reactivated or reborn under the influence of their foreign stylistic counterparts or equivalents. For instance the following expressions:

At the same time

wa fi al-waqti nafsihi waṣala Zaidun.
"Zaid arrived at the same time"

To kill the time
qatala al-waqta.

It is so-and-so
huwa kaḏā wa kaḏā

Type 3 consists of expressions undeniably of non-Arabic origin. For example:

To be supported by public opinion
fulānun yu'ayyiduhu al-ra'yu al-'Āmmu.
"somebody was supported by public opinion."

Under the auspices of
kāna al-ḥaflu taḥta išrāf fulānin (under the auspices of someone)
or taḥta ri'āyati sa'ādati al-midīri al-'āmm (under the auspices of His Excellency the Director-General)

To play a role
Zaid la'iba dawran fī hādihi al-qaḍiyyah (Zaid played a role in this matter).

The stylistic borrowings have played a tremendous role in the Arabic language. They have unquestionably affected the Arabic syntactic structure, in terms of word order and frequent use of the gerund. For instance:

On the one hand . . . . . . and . . . . . . on the other
min nāḥiya . . . . wa min nāḥiyatin uxrā

In vain do I wait
'abaṯan antaẓiru al-āna fa najmī laysa yaṭla'u
(an expression used by Nāzik al-Malaika in her *Dīwān* or anthology *'Āshiqatu al-Layl).*

I am thankful to you for this
innī šākirun laka hāḏā

The rapid development in the Arabic speaking countries has also played a great part in the excessive use of literal translations from foreign languages despite the existence of Arabic equivalents. For instance: *Zaid ṭalaba yada laylā* "Zaid asked for the hand of Laila" instead of *"Zaid xaṭabahā".*

Modern Arabic also lends itself to extensive stylistic borrowings through semantic extension and abstraction. Note the words of the late Ṭāha Ḥusain:

Wa yaltamisu nafsahu, kamā yaqūlu al-Firansiyyūna, fī hāḏa al-taqlīdi, meaning "He tries to find himself, as the French say, within this tradition."

Here Ṭāha Ḥusain still reminds his readers that the phrase "tries to find himself" is taken from French.

Modern Arabic has also borrowed proverbials and idiomatic expressions. For instance:

Their efforts were crowned with success
kullilat masāʼīhim bi al-najāḥ.

Last but not least
wa axīran wa laysa āxiran.

In poetry, the modern English and French influence is clear in various movements. One of these is the introduction of Free verse into modern Arabic literature, a movement with a growing number of followers and supporters across the Arabic speaking world.

REFERENCES

Bakalla, M.H. 1981. *Arabic Linguistics: An Introduction and Bibliography.* London.

Chejne, Anwar. 1969. *The Arabic Language: Its Role in History.* Minneapolis.

Fahmi, Hasan Husain. 1958. *Manual of Arabization of Scientific and Technical Terms* (in Arabic). Cairo: Egyptian Renaissance Press.

Haywood, J.A. 1971. *Modern Arabic Literature 1800–1970.* London.

Stetkevych, Jaroslav. 1970. *The Modern Arabic Literary Language: Lexical and Stylistic Developments.* Chicago & London.

XXXVI

ARABIC LITERARY CRITICISM

Literary criticism is used here as a cover term for the field of literary appreciation, analysis, judgment and comparison of literary texts, both in terms of theory and practice. The Arabic science *Balāġah,* a formal science primarily concerned with formal distinctions and classifications of various figures of speech, is still a matter of controversy.

Arabic literary criticism has a long history and it seems to go back as far as the beginning of Arabic literature itself. The ancient historians of Arabic literature referred to the observations made by literary critics, especially in the Annual Tournaments at *Ukāẓ Fair* near Taif and other Seasonal Assemblies or markets of the pre-Islamic poets, critics, and orators. In these markets the poets used to gather to present their poems, and the judges or critics used to choose the best poem or poems in accordance with certain principles. In some instances this poem was hanged on the *Ka'ba* in Mecca. There were at least 10 *Mu'allaqāt,* or hanged poems (cf. Chapters XVI – XVIII). Amongst the famous critics were al-Khansā' the daughter of 'Amr ibn al-Sharīd (born towards the end of the 6th Century A.D.) and al-Nābighah (died about 604 A.D.), who were also great poets. The literary critical material of the pre-Islamic era is noticeably meagre, and need not detain us here.

The second phase in Arabic literary criticism started with the advent of Islam and the revelation of the *Holy Book* "the Qur'ān" which was completely different from all existing forms of literature as it was neither poetry nor pure prose. The *Holy Qur'ān* was destined to play an important role in the life of the Arabic language and literature, and consequently in the enrichment of Arabic literary criticism.

The Second Caliph Omar, a companion of the Prophet (Peace Be Upon Him), was renowned for his appreciation and sound judgment of ancient and contemporary literature. He once made the following remark about the pre-Islamic poet, al-Nābighah (Ashmāwī 1960: 52):

"He was the greatest of Jāhiliyya poets, because he never inserted redundant words, always avoided the uncouth and unfamiliar in poetry, and never praised a man except for his merit."

With the rapid expansion of the Islamic world by the end of the seventh century, and the progress of research in various sciences such as grammar and philology or linguistics, the interest in Arabic literature increased. During the eighth and ninth centuries the grammarians and philologists started to collect oral poetry of the pre-Islamic and early Islamic eras. They also gathered the observations of early literary critics together with those of their contemporaries. Amongst these scholars were, Abū 'Amr ibn al-'Alā', Yūnus ibn Ḥabīb, al-Aṣma'ī and Ibn Sallām al-Jumaḥī (died about 857 A.D.). Ibn Sallām wrote a very important book *Ṭabaqāt Fuḥūl al-Shu'arā'* (The Classification of Great Poets), which is considered one of the first works on literary criticism and representative of the critical observations of his period. He possessed some of the qualities that every critic must have, and he also laid down some of the principles upon which criticism should be based. In his opinion, criticism must not be based on taste alone. It needed long training and experience, and a critic must be an expert on his subject and skilled in the practice of his art. Among the famous literary critics of the ninth century A.D. are al-Jāḥiẓ, Ibn Qutaiba and Ibn al-Mu'tazz.

One of al-Jāḥiẓ's books, *al-Bayān wal-Tabyīn,* dealt with literary criticism in pre-Islamic times till the eighth century. He made a number of observations on effective and defective public speaking. They can be grouped under four headings:

1. The correctness of pronunciation and the defects of speech and their causes.
2. The proper and improper language and its elements.
3. Syntax and the relations between words and their meanings.
4. The proper appearance of the orator and his use of gestures.

Ibn Qutaiba in his book on *Arabic Poetry and Poets,* attacked the philosophers' approach to criticism and rigid logical methods in their judgment and analysis, and urged the critics to form independent judgments and use their own powers of appreciation.

The Prince and poet Ibn al-Mu'tazz wrote his book *al-Badī'* or "Good Style" in which he discussed the dispute between traditionalists and modernists. He also discussed the following subjects:

First: The metaphor or *isti'ārah* which is the essence of poetry.
Second: The formal aspects of poetry such as *tajnīs* or assonance; *muṭābaqa* or antithesis.
Third: The logical argument of poetry or discourse.

In the early tenth century, Qudāma ibn Ja'far, influenced by the new Aristotalian philosophical approach to literature, wrote his two books, *Naqd al-Shi'r* "Criticism of Poetry" and *Naqd al-Nathr* "Criticism of Prose." In his first book, he defined poetry as "a regular speech with metres, rhymes and meanings." He also stated that "the basic elements of poetry are: words, metre, rhyme, and meaning." To these interrelated simple elements, he added what he called the four complex elements (Ashmāwī 1960: 56):

1. The suitability of words and meanings.
2. The suitability of words and metre.
3. The suitability of meaning and metre.
4. The suitability of meaning and rhyme.

He also used certain statistical measurements in his formal analysis.

The tenth century A.D. also produced three great critics, al-Āmidi, al-Jurjānī, Abū al-Faraj al-Aṣfahānī, as well as al-'Askari and al-Bāqillānī who are considered the first exponents of methodical literary criticism.

Al-Āmidī wrote a book entitled *al-Muwāzanah* on "The Comparison Between Abū Tammām and Buḥturī", the two great poets who were representatives of two schools of poetical art. In his analysis, al-Āmidī relied for his methodical criticism on pure Arabic taste and on an essentially practical way of analysing and criticising literary texts. The criteria which guided his comparisons were the traditional models, his wide knowledge of Arabic poetry and his cultivated literary taste.

Abd al-Azīz al-Jurjānī, in his book *al-Wasāṭa* "One the Mediation between the Poet al-Mutanabbī and his Antagonists", defended al-Mutanabbī and his poetry. His method was to compare the merits of his poet with the defects of others without going beyond the appreciation of the subtleties of poetry. His honesty, fair judgment,, and impartiality has increased the value of his work and imparted to it the qualities of scientific research. His introduction to *Wasāṭa* contained a good deal of theorising about literature and literary criticism. An example of that is his interesting, and almost modern, analysis of poetical ability into its five components: natural aptitude, intelligence, acquaitance with art, memorisation of past models, and practical training. These he maintained were factors of a general nature, applicable to all humanity, and not confined to a certain age or generation.

The two books by al-Āmidī and al-Jurjānī appear to represent the peak of practical Arabic criticism and illustrate the early Arabs' mature efforts in the field of literary criticism.

Abū al-Faraj al-Aṣfahānī also in the tenth century A.D. wrote *Kitāb al-Aġānī* "The Book of Songs", a literary Encyclopedia of more than 20 volumes dealing essentially with lyrical poetry which was set to music and song in the early centuries of Islam. Under each poem or song al-Aṣfahānī also collected a large amount of critical and biographical information about a great number of Arab poets and scholars.

Al-'Askarī's book *al-Ṣinā'atain* "On the Arts of Poetry and Prose" tried to systematize and enlarge upon the earlier attempts of literary critics. Like Qudāma, he followed a rigid, systematic method, and a didactic approach which is interesting in its definitions and classifications.

He was quite successful on the problem of poetical plagiarism when he states his view (Ashmāwī 1960: 59):

> "The meanings of poetry are common among the rational. The good meaning may occur to the vulgar, Nabatean and Negro, and the choice and distinction between them came to light in form and poetic expression."

Their contemporary al-Bāqillānī, wrote his book *On the Unique Excellence of the Holy Qur'ān,* which was considered to be amongst the major works on literary criticism, as it attempted to apply the critical concepts to revealing some of the secrets of the Qur'anic literary styles.

The climax of Arab and Muslim achievement in the field of literary criticism culminated in the eleventh century at the hands of Abd al-al-Qāhir al-Jurjānī (died 1078 A.D.), the author of the two well known books *The Secrets of Rhetoric* and *The Signs of the Unique Excellence of the Qur'ān.* He is reputed for his formal "Theory of Construction" which is regarded as a landmark in the history of literary criticism.

The Theory of Construction is that the context in itself is the only repository from which every possible shade of beauty in literature comes forth. To prove this Abd al-Qāhir depended on a thorough investigation of the philological traits and attempted to display, through interpretation and analysis, that literary expression varied aesthetically and emotionally according to the differences of these philological traits.

Arabic literary criticism continued from the sixth century till the end of the 19th century but during this time it reached its lowest ebb. Scores of literary critics emerged during this period but none could reach the peak or climax set by the forerunners.

The awakening of the Arabs and Muslims during the nineteenth century as a result of the contact with the Western cultures gave rise to a new outlook in literary criticism. It stimulated creativeness in literature and liberation from the rigid rules of formal rhetoric. It also led to the revival of the study of the early ideas and concepts on the subjects, in the light of modern theories of literary criticism. Moreover, modern schools of literary criticism were formed. The school founded by al-'Aqqād, al-Māzinī and Shukrī attacked traditional poets. According to this school, some of the requisites of a good poem were: organic unity, sincerity, the avoidance of exaggeration, artificiality and inflated language. Modern Arabic literary criticism also extended its frontiers in order to include other literary forms besides poetry, such as drama, the novel, the short story and the essay. Literary criticism has also become a subject which is studied in colleges and universities, and Arab specialists in literary criticism are on the increase throughout the Arabic speaking world and their contributions to this subject are notable.

REFERENCES

Abū Dīb, Kamal. 1979. *Al-Jurjānī's Theory of Poetic Imagery. Approaches to Arabic Literature, no. 1.* Warminster, Wilts., England.

El-Ashmāwī, M.Z. 1960. *"Arab contribution to literary criticism",* in *Bulletin of the Faculty of Arts, University of Alexandria* (Alexandria, Egypt) 14. 51–68.

Kanazi, George. 1975. *"Abū Hilāl al-'Askarī's attitude towards poetry and poets",* in *Journal of Semitic Studies* (Manchester) 20. 73–80.

Khalafallah, Mohammad. 1961. *"Some landmarks of Arab achievement in the field of literary criticism",* in *Bulletin of the Faculty of Arts, University of Alexandria* (Alexandria, Egypt) 15. 3–19.

XXXVII

ARABIC TRAVEL LITERATURE

Arabic travel literature constitutes a large segment of the general main stream of Arabic literature. But although scores of Arab and Muslim travellers contributed in varying degrees to our knowledge of the people and places with which they came into contact at certain periods of time within the fourteen centuries of Islamic history, the Arabic travel literature engendered is still not considered a part of the literary heritage or even within its domain. It has normally been classified amongst the works on history and/or geography.

Recorded travel literature goes back to the time when the Prophet Muḥammad (Peace Be Upon Him) used to travel to Syria with the commercial caravans of his Meccan tribe, Quraish. A number of stories were related about the Prophet's encounters with the people he met, whether Christians or non-Christians. But among the most famous and outstanding works of medieval Arabic travel literature are the two books by the Andalusian Ibn Jubair and the Moroccan Ibn Baṭṭūṭa (cf. chapter XXV). They are both available in Arabic and a number of European languages.

The Arab traveller Ibn Jubair of Valencia (1145–1217 A.D.) left us an important account of his travels to Egypt, Hijaz and Syria. His travels covered the period between 1183 and 1185 whilst he was on his way to Hijaz to perform pilgrimage. On his return to Granada, he wrote the account of his adventures at sea and on land.[1]

Muḥammad Ibn Abdallah, known as Ibn Baṭṭūṭa was born in Tangier, Morocco on February 24th, 1304 and died in Morocco in 1369. He came from a learned family and at the age of 21 he set out from his native land to perform pilgrimage at Mecca. It is to be noted that pilgrimage has always been, for the Muslims all over the world, one of the greatest stimuli to travel. Particularly during the Medieval period, the commercial routes of Africa and Asia were in the hands of the Muslims. The extensive travels by many Muslim scholars, merchants, and travellers were then largely protected by the excellent caravan and naval services of the Muslim merchants.

Ibn Baṭṭūṭa travelled widely in Africa, Asia and Europe. Amongst the places he visited were India, the Maldive Islands, Ceylon, Assam, Sumatra and China to mention just a few. In 1342 (during the Yüan dynasty)[2] he headed a mission to one of the greatest and most powerful rulers of his time, the Mongol Emperor of China, or the Great Khān (Qān).[3] On the Chinese Mainland, he visited Kwangtung, Shanghai, and Peking as well as other towns and ports. He was very impressed by the Chinese official hospitality and he stressed their generosity, and the respect and assistance given to overseas merchants and visitors.

Ibn Baṭṭūṭa's long journey lasted for about 29 years, covering a distance estimated at 75,000 miles, both on land and sea, a figure unparalleled in history prior to the advent of the age of steam.[4]

Unfortunately, Ibn Baṭṭūṭa lost his notes and documents before he returned to his home-town in 1349. The account of his travels were dictated later on to one of the Sultan's secretaries, Muḥammad Ibn Juzayy who also added his personal touch to them.[5]

One of Ibn Baṭṭūṭa's primary aims was to describe the contemporary scenes of the Islamic World and beyond. His work is still of interest not only to historians, geographers, anthropologists and folklorists, but also to students of literature and stylistics. His simple literary style of both prose and poetry is a reflection of his age, culture and society. Professor Gibb (1974: 152) states:

> "In mere extent of his travels Ibn Baṭṭūṭa surpassed all ancient and medieval travellers. That his work should contain errors was inevitable, especially as the loss of his notes at the hands of pirates in the Indian Ocean compelled him to trust entirely to his memory; but they are so few and rarely important that the work ranks as an authority for the social and cultural history of post-Mongol Islam. His very faults are, if faults at all, those of his age; his sincerity is above suspicion. The book has, too, a literary interest of its own. Ibn Juzayy, it is true, decked it out with poetical citations, purple passages from Ibn Jubair and others, and naive interpolations of his own, but the work remains substantially a simple narrative, full of

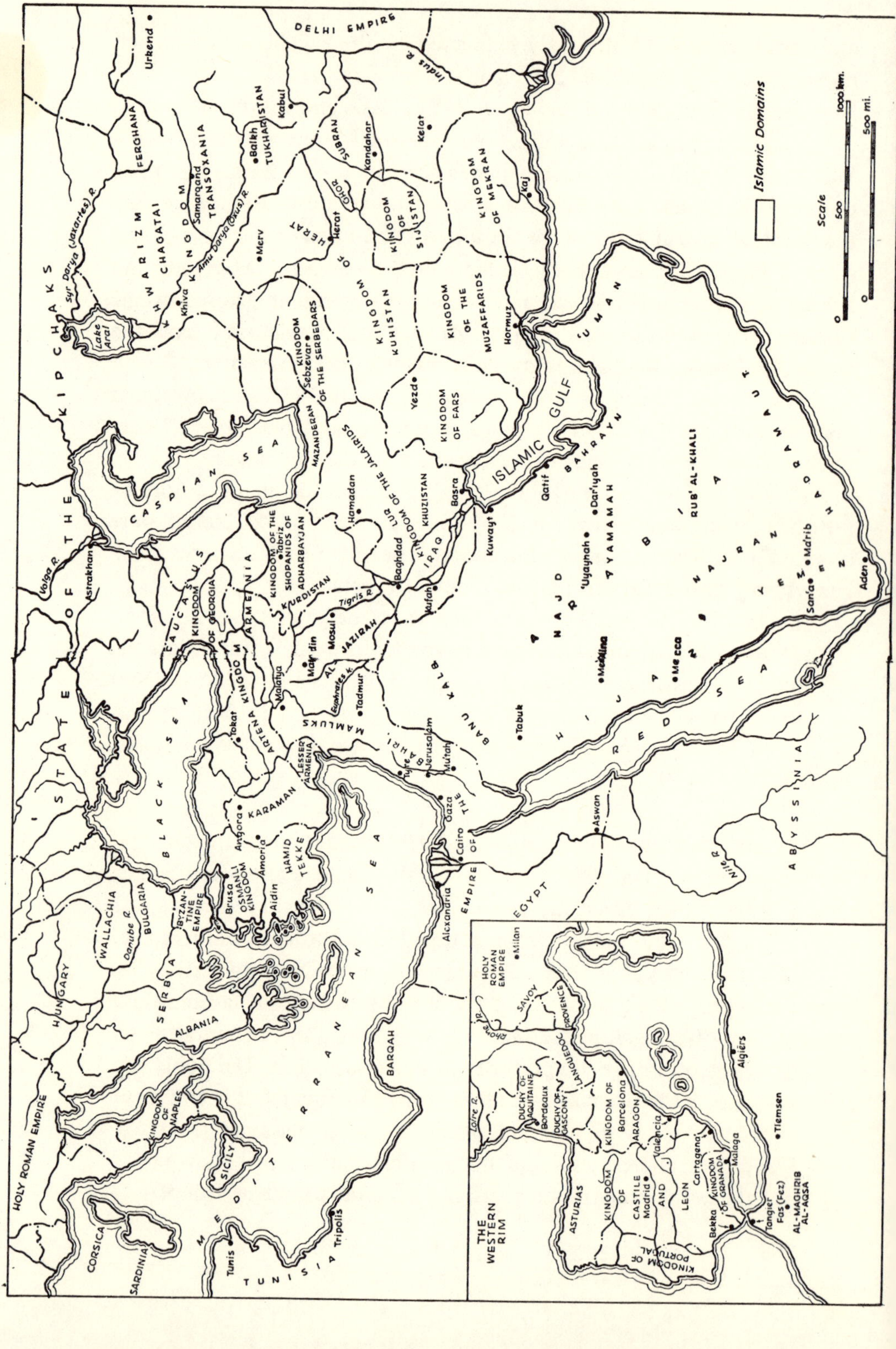
DELHI EMPIRE
Urkend
Indus R.
Islamic Domains
Scale
0
500
1000 km.
500 mi.
KIPCHAKS
FERGHANA
Kabul
TUKHARISTAN
Balkh
Samarqand
TRANSOXANIA
CHAGATAI
KINGDOM
KHWARIZM
Syr Darya (Jaxartes) R.
Amu Darya (Oxus) R.
Khiva
Lake Aral
Merv
Herat
HERAT
GHOR
SUBRAN
Kandahar
Kelat
KINGDOM OF SIJISTAN
KINGDOM OF MEKRAN
Kaj
KINGDOM KUHISTAN
KINGDOM OF THE MUZAFFARIDS
Hormuz
'UMAN
KINGDOM OF THE SERBEDARS
Sebzevar
MAZANDERAN
CASPIAN SEA
Yezd
KINGDOM OF FARS
ISLAMIC GULF
Qatif
BAHRAYN
RUB' AL-KHALI
HADRAMAUT
JALAIRIDS
Hamadan
LUR
KHUZISTAN
Basra
Kuwayt
Dar'iyah
YAMAMAH
'Uyaynah
NAJD
NAJRAN
Ma'rib
YEMEN
San'a'
Aden
KINGDOM OF THE SHOPANIDS OF ADHARBAYJAN
Tabriz
IRAQ
Baghdad
KURDISTAN
Tigris R.
Kufah
Mosul
JAZIRAH
Mardin
Euphrates R.
Tadmur
Malatya
Astrakhan
Volga R.
CAUCASUS
KINGDOM OF GEORGIA
ARMENIA
KINGDOM
Tokat
ARTENA
MAMLUKS
BAHRI
BANU KALB
Tabuk
Medina
Mecca
HIJAZ
RED SEA
LESSER ARMENIA
Jerusalem
Tyre
Mu'tah
Gaza
KARAMAN
Angora
Amoria
HAMID
TEKKE
Brusa
OSMANLI KINGDOM
Aidin
BLACK SEA
STATE OF THE KIPCHAKS
BYZANTINE EMPIRE
BULGARIA
WALLACHIA
Danube R.
HUNGARY
SERBIA
ALBANIA
Cairo
Alexandria
EMPIRE OF THE MAMLUKS
EGYPT
Aswan
ABYSSINIA
Nile R.
MEDITERRANEAN SEA
BARQAH
KINGDOM OF NAPLES
SICILY
HOLY ROMAN EMPIRE
CORSICA
SARDINIA
Tunis
Tripolis
TUNISIA
THE WESTERN RIM
Milan
HOLY ROMAN EMPIRE
SAVOY
PROVENCE
Rhone R.
LANGUEDOC
DUCHY OF AQUITAINE
Bordeaux
DUCHY OF GASCONY
Loire R.
KINGDOM OF ARAGON
Barcelona
Valencia
Cartagena
KINGDOM OF GRANADA
Malaga
Algiers
Tlemsen
ASTURIAS
KINGDOM OF CASTILE AND LEON
Madrid
KINGDOM OF PORTUGAL
Bekka
Tangier
Fas (Fez)
AL-MAGHRIB AL-AQSA

racy incident and touches of humour, without pretensions to style, and interspersed with anecdotes that throw an abundance of light on the manners of the times."

The contacts between the Arabs and the Chinese go back deep in history, even to the pre-Islamic era. During the Middle Ages the Arabs and Muslims spread their power and Empire over the largest part of the Ancient World. This made the contact with the Chinese even greater. As a result of the contacts with the Orient and the Occident, the Arabs and Muslims improved upon the old sciences and developed new ones during this period. The Arabs and Muslims also acted then as *the* bridge or link between the East and West which later on had much to contribute towards the awakening of Europe in particular and the West in general. Liang Ch'i-Ch'ao[6] once hastily remarked (Levenson 1970:126):

> "The great tools of modern European civilisation: compass, firearms, printing came to Europe via the Arabs, who learned their secrets from the Chinese."

To conclude, here is an account extracted from Ibn Baṭṭūṭa's book on his visit to China (1929:282–301).

Ibn Baṭṭūṭa's Visit to China

"The land of China is of vast extent, and abounding in produce, fruits, grain, gold and silver. In this respect there is no country in the world that can rival it. It is traversed by the river called the "Water of Life," which rises in some mountains, called the "Mountain of Apes," near the city of Khān-Bāliq (Peking) and flows through the centre of China for the space of six months' journey, until finally it reaches Ṣīn as-Ṣīn (Canton). It is bordered by villages, fields, fruit gardens, and bazaars, just like the Egyptian Nile, only that the country through which runs this river is even more richly cultivated and populous, and there are many waterwheels on it. In the land of China there is abundant sugar-cane, equal, nay superior, in quality to that of Egypt, as well as grapes and plums. I used to think that the 'Othmānī plums of Damascus had no equal, until I saw the plums in China. It has wonderful melons

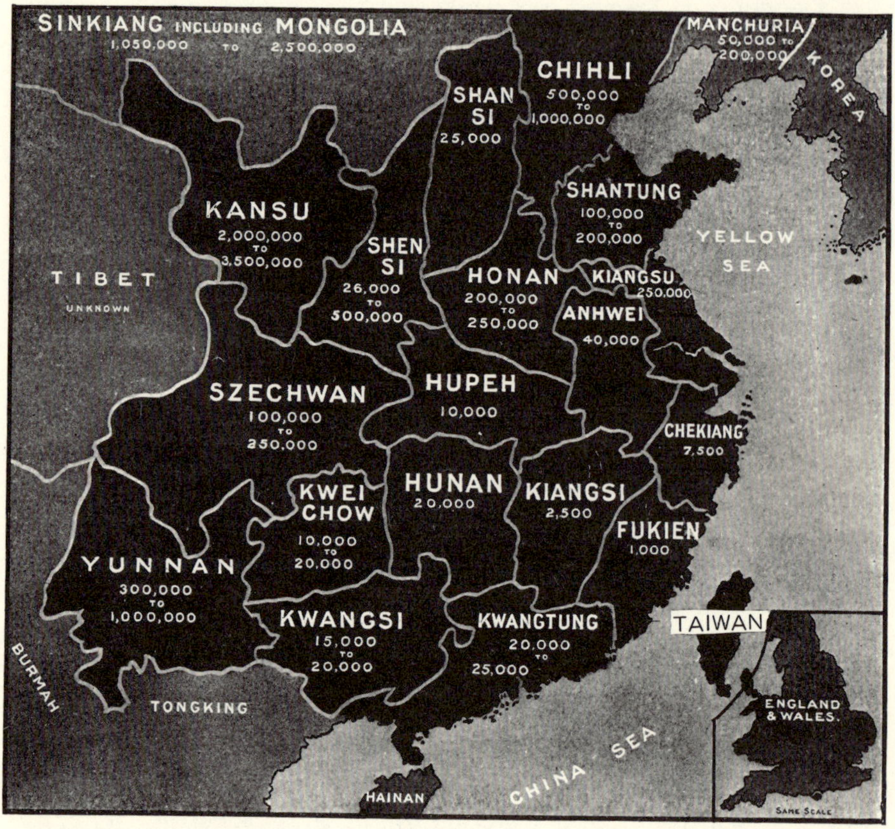

MAP 7. The Estimated Numbers and Distribution of the Muslim Population in China.
The figures on the map represent the estimated minimum and maximum Muslim population between 1900–1910. According to some recent estimates, there are more than 20 million Muslims in China, about 55,000 of whom are in Taiwan.

too, like those of Khwārizm and Iṣfahān. All the fruits which we have in our country are to be found there, either much the same or of better quality. Wheat is very abundant in China, indeed better wheat I have never seen, and the same may be said of their lentils and chick-peas.

The Chinese pottery (porcelain) is manufactured only in the towns of Zaytūn[7] and Sīn-kalān. It is made of the soil of some mountains in that district, which takes fire like charcoal, as we shall relate subsequently. They mix this with some stones which they have, burn the whole for three days, then pour water over it. This gives a kind of clay which they cause to ferment. The best quality of (porcelain is made from) clay that has fermented for a complete month, but no more, the poorer quality (from clay) that has fermented for ten days. The price of this porcelain there is the same as, or even less than, that of ordinary pottery in our country. It is exported to India and other countries, even reaching as far as our own lands in the West, and it is the finest of all makes of pottery.

The hens and cocks in China are very big indeed, bigger than geese in our country, and hens' eggs there are bigger than our goose eggs. On the other hand their geese are not at all large. We bought a hen once and set about cooking it, but it was too big for one pot, so we put it in two. Cocks over there are about the size of ostriches; often a cock will shed its feathers and (nothing but) a great red body remains. The first time I saw a Chinese cock was in the city of Kawlam. I took it for an ostrich and was amazed at it, but its owner told me that in China there were some even bigger than that, and when I got to China I saw for myself the truth of what he had told me about them.

The Chinese themselves are infidels, who worship idols and burn their dead like the Hindus. The king of China is a Tatar, one of the descendants of Jinkīz (Chingiz) Khān. In every Chinese city there is a quarter for Muslims in which they live by themselves, and in which they have mosques both for the Friday services and for other religious purposes. The Muslims are honoured and respected. The Chinese infidels eat the flesh of swine and dogs, and sell it in their markets. They are wealthy folk and well-to-do, but they make no display either in their food or their clothes. You will see one of their principal merchants, a man so rich that his wealth cannot be counted, wearing a coarse cotton tunic. But there is one thing that the Chinese take a pride in, that is,

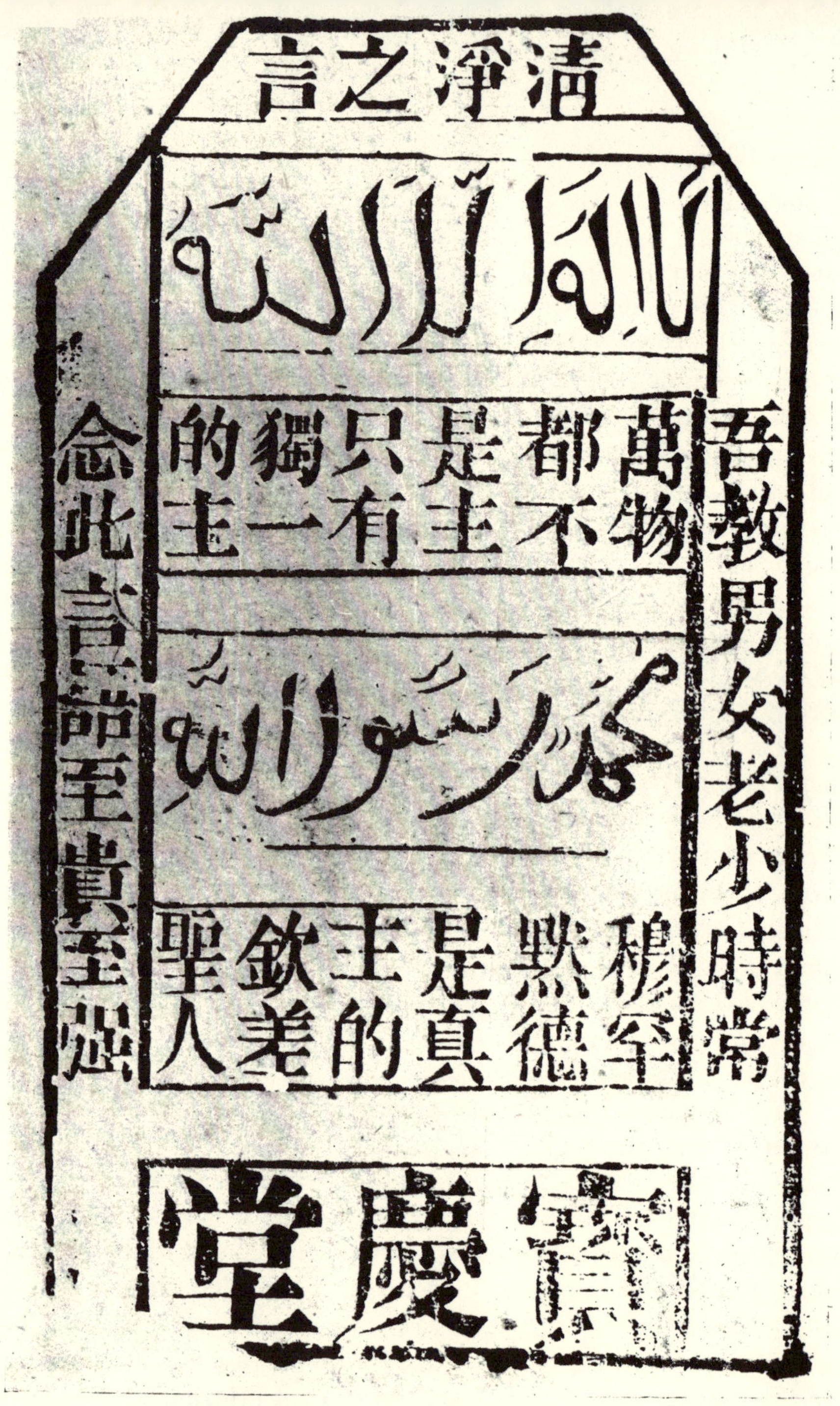

PLATE 3. *The Kalima* in Arabic and Chinese.
The two double rows of Chinese characters in the centre read: "Ten thousand things (i.e. created things) are not God. There is only one God. Muhammad is the true God's officially appointed Prophet." The Chinese characters in the right and left columns merely state that the constant repetition of these words is of great merit. The Arabic reads: "There is no deity but God, Muhammad is the Messenger of God."

gold and silver plate. Every one of them carries a stick, on which they lean in walking, and which they call "the third leg." Silk is very plentiful among them, because the silk-worm attaches itself to fruits and feeds on them without requiring much care. For that reason it is so common to be worn by even the very poorest there. Were it not for the merchants it would have no value at all, for a single piece of cotton cloth is sold in their country for the price of many pieces of silk. It is customary amongst them for a merchant to cast what gold and silver he has into ingots, each weighing a hundredweight or more or less, and to put those ingots above the door of his house.

The Chinese use neither (gold) dinars nor (silver) dirhams in their commerce. All the gold and silver that comes into their country is cast by them into ingots, as we have described. Their buying and selling is carried on exclusively by means of pieces of paper, each of the size of the palm of the hand, and stamped with the sultan's seal. Twenty-five of these pieces of paper are called a *bālisht,* which takes the place of the dinar with us (as the unit of currency).[8] When these notes become torn by handling, one takes them to an office corresponding to our mint, and receives their equivalent in new notes on delivering up the old ones. This transaction is made without charge and involves no expense, for those who have the duty of making the notes receive regular salaries from the sultan. Indeed the direction of that office is given to one of their principal amīrs. If anyone goes to the bazaar with a silver dirham or a dinar, intending to buy something, no one will accept it from him or pay any attention to him until he changes if for *bālisht,* and with that he may buy what he will.

All the inhabitants of China and of Cathay[9] use in place of charcoal a kind of lumpy earth found in their country. It resembles our fuller's earth, and its colour too is the colour of fuller's earth. Elephants (are used to) carry loads of it. They break it up into pieces about the size of pieces of charcoal with us, and set it on fire and it burns like charcoal, only giving out more heat than a charcoal fire. When it is reduced to cinders, they knead it with water, dry it, and use it again for cooking, and so on over and over again until it is entirely consumed. It is from this clay that they make the Chinese porcelain ware, after adding to it some other stones, as we have related.

The Chinese are of all people the most skilful in the arts and possessed of the greatest mastery of them. This characteristic of theirs is well known, and has frequently been described at length in the works of various writers. In regard to portraiture there is none, whether Greek or any other, who can match them in precision, for in this art they show a marvellous talent. I myself saw an extraordinary example of this gift of theirs. I never returned to any of their cities after I had visited it a first time without finding my portrait and the portraits of my companions drawn on the walls and on sheets of paper exhibited in the bazaars. When I visited the sultan's city I passed with my companions through the painters' bazaar on my way to the sultan's palace. We were dressed after the 'Irāqī fashion. On returning from the palace in the evening, I passed through the same bazaar, and saw my portrait and those of my companions drawn on a sheet of paper which they had affixed to the wall. Each of us set to examining the other's portrait (and found that) the likeness was perfect in every respect. I was told that the sultan had ordered them to do this, and that they had come to the palace while we were there and had been observing us and drawing our portraits without our noticing it. This is a custom of theirs, I mean making portraits of all who pass through their country. In fact they have brought this to such perfection that if a stranger commits any offence that obliges him to flee from China, they send his portrait far and wide. A search is then made for him and wheresoever the person bearing a resemblance to that portrait is found he is arrested.

When a Muslim merchant enters any town in China, he is given the choice between staying with some specified merchant among the Muslims domiciled there, or going to a hostelry. If he chooses to stay with the merchant, his money is taken into custody and put under the charge of the resident merchant. The latter then pays from it all his expenses with honesty and charity. When the visitor wishes to depart, his money is examined, and if any of it is found to be missing, the resident merchant who was put in charge of it is obliged to make good the deficit. If the visitor chooses to go to the hostelry, his property is deposited under the charge of the keeper of the hostelry. The keeper buys for him whatever he desires and presents him with an account. If he desires to take a concubine, the keeper purchases a slave-girl for him and lodges him in an apartment opening out of the hostelry, and purveys for them both. Slave-girls fetch a low price; yet all the Chinese sell their sons and daughters, and consider it no disgrace. They are not compelled, however, to travel with those who buy them, nor on the other hand, are they hindered from going if they choose to do so. In the same way, if a stranger desires to marry, marry he may; but as for spending his money in debauchery, no, that he may not do. They say "We will not have it noised about amongst Muslims that their people waste their substance in our country, because it is a land of riotous living and women of surpassing beauty."

China is the safest and best regulated of countries for a traveller. A man may go by himself a nine months' journey, carrying with him large sums of money, without any fear on that account. The system by which they ensure his safety is as follows. At every post-station in their country they have a hostelry controlled by an officer, who is stationed there with a company of horsemen and footsoldiers. After sunset or later in the evening the officer visits the hostelry with his clerk, registers the names of all travellers staying there for the night, seals up the list, and locks them into the hostelry. After sunrise he returns with his clerk, calls each person by name, and writes a detailed description of them on the list. He then sends a man with them to conduct them to the next post-station and bring back a clearance certificate from the controller there to the effect that all these persons have arrived at that station. If the guide does not produce this document, he is held responsible for them. This is the practice at every station in their country from Sīn as-Sīn to Khān-Bāliq. In these hostelries there is everything that the traveller requires in the way of provisions, especially fowls and geese. Sheep on the other hand, are scarce with them.

To return to the account of our journey. The first city which we reached after our sea voyage was the city of Zaytūn. (Now although *zaytūn* means "olives") there are no olives in this city, nor indeed in all the lands of the Chinese nor in India; it is simply a name which has been given to the place. Zaytūn is an immense city. In it are woven the damask silk and satin fabrics which go by its name, and which are superior to the fabrics of Khansā and Khān-Bāliq. The port of Zaytūn is one of the largest in the world, or perhaps the very largest. I saw in it about a hundred large junks; as for small junks, they could not be counted for multitude. It is formed by a large inlet of the sea which penetrates the land to the point where it unites with the great river. In this city, as in all Chinese towns, a man will have a fruit-garden and a field with his house set in the middle of it, just as in the town of Sijilmāsa in our own country.[10] For this reason their towns are extensive. The Muslims live in a town apart from the others.

On the day that I reached Zaytūn I saw there the amīr who had come to India as an envoy with the present to the sultan, and who afterwards travelled with our party and was shipwrecked on the junk. He greeted me, and introduced me to the controller of the *douane* and saw that I was given good apartments there[11] I received visits from the qāḍī of the Muslims, the shaykh al-Islam, and the principal merchants. Amongst the latter was Sharaf ad-Dīn of Tabrīz, one of the merchants from whom I had borrowed at the time of my arrival in India, and the one who had treated me most fairly. He knew the Qur'ān by heart and used to recite it constantly. These merchants, living as they do in a land of infidels, are overjoyed when a Muslim comes to them. They say "He has come from the land of Islam," and they make *him* the recipient of the tithes on their properties, so that he becomes as rich as themselves. There was living at Zaytūn, amongst other eminent shaykhs, Burhān ad-ad-Dīn of Kāzarūn, who has a hermitage outside the town, and it is to him that the merchants pay the sums they vow to Shaykh Abū Isḥāq of Kāzarūn.

When the controller of the *douane* learned my story he wrote to the Qān,[12] who is their Emperor, to inform him of my arrival on a mission from the king of India. I asked him to send with me someone to conduct me to the district of Sīn (Sīn as-Sīn), which they call Sīn-kalān,[13] so that I might see that district, which is in his province, in the interval before the arrival of the Qān's reply. He granted my request, and sent one of his officers to conduct me. I sailed up the river on a vessel resembling the war galleys in our country, except that in this the rowers plied their oars standing upright, their place being in the centre of the vessel, while the passengers were at the forepart and the stern. They spread over the ship awnings made from a plant which grows in their country, resembling but different from flax, and finer than hemp (perhaps grass-cloth). We sailed up this river for twenty-seven days. Every day we used to tie up about noon by a village where we could buy what we needed and pray the noon prayers, then in the evenings we went ashore at another village and so on, until we reached the city of Sīn-kalān or Sin as-Sīn. Porcelain is manufactured there as well as at Zaytūn, and hereabouts the river of the "Water of Life" flows into the sea, so they call the place "The Meeting of the Waters." Sīn-kalān is a city of the first rank, in regard to size and the quality of its bazaars. One of the largest of these is the porcelain bazaar, from which porcelain is exported to all parts of China, to India, and to Yemen. In the centre of this city there is an enormous temple with nine portals, inside each of which there is a portico with benches where the inmates of the temple sit. Between the second and third portals there is a place containing chambers, which are occupied by the blind and crippled. Each of the occupants receives subsistence and clothing from the endowment of the temple. There are similar establishments between all the portals. In the interior there is a hospital for the sick and a kitchen for cooking food, and it has a staff of doctors and servitors. I was told that aged persons who are incapacitated from gaining their livelihood receive subsistence and clothing at the temple, likewise orphans and destitute widows.

This temple was built by one of their kings, who moreover endowed it with the revenues of this city and the villages and fruit gardens belonging to it. The portrait of this king is painted in the temple we have described, and they worship it.

In one of the quarters of this city is the Muslim town, where the Muslims have their cathedral mosque, hospice and bazaar. They have also a qāḍī and a shaykh, for in every one of the cities of China there must always be a Shaykh al-Islam, to whom all matters concerning the Muslims are referred (*i.e.* who acts as intermediary between the government and the Muslim community), and a qāḍī to decide legal cases between them. My quarters were in the house of Awḥad ad-Dīn of Sinjār, one of their principal men, of excellent character and immensely wealthy. I stayed with him for fourteen days, during which gifts were poured upon me one after the other from the qāḍī and other Muslims. Every day they made a new entertainment, to which they came in beautifully-appointed boats, bringing musicians with them. Beyond the city of Sīn-kalān there is no other city, either infidel or Muslim. It is sixty days' journey, so I was told, from there to the Rampart of Gog and Magog, the intervening territory being occupied by nomadic infidels, who eat men when they get hold of them. On that account no one ever crosses their country or visits it, and I did not find in Sīn-kalān

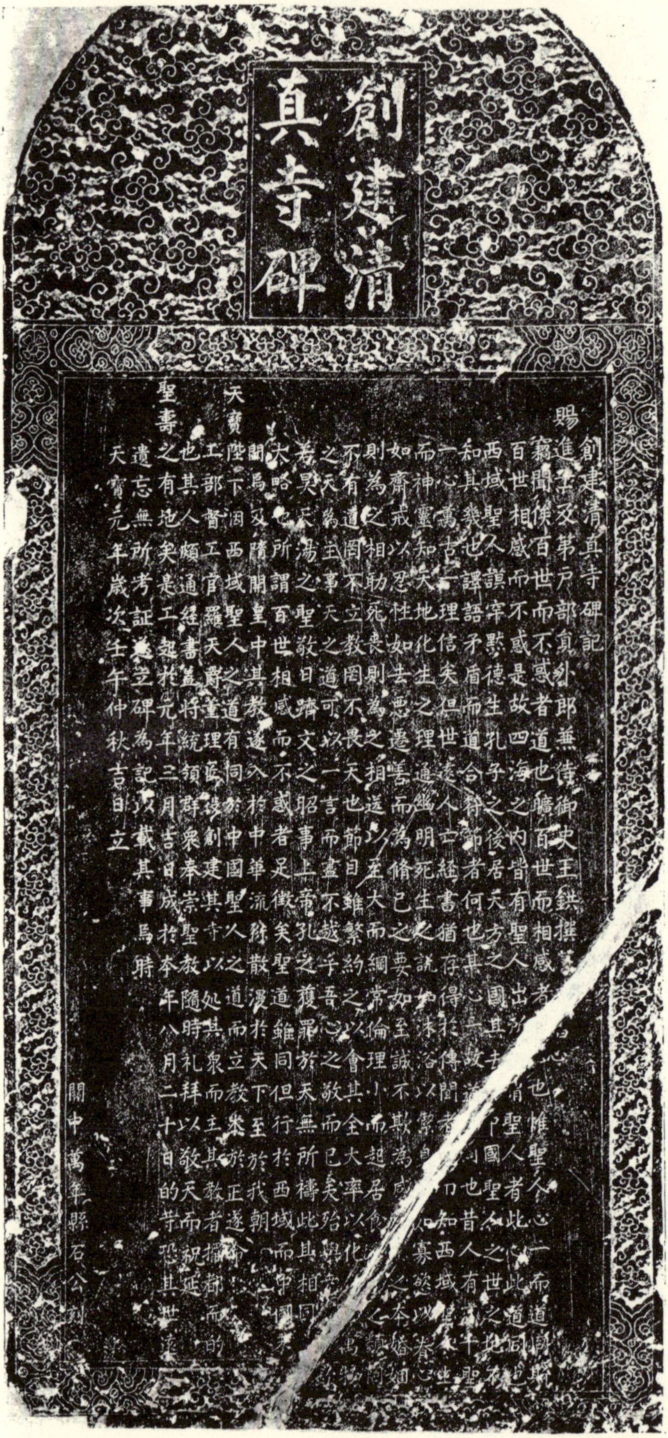

PLATE 4. A Monument to Record the Building of the First Mosque in China. The Monument is in the Old Mosque at Sianfu Shensi, Dated 742 A.D.

anyone who had himself seen the Rampart or even seen anyone who had seen it.

A few days after my return to Zaytūn, the Qān's order arrived with instructions to convey me to his capital with all honour and dignity, by water if I preferred, otherwise by land. I chose to sail up the river, so they made ready for me a fine vessel of the sort that is designed for the use of governors. The governor sent his staff with us, and he, and likewise the qāḍī and the Muslim merchants, sent us large quantities of provisions. We travelled as state-guests, eating our midday meal at one village, and our evening meal at another. After ten days' journey we reached Qānjanfū, a large and beautiful city set in a broad plain and surrounded by fruit-gardens,[14] which gave the place the look of the Ghūta at Damascus. On our arrival, we were met outside the town by the qāḍī, the Shaykh al-Islam, and the merchants, with standards, drums, trumpets, and bugles, and musicians. They brought horses for us, so we rode in on horseback while they walked on foot before us. No one rode along with us but the qāḍī and the Shaykh al-Islam. The governor of the city with his staff also came out to meet us, for the sultan's guest is held in very high honour by them, and so we entered the city. It has four walls; between the first and second live the sultan's slaves, who are some of them day-guards and others night-guards of the city; between the second and third are the quarters of the mounted troops and the general who governs the city; within the third wall live the Muslims (it was here that we lodged at the house of their shaykh), and within the fourth is the Chinese quarter, which is the largest of these four cities in one. The distance separating each gate in this city from the next is three or four miles, and every inhabitant, as we have said, has his own orchard, house, and grounds.

One day as I was staying at Qānjanfū, a very large vessel came in, belonging to one of their most respected doctors. I was asked if he might see me, and he was announced as "Mawlānā (Our master *i.e.* The reverend) Qiwām ad-Dīn of Ceuta." His name roused my interest, and when he came in and we fell to conversation after the usual greetings, it struck me that I knew him. I kept looking at him intently, and at last he said "I see you are looking at me as if you knew me." So I said to him "Where do you come from?" He replied "From Ceuta." "And I" said I "from Tangier." Whereupon he broke into fresh greetings to me, and wept until I wept in sympathy with him. I then said to him "Did you go to India?" He replied "Yes, I went to the capital, Delhi." Then when he told me that, I remembered him and said "Are you al-Bushrī?" and he replied "Yes." I remembered he had come to Delhi with his mother's brother, Abū al-Qāsim of Murcia, as a beardless youth and a very clever student. I had spoken of him to the sultan of India, who gave him three thousand dinars and invited him to stay at his court, but he refused, as he was set on going to China, where he prospered exceedingly, and acquired enormous wealth. He told me that he had about fifty white slaves and as many slave-girls, and presented me with two of each, along with many other gifts. I met his brother in after years in the Negrolands—what a distance lies between them!

I stayed at Qānjanfū for fifteen days and then continued my journey. The land of China, in spite of all that is agreeable in it, did not attract me. On the contrary I was sorely grieved that heathendom had so strong a hold over it. Whenever I went out of my house I used to see any number of revolting things, and that distressed me so much that I used to keep indoors and go out only in case of necessity. When I met Muslims in China I always felt just as though I were meeting my own faith and kin. So great was the kindness of this doctor al-Bushrī that when I left Qānjanfū he accompanied me for four days, until I reached the town of Baywam Qutlū. This is a small town, inhabited by Chinese, a proportion of them being troops, the rest common people. The Muslim community there consists of four houses only, the inhabitants of which are agents of my learned friend. We put up at the house of one of them, and stayed with him for three days, after which I bade the doctor adieu and set out again.

I sailed up the river with the usual routine, stopping for dinner at one village, and for supper at another. After seventeen days of this, we reached the city of Khansā (Hang-chow), which is the biggest city I have ever seen on the face of the earth. It is so long that it takes three days to traverse in the ordinary routine of marches and halts. It is built after the Chinese fashion already described, each person, that is, having his own house and garden. It is divided into six cities, as we shall describe later. On our arrival a party came out to meet us, consisting of the qāḍī and the Shaykh al-Islam of the city, and the family of 'Othmān ibn 'Affān of Egypt, who are the principal Muslim residents there, accompanied by a white flag, drums, bugles, and trumpets. The governor of the city also came out to meet us with his escort, and so we entered the town.

Khansā consists of six cities, each with its own wall, and an outer wall surrounding the whole. In the first city are the quarters of the city guards and their commander; I was told by the qāḍī and others that they mustered twelve thousand men on the register of troops. We passed the first night after our entry in the house of their commander. On the second day we entered the second city through a gate called the Jews' Gate. In this city live the Jews, Christians, and sun-worshipping Turks, a large number in all; its governor is a Chinese and we passed the second night in his house. On the third day we entered the third city, and this is inhabited by the Muslims. Theirs is a fine city, and their bazaars are arranged just as they are in Islamic countries; they have mosques in it and muezzins—we heard them calling to the noon prayers as we entered. We stayed here in the mansion of the family of 'Othmān ibn 'Affān of Egypt. He was a wealthy merchant, who conceived a liking for this city and made his home in it, so that it came be be called 'Othmānīya after him, and he transmitted to his posterity the influence and respect which he enjoyed there. It was he who built the cathedral mosque of Khansā, and endowed it with large benefactions. The number of Muslims in this city is very large, and our stay with them lasted fifteen days. Every day and night we were the guests at a new entertainment, and they continuously provided the most sumptuous meats, and went out with us every day on pleasure rides into different quarters of the city.

One day they rode out with me and we entered the fourth city, which is the seat of government, and in which the chief governor Qurtay resides. When we entered the gate leading to it, my companions were separated from me, and I was found by the wazīr, who conducted me to the palace of the chief governor Qurtay. It was on this occasion that he took from me the mantle which the Imām Jalāl ad-Dīn of Shiraz had given me. No one resides in this city, which is the most beautiful of the six, except the sultan's slaves and servants. It is traversed by three streams, one of them being a canal taken off from the great river, which is used by small boats bringing provisions and coal to the town, and there are pleasure boats on it as well. The citadel lies in the centre of this city. It is of enormous size, and the government house stands in the middle of it, surrounded by the court of the citadel on all sides. Within it there are arcades, in which sit workmen making rich garments and weapons. The amīr Qurtay told me that there were sixteen hundred master-workmen there, each with three or four apprentices working under him. They are all without exception the slaves of the Qān; they have chains on their feet, and they live outside the fortress. They are permitted to go out to the bazaars in the city, but may not go beyond its gate. They are passed in review before the governor every day, a hundred at a time, and if any one of them is missing, his commander is held responsible for him. Their custom is that when one of them has served for ten years, he is freed from his chains and given the choice between staying in service, without chains, or going wherever he will within the Qān's dominions, but not outside them. When he reaches the age of fifty he is exempted from work and maintained by the state. In the same way anyone else who has attained this age or thereabouts is maintained. Anyone who reaches the age of sixty is regarded by them as a child, and legal penalties cease to be applicable to him. Old men in China are greatly respected, and each one of them is called Ata, which means "Father."

The amīr Qurtay is the principal amīr in China. He entertained us in his palace, and prepared a banquet (their name for it is *towa*),[15] which was attended by the principal men of the city. He had Muslim cooks brought, who slaughtered the animals in accordance with Muslim ritual, so that the food should be ceremonially clean and cooked the food. This amīr, in spite of his exalted rank, presented the dishes to us with his own hand, and with his own hand carved the meat. We stayed with him as his guests for three days. He sent his son with us to the canal, where we went on board a ship resembling a fire-ship, and the amīr's son went on another along with musicians and singers. They sang in Chinese, Arabic, and Persian. The amīr's son was a great admirer of Persian melody, and when they sang a certain Persian poem he commanded them to repeat it over and over again, until I learned it from them by heart. It has a pleasant lilt, and goes like this:

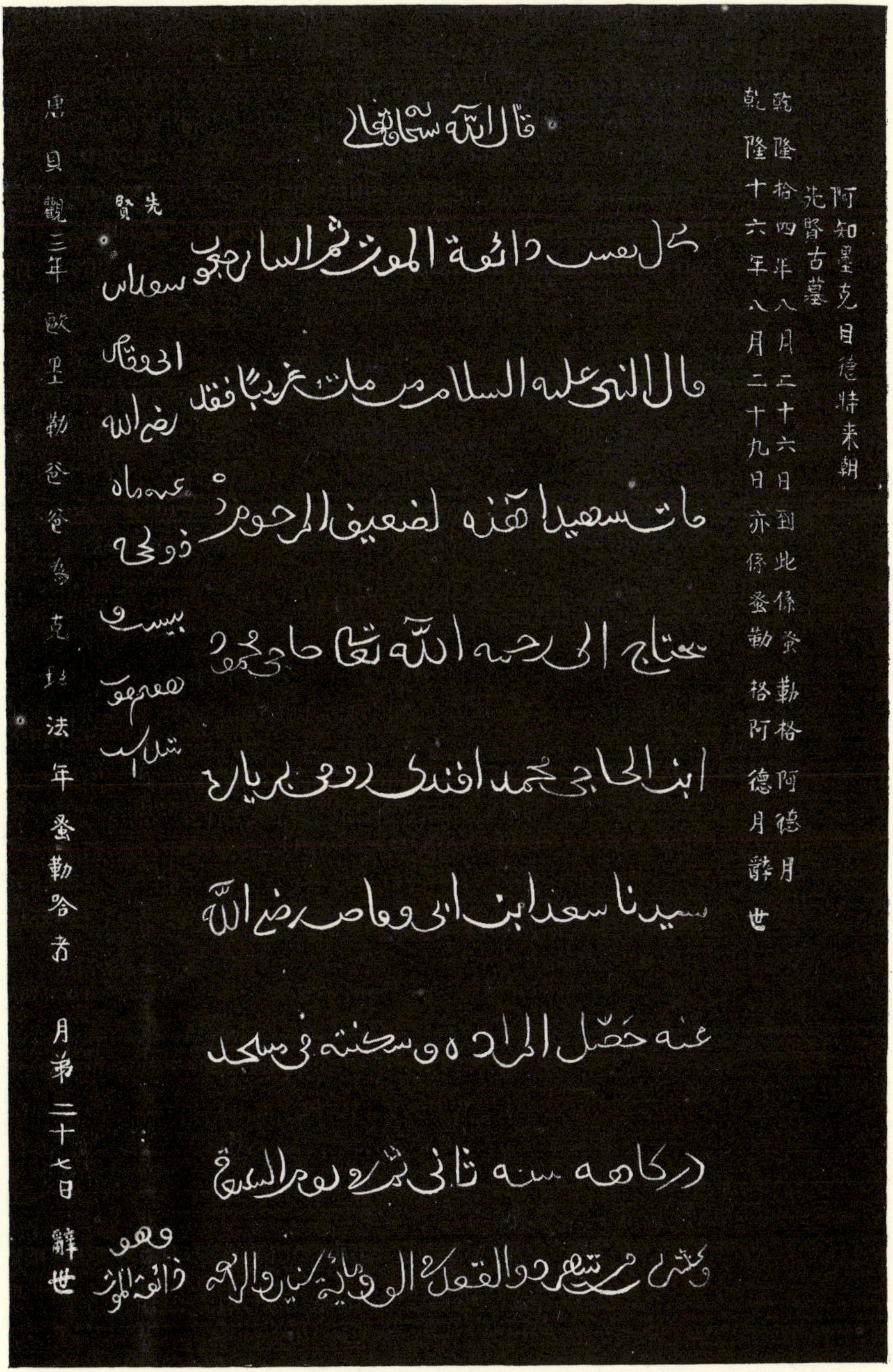

PLATE 5. A Trilingual Inscription at Canton, Dated 1750 A.D. The Three Languages are Arabic, Persian and Chinese.

Ta dil bimihnat dadim
dai bahr-i fikr uftadim
Chun dar namaz istadim
qavi bimihrab andarim.[16]

On this canal there was assembled a large crowd in ships with brightly-coloured sails and silk awnings, and their ships too were admirably painted. They began a mimic battle and bombarded each other with oranges and lemons. We returned in the evening to the amīr's palace, and spent the night there. The musicians were there, and sang all kinds of pleasing melodies.

That same night a certain juggler, one of the Qān's slaves, was there. The amīr said to him "Show us some of your feats." So he took a wooden ball with holes in which there were long leather thongs, and threw it into the air. It rose right out of our sight, for we were sitting in the middle of the palace court, during the season of intense heat. When nothing, but a short piece of the cord remained in his hand, he ordered one of his apprentices to go up the rope, which he did until he too disappeared from our sight. The juggler called him three times without receiving any reply, so he took a knife in his hand, as if he were enraged, and climbed up the rope until he disappeared as well. The next thing was that he threw the boy's hand to the ground, and then threw down his foot, followed by his other hand, then his other foot, then his trunk, and finally his head. After that he came down himself puffing and blowing, with his clothes all smeared with blood, and kissed the ground in front of the amīr, saying something to him in Chinese. The amir gave him some order, and thereupon he took the boy's limbs, placed them each touching the other, and gave him a kick, and up he rose as sound as ever. I was amazed and took palpitation of the heart, just as had happened to me when I saw something similar at the court of the king of India, so they administered some potion to me which removed my distress. The qāḍī Afkhar ad-Dīn was sitting beside me, and he said to me: "By God, there was no climbing or coming down or cutting up of limbs at all; the whole thing is just hocus-pocus."

On the following day we entered the fifth and largest city, which is inhabited by the common folk. Its bazaars are good and contain very skilful artificers; it is there that the fabrics which take their name from this town are woven. We passed a night in this city as the guests of its governor, and on the morrow entered the sixth city through a gate called Boatmen's gate. This sixth city, which lies on the banks of the great river, is inhabited by seamen, fishermen, caulkers, and carpenters, along with archers and footsoldiers, all of them being slaves of the sultan. No other persons live in this town with them, and their numbers are very great. We spent a night there as the guests of its governor. The amīr Qurtay equipped a vessel for us with all that was needed in the way of provisions, etc., and sent his suite with us to arrange for our hospitable reception on the journey. So we left this city, which is the last of the provinces of China proper, and entered the land of Khitā (Cathay).

Cathay is the best cultivated country in the world. There is not a spot in the whole extent of it that is not brought under cultivation. The reason is that if any part is left uncultivated its inhabitants or their neighbours are assessed for the land-tax due thereon. Fruit-gardens, villages, and fields extend along both banks of this river without interruption from the city of Khansā to the city of Khān-Bāliq (Peking), which is a space of sixty-four days' journey. There are no Muslims to be found in these districts, except casual travellers, since the country is not suitable for their permanent residence, and there is no large city in it, only villages and wide spaces, covered with corn, fruit-trees, and sugarcane. I have never seen anything in the world like it, except a space of four days' journey between Anbār and 'Āna (in 'Irāq). We used to disembark every night and stay in the villages in order to receive our provisions as guests of the sultan.

Thus we completed our journey to the city of Khān-Bāliq, also called Khāniqū,[17] the capital of the Qān—he being their emperor, whose dominion extends over the countries of China and Cathay. When we arrived there we moored at a distance of ten miles from the city, as is their custom, and a written report of our arrival was sent to the admirals, who gave us permission to enter the port of the city. Having done so, we disembarked and entered the town, which is one of the largest towns in the world. It is not laid out, however, after the Chinese fashion, with gardens inside the city, but is just like the cities in other countries with gardens outside the walls. The sultan's city lies in the centre, like a citadel, as we shall relate. I stayed with Shaykh Burhān ad-Dīn of Sāgharj—the same man to whom the king of India sent 40,000 dinars with an invitation to him to come to India, and who took the money and paid his debts with them, but refused to go to the king and set out instead for China. The Qān set him at the head of all the Muslims who live in his territories, and gave him the title of *Ṣadr al-Jihān*. The word *qān* is a term applied by them to every person who exercises the sovereignty over all the provinces, just as every ruler of the country of Lūr is called *atābeg*. His name is Pāshāy,[18] and there is no infidel on the face of the earth who owns an empire greater than his. His palace lies in the centre of the inner city, which is appropriated to his residence. The greater part of it is constructed of carved wood, and it is excellently planned.

When we reached the capital Khān-Bāliq, we found that the Qān was absent from it at that time, as he had gone out to fight his cousin Fīrūz, who had rebelled against him in the district of Qarāqorum and Bish-Bāligh in Cathay.[19] The distance between these places and the capital is a three months' journey through cultivated districts. After his departure the majority of his amīrs threw off their allegiance to him and agreed to depose him because he had departed from the precepts of the *Yasāq*, that is, the precepts which were laid down by their ancestor Jinkīz (Chingiz) Khān, who laid waste the lands of Islam. They went over to his rebel nephew and wrote to the Qān to the effect that he should abdicate and retain the city of Khansā as an appanage. He refused to do so, fought them, and was defeated and killed.

It was a few days after our arrival at his capital that the news of this was received. The city was decorated; trumpets, bugles and drums were played, and games and entertainments held for the space of a month. Thereafter the slain Qān was brought, with about a hundred other slain, his cousins, relatives, and intimates. A great *nā'ūs*, that is, a subterranean chamber, was dug for him and richly furnished. The Qān was laid in it with his weapons, and all the gold and silver plate from his palace was deposited in it with him. With him also were put four slave-girls and six of the principal mamlūks, who carried drinking vessels, then the door of the chamber was built up and the whole thing covered over with earth until it reached the size of a large mound. After that they brought four horses and drove them about the Qān's grave until they stopped from exhaustion, then they set up a wooden erection over the grave and suspended the horses on it, having first driven a piece of wood through each horse from tail to mouth. The abovementioned relatives of the Qān were also placed in subterranean chambers along with their weapons and house utensils, and they impaled over the tombs of the principal members, of whom there were ten, three horses each, and over the tombs of the rest one horse each.

This day was observed as a solemn holiday, and not one person was absent from the ceremony, men or women, Muslim or heathen. They were all dressed in mourning robes, which are white capes in the case of the infidels and long white garments in the case of the Muslims. The Qān's khātūns and courtiers lived in tents near his grave for forty days, some even more than that, up to a year; and a bazaar was established there to supply the food and other things which they required. Such practices as these are observed, so far as I can record, by no other people in these days. The heathen Indians and Chinese, on the other hand, burn their dead; other people do indeed bury the dead man, but they do not put anyone in with him. However, I have been told by trust-worthy persons in the Negrolands that the heathen there, when their king died, used to make a *nā'ūs* for him and put in with him some of his courtiers and servants, along with thirty of the sons and daughters of their principal families, first breaking their hands and feet, and they put in drinking vessels along with them.

When the Qān was slain, as we have related, and his nephew Fīrūz obtained the sovereign power, he chose to make his capital at the city of Qarāqorum, on account of its proximity to the territories of his cousins, the kings of Turkistan and Transoxania. Afterwards several of the amīrs who were not present when the Qān was killed revolted against him and intercepted communications and the disorders grew to serious proportions.

When the revolt broke out and the flames of disorder were kindled, Shaykh Burhān ad-Dīn and others advised me to return to Southern China before the disturbances became chronic. They presented themselves with me to the representatives of Sultan Fīrūz, who sent three of his suite to escort me and wrote orders for my treatment as a guest on the journey. We travelled down the river to Khansā, and thence to Qānjanfū and Zaytūn, and on reaching the last I found the junks ready to sail for India. Amongst them was a junk belonging to al-Malik az-

Zāhir, the ruler of Jawa Sumatra, the crew of which were Muslims. His agent knew me and was delighted at my arrival. We sailed with fair winds."

NOTES

1) Cf. Gibb (1974: 139f). Ibn Jubair's book of his travels was translated into English by R.J.C. Broadhurst, published in London in 1952.
2) Yüan was the dynastic title taken by the Mongols during their rule of China.
3) Ibn Baṭṭūṭa's complete travels in China and India were translated into German and annotated by H. von Mzik. It appeared under the title: *Die Reise der Arabers Ibn Batuta durch Indien und China,* Hamburg, 1911.
4) Cf. Gibb's introduction to Ibn Baṭṭūṭa's book (1929:9).
5) One of the earliest abridged texts was translated by Samuel Lee, entitled *The Travels of Ibn Batuta,* published in London, 1829. A few years later, a complete text was discovered in Algeria and translated into French by Charles Defremery & B.R. Sanguinetti entitled *Les Voyages d'Ibn Batouta,* in 4 vols., Paris 1853 & c. Professor Gibb's edition and translation of Ibn Battuta's book into English is the most important and comprehensive work so far with its long introduction and extensive notes and critical views on the travels. The first volume appeared in 1929. Another volume was published in London, 1958. It is interesting to note that Marco Polo also dictated his Travels to a scribe.
6) Liang (1873–1929) is a Chinese scholar, journalist, and political figure in modern Chinese history.
7) Zaytūn in Arabic literally means "olives". Here it is identified as Ts'wan-chow.
8) The *bališt* or *bališ,* originally an ingot of metal weighing about 4½ lbs., was the currency of the steppes at the beginning of the 13th century. The word was probably brought into China by the Mongols.
9) Cathay or *Khitāy* in Arabic, a term used first by the Muslims and taken from them by European travellers and missionaries be-

tween the 13th to 16th centuries, denoted the northern part of China, in contrast to Ṣīn or China proper in the South. The name was derived from the Kitay or Khitay Turks, who founded the Liao dynasty which reigned at Peking during the 10th and 11th centuries. The name Ṣīn (China in Arabic) appears to be derived from the Ts'in dynasty (255–209 B.C.)

10) Sijilmāsa was in the neighbourhood of Tafilelt, in Southern Morocco.

11) Douane, or Arabic Dīwān, was at one and the same time custom-house, waterhouse, lodging house and bourse for foreign merchants, and its controller was one of the principal officers of the realm.

12) The Arabic and Persian writers, like Marco Polo in his travels to China in the 13th century, conventionally use the term Qān or Qā'ān for the Great Khan of the Mongols.

13) Ṣīn Kalān is an Arabicized form of the Persian Chin-Kalan, for Sanskrit Mahacina = Great China, which is also the meaning of the Arabic name Sin al-Sin.

14) Identified as Fuchow.

15) Qurtay appears to be a contraction of Qarātāy, a common Turkish title for "commander". Towa or Tuwi is a Turkish title for "king".

16) The lines may be rendered as follows:

My heart given up to emotion,
Was overwhelmed in waves like the ocean's;
But betaking me to my devotions,
My trouble were gone from me!

17) Peking was called by the Mongols Khān Bāliq "city of the Khan". The word Khāniqū is an adjective "(city) of the Khan".

18) Probably a corrupted form of the Persian *padshah* "king".

19) The reigning Emperor was Togon Timur who reigned between 1333–71. Qarāqorum is the first capital of the Mongols. Bishbāliq was situated on or near the present Guchen, to the east of Urumtsi in Dzungaria.

REFERENCES

Broomhall, Marshall. 1910. *Islam in China: A Neglected Problem.* London: Morgan & Scott Ltd. See especially chapters I, II (*China and the Arabs*), III (*Some Early Travellers*), and VIII (*The Yunnan Rebellions*).

Eberhard, Wolfram. 1977. *A History of China.* 4th edn. Berkeley & Los Angeles: University of California Press. See Chapter Ten, especially pp. 237–243.

Gibb, H.A.R. 1974. *Arabic Literature: An Introduction.* London, Oxford & New York: Oxford University Press. See especially Chapters 6.4 & 7.2.

Hsu, Immanuel C. Y. 1970. *The Rise of Modern China.* Published by Oxford University Press. Taiwan edn. Taipei: Rainbow-Bridge Book Co. Cf. Chapter One. especially pp. 6–7.

Ibn Baṭṭūṭa. 1929. *Travels in Asia and Africa* (1325–1354). Translated and selected by H.A.R. Gibb, with an Introduction and Notes. The Broadway Travellers series. London: George Routledge & Son, Ltd.

Levenson, Joseph R. 1970. *Liang Ch'i-Ch'ao and the Mind of Modern China.* 2nd printing. Taipei: Rainbow-Bridge Book Co., See Part Two, Chapter IV.

Marco Polo. 1980. *The Travels of Marco Polo.* Translated and with Introduction by Ronald Latham. Penguin Classics. Reprint of 1958 edn. Harmondsworth, Middlesex, England: Penguin Books Ltd. See the translator Introduction, especially pp. 7 ff.

Renaudot Eusebius. 1733. *"Ancient accounts of India and China by Two Muhammadan Travellers".* Translated from the Arabic. London.

Zwemer, S.M. 1934. *'The fourth religion of China",* in the *Muslim World* (Hartford, Connecticut) 24.1–12.

Classified Select Bibliography

CLASSIFIED SELECT BIBLIOGRAPHY

1.0 GENERAL BACKGROUND OF THE ARAB & MUSLIM WORLD

1.1 The Qur'ān

The Holy Qur'ān (Koran). The meanings of the Holy Book have been translated fully or in parts into many languages. The outstanding translations in English are those by Arthur J. Arberry (London: Cambridge University Press), Muhammad (Marmaduke) Pickthall (1930), G. Sale (London 1734), N.J. Dawood (A Penguin Class), J.M. Rodwell (London and Hertford, 1861), E.H. Palmer (Oxford, 1880, and reprinted in The World's Classics, vol. 328), and Abdullah Yusuf Ali (1934).

Balyon, J.M.B. 1961. *Modern Muslim Koran Interpretation, 1880–1960.* Leiden: E.J. Brill.

Bell, R. 1953. *Introduction to the Qur'ān* Edinburgh: Edinburgh University Press.

El-Chouémi, Moustafa. 1966. *Le Verbe dans le Coran: Racine et Formes.* Études Arabes et Islamiques, Série 3: Études et Documents, 6. Paris: Librairie C. Klincksieck.

Cragg, Kenneth. 1971. *The Event of the Qur'ān: Islam in its Scriptures.* London: George Allen & Unwin.

———. 1973. *The Mind of the Qur'ān: Chapters in Reflection.* London: George Allen & Unwin.

Goldziher, Ignaz. 1926. *Die Richtungen der islamischen Koranauslegung.* Leiden.

Izutsu, Toshihiko. 1959. *The Structure of the Ethical Terms in the Koran: A Study in Semantics.* Tokyo: Keio Institute of Philological Studies.

———. 1964. *God and Man in the Koran. Semantics of the Koranic*

Weltanschauung. Tokyo: Keio Institute of Cultural and Linguistic Studies.

———. 1965. *The Concept of Belief in Islamic Theology: A Semantic Analysis of Īmān and Islam.* Tokyo: Keio Institute of Cultural and Linguistic Studies.

———. 1966. *Ethico-Religious Concepts in the Qur'ān.* McGill Islamic Studies, I. Montreal: McGill University Press.

Jeffery, Arthur. 1938. *The Foreign Vocabulary of the Qur'ān.* Gaekwad's Oriental Series, 79. Baroda: Oriental Institute. Reprinted.

Kramers, J.H. 1940. *De Taal van den Koran.* Leiden: E.J. Brill.

Makino, Shinya. 1970. *Creation and Termination: A Semantic Study of the Structure of the Qur'ānic World View.* Studies in the Humanities and Social Relations. Tokyo: Keio Institute of Cultural and Linguistic Studies.

Margoliouth, D.S. 1939. *"Some additions to Professor Jeffery's (Foreign Vocabulary of the Qur'ān)"*, in *Journal of the Royal Asiatic Society* (London) 53–61.

Müller, Friedrun R. 1969. *Untersuchungen zur Reimprosa im Koran.* Ph.D. diss., Eberhard-Karls-Universität zu Tübingen. Bonner Orientalische Studien., N.S. 20. Bonn: Orientalisches Seminar der Universität, Tübingen.

Nöldeke, Theodor. 1909–38. *Geschichte des Qoran* (Qur'ān). 3 vols. 2nd edn. Leipzig.

Roberts, R. 1925. *The Social Laws of the Qur'ān.* London.

Sabbagh, T. 1943. *La Metaphore dans le Coran.* Paris: Adrien-Maisonneuve.

Sarwar, Alhaj G. 1965. *Philosophy of the Qur'ān.* Lahore: Muhammad Ashraf.

Seale, Morris S. 1979. *Qur'ān and Bible: Studies in Interpretation and Dialogue.* London: Croom Helm Ltd.

Stanton, H.U.W. 1919. *The Teaching of the Qur'ān.* London: S.P.C.K.

1.2 The Traditions & Islamic Law

Ali, M. Muhammad. n.d. *A Manual of Ḥadīth.* Lahore.

Ali, Syed Ameer. 1880. *Personal Law of the Muhammadans.* London.

Anderson, J.N.D. 1959. *Islamic Law in the Modern World.* New York

University Press.

Andrae, Tor. 1918. *Die Person Muhammeds in Lehre und Glauben seiner Gemeinde.* Uppsala & Stockholm. Translated into English under the title *Mohammed: The Man and His Faith,* London, 1936.

Al-Bukhārī. 1903–14. *Les Traditions islamiques.* Translated into French by O. Houdas and W. Marcais. Paris. A complete English translation is now available.

Fyzee, A.A.A. 1949. *Outlines of Muhammadan Law.* London: Oxford University Press.

Grimme, Hubert. 1892–5. *Mohammed.* Münster: Aschendorff.

Guillaume, Alfred 1924. *The Traditions of Islam.* Oxford.

———. 1960. *New Light on the Life of Muhammad.* Manchester: Manchester University Press.

Hamidullah, Muhammad. 1959. *Le Prophête de l'Islam.* Paris: Librairie Philosophique J. Vrin.

Hebbo, Ahmad Irhayem. 1970. *Die Fremdwörter in der Arabischen Propheten-biographie des Ibn Hischam.* Ph. D. diss., Ruprecht-Karl-Universitat zu Heidelberg.

Ibrahim, Ezzedin & Denys Johnson-Davies, translators. 1976. *Al-Nawawī's Forty Ḥadīth.* Damascus: The Holy Koran Publishing House.

Ibn Taimiyya. 1939. *Contributions à une Étude de la Méthodologie canonique.* Translated into French by H. Laoust. Cairo.

Lammens, Henri 1929. *Islam: Beliefs and Institutions.* Translated by E. Denison Ross. London: Methuen & Co. Ltd.

Macdonald, D.B. 1903. *Development of Muslim Theology, Jurisprudence, and Constitutional Theory.* London & New York: Charles Scribner's Sons.

Margoliouth, David Samuel. 1905. *Mohammad and the Rise of Islam.* 3rd edn. Heroes of the Nations' Series. London & New York: Putnam.

Muslim. 1966. *Ṣaḥīḥ Muslim.* Translated into English by M. Abdul Hamid Siddiqui. Lahore: Ashraf Kashmiri Bazar. Reprinted, 1973.

Nadvi, Abul Hasan Ali. 1974. *The Four Pillars of Islam.* Lucknow: Academy.

Rodinson, Maxime. 1977. *Mohammed.* Reprint of 1971 edn. Hammondsworth, Middlesex, England: Penguin Books Ltd. Translated from the French original *Mohamet,* Paris: Club français du livre, 1961.

Schacht, Joseph 1950. *The Origins of Muhammadan Jurisprudence.* Oxford: Clarendon Press.

———. 1964. *An Introduction to Islamic Law.* Oxford; Clarendon Press.

Sprenger, A. 1861–65. *Das Leben und die Lehre des Mohammad,* 3 vols. Berlin.

Watt, W. Montgomery. 1953. *Muhammed at Mecca.* Oxford: Clarendon Press.

———. 1956. *Muhammed at Medina.* Oxford: Clarendon Press.

Wellhausen, Julius., Translator. 1882. *Muhammed in Medina.* An abridged translation of *Kitāb al-Maghāzī,* by al-Wāqidī. Berlin: G. Reimer.

1.3 Basic Bibliographies

Arberry, Arthur John. 1943. *British Orientalists.* London: William Collins.

Barthold, V.–V. 1947. *La Découverte de l'Asie: Histoire de l'orientalisme en Europe et en Russie.* Translated into French by B. Nikitine. Paris: Payot.

Benfey, Theodor. 1869. *Geschichte der Sprachwissenschaft und Orientalischen Philologie in Deutschland.* Munich: Gottafschen.

Chamieh, Jebran, ed. 1979. *Sa'udi Arabia Yearbook 1979/1980.* Beirut, Riyad & London: The Research & Publishing House.

Dugat, Gustave. 1868–70. *Histoire des orientalistes de l'Europe du XIIe au XIXe siècle,* 2 vols. Paris: Adrien Maisonneuve.

Europa Publications Limited. 1980. *The Middle East and North Africa, 1980–81.* 27th edn. London: Europa Publications Ltd.

Fück, Johann. 1955. *Die Arabischen Studien in Europa bis in den Anfang des 20 Jahrhunderts.* Leipzig: Otto Harrassowitz.

Gafurov, B.G. & U.V. Gankovsky. 1968. *Fifty Years of Soviet Oriental Studies.* USSR Academy of Sciences, Institute of the Peoples of Asia. Moscow: Nauka Publishing House.

Gérard, René. 1963. *L'Orient et la pensée romantique allemande.* Paris: Didier.

Hopwood, Derek & Diana Grimwood-Jones, eds. 1972. *Middle East and*

Islam. A Bibliographical Introduction. Middle East Libraries Committee. Bibliotheca Asiatica, 9. Zug, Switzerland: Inter Documentation Company A.G.

Mohl, Jules. 1879–80. *Vingt-sept Ans d'histoire des études orientales: Rapports fait à la Société asiatique de Paris de 1840 à 1867,* 2 vols. Paris: Reinwald.

Monroe, James T. 1970. *Islam and the Arabs in Spanish Scholarship.* Leiden: E.J. Brill.

Morrison, S.A. 1954. *Middle East Survey.* London: SCM Press.

Paret, Rudi. 1966. *Arabistik und Islamkunde im Deutschen Universitäten.* Wiesbaden: Franz Steiner.

Pearson, J.D. 1958–. *Index Islamicus* (in progress). London: Mansell Publishing Ltd.

Schwab, Raymond. 1950. *La Renaissance orientale.* Paris: Payot.

Sezgin, Fuat. 1967–. *Geschichte Arabischen Schrifttums,* 6 vols. Further volumes, in progress. Leiden: E.J. Brill.

Smith, Pamela Ann, ed. 1980. *The Middle East Yearbook.* London: IC Magazine Ltd.

1.4 History, Society & Culture

'Abduh, Muḥammad. 1925. *Risālat al-Tawḥīd.* Translated into French by B. Michel. Paris. English translations are also available.

Abramovich, Z. & I. Guelfat. 1944. *Arab Economics* (in Hebrew). Tel Aviv.

Abu-Lughod, Ibrahim. 1963. *Arab Rediscovery of Europe: A Study in Cultural Encounters.* Princeton, N.J.: Princeton University Press.

Abū Yūsuf Ya'qūb. 1921. *Le Livre de l'Impôt Foncier.* Translated from the Arabic into French by E. Fagnan. Paris.

Adams, C.C. 1933. *Islam and Modernism in Egypt.* London: Oxford University Press.

Affifi, A.E. 1939. *The Mystical Philosophy of Muḥyid Dīn ibnul 'Arabī.* Cambridge.

Ahmad, Aziz. 1967. *Islamic Modernism in India and Pakistan, 1857–1964.* Oxford.

Alderson, A.D. 1956. *The Structure of the Ottoman Dynasty.* Oxford.

Ali, Syed Ameer. 1922. *The Spirit of Islam.* Revised edn. London.

Amari, M. 1854–72. *Storia degli Musulmani di Sicilia,* 3 vols. Florence. New edn., by Carl A. Nallino, Catania, 1933–39.

Ammar, Hamed. 1954. *Growing up in an Egyptian Village.* London: Routledge & Kegan Paul, Ltd.

Andrae, Tor. 1926. *Der Ursprung des Islams und das Christentum.* Uppsala & Stockholm: Almqvist & Wiksell. French translation, *Les Origines de l'Islam et le Christianisme.* Paris: Adrien-Maisonneuve, 1955.

Antonius, George. 1938. *The Arab Awakening.* London. Also, New York, 1946. Beirut, 1955.

'Arabfaqīh. 1897–9. *Conquête de l'Abyssinie.* Translated into French by R. Basset. Paris.

Arberry, Arthur John. 1935. *The Mawáqif of al-Niffari.* London.

———. 1950. *Sufism.* London.

———. 1955. *Revelation and Reason in Islam.* London: George Allen & Unwin.

———. 1964. *Aspects of Islamic Civilization as Depicted in the Original Texts.* London: George Allen & Unwin.

———. & R. Landau, eds. 1943. *Islam-To-Day.* London.

Arnold, Sir Thomas W. 1913. *The Preaching of Islam.* 2nd edn. London.

———. 1924. *The Caliphate.* Oxford.

———, & A. Guillaume. 1931. *The Legacy of Islam.* Oxford.

Ashkenazi, Tovia. 1938. *Tribus semi-nomades de la Palestine du Nord.* Paris: Geuthner.

Atiye, A.S. 1938. *The Crusade in the Late Middle Ages.* London.

Ayrout, H.H. 1945. *The Fellaheen.* Translated by Hilary Wayment. Cairo: R. Shindler.

Baer, Gabriel. 1964. *Population and Society in the Arab East.* Translated by Hanna Szoke. New York: Frederick A. Praeger.

Al-Baghdādī. 1920. *Moslems Sects and Schisms.* Translated by K. Seeley. Columbia.

Al-Balādhurī. 1916–24. *The Origins of the Islamic State.* Translated into English from the Arabic by Philip K. Hitti and F.C. Murgotten. New York.

Baldensperger, Philip J. 1900. *Women in the East.* London: Palestine Exploration Fund Quarterly Statement.

Barthold, V.W. 1911. *The Geographical and Historical Study of the*

East (in Russian). St. Petersburg. Reprinted, Leningrad, 1925. German translation, 1913.

Barthold, W. 1934. *Mussulman Culture.* Calcutta.

Becker, C.H. 1924–32. *Islamstudien,* 2 vols. Leipzig.

Behrmann, R.A. 1932. *The Mahdi of Allah.* London.

Bell, Gertrude. 1907. *Syria: The Desert and the Sown.* London.

Bell, R. 1926. *The Origin of Islam in its Christian Environment.* London.

Berger, Morroe. 1962. *The Arab World Today.* New York: Doubleday Anchor Books.

Birge, J.K. 1937. *The Bektashi Order of Dervishes.* London.

Al-Bīrūnī. 1879. *The Chronology of Ancient Nations.* Translated by E. Sachau. London.

———. 1888. *Al-Bīrūnī's India,* 2 vols. Translated into English by C.E. Sachau. London.

Bonne, Alfred 1945. *The Economic Development of the Middle East.* New York.

———. 1955. *State and Economics in the Middle East: A Society in Transition.* London: Routledge & Kegan Paul.

Bosworth, Clifford Edmund. 1967. *The Islamic Dynasties: A Chronological and Genealogical Handbook.* Edinburgh: The University Press. Revised edn., 1980.

Bravmann, Meir M. 1972. *The Spiritual Background of Early Islam: Studies in Ancient Arab Concepts.* Leiden: E.J. Brill.

Brocklemann, Carl, ed. 1948. *History of the Islamic Peoples.* Translated by Joel Carmichael & Moshe Perlmann. London & Henley: Routledge & Kegan Paul. Reprinted, 1980.

Burckhardt, T. 1960. *Fes: Stadt des Islam.* Olten.

———. 1972. *Moorish Culture in Spain.* Translated into English by A. Jaffa. London.

Caetani, Leone, Principe di Teano, Duca di Sermoneta. 1905–26. *Annali dell'Islam,* 10 vols. Milan.

———. 1911–14. *Studi di storia orientale,* vols. I & III. Milan.

———. 1912. *Chronographia Islamica.* Paris.

Calvert, A.F. 1905. *Moorish Remains in Spain.* London.

Chatila, Khaled. 1934. *Le mariage chez les musulmans en Syrie.* Paris: Geuthner.

Chehabe ed-Dine, S. 1960. *Géographie humaine de Beyrouth.* Beirut.

Chew, Samuel C. 1937. *The Crescent and the Rose: Islam and England During the Renaissance.* New York: Oxford University Press.

Christopher, John B. 1966. *Lebanon Yesterday and Today.* New York.

Cleland, W. 1936. *The Population Problem in Egypt.* Lancaster, Pa.

Clergé, M. 1934. *Le Caire. Etude de géographie urbaine et d'histoire économique.* Cairo.

Cohen, I. 1946. *The Zionist Movement.* New York.

Coon, Carleton S. 1952. *Caravan: The Story of the Middle East.* New York.

Cour, A. 1904. *L'Etablissement de la dynastie des cherifs au maroc et leur rivalité avec les Turcs de la Régence d'Alger, 1505–1830.* Algiers.

Cragg, Kenneth. 1968. *The Privilege of Man. A Theme in Judaism, Islam and Christianity.* London: The University of London Athlone Press.

———. 1969. *The House of Islam.* California: Dickenson Publishing Inc.

Cumming, H.H. 1938. *Franco-British in the Post-War Near East.* London.

Daghestani, Kazem. 1932. *Étude sociologique sur la famille musulmane contemporaine en Syrie.* Paris.

Daher, Adel. 1969. *Current Trends in Arab Intellectual Thought.* RAND study. RM–5979–FF, December, 1969.

Daniel, Norman. 1960. *Islam and the West: The Making of an Image.* Edinburgh: University Press.

———. 1975. *The Arabs and Medieval Europe.* London: Longmans, Green & Co.

Davis, H.M. 1947. *Constitutions, Electoral Laws, Treaties of States in the Near and Middle East.* Durham, N.C.

Department of Public Relations of the Armed Forces, Cairo, Egypt. 1955: *Gamal Abdel Nasser: Leader of the Revolution.* Cairo.

Depont, O. et X. Coppolani. 1897. *Les Confréries religieuses musulmanes.* Algiers.

Dermenghem, Emile. 1958. *Muhammad and the Islamic Tradition.* Translated by Jean M. Watt. London: Harbor & Brothers.

Diercks, G. 1882. *Die Araber im Mittelalter und ihr Einflüss auf die Cultur Europa's.* 2nd edn. Leipzig.

Dodwell, H.H. 1931. *The Founder of Modern Egypt*. Cambridge.

Donaldson, D.M. 1933. *The Shi'ite Religion*. London.

Dozy, R. 1932. *Histoire des Musulmans d'Espagne jusqu'à la conquête de l'Andalousie par les Almoravids, 711–1110*. New edn., prepared by E. Levi-Provençal. English translation, 1913, as *Spanish Islam*.

Faris, N.A. ,ed. 1944. *The Arab Heritage*. Princeton, N.J.: Princeton University Press.

Farrukh, Omar A. 1937. *Das Bild des Fruhislam in der arabische Dichtung*. Leipzig: A Pries.

Faure-Biquet, G. 1905. *Histoire de l'Afrique septentrionale sous la domination musulmane, 740 à 1835*. Paris.

Fawzi, Saad ed-Din. 1957. *The Labour Movement in the Sudan 1946–1955*. London.

Fournel, L. 1877–81. *Les Berbers*. Paris.

Fuller, A.H. 1961. *Buarij: Portrait of a Lebanese Muslim Village*. Cambridge, Mass.: Harvard University Press.

Fyzee, A.A.A. 1942. *A Shi'ite Creed*. London: Oxford University Press.

Al-Ghazālī (Al-Ghazzālī). 1909. *The Confessions of al-Ghazzālī*. Translated by C. Field. London.

Ghorbal, S. 1928. *The Beginnings of the Egyptian Question and the Rise of Mehemet Ali*. London.

Gibb, Hamilton A.R., ed. 1932. *Whither Islam?* London.

———. 1945. *Modern Trends in Islam*. Chicago: University of Chicago Press.

———. 1949. *Islam: A Historical Survey* (formerly entitled *Muhammedanism*). Oxford: Oxford University Press. Reprinted, 1978.

———. 1962. *Studies in the Civilization of Islam*. Edited by S.J. Shaw and W.K. Polk. Berton: Beacon Press.

———, & Harold Bowen. 1950. *Islamic Society and the West: Islamic Society in the Eighteenth Century*. London: Oxford University Press.

Glubb, John Bagot. 1963. *The Great Arab Conquests*. London, Melbourne & New York: Quartet Books. Reprinted, 1980.

Goeje, M.J. de. 1886. *Mémoire sur les Carmathes du Bahrain et les Fatimides*. Leiden: E.J. Brill.

Goitein, S.D. 1968. *Studies in Islamic History and Institutions*. Leiden: E.J. Brill.

Goldziher, Ignaz. 1884. *Die Zahiriten*. Leipzig.

———. 1888–90. *Muhammedanische Studien*, 2 vols. Halle. Reprinted, Hildesheim: G. Olm, 1961.

———. 1910. *Vorlesungen uber den Islam*. Heidelberg. 2nd edn., prepared by F. Babinger, 1925.

Granqvist, Hilma. 1931. *Marriage Conditions in a Palestinian Village*. Helsingfors: Societas Fennica.

Grousset, R. 1934 – 36. *Histoire des croisades et du régime franque a Jerusalem*, 3 vols. Paris.

Grünebaum, Gustave E. von. 1946. *Medieval Islam: A Study in Cultural Orientation*. Chicago: University of Chicago Press. 2nd edn., 1953.

———. 1951. *Muhammedan Festivals*. New York: Henry Schuman.

———. 1955. *Unity and Variety in Muslim Civilization*. Chicago & London: University of Chicago Press.

———. 1961. *Islam: Essays in the Nature of Growth of a Cultural Tradition*. London: Routledge & Kegan Paul.

———. 1962. *Modern Islam*. Los Angeles & Berkeley: University of California Press.

———. 1966. *'Problems of Muslim nationalism in social change"*, in *The Colonial Situation*, edited by J. Wallestein. New York: John Wiley.

Gulick, John. 1953. *The Lebanese Village: An Introduction*, in *American Anthropologist*, vol. 55 (August).

———. 1955. *Social Structure and Culture Change in a Lebanese Village*. Viking Fund Publication in Anthropology, no. 21. New York.

Halpern, M. 1963. *The Politics of Social Change in the Middle East and North Africa*. Princeton, N.J.: Princeton University Press.

Hamadi, Sania. 1960. *Temperament and Character of the Arabs*. New York: Twayne Publishers.

Hamid, Khawaja A. 1940. *'The conception of man in Islam"*, in *Islamic Culture* (Heyderabad) 19.133–66.

Hammar-Purgstall, J. von. 1827–35. *Geschichte des osmanischen Reiches*, 10 vols. Pest. 2nd edn., 4 vols., 1840. French edn. Paris, 1844.

Hanna, P.L. 1942. *British Policy in Palestine*. Washington.

Hasluck, F.W. 1929. *Christianity and Islam under the Sultans*, 2 vols.

Oxford.

Hitti, Philip K. 1943. *The Arabs*. Reprinted, 1946. Princeton; N.J.: Princeton University Press.

———. 1953. *History of the Arabs*. 5th edn. London.

Hodgson, M.G.S. 1955. *The Order of Assassins*. The Hague.

Hoenerbach, Wilhelm. 1965. *Spanisch-Islamische Urkunden aus der Zeit der Nasriden und Moriscos*. Bonner Orientalistische Studien, N.S. 15. Bonn: Selbstverlag des Orientalischen Seminars der Universität Bonn.

Hogben, S.J. 1929. *The Muhammadan Emirates of Nigeria*. Oxford.

Holt, P.M. 1965. *The Study of Modern Arab History*. London: School of Oriental and African Studies.

———. Anne Lambton & B. Lewis, eds. 1970. *The Cambridge History of Islam*. Cambridge: Cambridge University Press.

Hourani, Albert H. 1946. *Syria and Lebanon*. London: Oxford University Press.

———. 1947. *Minorities in the Arab World*. London: Oxford University Press.

———. 1961. *A Vision of History: Near Eastern and Other Essays*. Beirut: Khayat's.

———. 1962. *Arab Thought in the Liberal Age* (1789–1838). Oxford. Reprinted, 1967.

Huart, Clément. 1901. *Histoire de Baghdad depuis la domination des Khans mongols jusqu'au massacre des Mamlouks*. Paris.

———. 1912–13. *Histoire des Arabes*, 2 vols. Paris.

Huber, R. 1943. *Arabisches Wirtschaftsleben*. Heidelberg.

Hunter, W.W., 1945. *The Indian Mussalmans*. Calcutta.

Hurgronje, Christian Snouck. 1906. *The Achehnese*, 2 vols. Leiden: E.J. Brill.

———. 1923–27. *Verspreide Geschriften*, 6 vols. Bonn.

———. 1931. *Mekka in the Latter Part of the 19th Century* (English translation). London. Reprinted, Leiden: E.J. Brill.

El-Ibiani, E. 1919. *Commentaire du Statut Personnel Musulman*. Cairo.

Ibn Hudhail. 1924. *La Parure des Cavaliers*. Translated into French by L. Mercier. Paris.

Ibn Khaldūn. 1852. *Histoire des Berbères*, 4 vols. Translated into French by MacGuckin de Slane. Algiers. Revised edn., Paris, 1925–56.

———. 1958. *The Muqaddimah: An Introduction to History*.

Translated into English by Franz Rosenthal. New York: Pantheon Books.

———. 1958. *Prolegomènes d'Ebn Khaldoun.* Notices et Extraits des manuscrits de la Bibliothèque Impériale. Vol. 8. Edited by E. Quatremère. Paris: Académie des Inscriptions et Belles-Lettres.

Ibn Munqidh, Usāma. 1929. *An Arab-Syrian Gentleman.* Translated by Philip K. Hitti. New York.

Ibn Sa'īd. 1953. *The Pennants.* Translated by A.J. Arberry. Cambridge.

Imamuddin, S.M. 1965. *Some Aspects of Socio-Economic and Cultural History of Muslim Spain.* Leiden: E.J. Brill.

Iqbal, Sir Muhammad. 1920. *The Secrets of the Self.* Translated by R.A. Nicholson. London.

———. 1958. *Reconstruction of Religious Thought in Islam.* Lahore: Muhammad Ashraf. Also published by Oxford University Press, London, 2nd edn 1934.

Ireland, P.W., ed. 1942. *The Near East: Problems and Prospects.* Chicago.

Issawi, Charles. 1947. *Egypt: An Economic and Social Analysis.* London: Oxford University Press for the Royal Institute of International Affairs.

Al-Jabartī, Abdul-Raḥmān. 1838. *Journal d'Abdurrahman Gabarti.* Translated by A. Cardin. Paris.

Jabre, F. 1958. *La notion de la certitude selon Ghazali.* Paris.

Jackh, E. 1944. *The Rising Crescent.* New York.

Jacob, G. 1897. *Studien in arabischen Dichtern.* Heft iii, *Altarabisches Beduinen-leben nach den Quellen geschildert.* Berlin.

Jaussen, P. Antonin le. 1908. *Coutumes des arabes au pays de Moab.* Paris: Lecoffre.

———. 1927. *Coutumes palestiniennes.* Vol. I: *Naplouse et son district.* Paris: Geuthner.

———, & Savignac. 1914. *Coutumes des Fuqara.* Paris: Geuthner.

Jeffery, Arthur. 1962. *A Reader on Islam.* The Hague: Mouton.

Jovelet, L. 1933. *L'Evolution sociale et politique des "pays arabes", 1930–33,* in *Revue des études islamiques* (Paris).

Jung, E. 1924–25. *La Revolte arabe,* 2 vols., Paris.

———. 1927. *L'Islam et l'Asie devant l'imperialisme.* Paris.

Al-Jurjānī. 1959. *Geheimnisse der Wortkunst.* Translated by H. Ritter. Wiesbaden.

Keddie, Nikki R. 1972. *Scholars, Saints and Sufis. Muslim Religious Institutions in the Middle East since 950 A.D.* Berkeley, Los Angeles & London: University of California Press.

Klein, F.A. 1883. *Mitteilungen über Leben, Sitten und Gebräuche der Fellachen in Palästina*, in *Zeitschrift des Deutschen Palästina Vereins.*

Kohn, H. 1929. *A History of Nationalism in the East.* London.

———. 1932. *Nationalism and Imperialism in the Hither East.* London.

———. 1936. *Western Civilization in the Near East.* New York.

Kremer, A. von. 1868. *Geschichte der herrschenden Ideen des Islams.* Leipzig.

———. 1873. *Culturgeschichtliche Streifzuge auf dem Gebiete des Islams.* Leipzig. Translated into English by S.K. Buksh as *Contributions to the History of Islamic Civilization,* vol. I. Calcutta, 1905. Reprinted, 1929.

———. 1874–77. *Culturgeschichte des Islams unter den Chalifen,* 2 vols. Vienna. Vol. I, translated into English by S. Khuda Buksh as *The Orient under the Caliphs.* Calcutta, 1920. Vol II, translated by S.K. Buksh in *Studies: Indian and Islamic,* London, 1927.

Kritzeck, James. 1964. *Peter the Venerable and Islam.* Princeton, N.J.: Princeton University Press.

Laffin, John. 1976. *The Arab Mind: A Need for Understanding.* New York: Taplinger Publishing Co. Also published in London by Cassell & Co. Ltd., 1975, 1977 and 1978.

Lammens, Henri. 1914. *Le Berceau de l'islam,* vol. I. Rome.

———. 1930. *Études sur le siécle des Omayyades.* Beirut.

Lane, Edward William. 1883. *Arabian Society in the Middle Ages.* Edited by Stanley Lane-Poole, London.

Lane-Poole, Stanley. 1894. *The Mohammadan Dynasties.* London.

———. 1899. *The Moors in Spain.* New York.

———. 1901. *Egypt in the Middle Ages.* London. Reprinted, 1925.

Lea, H.C. 1901. *The Moriscos of Spain, their Conversion and Expulsion.* Philadelphia.

Letourneau, R. 1950. *L'islam contemporain.* Paris.

Levi-Provençal, E. 1932. *L'Espagne musulmane au Xe siécle, institutions et vie sociale.* Paris.

———. 1938. *La Civilization arabe en Espagne.* Cairo.

Levy, R. 1931–33. *An Introduction to the Sociology of Islam,* 2 vols. London.

———. 1958. *The Social Structure of Islam.* Cambridge.

Lewicki, T. 1974. *Arabic External Sources for the History of Africa South of the Sahara.* London.

Lewis, Bernard. 1950. *The Arabs in History.* London. Reprinted several times.

———. 1967. *The Assassins.* London.

———, & P.M. Holt, eds. 1962. *Historians of the Middle East.* London: Oxford University Press.

Lichtenstadter, Ilse. 1935. *Women in the Aiyām al-'Arab.* London.

———. 1958. *Islam and the Modern Age.* New York: Bookman Associates.

Liebesny, H.S. 1943. *The Government of French North Africa.* Philadelphia.

Lutfiyya, Abdulla M. 1966. *Baytin: A Jordanian Village.* The Hague: Mouton & Co.

———, & Charles W. Churchill, eds. 1970. *Readings in Arab Middle Eastern Societies and Cultures.* The Hague & Paris: Mouton.

Macdonald, D.B. 1909. *Religious Attitude in Islam.* Chicago.

Macmichael, H.A. 1922. *A History of the Arabs in the Sudan.* London.

Al-Maqqarī. 1840. *The History of the Mohammedan Dynasties in Spain.* Translated by Pascual de Gayzangos. London.

Margoliouth, D.S. 1914. *The Early Development of Mohammedanism.* London.

Masse, Henri. 1938. *Islam.* Translated by Halide Edib. New York: G.P. Putnam's Sons.

Massignon, Louis. 1922. *Al-Ḥallāj: Martyr mystique de l'Islam,* 2 vols. Paris.

———. 1922. *La Passion d'al-Hosayn ibn Mansour al-Ḥallāj.* Paris: Paul Geuthner.

———. 1927. *L'Islam et la Politique Contemporaine.* Paris.

———. 1955. *Annuaire du Monde Musulman.* Paris.

Masumi, S.H. 1963. *'The concept of society in Islam",* in *Journal of the Pakistan Philosophical Society* 7/4. 42–50.

McCarthy, R.J. 1953. *The Theology of al-Ash'ari.* Beirut.

Meaken, Budget. 1899. *The Moorish Empire.* London.

Metlitzki, Dorothee. 1977. *The Matter of Araby in Medieval England.* New Haven, Conn.: Yale University Press.

Mez, Adam. 1922. *Die Renaissance des Islams.* Heidelberg. Also translated into English (London) and Arabic (Cairo).

Miller, W. 1923. *The Ottoman Empire and its Successors, 1801–1927.* Cambridge. Reprinted, 1936.

Miller, W.M. 1931. *Bahaism: Its Origin, History, Teachings.* New York.

Monroe, E. 1938. *The Mediterranean in Politics.* London.

Morgan, Kenneth W., ed. 1958. *Islam. The Straight Path.* New York: Ronald Press Co.

Muir, Sir William. 1896. *The Mameluke or Slave Dynasty of Egypt.* London.

Muller, A. 1885–87. *Der Islam im Morgen- und Abendland,* 2 vols. Berlin.

Murray, G.W. 1935. *Sons of Ishmael: A Study of the Egyptian Bedouin.* London: George Routledge.

Nallino, Carl A. 1939–44. *Raccolta di scritti editi e inediti,* 5 vols. Rome.

Nasr, S.H. 1967. *Ideals and Realities of Islam.* London.

———. 1968. *The Encounter of Man and Nature, the Spiritual Crises of Modern Man.* London.

Nathan, R., O. Gass & D. Creamer. 1946. *Palestine: Problem and Promise.* Washington, D.C.

Neilsen, D., ed. 1927. *Handbuch der altarabischen Altertumskunde,* vol. I. Copenhagen, Leipzig & Paris.

Nicholson, Reynold A. 1921. *Studies in Islamic Mysticism.* Cambridge.

———. 1923. *The Idea of Personality in Sufism.* Cambridge.

Nöldeke, Theodor. 1879. *Geschichte der Perser unde Araber zur Zeit der Sasaniden.* Leiden: E.J. Brill.

Nuseibeh, Hazem Zeki. 1959. *The Ideas of Arab Nationalism.* Ithaca, New York: Cornell University Press.

O'Leary, De Lacy 1927. *Arabia before Muhammad.* London.

Ostrorog, L. 1927. *The Angora Reform.* London.

Patai, Raphael. 1951. *'Nomadism: Middle Eastern and Central Asian",* in *Southwestern Journal of Anthropology* (USA) 7.408ff.

———. 1952. *'The Middle East as a culture area",* in *The Middle*

East Journal (Washington, D.C.) 6.1–21.

———. 1953. *Israel between East and West: A Study in Human Relations*. Philadelphia.

———. 1954. *"Religion in Middle Eastern, Far Eastern, and Western culture"*, in *Southwestern Journal of Anthropology* (USA) 10.233–54 (Autumn).

———. 1973. *The Arab Mind.* New York: Charles Scribner's Sons.

Paton, A.A. 1870. *History of the Egyptian Revolution from the Period of the Mamelukes to the Death of Mohammed Ali,* 2 vols. London.

Peters, F.E. 1973. *Allah's Commonwealth.* New York.

Pirenne, Henri. 1937. *Mohamet et Charlemagne.* Paris, Alcan and Brussels: Nouvelle Société d'Editions, 2nd edn. English translation, *Mohammed and Charlemagne,* by Bernard Miall. New York: W.W. Norton & Co.

Poliak, A.N. 1946. *History of the Arabs* (in Hebrew). Jerusalem.

Polk, W.R. 1963. *The Opening of South Lebanon, 1788–1840.* Harvard.

Prothro, E. Terry 1961. *Child-Rearing in the Lebanon.* Cambridge, Mass.: Harvard University Press.

Puryear, V.J. 1941. *France and the Levant from the Bourbon Restoration to the Peace of Kutiah.* Berkeley.

Qureshi, I.H. 1961. *The Muslim Community of the Indo-Pakistan Sub-Continent.* The Hague.

Rabbath, E. 1937 *Unité Syrienne et le devenir Arabe.* Paris.

Rahman, Fazlur 1958. *Prophecy in Islam.* London.

Reinaud, J. 1828. *Monuments arabes, Persans et turcs du Cabinet de M. le duc de Blacas.* Paris: Imprimerie royale.

Roman, Jean. 1954. *Le Pèlerinage aux lieux saints de l'Islam.* Algiers: Baconnier.

Rondot, P. 1947. *Les institutions politiques du Liban.* Paris.

Rosenthal, Franz. 1952. *History of Muslim Historiography.* Leiden: E.J. Brill. Arabic translation is also available.

———. 1971. *The Herb: Hashish versus Medieval Muslim Society.* Leiden: E.J. Brill.

Rossi, E. 1944. *Documenti sull' origine e gli sviluppi della questione araba, 1875–1944.* Rome.

Al-Sa'dī. 1900. *Tārīkh al-Soudān* (histoire du Afrique). Translated into French by O. Houdas.

Salim, S.S. 1955. *Economic and Political Organization of Echchbaysh, a Marsh Village Community in South Iraq*. Ph. D. thesis, University of London.

Sanaullah, M.F. 1938. *The Decline of the Seljuqid Empire*. Calcutta.

Santillana, D. 1926–38. *Instituzioni di diritto musulmano malichita*, 2 vols. Rome.

Al-Sayyid, Afaf Lutfi. 1968. *Egypt and Cromer: A Study in Anglo-Egyptian Relations*. London.

Schacht, Joseph & C.E. Bosworth. 1974. *The Legacy of Islam*. Oxford: Clarendon Press.

Schuon, F. 1961. *Understanding Islam*. London.

Schuon, S. 1970. *Dimensions of Islam*. London.

Schwarz, Walter. 1959. *The Arabs in Israel*. London.

Scott, S.P. 1904. *History of the Moorish Empire in Europe*. 3 vols. New York.

Seligman, Brenda Z. 1923–25. *"Studies in Semitic Kinship"*, in *Bulletin of the School of Oriental Studies* (London) 3.169–270.

Seligman, Charles G. & Brenda Z. 1918. *The Kababish: A Sudan Arab Tribe*. Harvard African Studies, vol. 2. Cambridge, Mass.: Harvard University Press.

Shim' oni, J. 1947. *The Arabs of Palestine* (in Hebrew). Tel Aviv.

Shustery, Muhammad Abbas. 1938. *Outlines of Islamic Culture*, 2 vols. Bangalore.

Singh, A., ed. 1976. *Socio-Cultural Impact of Islam upon India*. Panjab University, Chandrigarh, India.

Smith, H.B. 1954. *'The Muslim doctrine of man"*, in *Muslim World* (Hartford, Connecticut) 44.202–48.

Smith, Margaret. 1928. *Rābi'a the Mystic*. Cambridge.

———————. 1935. *An Early Mystic of Baghdad*. London.

———————. 1944. *Al-Ghazālī the Mystic*. London.

Smith, W.C. 1946. *Modern Islam in India*. 2nd edn. London.

Smith, William Robertson. 1885. *Kinship and Marriage in Early Arabia*. Cambridge: Cambridge University Press. 2nd edn., London 1903. A new edn., edited by Stanley Cook, London, 1907. Reprinted, Oosterhout, Netherlands: Anthropological Publications, 1966.

———————. 1912. *Lectures and Essays*. Edited by J.S. Black and George Chrystal. London.

——————. 1927. *Lectures on the Religion of the Semites.* 3rd edn. revised by S.A. Cook, London.

Southern, R.W. 1962. *Western Views of Islam in the Middle Ages.* Cambridge, Mass.: Harvard University Press.

Speiser, E.A. 1947. *The United States and the Near East.* Cambridge, Mass: Harvard University Press.

Stevenson, W.B. 1907. *The Crusaders in the East.* Cambridge.

Strange, G.Le. 1890. *Palestine under the Moslems.* London.

———————. 1905. *Baghdad during the Abbasid Caliphate.* Oxford.

Stripling, G.W.F. 1942. *The Ottoman Turks and the Arabs, 1511–1574.* Urbana, Illinois.

Al-Suyūṭī. 1881. *History of the Caliphs.* Translated into English by H.S. Jarrett. Calcutta.

Sweet, Louise E. 1960. *Tell Toqaan. A Syrian Village.* Ann Arbor, Michigan: University of Michigan Press.

Al-Ṭabarī, 'Ali. 1922. *The Book of Religion and Empire.* Translated by Al Mingana. London.

Al-Ṭāhir, Abdul Jalīl. 1955. *Bedouins and Tribes in Arab Countries* (in Arabic). Cairo: The Arab League.

Tannous, Afif I. 1942. *"Group behavoiur in the village community of Lebanon",* in *American Journal of Sociology* 48.231–39.

———————. 1943 (1944). *'The Arab village community of the Middle East",* in *Annual Report of the Smithsonian Institution,* 524–43.

Temperley, H.W.V. 1936. *England and the Near East: The Crimea.* London.

Thayer, Philip W., ed. 1959. *Tensions in the Middle East.* Baltimore: The John Hopkins Press.

Thomas, B. 1937. *The Arabs.* London.

Titus, Murray. 1930. *Indian Islam.* London: Oxford University Press.

Topf, E. 1929. *Die Staatenbildung in den arabischen Teilen der Turkei seit dem Weltkriege.* Hamburg.

Toynbee, J.A. 1934–. *The Study of History.* Oxford. An abridged edn., New York & London, 1947.

Tritton, Arthur S. 1930. *The Caliphs and their non-Muslim Subjects.* Oxford.

Al-Turk, Yusuf. 1950. *Chroniques d'Egypt, 1789–1804.* Translated by G. Wiet. Cairo.

Van Ess, J. 1943. *Meet the Arab*. New York.

Volten, G. van. 1890. *De Opkomst der Abbasiden in Chorasan*. Leiden.

———. 1894. *Recherches sur la domination arabe, le chitisme et les croyances messianiques sous le califat des Omaiyades*. Amsterdam.

Warriner, Doreen. 1957. *Land Reform and Development in the Middle East*. Royal Institute of International Affairs. London: Oxford University Press.

Watt, W. Montgomery. 1948. *Free Will and Predestination in Early Islam*. London.

———. 1953. *The Faith and Practice of al-Ghazali*. London.

———. 1963. *Muslim Intellectual: A Study of Ghazali*. Chicago & Edinburgh.

Weil, Gotthold. 1848–51. *Geschichte der Chalifen*, 3 vols. Mannheim.

Wellhausen, Julius. 1897. *Reste arabischen Heidentums*. 2nd edn. Berlin.

———. 1902. *Das arabische Reich und sein Sturz*. Berlin. English translation as *The Arab Kingdom and its Fall*. Calcutta, 1927. Arabic translation is also available, Cairo.

Wensinck, A.J. 1932. *The Muslim Creed*. Cambridge.

———. 1940. *La Pensée de Ghazzali*. Paris.

Westermarck, Edward. 1914. *Marriage Ceremonies in Morocco*. London: Macmillan.

———. 1930. *Wit and Wisdom in Morocco*. London.

Weulersse, Jacques. 1946. *Paysans de Syrie et du Proche-Orient*. Paris: Gallimard.

Wiet, G. 1938. *L'Egypte de la conquête arabe à la conquête ottomane, 642–1517*. Histoire de la nation égyptienne, vol. IV, edited by G. Hanotaux. Paris.

Wilcken, G.A. 1884. *Het Matriarchat bij de oude Araberen*. Amsterdam. German translation. *Das Matriarchat . . .bei den alten Arabern*. Leipzig, 1884.

Winer, L. 1917. *Contributions Towards a History of Arabico-Gothic Culture*. New York.

Woodsmall, E. 1936. *Moslem Women Enter a New World*. New York.

Wüstenfeld, F. 1881. *Geschichte der Fatimidenchalifen*. Göttingen.

———. 1882. *Die Geschichtschreiber der Araber und ihre Werke*.

Göttingen.
El-Yan. 1926. *La condition Privée de la Femme dans le Droit de l'Islam.* Paris.
Yaukey, David. 1961. *Fertility Differences in a Modernizing Country (Lebanon).* Princeton, N.J.: Princeton University Press.
Zaidān, Jurjī. 1917. *Der letzte Mameluck.* Translated into German by M. Thilo. Barmen.
Al-Zamakhsharī. 1876. *Les Colliers d'Or.* Translated by C. Barbier de Meynard. Paris.
Zambaur, E. de. 1927. *Manuel de généalogie et de chronologie pour l'histoire de l'islam.* Hanover.
Zinkeisen, J. 1840–63. *Geschichte des osmanischen Reiches in Europa,* 7 vols. Gotha.
Zurayk, Constantine K. 1956. *The Meaning of the Disaster.* Translated by R. Bayly Winder. Beirut.
Zwemer, S.M. 1920. *A Moslem Seeker After God.* New York.

1.5 Islam in China

Andrews, G.F. 1921. *The Crescent in Northwest China.* London: China Inland Mission.
Bales, W.L. 1937. *Tso Tsung-t'ang: Soldier and Statesman of Old China.* Shanghai.
Barthold, W. 1928. *Turkestan down to the Time of the Mongol Invasion.* Translated by H.A.R. Gibb in the E.J.W. Gibb Memorial Series, New Series, vol. V. London.
———. 1935. *Ulug Beg und seine Zeit.* Leipzig.
Boulger, Demetrius C. 1878. *The Life of Yakoob Beg.* London: W.H. Allen & Co.
———. 1893. *A Short History of China.* London: W.H. Allen & Co.
Broomhall, Marshall. 1910. *Islam in China: A Neglected Problem.* London: Morgan & Scott, Ltd.
Chiang, Siang-tseh. 1951. *The Organization of the Nien Rebellion and the Struggle between the Nien and the Loyalists* (1851–68). Ph.D. diss., University of Washington. Published as *The Nien Rebellion,* Seattle, 1954.

Chu, Wen-Djang. 1966. *The Moslem Rebellion in Northwest China 1862–1878. A Study of Government Minority Policy.* Taipei: Rainbow-Bridge Book Co.

Dawson, Raymond, ed. 1964. *The Legacy of China.* Oxford: Clarendon Press. Reprinted, Taipei, Taiwan: Swang Yeh.

Grousset, R. 1938. *L'Empire des Steppes.* Paris.

———. 1941. *L'Empire mongol.* Paris.

Howarth, H.H. 1876–1927. *History of the Mongols.* London.

Hu, Huan-yung & Ch'eng-k'ang T'ung. 1943. *Books and Articles on Sinkiang in Western Languages.* National Central University, Chungking.

Ibn 'Arabshāh. 1658. *Histoire du grand Tamerlan.* Translated into French by P. Vattier. Paris.

Krause, F.A. 1935. *Cingis Han, Die Geschichte seines Lebens nach den chinesischen Reichannalen.* Heidelberger Akten der Portheim-Stiftung.

Mason, Isaac. 1938. *Notes on Chinese Mohammedan Literature.* (Reprinted from Journal of the North-China Branch of the Royal Asiatic Society, vol. LIV, 1925). Peking: Wen-tien ko Bookstore.

Ollone, H.M.G. d'. 1911. *Recherches sur les Musulmans Chinois.* Paris: Ernest Leroux.

Pickens, Claude L. Jr. 1950. *Annotated Bibliography of Literature on Islam in China.* Hankow, Hupeh: Society of Friends of the Moslems in China.

Shaffer, E.S. 1975. *Kublai Khan and the Fall of Jerusalem: The Mythological School in Biblical Criticism and Secular Literature, 1770–1880.* Cambridge: Cambridge University Press.

Thiersant, P. Dabry de. 1878. *Le Mahometisme en chine et dans le Turkestan Oriental,* 2 vols. Paris: Ernest Leroux.

Vladimirtzow, B. 1930. *The Life of Chingis Khan.* London.

———. 1934. *Social Organization of the Mongols* (in Russian). Leningrad.

Yüan, T.L. & H. Watanabe. 1962. *Classified Bibliography of Japanese Books and Articles Concerning Sinkiang* 1886–1962. *Tokyo.*

1.6 Education

Ahmed, M. 1968. *Muslim Education and the Scholars' Social Status up to the 5th Century Muslim Era (11th Century Christian Era) in the Light of Tarikh Baghdad.* Zurich.

Al-Attas, Syed Muhammad al-Naquib. 1977. *Aims and Objectives of Islamic Education.* Islamic Education Series. Sevenoaks, Kent, England: Hodder & Stoughton Ltd. Jeddah: King Abdulaziz University.

Baloch, N.A. 1962. *"Nahj al-Ta'allum. A mid-sixteenth century work on education"*, in *Sind University Research Journal, Arta Series* 2.47–60.

Dodge, R. 1962. *Muslim Education in Medieval Times.* Washington.

Elder, E.E. 1927. *"The conception of University in early Islam"*, in *Muslim World* (Hartford, Connecticut) 17.11–30.

Gibb, Hamilton A. R. 1939. *The University in the Arab Muslim World.* Cambridge.

Haskins, C.H. 1923. *The Rise of Universities.* New York.

Heyworth-Dunne, J. 1938. *An Introduction to the History of Education in Modern Egypt.* London.

Jabre, F. 1958. *La notion de Marifah chez Ghazālī.* Paris.

Law, N.N. 1916. *Promotion of Learning in India During Muhammadan Rule, by Muhammadens.* London.

Mathews, Roderic D. & Matta Akrawi. *Education in Arab Countries of the Near East.* Washington.

Nakosteen, M. 1964. *History of Islamic Origins of Western Education A.D. 800–1350. With an Introduction to Medieval Muslim Education.* Boulder, Colorado.

Qubain, F.I. 1966. *Education and Science in the Arab World.* Baltimore.

Quraishi, Mansoor Ahmad. 1970. *Some Aspects of Muslim Education.* M.S. thesis. Centre of Advanced Study in Education. Faculty of Education, University of Baroda, India.

Rosenthal, Franz. 1970. *Knowledge Triumphant: The Concept of Knowledge in Medieval Islam.* Leiden: E.J. Brill.

Saqeb, G.N. 1977. *Modernization of Muslim Education.* London.

Sayili, A. 1942. *The Institutions of Science and Learning in the Muslim World.* Ph. D. diss., Harvard University, Cambridge, Mass.

Shalaby, A. 1954. *History of Muslim Education.* Beirut.

Talas, A. 1939. *L'enseignement chez les Arabes. La Madrasa Nizāmiyya et son histoire*. Ph. D. diss., University of Paris.

Tibawi, A.L. 1972. *Islamic Education: Its Traditions and Modernization into the Arab National Systems*. London.

Totah, K.A. 1926. *The Contribution of the Arabs to Education*. New York.

Tritton, Arthur S. 1957. *Materials on Muslim Education in the Middle Ages*. London.

Waheed, A. 1945. *The Evolution of Muslim Education. A Historical, Psychological and Cultural Study of the Influences which have Shaped Muslim Education*. Lahore: Islamic College Peshawar, Feraze & Sons.

Wüstenfeld, F. 1837. *Die Akademien der Araber und ihre Lehrer*. Göttingen. Reprinted, 1970.

Yasamee, Abdullah Khan. 1972. *Contribution of the Spanish Arabs to Western Thought and Education*. M. Phil. thesis, University of London.

Al-Zarnūjī. 1947. *Ta'līm al-Muta'allim Ṭarīq al-Ta'allum* (Instructing the student in the method of learning). Translated by G.E. von Grünebaum and T.M. Abel. New York.

1.7 Sciences, Industry and Arts

Arberry, A.J. 1950. *The Spiritual Physick of Rhazes* (al-Rāzī). London.

———————. 1951. *Avicenna on Theology*. London.

Arnaldez, R. & L. Massignon. 1957. *"La science arabe"* in *La Science antique et médiévale: des origines à 1450*, vol. I, edited by R. Taton. Histoire générale des sciences series, I. Paris. English translation by A. Pomerons as *Ancient and Medieval Science*. New York, 1963 & London, 1965.

Arnold, Sir Thomas W. 1928. *Painting in Islam*. Oxford.

Binzagr, Safeya. 1979. *Saudi Arabia: An Artist's View of the Past*. Lausanne, Switzerland: Three Continents Publishers with the collaboration of Arabian Resource Management S.A. Geneva.

Al-Bīrūnī. 1934. *The Book of Instruction in the Elements of the Art of Astrology*. Translated into English by R.R. Wright. London.

Boer, T.J. de. 1903. *The History of Philosophy in Islam*. Translated by

E.K. Jones. London: Luzac.

Briggs, M. 1924. *Muhammadan Architecture in Egypt and Palestine.* Oxford.

Browne, E.G. 1921. *Arabian Medicine.* Cambridge.

Cobb, Stanwood. 1963. *Islamic Contributions to Civilization.* Washington, D.C.: Avion Press.

Corbin, Henry, S.H. Nasr & O. Yahya. 1964. *Histoire de la Philosophie Islamique.* Paris: Gallimard.

Creswell, K.A.C. 1932–40. *Early Muhammadan Architecture,* 2 vols. Oxford.

Al-Daffā', 'Alī Abdalla. 1976. *Contributions of Arabs and Muslims to Mathematics!* London.

Dimand, M.S. 1958. *A Handbook of Muhammadan Art.* New York: The Metropolitan Museum of Art.

Diez, E. 1915. *Die Kunst der islamischen Völker.* Berlin.

———. & H. Gluck. 1925. *Die Kunst des Islam.* Berlin.

Ducousso, Gaston. 1913. *L'industrie de la soie en Syrie.* Beyrouth: Imprimerie Catholique.

Dunlop, D.M. 1958. *Arabic Science in the West.* Karachi.

Elgood, C. 1951. *A Medical History of Persia and the Eastern Caliphate.* Cambridge.

Farmer, H.G. 1929. *A History of Arabian Music to the 13th Century.* London: Luzac & Co.

Gardet, Louis. 1951. *La Pensée religieuse d'Avicenne.* Paris: Librairie Philosophie J. Vrin.

Grohmann, Adolf. 1967. *Arabische Paläographie.* Wien, Graz & Köln: Böhlau.

Gruner, O.C. 1930. *A Treatise on the Canon of Medicine of Avicenna. Incorporating a Translation of the First Book.* London.

Haymond, Robert. 1947. *The Philosophy of Al-Farubi and its Influence on Medieval Thought.* New York.

Hodgen, Margaret T. 1964. *Early Anthropology in the Sixteenth and Seventeenth Centuries.* Philadelphia: University of Pennsylvania Press.

Ibn 'Arabī. 1911. *Tarjumān al-Ashwāq.* Translated by Reynold A. Nicholson. London.

Ibn Bajja (Avempace). 1968. *Opera Metaphysica.* Edited by Mājid Fakhry. Beirut: Dār al-Mahl.

Ibn Rushd (Averroes). 1859. *Thalāth Rasā'il* (Philosophie und Theologie). Edited by M.J. Müller. Königlich-Bayerische Akademie Wissenschaften: Monumenta Saecularia, I. Classe no. 3. München.

———. 1912. *Die Metaphysik des Averroes.* Edited by M. Horten. Halle.

———. 1954. *Tahāfut al-Tahāfut.* Translated by S. van den Bergh. London.

———. 1961. *On the Harmony of Religion and Philosophy.* Translated into English by George F. Hourani. London. Reprinted, 1967.

Ibn Sab'īn. 1880. *"Correspondance du philosophie soufi Ibn Sab'īn".* Translated by A.F. Mehren in *Journal Asiatique,* Paris.

Ibn Ẓafar. 1852. *Solwan, or Waters of Comfort.* Translated by M. Amari. London.

Ikhwān al-Ṣafā'. 1928. *Rasā'il.* Edited by Kair al-Dīn al-Zarkalī. 3 vols. Cairo.

Issawi, Charles, translator. 1950. *An Arab Philosophy of History: Selections from the Prolegomena of Ibn Khaldūn of Tunis 1332–1406.* London: John Murray.

Al-Khawārizmī. 1831. *The Algebra of Mohammed ben Mūsā.* Edited and translated by F. Rosen. London.

Al-Kindī. 1966. *The Medical Formulary or Aqrabadhin of al-Kindī.* Translated with a study of its materia medica by Martin Levey. Madison, Wisconsin: University of Wisconsin Press

Kuhnel, E. 1925. *Islamische Kleinkunst.* Berlin.

Mahdi, Muhsin. 1957. *Ibn Khaldūn's Philosophy of History.* London: Allen & Unwin.

Marçais, G. 1926–27. *Manuel d'art musulman. L'Architecture,* 2 vols. Paris.

Miéli, A. 1938. *La science arabe et son rôle dans l'évolution scientifique mondiale.* Leiden: E.J. Brill. 2nd edn, 1966.

Migeon, G. 1927. *Manuel d'art musulman, Arts plastiques et industriels,* 2 vols. Paris.

Morewedge, P., translator. 1973. *The Metaphysics of Avicenna.* London.

Nasr, S.H. 1964. *An Introduction to Islamic Cosmological Doctrines.* Cambridge, Mass.

———. 1968. *Science and Civilization in Islam.* Cambridge, Mass.: Harvard University Press.

———. 1975. *An Annotated Bibliography of Islamic Science,* vol. I. Tehran.

———. 1976. *Islamic Science.* London: World of Islam Festival Publishing Co.

O'Leary, De Lacy. 1980. *How Greek Science Passed to the Arabs.* London, Boston & Henley: Routledge & Kegan Paul. First published in 1949.

Peters, F.E. 1968. *Aristotle and the Arabs: The Aristotelian Tradition in Islam.* New York & London.

Pope, A.U. 1928–36. *A Survey of Persian Art.* London & New York.

Rahman, Fazlur. 1952. *Avicenna's Psychology.* London.

Richmond, E.T. 1926. *Moslem Architecture.* London.

Rivoira, G.T. 1919. *Moslem Architecture.* Translated by G.M. Rushforth. Oxford.

Rohman, S. 1956. *An Introduction to Islamic Philosophy.* Dacca: Mallick Bross.

Saaty, H. & G. Hirabayashi. 1959. *Industrialization in Alexandria.* Cairo: Social Research Center.

Sarton, George. 1927–48. *Introduction to the History of Science,* 3 vols. Baltimore. An Arabic translation is now available, Cairo: Dār al-al-Ma'ārif.

Schimmel, Annemarie. 1970. *Islamic Calligraphy.* Leiden: E.J. Brill.

Schuon, F. 1976. *Islam and the Perennial Philosophy.* London World of Islam Festival Publishing Co.

Al-Shahristānī. 1850–1. *Religionsparteien und Philosophenschule.* Translated by Th. Haarbrücker. Halle.

Sharif, M.M., ed. 1963. *A History of Muslim Philosophy,* 2 vols. Wiesbaden: Otto Harrassowitz.

Stillman, Yedida Kalfon. 1979. *Palestinian Costume and Jewelry.* Albuquerque: University of New Mexico Press.

Walzer, R. 1962. *Greek into Arabic.* Oxford.

Wolfson, H.A. 1929. *Crescas' Critique of Aristotle: Problems of Aristotle's Physics in Jewish and Arabic Philosophy.* Cambridge, Mass.

Worthington, E.B.. 1946. *Middle East Science.* London: Her Majesty's Stationary Office.

1.8 Bio-Bibliographies

Afnan, S.M. 1958. *Avicenna: His Life and Works.* London.

Arberry, Arthur J. 1960. *Oriental Essays: Portraits of Seven Scholars.* New York: Macmillan Co.

Atiyeh, G.N. 1966. *Al-Kindi: The Philosopher of the Arabs.* Rawalpindi.

Bahā al-Dīn of Mosul. 1892. *The Life of Saladin.* Translated by C.R. Conder. London.

Bowen, H. 1928. *The Life and Times of Alī ibn 'Īsā, "the Good Vizier".* Cambridge.

Dehéran, Henri. 1938. *Silvestre de Sacy: ses contemporains et ses disciples.* Paris.

Gardner, W.R.W. 1919. *An Account of Ghazzālī's Life and Works.* Madras.

Gauthier, L. 1948. *Ibn Rochd* (Averroes). Paris.

Hājjī Khalīfa. 1835–58. *Lexicon Bibliographicum et Encyclopoedicum.* 7 vols. Arabic text and Latin translation, by G. Flügel. Leipzig & London.

Ibn Khallikān. 1842–71. *Biographical Dictionary (The Obituaries of Eminent Men),* 4 vols. Translated from the Arabic by Baron MacGuckin de Slane. London: Oriental Translation Fund.

Ibn al-Nadīm. 1960. *Al-Fihrist* (an Arabic Encyclopaedia). Cairo. Also edited by G. Flügel, Leipzig. Available in English translation.

Inan (Enan), M.A. 1944. *Ibn Khaldūn: His Life and Work.* (Translated from Arabic, Cairo, 1933). Lahore.

Al-Jabartī, Abdul-Raḥmān. 1888–94. *Merveilles bibliographiques et historiques,* 9 vols. Translated into French by Chefik Mansour Bey, Abdulaziz Khalil Bey, Gabriel Khalil Bey and Iskander Mamoun Effendi. Cairo.

Keddie, Nikki R. 1972. *Sayyid Jamāl al-Dīn al-Afghānī. A Political Biography.* Berkeley, Los Angeles & London: University of California Press.

Pakdaman, Homa. 1969. *Djamāl-ed-Dīn Assad Abadi dit Afghānī.* Paris.

Rahman, Fazlur. 1975. *The Philosophy of Mulla Sadra.* Albany.

Renan, Ernest. 1952. *Averroes et Averroesme.* Paris.

Said, Edward W. 1978. *Orientalism.* London & Henley, England: Routledge & Kegan Paul.

Schmidt, N. 1930. *Ibn Khaldūn: Historian, Sociologist and Philosopher.* New York.

Al-Suyūṭī, Jalāl al-Dīn. 1964. *A Biographical Dictionary of Lexicographers and Grammarians* (in Arabic). Edited by Muḥammad Abū al-Faḍl Ibrāhīm. Cairo: 'Īsā al-Ḥalabī Press.

Yāqūt. *Dictionary of Learned Men* (in Arabic). Edited by D.S. Margoliouth. Leiden: E.J. Brill. Reprinted in Beirut, in 15 vols.

Al-Zubaidī, Abū Bakr. 1954. *Biographies of the Arab Grammarians and Lexicographers* (in Arabic). Edited by Muḥammad Abū al-Faḍl Ibrāhīm. Cairo: al-Khānjī.

1.9 Geography

Abū al-Fidā. 1848–83. *Géographie d'Aboulfeda,* 2 vols. Traduite l'arabe by Joseph Reinaud and S. Guyard. Latin translation. Paris.

Al-Dimishqī. 1874. *Manuel de la Cosmographie du Moyen Âge.* Translated by A.F. Mehren. Copenhagen.

Fisher, W.B. 1950. *The Middle East: A Physical, Social and Regional Geography.* New York.

Al-Idrīsī. 1836-40. *Géographie.* Translated by P.A. Jaubert. Paris.

———. 1866. *Description de l'Afrique et de l'Espagne.* Translated by R. Dozy et M.J. de Goeje. Leyden.

Al-Iṣṭakhrī. 1800. *The Oriental Geography of Ibn Ḥawqal.* Translated into English by William Ouseley. London.

Leo Africanus (Jean-Leon l'Africain). 1956. *Description de l'Afrique,* 2 vols. Translated into French by A. Epaulard. New Arabic edn., Imam Muhammad Ibn Saud Islamic University, Riyadh, Saudi Arabia, 1978.

Al-Qalqashandī. 1879. *Die Geographie und Verwaltung von Ägypten.* Translated by F. Wustenfeld. Göttingen.

Al-Ya'qūbī. 1937. *Les Pays.* Translated by G. Wiet. Cairo.

Yāqūt. 1959. *Introductory Chapters of Mu'jam al-Buldān.* Translated by W. Jwaideh. Leiden: E.J. Brill.

1.10 Travels

Berg, L.W.C. van den. 1886. *Le Hadramaut et les colonies arabes dans l'Archipel Indien.* Batavia.

Blunt, Lady Anne. 1879. *Bedouin Tribes of the Euphrates.* Edited by Wilfrid Scawen Blunt. London.

———. 1881. *A Pilgrimage to Nejd,* 2 vols. London.

Burckhardt, John Lewis. 1830. *Notes on the Bedouins and Wahabys.* London.

Burton, Sir Richard F. 1855–56. *Personal Narrative of a Pilgrimage to al-Madinah and Meccah,* 2 vols. London. Reprinted, 1913.

Dickson, H.R.P. 1949. *The Arab of the Desert.* London: Allen & Unwin.

Doughty, Charles, M. 1888. *Travels in Arabia Deserta,* 2 vols. Cambridge: Cambridge University Press. Reprinted, 1979.

Ferrand, G., translator. 1922. *Voyage du marchand Sulayman en Inde et en Chine.* Paris.

Ibn Jubair. 1852. *Travels of Ibn Jubair.* Edited by William Wright. Leiden: E.J. Brill. 2nd edn., edited by M.J. de Goeje, Leiden, 1907.

Ingrams, H. 1942. *Arabia and the Isles.* London.

Kiernan, R.H. 1937. *The Unveiling of Arabia.* London: Harrap.

Lane, Edward William. 1836. *An Account of the Manners and Customs of the Modern Egyptians* (written in Egypt during the years 1833–1835). London. Reprinted by East-West Publications, London & Livres de France, Cairo, 1978.

Musil, Alois. 1908. *Arabia Petraea,* 3 vols. Wien.

———. 1927. *Arabia Deserta.* New York: American Geographical Society.

———. 1928. *Manners and Customs of the Rwala Bedouins.* New York: American Geographical Society.

Philby, H.St. John B. 1930. *Arabia.* London.

Stark, F. 1945. *The Southern Gates of Arabia.* 2nd edn. Harmondsworth, England: Penguin Books.

Thomas, Bertram. 1931. *Alarms and Excursions in Arabia.* London.

———. 1932. *Arabia Felix.* New York: Charles Scribner's Sons.

———. 1937. *The Arabs.* London: Butterworth.

ADDENDA

Abdul-Wāsi', Abdul-Wahāb. 1971. *Education in Saudi Arabia.* London: Macmillan.

Al-Farsy, Fouad. 1978. *Saudi Arabia: A Case Study in Development.* London: Stacey International.

Aramco Handbook. 1968. Dhahran: The Arabian American Oil Company. Revised edition, 1980.

Armstrong, H.C. 1954. *Lord of Arabia.* Beirut: Khayyat.

Asad, Muhammad. 1954. *The Road to Mecca.* New York: Simon and Schuster.

Assah, Ahmed. 1969. *Miracle of the Desert Kingdom.* London: Jonson.

Awwad, Mohammad Amin M.B. 1973. *Relativisation and Related Matters in Classical, Modern Standard and Palestinian Colloquial Arabic.* Ph.D. diss., Brown University (USA).

Azzam, Abdel Rahman. 1964. *The Eternal Message of Muhammad.* New York: Devin-Adair.

Bremond, E. 1937. *Yemen et Saoudia.* Paris.

Brown, W.R. 1948. *The Horse of the Desert.* New York: Macmillan.

Bullard, Sir Reader. 1961. *The Camels Must Go.* London: Faber & Faber.

Buttiker, W. 1979–(in progress). *Fauna of Saudi Arabia.* Switzerland.

Cheeseman, R.E. 1926. *In Unknown Arabia.* London: Macmillan.

Collins, Robert O., ed. 1969. *An Arabian Diary: Sir Gilbert Clayton.* California.

Cragg, Kenneth. 1956. *The Call of the Minaret.* Oxford University Press.

De Gaury, Gerald. 1946. *Arabia Phoenix.* London: Harrap.

———. 1950. *Arabian Journey and Other Desert Travels.* London: Harrap.

———. 1966. *Faisal, King of Saudi Arabia.* London: Arthur Barker.

Esin, Emel. 1963. *Mecca the Blessed, Madinah the Radiant.* London: Elek.

Fisher, Sydney N. 1969. *The Middle East: A History.* New York: Knopf.

Glubb, Sir John Bagot. 1963. *The Life and Times of Muhammad.* London: Hodder & Stoughton.

Graves, P. 1942. *Life of Sir Percy Cox.* London.

Hartshorn, J.E. 1967. *Oil Companies and Governments.* 2nd revised edn. London: Faber & Faber.

Hogarth, D.G. 1904. *The Penetration of Arabia.* New York: F.A. Stokes.

Hopwood, Derek, ed. 1972. *The Arabian Peninsula.* London: Allen & Unwin.

Howarth, David. 1964. *The Desert King.* London: Collins.

Keiser, Helene. 1971. *Arabia.* Zurich: Silva.

Lebkicker, Rentz and Steincke. *The Arabia of Ibn Saud.* USA: Russell and Moore.

Le Bon, Gustave. 1974. *The World of Islamic Civilization.* Geneva: Minerva.

Lenczowski, George. 1960. *Oil and State in the Middle East.* New York: Cornell University Press.

———. 1962. *The Middle East in World Affairs.* New York: Cornell University Press.

Longrigg, S. 1968. *Oil in the Middle East.* 3rd edn. Oxford University Press.

Meinertzhagen, Richard. 1954. *The Birds of Arabia.* Edinburgh: Oliver & Boyd.

Meulen, D. van der. 1961. *Faces in Shem.* London: John Murray.

Monroe, Elizabeth. 1973. *Philby of Arabia.* London: Faber & Faber.

Musil, Alois. 1926. *The Northern Hijaz.* New York: American Geographical Society.

Pesce, Angelo. 1972. *Colours of the Arab Fatherland.* Riyadh, Saudi Arabia.

———. 1974. *Jiddah: Portrait of an Arabian City.* Falcon Press.

Philby, H. St. John B. 1922. *The Heart of Arabia.* London: Constable.

———. 1933. *The Empty Quarter.* New York: Henry Holt.

———. 1952. *Arabian Jubilee.* London: Robert Hale.

———. 1955. *Saudi Arabia.* London: Ernest Benn.

———. 1964. *Arabian Oil Ventures.* Washington: Middle East Institute.

Philips, C.H., ed. 1963. *Handbook of Oriental History.* London: Royal Historical Society.

Purdy, Anthony, ed. 1976. *The Business Man's Guide to Saudi Arabia.* London: Arlington Books.

Ross, Heather Colyer. 1978. *Bedouin Jewellery in Saudi Arabia.* London: Stacey International. 2nd revised edn. is in press.

Ryan, Sir A. 1951. *The Last of the Dragomans.* London.

Sanger, Richard. 1954. *The Arabian Peninsula.* New York: Cornell University Press.

Shroeder, Eric. 1955. *Muhammad's People: A Tale by Anthology.* Portland, Maine(USA): Bond Wheelwright.

Smith, Wilfred Cantwell. 1957. *Islam in Modern History.* Princeton: Princeton University Press.

Thesiger, Wilfred. 1959. *Arabian Sands.* London: Book Club Associates.

Twitchell, K.S. 1958. *Saudi Arabia.* 3rd edn. Princeton: Princeton University Press.

Vidal, F.S. 1955. *The Oasis of Al-Ḥasa.* Dhahran: Arabian American Oil Company.

Vincett, Betty. 1977. *The Flowers of Arabia.*

Wahba, Hafiz. 1964. *Arabian Days.* London: Arthur Barker.

Wellsted, J.R. 1838. *Travels in Arabia.* London: John Murray.

Winder, R. Bayly. 1965. *Saudi Arabia in the Nineteenth Century.* New York: St. Martin's Press.

Yale, William. 1958. *The Near East: A Modern History.* Michigan, Ann Arbor: University of Michigan Press.

Ziriklī, Khair al-Dīn. 1970. *Arabia under King Abdul Azīz* (in Arabic). 4 vols. Beirut.

2.0 ARABIC LANGUAGE & LINGUISTICS

2.1 General & Bibliographies

Abbott, Nabia. 1939. *The Rise of the North Arabic Script and its Kuranic Development.* Oriental Institute Publications, 50. Chicago: University of Chicago Press.

———. 1972. *Studies in Arabic Literary Papyri.* Oriental Institute Publications, 77. Chicago: University of Chicago Press.

Abboud, Peter F. 1970. "Spoken Arabic", in *Current Trends in Linguistics: Linguistics in South West Asia and North Africa,* vol. 6, 439–66. edited by Thomas A. Sebeok, Charles A. Ferguson, C.T. Hodge, et al. The Hague: Mouton.

Arif, Aida S. 1967. *Arabic Lapidary in Africa: Egypt, North Africa, Sudan. A Study of the Development of the Kufic Script.* London: Luzac.

Bakalla, M.H. 1975. *Bibliography of Arabic Linguistics.* London: Mansell Publishing Ltd.

———. 1981. *Arabic Linguistics: An Introduction and Bibliography.* London: Mansell Publishing Ltd.

Bateson, Mary Catherine. 1967. *Arabic Language Handbook.* Washington: Center for Applied Linguistics.

Beeston, A.F.L. 1970. *The Arabic Language Today.* Hutchinson University Library: Modern Languages. London: Hutchinson & Co. (Publishers) Ltd.

Blanc, Haim. 1970. "Semitic", in *Current Trends in Linguistics,* vol. I. 374–91. Edited by Thomas A. Sebeok, Paul Garvin, Horace Lunt and Edward Stankiewicz. The Hague & Paris: Mouton.

———. 1975. "Linguistics among the Arabs", in *Current Trends in Linguistics: Historiography of Linguistics,* vol. 13. 1265–83, edited by Thomas A. Sebeok, Hans Aarsleff, et al. The Hague: Mouton.

Blau, Joshua. 1965. *The Emergence and Linguistic Background of Judeo-Arabic: A Study of the Origins of Middle Arabic.* London: Oxford University Press.

Chejne, Anwar G. 1969. *The Arabic Language: its Role in History.* Minneapolis: University of Minnesota Press.

Cohen, David. 1970. *Études de Linguistique Semitique et Arabe.* Janua

Linguarum, Series Practica, 81. The Hague: Mouton.

Darwish, Abdalla A.F. 1955. *Al-Khalil ibn Ahmad and the Evolution of Arabic Lexicography*. Ph.D. diss., University of London.

Fleisch, Henri. 1961, 1978. *Traité de philologie arabe.* 2 vols. Beirut: Imprimerie Catholique.

Fück, Johann. 1950. *Arabiya. Untersuchungen zur Arabischen Sprach- und Stilgeschichte.* Abhandlungen der Sachsischen Akademie der Wissenschaften zu Leipzig. Phil.-hist. Klasse XLV, 1. Berlin: Akademie -Verlag. French translation by Claude Denizeau, as *Arabiya. Recherches sur l'Histoire de la Langue et du style Arabe.* Publications of l'Institut des Hautes Études Marocanes, Notes et documents, 16. Paris: Didier, 1955. Arabic translation by A.H. al-Najjār, Cairo: Arab Book Press, 1951.

Goldziher, Ignaz. 1896–99. *Abhandlungen zur Arabischen Philologie*, 2 vols. Leiden: E.J. Brill.

Gordon, David C. 1964. *The Search for Identity: Arabization and Modernization in North Africa.* 2nd printing. Cambridge, Mass.: Harvard University Press.

Gray, Louis Herbert. 1934. *Introduction to Semitic Comparative Linguistics. A Basical Grammar of the Semitic Languages, printed in transcription with emphasis on Arabic and Hebrew.* Colombia University Studies in Comparative Linguistics, 1. Reprinted, Amsterdam: Philo Press, 1971.

Hamzaoui, Rachad. 1965. *L'académie arabe de Damas et le problème de la modernisation de la langue arabe.* Leiden: E.J. Brill.

———. 1972. *L'académie de langue arabe du Caire.* Ph.D. diss., University of Paris.

———. , Z. Riahi & H. Ounali. 1970. *Quelques aspects du bilinguisme en Tunisie.* Tunis: Cahiers du CERES, Série linguistique, 3.

Hanna, Sami Ayyad, ed. 1972. *Medieval and Middle Eastern Studies in Honour of Aziz Suryal Atiya.* Leiden: E. J. Brill.

Haywood, John A. 1960. *Arabic Lexicography: Its History and its Place in the General History of Lexicography.* Leiden: E.J. Brill. 2nd edn., 1965.

Hunwick, John O. 1964. *"The influence of Arabic in West Africa"*, in *Transactions of the Historical Society of Ghana* (Legon) 7.24–41.

Inayatullah, Shaikh. 1969. *Why We Learn the Arabic Language.* Lahore:

Shaikh Muhammad Ashraf.

Killean, Carolyn G. 1970. *"Classical Arabic"*, in *Current Trends in Linguistics: Linguistics in South West Asia and North Africa,* vol. 6. 413–38, edited by Thomas A. Sebeok, Charles A. Ferguson, C.T. Hodge, et al. The Hague: Mouton.

Krackovskij, I.J. 1950. *Očerki po istorii russkoj arabistiki.* Moscow. Translated into German as *Die Russische Arabistik: Umriss ihrer Entwicklung.* Leipzig.

Levin, Saul. 1971. *The Indo-European and Semitic Languages.* Albany, New York: State University of New York Press.

Löwinger, S. & J. Somogyi, eds. 1948. *Ignace Goldzeher Memorial Volume,* Part I. Budapest.

Monteil, Vincent. 1960. *L'arabe moderne.* Association pour l'avancement des études Islamiques, série 3, Études et documents. Paris: Librairie C. Klincksieck.

Moscati, Sabatino, A. Spitaler, E. Ullendorff & W. von Soden. 1964. *An Introduction to the Comparative Grammar of the Semitic Languages.* Wiesbaden: Otto Harrassowitz.

Mulder, J.A. 1949. *Het Indonesisch-Arabische Schrift.* Djakarta.

Nöldeke, Theodor. 1887. *"Semitic languages"* in *Encyclopaedia Britannica,* 11th edn. Translation of his *Die semitischen Sprachen,* 1887.

———. 1899. *Die Semitischen Sprachen.* 2nd edn. Leipzig.

Oman, Giovanni. 1966. *L'Ittionimia Nei Paesi Arabi del Mediterraneo.* Quaderni dell' Archivio Linguistico Veneto, 3. Firenze.

Pérès, Henri. 1958. *L'Arabe Dialectal Algérien et Saharien: Bibliographie Analytique avec un Index Méthodique.* Alger: La Maison des Livres.

Prochazka, Theodore, Jr. 1967. *Selected Bibliography of Arabic, 1960-1967.* Washington, D.C.: ERIC Clearinghouse for Linguistics, Center for Applied Linguistics.

Šarbatov, G.Š. 1959. *Arabistika v SSSR (Filologija), 1917–1959.* Moscow.

Al-Sasi, Omar. 1972. *Sprichwörter und andere Volkskundliche Texte aux Mekka.* Ph.D. diss., Münster, Arabistik und Islamwissenschaft.

Selim, George Dimitri. 1970. *American Doctoral Dissertations on the Arab World, 1883–1968.* Washington: Library of Congress. Revised edn., 1978.

Sobelman, Harvey, ed. 1962. *Arabic Dialect Studies: A Selected Biblio-*

graphy. Washington, D.C.: Center for Applied Linguistics of the Modern Language Association and the Middle East Institute.

Wehr, Hans. 1934. *Die Besonderheiten des heutigen Hocharabischen mit Berücksichtigung der Einwirkung der europäischen Sprachen.* Berlin.

Wexler, Paul. 1976. *"Research frontiers in Sino-Islamic linguistics"*, in *Journal of Chinese Linguistics (USA)* 4.47–82.

Yushmanov, N.W. 1961. *The Structure of the Arabic Language.* Translated from the Russian by Moshe Perlmann. Washington, D.C.: Center for Applied Linguistics.

Zaki, Ahmad. 1953. *"The renovation of Arabic"*, in *The Use of Vernacular Languages in Education,* 87–95. UNESCO Monograph on Fundamental Education, VIII. Paris: UNESCO.

2.2.1 Linguistics (Ancient)

Arnaldez, Roger. 1956. *Grammaire et Théologie chez Ibn Ḥazm de Cordoue. Essai sur la Structure et les Conditions de la Pensée Musulmane.* Paris: Librairie Philosophie J. Vrin.

Bakalla, M.H. 1973. *The Phonetics and Phonology of Classical Arabic as Described by Ibn Jinnī's Sirr al-Ṣinā'ah.* M. Phil. thesis, University of London.

Birkeland, Harris. 1940. *Altarabische Pausalformen.* Oslo: Dybwad.

Bravmann, Max. 1934. *Materialien und Untersuchungen zu den Phonetischen Lehren der Araber.* Ph.D. diss., Friedrich-Wilhelms-Universität zu Breslau. Göttingen: W. Fr. Kaestner.

Carter, Michael G. 1968. *A Study of Sībawaihi's Principles of Grammatical Analysis.* Ph.D. thesis, University of Oxford.

Diem, Werner. 1968. *Das Kitāb al-Jīm des Abū 'Amr al-Shaibānī: ein Beitrag zur Arabischen Lexicographie.* Ph.D. diss., Ludwig-Maximilians-Universität zu München.

Flügel, Gustav Leberecht. 1862. *Die Grammatischen Schulen der Araber.* Abhandlungen der Deutschen Morgenlandischen Gesselschaft, II. Band no. 4. Leipzig.

Ghul, Mahmoud A. 1963. *Early Southern Arabian Languages and Classical Arabic Sources: A Critical Examination of Literary and Lexicographical Sources by Comparison with the Inscriptions.* Ph.D. diss.,

University of London.

Ḥillāwi, N. 1966. *A Study of Abū 'Ubaida Ma'mar ibn al-Muthannā as a Philologist and and Transmitter of Literary Material.* Ph.D. diss., University of London.

Huffman, Henry Russell. 1973. *Syntactical Influence of Arabic on Medieval and Later Spanish Prose.* Ph.D. diss., University of Wisconsin, Madison.

Marshall, David R. 1963. *The Accusative in Arabic Grammatical Literature.* Ph.D. diss., University of Durham, England.

Mehiri, Abdelkader. 1970. *Les Theories Grammaticales d'Ibn Jinni.* Ph.D diss., University of Paris (Sorbonne). Published, Tunis: The University Press, 1973.

Omar, Ahmad Mukhtar. 1966. *Arabic Linguistic Studies in Egypt to the End of the Tenth Century A.D.* Ph.D. diss., University of Cambridge.

Paz Torres Palomo, Maria. 1971. *Bartolome Dorador y el Arabe Dialectal Andaluz.* Ph.D. diss., Universidad de Granada. Granada: Editado e impreso por el Secretariado de Publicationes de la Universidad.

Rescher, Oscar. 1908. *Studien über Ibn Jinnī und sein Verhältnis zu den Theorien de zu Basri und Baghdadi.* Strassburg: Verlag von Karl J. Trübner.

Reuschel, Wolfgang. 1959. *Al-Khalīl ibn Aḥmad, der Lehrer Sībawaih, als Grammatiker.* Berlin: Akademic Verlag.

El-Saaran, Mahmoud H.A. 1951. *A Critical Study of the Phonetic Observations of the Arab Grammarians.* Ph.D. diss., University of London.

Schaade, A. 1911. *Sībawaihi's Lautlehre.* Leiden: E.J. Brill.

Semaan, Khalil I.H. 1963. *Arabic Phonetics. Ibn Sīnā's Risālah on the Points of Articulation of the Speech Sounds.* Translated from the Medieval Arabic. Arthur Jeffery Memorial Monographs, no. 3. Lahore: Sheikh Muhammad Ashraf.

———————. 1968. *Linguistics in the Middle Ages: Phonetic Studies in Early Islam.* Leiden: E.J. Brill.

Sībawaihi. 1881–1889. *Kītab Sībawaihi.* Le Livre de Sībawaihi. Traité de Grammaire Arabe. Edited by Hartwig Derenbourg. 2 vols. Paris: Imprimé par Autorisation du Gouvernment à l'Imprimerie Nationale.

———————. 1895–1900. *Kitāb Sībawayh.* The Book of Arabic Grammar. Translated into German by G. Jahn. 2 vols. Berlin.

———. 1897. *Kitāb Sībawaihi*. The Book of Arabic Grammar with the commentaries of al-Sīrāfi and al-Shantamarī. Cairo: Būlāq Press.

Thompson, Billy Bussell. 1970. *Billingualism in Moorish Spain*. Ph.D. diss., University of Virginia.

Walsh, John Kevin. 1967. *The Loss of Arabisms in the Spanish Lexicon*. Ph.D. diss., University of Virginia.

Wechter, Pinchas. 1940. *Ibn Barun's Book of Comparison between the Hebrew and the Arabic Languages*. Ph.D. diss., The Dropsie College for Hebrew and Cognate Learning, Philadelphia.

———. 1964. *Ibn Barun's Arabic Works on Hebrew Grammar and Lexicography*. Oxford: Oxford University Press.

Weil, Gotthold. 1913. *Die grammatischen Schulen von Kufa und Basra. Zugleich* Einleitung zu der Ausgabe des Kitab al-Insaf von al-Anbari. Leiden: E.J. Brill.

Weiss, Bernard George. 1966. *Language in Orthodox Muslim Thought: A Study of 'Wad' al-Lughah" and its Development*. Ph.D. diss., Princeton University, New Jersey.

Wild, Stefan. 1965. *Das Kitāb al-'Ain und die Arabische Lexicographie*. Ph.D. diss., München. Published, Wiesbaden: Otto Harrassowitz.

2.2.2 Linguistics (Modern)

Abboud, Peter. 1964. *The Syntax of Najdi Arabic*. Ph.D. diss., University of Texas at Austin.

Abdel-Hamid, Ahmed Kamal. 1974. *A Transfer Grammar of English and Arabic*. Ph.D. diss., University of Texas at Austin.

Abdo, Daud A. 1969. *On Stress and Arabic Phonology: A Generative Approach*. Beirut: Khayats.

Aboul-Fetouh, Hilmi M. 1969. *A Morphological Study of Egyptian Colloquial Arabic*. The Hague: Mouton.

Abubakr, El-Rashid. 1970. *The Noun Phrase in the Spoken Arabic of the Sudan*. Ph.D. diss., University of London.

Ali, Latif H. & R.G. Daniloff. 1972. *"A contrastive cinefluorographic investigation of the articulation of emphatic/non-emphatic cognate consonants"*, in *Studia Lingustica* (Lund) 26.81–105.

Al-Ani, Salman Hassan. 1970. *Arabic Phonology: An Acoustical and Physiological Investigation*. Janua Linguarum, Series Practica, 61.

The Hague: Mouton.

———. 1978. *Readings in Arabic Linguistics.* Bloomington, Indiana: Indiana University Linguistics Club.

Badawi, El-Said Mohammad. 1965. *An Intonational Study of Colloquial Riyadhi Arabic.* Ph.D. diss., University of London.

Bakalla, M.H. 1979. *The Morphological and Phonological Components of the Arabic Verb.* London & Beirut: Longman & Librairie du Liban.

———. Forthcoming. *Arabic Linguistics: A Book of Readings, vol. I.* Library of Arabic Linguistics, 1. London: Routledge & Kegan Paul.

———. Forthcoming. *Arabic Phonetics: A Book of Readings, vol. I.* Library of Arabic Linguistics, 2. London: Routledge & Kegan Paul.

Bathurst, R.D. 1971. *"Automatic alphabetization of Arabic word",* pp. 185–90, in *The Computer in Literary and Linguistic Analysis,* edited by R.A. Wisbey. Cambridge: Cambridge University Press.

Becker (–Makkai), Valerie. 1964. *A Transfer Grammar of the Verb Structures of Modern Literary Arabic and Lebanese Colloquial Arabic.* Ph.D. diss., Yale University.

Belkin, Vladimir Mikhailovich. 1974. *Arabskaya Lexikologiya* (Arabic Lexicology). Moscow: Izdatelstvo Moskovskogo universiteta.

Bergsträsser, Gottholf. 1915. *Sprachatlas von Syrien und Palästina.* Leipzig.

Birkeland, Harris. 1952. *Growth and Structure of the Egytian Arabic Dialect.* Oslo: Dybwad.

———. 1954. *Stress Patterns in Arabic.* Oslo: Dybwad.

Brame, Michael K. 1970. *Arabic Phonology: Implications for Phonological Theory and Historical Semitic.* Ph.D. diss., Massachusetts Institute of Technology, Cambridge, Mass.

Bratton, Neil John Quinn. 1968. *Structures and Messages in English and Arabic.* Ph.D. diss., Georgetown University.

Bulos, Afif. 1965. *The Arabic Triliteral Verb.* Beirut: Khayats.

Cadora, Frederic Joseph. 1979. *An Analytical Study of Interdialectal Lexical Compatibility in Arabic.* Leiden: E.J. Brill.

Cantineau, Jean. 1960. *Course de Phonetique Arabe.* Paris: Librairie C. Klincksieck.

———. 1960. *Études de linguistique arabe.* Paris: Librairie C. Klincksieck.

Cereteli, G.V. 1959. *Arabskie dialekty Srednej Azii.* Vol. I: *Buxarskij arabskij dialekt*. Tbilisi.

Coady, James Martin. 1967. *Emphasis in Four Arabic Dialects: An Acoustic Study*. M.A. diss., Indiana University at Bloomington.

Cowan, William George. 1960. *A Reconstruction of Proto-Colloquial Arabic*. Ph.D. diss., Cornell University.

El-Derwi, Ahmad M.A. 1965. *Number in Cairene Colloquial Arabic with Comparative Reference to English*. M.A. diss., Brown University (USA).

Dikshit, Om. 1972. *The Usage of Perso-Arabic Elements with Special Reference to Honorifics in Hindi: A Study in Linguistics and Culture and its Pedagogical Implications*. Ph.D. diss., University of Texas at Austin.

Erickson, Jon Laroy. 1965. *English and Arabic: A Discussion of Contrastive Verbal Morphology*. Ph.D. diss., University of Texas at Austin.

Faris, Abdul Razzak H. 1966. *Numbers in Spoken Baghdadi Arabic*. M.S. diss., Georgetown University.

Ferguson, Charles A. 1971. *Language Structure and Language Use: Essays by C.A. Ferguson*. Selected and introduced by Anwar S. Dil. Stanford, California: Stanford University Press.

Fleisch, Henri. 1956. *L'Arabe Classique. Esquissique d'une Structure Linguistique*. Beirut: Dar el-Machreq. Revised edn., 1968. Arabic translation by Abd al-Ṣabūr Shāhīn, Beirut: Imprimerie Catholique, 1966.

Gaber, Abdelrahman M.A. 1966. *Syllabic Structure in Modern Standard Arabic and Colloquial Egyptian Arabic*. M.A. diss., Brown University (USA).

Gaber, A.R.M.A. 1972. *The Phonology of the Verbal Piece in Cairo Egyptian Arabic*. Ph.D. diss., University of London.

Gabuchan, Grachiya Mikaelovich. 1972. *Teoriya Artiklya i Problemui Arabskogo Sintaksisa*. Akademiya Nauk SSSR. Moskva: Izdatel'stvo Nauka.

Gairdner, W.H.T. 1925. *The Phonetics of Arabic*. London & Oxford: Oxford University Press.

El-Garh, Mohamed M.S. 1959. *The Ta Infix and Prefix in Arabic Verbal Forms Compared with Other Semitic Languages*. Ph.D. diss., University of London.

Ghaly, Muhammad M. 1961. *Substantive Morphology of Colloquial*

Egyptian Arabic. Ph.D. diss., University of Michigan at Ann Arbor.

Greis, Naguib A. 1963. *The Pedagogical Implications of a Contrastive Analysis of Cultivated Cairene Arabic and the English Language.* Ph.D. diss., University of Minnesota.

El-Hajjé, Hassan. 1954. *Le Parler Arabe de Tripoli (liban). Étude Linguistique.* Paris: Klincksieck.

Haleese, Y.A.K.El-. 1971. *A Phonetic and Phonological Study of the Verbal Piece in a Palestinian Dialect of Arabic: Yatta Dialect.* Ph.D. diss., University of London.

Hanna, Sami A. 1964. *Problems of American College Students in Learning Arabic: A Diagnostic Study of Reading Errors, Remedial Instruction and a Proposed Method of Teaching.* Ph.D. diss., University of Utah at Salt Lake City.

Harrell, Richard Slade. 1957. *The Phonology of Colloquial Egyptian Arabic.* New York: American Council of Learned Societies.

———————. & H. Blanc eds. 1960 *Contributions to Arabic Linguistics.* Harvard Center for Middle Eastern Studies. Cambridge, Mass.: Harvard University Press.

Il-Hazmy, Alayan M. 1972. *A Critical and Comparative Study of the Spoken Dialects of Badr and District in Saudi Arabia.* M. Phil. thesis, University of Leeds.

Helmy-Hassan, Saleh E. 1960. *Verb Morphology of Egyptian Colloquial Arabic, Cairene Dialect.* Ph.D. diss., University of Michigan at Ann Arbor.

Ingham, Bruce. 1974. *The Phonology and Morphology of the Verbal Piece in an Arabic Dialect of Khuzistan.* Ph.D. diss., University of London.

Janssens, Gerard. 1972. *Stress in Arabic and Word Structure in the Modern Arabic Dialects.* Leuven: Uitgeverij Peeters.

Jastrow, Otto. 1973. *Daragözü. Eine Arabische Mundart der Kozluk-Sason-Gruppe (Südostanatolien). Grammatik und Texte.* Erlanger Beitrage zur Sprach- und Kunstwissenschaft, Band 46. Nürnberg: Verlag Hans Carl.

Johnstone, T.M. 1967. *Eastern Arabian Dialect Studies.* London Oriental Series, 17. London: Oxford University Press.

Kamel, N. 1953. *Political Jargon in Contemporary Egypt.* Ph.D. diss., University of London.

Kaye, Alan Stewart. 1971. *Chadian and Sudanese Arabic in the Light of Comparative Arabic Dialectology*. Ph.D. diss., University of California at Berkeley. Revised edn., The Hague: Mouton, 1978.

Al-Khafājī, Abdur-Rasūl. 1972. *Descriptive and Comparative Analysis of Tense and Time in English and Arabic*. Ph.D. diss., University of Glasgow, Scotland.

Killean, Mary C.G. 1966. *The Deep Structure of the Noun Phrase in Modern Written Arabic*. Ph.D. diss., University of Michigan at Ann Arbor.

Laroui, A. 1971. *Cultural Problems and Social Structure: The Campaign of Arabization in Morocco*. Rabat: Mohammad V University.

Levy, Mary Mansnerus. 1971. *The Plural of the Noun in Modern Standard Arabic*. Ph.D. diss., University of Michigan at Ann Arbor.

Lewin, Bernhard. 1966. *Arabische Texte im Dialekte von Hama. Mit Einleitung und Glossar*. Beiruter Texte und Studien, 2. Wiesbaden: Franz Steiner Verlag.

———. 1969. *Notes on Cabali. The Arabic Dialect Spoken by the Alawis of Jebel Ansariye*. Acta Universitatis Gothoburgensis, Orientalia Gothoburgensia, 1. Stockholm: Almqvist and Wiksell.

Lewkowicz, Nancy Margaret Kennedy. 1967. *A Transformational Approach to the Syntax of Arabic Participles*. Ph.D. diss., University of Michigan at Ann Arbor.

Lotfi, M.K. 1948. *Changes Needed in Egyptian Readers to Increase their Value*. Ph.D. diss., University of Chicago.

Maamouri, Mohamed. 1967. *The Phonology of Tunisian Arabic*. Ph.D. diss., Cornell University.

Mahgoub, Fatma Muhammad. 1968. *A Linguistic Study of Cairene Proverbs*. Language Science Monographs, 1. Bloomington: Indiana University Research Center for the Language Sciences. The Hague: Mouton.

———. 1970. *A Kinemorphological Study of Cairene Gestures, with Pedagogical Applications*. Ph.D. diss., University of Texas at Austin.

Mainnz, E. 1931. *Zur Grammatik des Modernen Schrift-Arabisch*. Ph.D. diss., Hamburg.

Malaika, Nisar. 1963. *Grundzuge der Grammatik des Arabischen Dialektes von Bagdad*. Wiesbaden: Otto Harrassowitz.

Mansour, Bahija J. 1966. *Noun-Adjective Agreement in Colloquial Baghdad Arabic.* M.S. diss., Georgetown University.

Mazhar, Muhammad Ahmad. 1963. *Arabic the Source of all the Languages.* Lahore: Sunrise Art Printers.

————. 1967. *English Traced to Arabic.* Lahore: Sunrise Art Printers.

McKay, Jym Motheral. 1972. *Syntactic Similarities in Arabic Diglossia.* Ph.D. diss., University of Texas at Austin.

McLoughlin, Leslie John. 1969. *An Investigation of Some Features of Modern Standard Arabic.* M.A. thesis, University of Leeds.

Meynet, Ronald. 1971. *L'Écriture Arabe en Question. Les Projects de l'Académie de Langue Arabe du Caire de 1938 à 1968.* Beirut: Dar el-Machreq.

Morag, Shelomo. 1961. *The Vocalization of Arabic, Hebrew and Aramaic: Their Phonetic and Phonemic Principles.* Janua Linguarum, Series Minor, 13. The Hague: Mouton. Reprinted, 1972.

Al-Mozainy, Hamza Qublan. 1976. *Vowel Deletion and the Segmental Cycle in the Arabic Dialect of Hijaz (Saudi Arabia).* M.A. thesis, University of Texas at Austin.

Muhammad, R.A.R. 1973. *A Physiological and Spectographical Study of Baghdadi Vowels.* M.A. thesis, University College of North Wales, Bangor.

Murtonen, A. 1964. *Broken Plurals. Origin and Development of the System.* Leiden: E.J. Brill.

Obrecht, Dean H. 1968. *Effects of the Second Formant on the Perception of Velarization Consonants in Arabic.* The Hague: Mouton.

Omar, Margaret Kleffner. 1970. *The Acquisition of Egyptian Arabic as a Native Language.* Ph.D. diss., Georgetown University. Revised edn., The Hague: Mouton, 1973.

Parsons, A.J. 1966. *Some Observations on the Learning of Arabic with Particular Reference to Teach Yourself Arabic by A.S. Tritton.* Diploma thesis, University of Leeds.

Prochazka, Theodore, Jr. 1968. *Root Variants in Classical Arabic: A Phonological Study.* M.S. diss., Georgetown University.

Qafisheh, Hamdi Ahmad. 1968. *English Pre-Nominal Modifiers and Corresponding Modern Standard Arabic Structures: A Contrastive Analysis.* Ph.D. diss., University of Michigan at Ann Arbor.

Rabin, Chaim. 1951. *Ancient West Arabian.* London: Taylor's Foreign Press.

Rammuny, Raji Mahmud A. 1967. *An Analysis of the Differences in the Prosodies of General American English and Colloquial Jordanian Arabic and their Effect on Second-Language Acquisition.* Ph.D. diss., University of Michigan at Ann Arbor.

Reinhardt, Carl. 1894. *Ein Arabischer Dialekt Gesprochen in 'Oman und Zanzibar.* Lehrbrucher des Seminars fur Orientalischen Sprachen zu Berlin, 13. Stuttgart & Berlin. Reprinted, Stuttgart 1972.

Robertson-Smith, Alice Marian. 1970. *Classical Arabic and Colloquial Cairene: An Historical Linguistic Analysis.* Ph.D. diss., University of Utah at Salt Lake City.

Rouchdy, Aleya Aly. 1970. *A Case of Bilingualism: An Investigation in the Area of Lexical and Syntactic Interference in the Performance of a Bilingual (Arab) Child.* Ph.D. diss., University of Texas at Austin.

El-Rufai, M.A.H. 1969. *A Study of the Reading Abilities and Habits, in English and Arabic of Baghdadi Students.* Ph.D. thesis, University of London.

Sa'id, Majid Farhan. 1967. *Lexical Innovation Through Borrowing in Modern Standard Arabic.* Ph.D. diss., Princeton University. Published, Princeton Near East Papers, no. 6. Princeton University Press.

Satterthwait, Arnold Chase. 1962. *Parallel Sentence-Construction Grammars of Arabic and English.* Ph.D. diss., Harvard University.

El-Sayed (Elsayed), Dawood H. 1962. *A Descriptive Analysis of the Part-of-Speech System and the Grammatical Categories of Egyptian Colloquial Arabic.* Ph.D. diss., Cornell University.

Al-Sayed, Sahira Abdul Hamid. 1973. *A Lexicon and Analysis of English Words of Arabic Origin.* Ph.D. diss., University of Colorado.

Schreiber, Giselher. 1971. *Der Arabische Dialekt von Mekka Abriss der Grammatick mit Texten und Glossar.* Freiburg: Klaus Schwarz Verlag.

Semaan, Khalil I.H. 1954. *Teaching the Pronunciation of Arabic to Speakers of American English.* M.S. diss., Institute of Languages and Linguistics, Georgetown University.

Sieny, M.E. 1978. *The Syntax of Urban Hijazi Arabic (Saudi Arabia).* London & Beirut: Longman & Librairie du Liban.

Smeaton, B. Hunter. 1959. *Lexical Expansion due to Technical Changes: As Illustrated by the Arabic of al-Hasa, Saudi Arabia, during the Decade 1938–48.* Ph.D. diss., Columbia University. Published, Indiana University Publications, Language Science Monographs, no. 10. Bloomington: Indiana University Press.

Snow, James Adin. 1965. *A Grammar of Modern Written Arabic Clauses.* Ph.D. diss., University of Michigan at Ann Arbor.

Speers, Peter Carter, 1959. *Development and Present State of Modern Written Arabic.* Ph.D. diss., University London.

Al-Toma, Salih Jawad. 1957. *The Teaching of Classical Arabic to Speakers of the Colloquial in Iraq: A Study of the Problem of Linguistic Duality and its Impact on Language Education.* Ph.D. diss., Harvard University.

———————. 1969. *The Problem of Diglossia in Arabic: A Comparative Study of Classical Arabic and Iraqi Arabic.* Harvard Middle East Monographs, 21. Cambridge, Mass.: Harvard University Press.

Tsiapera, Maria. 1969. *A Descriptive Analysis of Cypriot Maronite Arabic.* Janua Linguarum, Series Practica, 66. The Hague: Mouton.

Al-Wahab, Abbas Sadik. 1971. *The Morphophonemics of the Iraqi Arabic Verb.* Ph.D. diss., University of Chicago, Chicago, Illinois.

Weaver, John. 1970. *Diglossia in Cyrenaica (Libya): An Exemplification.* M.A. thesis, University of Leeds.

Willms, Alfred. 1972. *Einführung in das Vulgärarabische von Nordwestafrika.* Leiden: E.J. Brill.

Wise, Hilary. 1975. *Syntax of the Verb Phrase of Colloquial Egyptian Arabic.* Special Publication of the Royal Philological Society, London. Oxford: Basil Blackwell.

Yassin, Mahmoud Aziz M. 1967. *A Study of Idioms in Colloquial Cairene Arabic.* M.A. thesis, University of London.

Al-Ziarah, Abdul Karim. 1953. *The English Loan-Words in the Arabic Language of Iraq.* M.A. diss., University of Texas at Austin.

El-Zorkani, Fatma A.H. 1965. *A Contrastive Study of Egyptian Cairene Arabic and English Verb Phrases.* M.A. diss., Brown University.

2.3 Grammar

Blanc, Haim. 1953. *Studies in North Palestinian Arabic. Linguistic inquiries among the Druzes of Western Galilee and Mount Carmel.* Jerusalem.

———. 1964. *Communal Dialects in Baghdad.* Harvard Middle Eastern Monographs, 10. Cambridge, Mass.: Harvard University Press.

Blau, Joshua. 1966–67. *A Grammar of Christian Arabic, Based Mainly on South Palestinian Texts from the First Millennium,* 3 vols. Louvain: Secretariat du Corpus Scriptorum Christianorum Orientalium.

Bloch, Ariel A. 1965. *Die Hypotaxe im Damaszenisch-Arabischen, mit Vergleichen zur Hypotaxe im Klassisch-Arabischen.* Wiesbaden: Franz Steiner.

Bravmann, Meir M. 1953. *Studies in Arabic and General Syntax.* Le Caire: Imprimerie de l'Institut Français d'Archéologie Orientale.

———. 1968. *The Arabic Elative. A New Approach.* Studies in Semitic Languages and Linguistics, vol. II. Leiden: E.J. Brill.

Brockelmann, Carl. 1948. *Arabische Grammatik. Paradigmen, Ubungsstucke und Glossar,* Leipzig: Otto Harrassowitz. Reprinted, 1969.

Cohen, David. 1963. *Le Dialecte Arabe Hassaniya de Mauritanie.* Avec la collaboration de Mohammed El Channafi. Paris: Librairie C. Klincksieck.

Cowan, David. 1968. *Modern Literary Arabic.* London & Cambridge: Cambridge University Press.

Diem, Werner. 1973. *Skizzen Jemenitischer Dialekte.* Beiruter Texte und Studien, Band 13. Beirut: Imprimerie Catholique.

Driver, C.R. 1925. *A Grammar of the Colloquial Arabic of Syria and Palestine.* London: Arthur Probsthain.

Erwin, Wallace M. 1963. *A Short Reference Grammar of Iraqi Arabic.* Washington: Georgetown University Press.

Gairdner, W.H.T. 1926. *Egyptian Colloquial Arabic: A Conversation Grammar.* London & Oxford: Oxford University Press.

Gatje, Helmut. 1973. *Zur Syntax der Determinationsverhaltnisse im Arabischen.* Mitteilungen des Deutschen Orient-Instituts, 2. Hamburg.

Grand'henry, Jacques. 1972. *Le Parler Arabe de Cherchell (Algerie).* Publication de l'Institut Orientaliste de Louvain, 5. Louvain-la-Neuve.

Grotzfeld, Heinz. 1965. *Syrisch-Arabische Grammatik (Dialekt von*

Damaskus). Porta Linguarum Orientalium, N.S. 8. Wiesbaden: Otto Harrassowitz.

Haywood, John A. & H.M. Nahmad. 1962. *A New Arabic Grammar of the Written Language.* London: Lund Humphries. 2nd edn., 1965.

Ibn Jinnī, 'Uthmān. 1885. *De Flexione Libellus.* Edited by Godofrendus Hoberg. Leipzig.

Lecomte, Gerard. 1968. *Grammaire de l'Arabe.* Que Sais-Je?Le point des connaissances Actuelles, 1275. Paris: Presses Universitaires de France.

Mainz, Ernst. 1931. *Zur Grammatik des modernen Schriftarabisch.* Hamburg.

Nasr, Raja Tawfik. 1967. *The Structure of Arabic: From Sound to Sentence.* Beirut: Librairie du Liban.

Piamenta, Moshe. 1966. *Studies in the Syntax of Palestinian Arabic: Simple Verb Forms in Subordinate and Main Clauses of Complex Sentences.* Jerusalem.

Reckendorf, H. 1921. *Arabische Syntax.* Heidelberg. Reprinted in Germany.

Scott, G.C. 1962. *Practical Arabic.* London: Longmans.

Thatcher, G.W. 1970. *Arabic Grammar of the Written Language. With Key.* Reprint. New York: Frederick Unger Publishing Co.

Wickens, G.M. 1980. *Arabic Grammar: A First Workbook.* Cambridge, London & c.: Cambridge University Press.

Wright, William. 1955. *A Grammar of the Arabic Language.* 3rd edn. 2 vols. Cambridge: Cambridge University Press.

2.4 Textbooks

Abboud, Peter F., N.A. Bezirgan, W.M. Erwin, M.A. Khouri, E.N. McCarus & R.M. Rammuny. 1968. *Elementary Modern Standard Arabic,* 2 parts. With Tapes. Ann Arbor, Michigan: Department of Near Eastern Studies, University of Michigan. Revised edn., 1975, by Abboud, Erwin, McCarus, Z.N. Abdel-Malek & G.N. Saad.

———. 1968. *Introduction to Modern Standard Arabic Pronunciation and Writing.* Ann Arbor, Michigan: Deaprtment of Near Eastern Studies, University of Michigan.

Beeston, A.F.L. 1969. *Arabic Historical Phraseology.* Supplement to

Written Arabic: An Approach to the Basic Structures. London: Cambridge University Press.

———. 1979. *Written Arabic: An Approach to the Basic Structures.* Reprint of 1968 edn. Cambridge: Cambridge University Press.

Bishai, Wilson B. 1971. *Concise Grammar of Literary Arabic. A New Approach.* Dubuque, Iowa: Kendall-Hunt Publishing Co.

Blachère, Régis. 1970. *Eléments de l'Arabe Classique: La Langue Arabe, Écriture, Lecture, Phonétique, Grammaire.* Paris: Adrien-Maisonneuve.

———. & M. Ceccaldi. 1970. *Exercices d'Arabe Classique.* 2nd edn. Paris: Adrien-Maisonneuve.

Bloch, Ariel A. & Heinz Grotzfeld. 1964. *Damaszenich-Arabische Texte. Mit Ubersetzung, Anmerkungen und Glossar herausgegeben.* Wiesbaden: Franz Steiner.

Cohen, David. 1964. *Le Parler Arabe des Juifs de Tunis: Textes et Documents Linguistiques et Ethnographiques.* The Hague: Mouton.

Daykin, Vernon. 1972. *Technical Arabic: A Language Reader Incorporating Technical and Scientific Terms.* London: Lund Humphries.

Englefield, Patrick, K. Ben Hamza & T. Abida. 1970. *Tunisian Arabic Basic Course,* 2 vols. Bloomington: Intensive Language Training Center, Indiana University.

Erwin, Wallace M. 1969. *A Basic Course in Iraqi Arabic.* Richard Harrell Arabic Series, 11. Washington, D.C.: Georgetown University Press.

Ess, John Van. 1971. *The Spoken Arabic of Iraq.* 2nd revised edn. London: Oxford University Press.

Ferguson, Charles A. & Moukhtar Ani. 1960. *Lessons in Contemporary Arabic. Lessons 1–8.* Washington, D.C.: Center for Applied Linguistics of the Modern Language Association of America.

Hanna, Sami Ayyad. 1965. *Beginning Arabic. A Linguistic Approach: From Cultivated Cairene to Formal Arabic.* Salt Lake City, Utah: University of Utah Printing Services.

———. 1965. *An Elementary Manual of Contemporary Literary Arabic.* Boulder, Colorado: Prutt Press.

———. & Naguib Greis. 1965. *Writing Arabic. A Linguistic Approach: From Sounds to Scripts.* Salt Lake City, Utah: University of Utah Printing Services. Revised edn., Leiden: E.J. Brill, 1972.

Harb, Hadia H. & Raja T. Nasr. 1973. *An Intermediate Colloquial*

Arabic Course. Beirut: Librairie du Liban.

Harder, E. 1968. *Arabische Sprachelehre. Mit Schlüssel.* 11th edn. Heidelberg.

Haywood, John A. & H.M. Nahmad. *Key to A New Arabic Grammar.* London: Lund Humphries.

Høybye, Poul. 1968. *Arabisk Kompendium.* København: Københavns Universitets Fond Tilvejebringelse af Laeremidler.

———. 1971. *Schlüssel zur Arabischen Sprache, Besonders fur Romanisten.* Bibliotheca Romanica, Series Prima, 11 A–B. Berne: A. Francke A.G. Verlag.

Kapliwatski, Jochanan. 1961–71. *Arabic Language and Grammar,* 4 vols. Jerusalem: Ruben Mas. Reprinted.

Kassab, Jean. 1970. *Manuel du Parler Arabe Moderne au Moyen-Orient,* vol. I. Publications du Centre Universitaire des Langues Orientales Vivantes, 6e serie, Tome VIII. Paris: Imprimerie Nationale, Librairie Orientaliste Paul Geuthner.

Klopfer, Helmut. 1963. *Modernes Arabisch. Eine Einführung ins heutige Zeitungs-Schriftarabisch (with tapes & records).* Heidelberg: Julius Groos Verlag. 2nd revised edn., 1970.

Koury, George J., ed. 1977. *An Arabic Reader for Beginners.* New York: Smyrna Press.

McCarus, Ernest, Hamdi Qafisheh & *Raji Rammuny. 1975. First Lessons in Literary Arabic.* Ann Arbor: Center for Near Eastern and North African Studies, University of Michigan.

The Middle East Centre for Arab Studies. 1965. *The MECAS Grammar of Modern Literary Arabic.* Beirut: Khayats.

Mitchell, T.F. 1970. *Writing Arabic: A Practical Introduction to Ruq'ah Script.* Reprint of 1953 edn. London, New York & Toronto: Oxford University Press.

Nasr, Raja Tawfik. 1978. *Learn to Read Arabic.* Beirut: Librairie du Liban & Troy, Michigan: International Book Centre.

———. 1978. *The Teaching of Arabic as a Foreign Language: Linguistic Elements.* Beirut: Librairie du Liban.

Pellat, Charles. 1956. *Introduction à l'arabe moderne.* Paris: Maisonneuve.

Qafisheh, Hamdi Ahmad. 1970. *Gulf Arabic, based on Colloquial Abū Dhabi Arabic.* Tuscon, Arizona: University of Arizona Environmental Research Laboratory.

Rabin, C. & H.M. Nahmad. 1947. *Arabic Reader.* Reprinted, 1978. London: Lund Humphries.

Rammuny, Raji M., A. Kh. al-Nami & M.I. Ali. 1978. *Al-Qirā'ah al-'Arabiyyah* (Reading Arabic). Ann Arbor, Michigan: The University of Michigan.

Saad, George N. 1979. *Arabic Sounds and Letters.* Amherst, Mass.: University of Massachusetts.

Siddiqui, Abdul Hameed & Mohammad Rafique. 1977. *Arabic for the Beginners.* Lahore: Kazi Publications.

Smith, Harlie L., Jr. 1969. *Modern Written Arabic.* Washington, D.C.: Department of State, Foreign Service Institute.

Tritton, Arthur S. 1943. *Arabic.* Teach Yourself Books. London: The English Universities Press. Reprinted.

Tubbs, Edward Joseph, Rev. 1972. *Visual Arabic Grammar-Lexicon.* Richmond, Surrey, England: Kingprint Ltd.

Velarde, A Khouri, L. Coleman & R. Nash Newton. 1980. *Arabic Phrase Book.* Teach Yourself Books. London: Hodder & Stoughton Ltd., New York: David McKay & Co. Inc.

Yellin, A. & L. Billig. 1931. *An Arabic Reader. Edited with Notes and a Glossary.* Jerusalem. Reprinted, 1979, by Johnson Reprint Corporation, New York.

Ziadeh, Farhat & R. B. Winder. 1957. *An Introduction to Modern Arabic.* Princeton, N.J.: Princeton University Press & London: Oxford University Press.

2.5 Dictionaries & Glossaries

Abcarius, J. John. 1974. *An English-Arabic Reader's Dictionary.* Beirut: Librairie du Liban.

'Āqil, Fākhir. 1971. *Dictionary of Psychological Expressions. English-Arabic-French.* Beirut: Dār al-Ilm lil-Malāyīn.

Badger, George Percy. 1881. *An English-Arabic Lexicon.* London. Reprinted, Beirut: Librairie du Liban, 1967.

Al-Ba'albakki, Munir. 1971. *Al-Mawrid. Modern English-Arabic Dictionary.* Beirut: Dar al-Ilm lil-Malayin.

Beg, Muhammad Abdul Jabbar. 1979. *Arabic Loan-Words in Malay: A*

Comparative Study. Kuala Lumpur: The University of Malaya Press.

Belot, Jean-Baptiste. 1952. *Dictionnaire Français-Arabe.* 2nd edn. Beirut: Imprimerie Catholique.

Benabdellah, Abdelaziz. 1969. *Lexique des Appareils, instruments et Outils.* Série Lexicographique, no. 8. Rabat: The Permanent Bureau for Arabization.

———. 1969. *Lexique sur la Nomenclature des Sciences, Arts, Doctrines et Systèmes.* Série Lexicographique, no. 9. Rabat: The Permanent Bureau for Arabization.

Bencheikh, T.E. 1968. *Glossaire Militaire de Langue Arabe.* Paris: Librairie de l'Armée.

El-Benhawy, Mohammed Amin. 1970. *Dictionary of Library Terms: English-Arabic.* Cairo: Dar al-Fikr al-'Arabi.

Blau, Joshua. 1970. *On Pseudo-Corrections in Some Semitic Languages.* Leiden: E.J. Brill.

Bocthor, Ellious. 1848. *Dictionnaire français-arabe.* Revised and supplemented by Caussin de Perceval. Paris.

Borisov, V.M. 1967. *Russko-Arabskij Slovar* (Russian-Arabic Dictionary). Moskva: Izdatel'stvo Sovetskaja enciklopedija.

Brill, Moshe, D. Neustadt & P. Schusser. 1940. *The Basic Word List of the Arabic Daily Newspaper.* Jerusalem: Hebrew University Press Association.

Cachia, Pierre J.E. 1974. *The Monitor. A Dictionary of Arabic Grammatical Terms. Arabic-English & English-Arabic.* London & Beirut: Longmans & Librairie du Liban.

Chebat, Anis. 1969. *Dictionnaire Technique Routier. Dictionnaire Français-Anglais-Arabe.* Rabat: The Permanent Bureau for Arabization.

Chéhabi, Yahya. 1967. *Vocabulaire des Archéologiques. Français-Arabe.* Publication de l'Academie Arabe de Damas. Damas: Imprimerie Taraki.

Corriente, Federico C. 1970. *Diccionario Español-Arabe.* Publications of Instituto Hispano-Arabe de Cutura in Madrid. Beirut: Imprimir por Dar Assakafa de Beirut en la Imprenta Goraieb.

Doniach, N.S., ed. 1972. *The Oxford English-Arabic Dictionary of Current Usage.* Oxford: Clarendon Press.

Dozy, Reinhart P.A. 1845. *Dictionnaire Détaillé des Noms des Vête-*

ments chez les Arabe. Amsterdam. Revised edn., 1971. Reprinted by Librairie du Liban, Beirut. Arabic translation is available, Baghdad.

———. 1881. *Supplement aux dictionnaires arabes.* 2 vols. Leiden: E.J. Brill.

———. & W.H. Engelmann. 1965. *Glossaire des Mots Espagnols et Portugais dérivés de l'Arabe.* Leiden: E.J. Brill.

Eguilaz, L. 1886. *Glossario Etimologico de las Palabras de Orgen Oriental.* Granada.

Elias, Elias Anton & Edward E. Elias. 1969. *Elias' Modern Dictionary: Arabic-English.* 9th edn. Cairo: Elias' Modern Press.

———. 1971. *Elias' Modern Dictionary: English-Arabic.* 17th edn. Cairo: Elias' Modern Press.

Faruqi, Harith S. 1970. *Faruqi's Law Dictionary: English-Arabic.* Beirut: Librairie du Liban.

Gateau, Albert. 1966. *Atlas et Glossaire Nautique Tunisiens,* 2 vols. Edited by Henri Charles. Beirut: Dar el-Machreq.

Hakki, Mamdouh. 1973. *Dictionnaire de Termes Juridiques et Commerciaux. Français-Arabe. Beirut:* Librairie du Liban.

Al-Ḥamawi, Ma'mūn. 1966. *Diplomatic Terms. English-Arabic.* Beirut: Khayats.

———. 1968. *Terms of International Relations and Politics. English-Arabic.* Beirut: Dar el-Machreq.

Harding, Gerald Lankester. 1971. *An Index and Concordance of Pre-Islamic Arabian Names and Inscriptions.* Near and Middle East Series, 8. Toronto & Buffalo: Toronto University Press.

Hawley, Donald. 1978. *Courtesies in the Gulf Area: A Dictionary of Colloquial Phrase and Usage.* London: Stacey International.

Henni, Mustapha. 1972. *Dictionnaire des Termes Économiques et Commerciaux. Français-Anglais-Arabe.* Beirut: Librairie du Liban.

Hitti, Yusuf K. 1972. *Hitti's English-Arabic Medical Dictionary.* Beirut: Librairie du Liban.

Al-Jawālīqī. 1969. *Al-Mu'arrab* (the Arabized words). Cairo.

Johannsen, H., A.B. Robertson & F.L. Brech, eds. 1972. *Management Glossary.* Translated by N. Ghattas. Beirut: Librairie du Liban.

Karam, Yusuf, M. Wahha & Y. Chlala. 1966. *Vocabulaire Philosophique. Français-Arabe.* Cairo: Costa Psoumas Press.

Karmi, Hasan S. 1971. *Al-Manār. An English-Arabic Dictionary.* London: Longman Group & Beirut: Librairie du Liban.

Al-Khaṭīb, Aḥmad Shafiq. 1971. *A New Dictionary of Scientific and Technical Terms. English-Arabic.* Beirut: Librairie du Liban.

Khaṭṭāb, Mahmoud Shīt, ed. 1970. *The Unifying Military Dictionary. Part I: English-Arabic.* Cairo: Dār al-Ma'ārif Press.

Krahl, Gunther. 1964. *Deutsh-Arabisches Wörterbuch.* Leipzig: Verlag Enzyklopädie. 2nd revised edn., Beirut: Librairie du Liban, 1971.

Kunitzsch, Paul. 1956. *Arabische Sternnamen in Europa.* Ph.D. diss., Freie Universität, Berlin.

Landau, Jacob M. 1959. *A Word Count of Modern Arabic Prose.* New York: American Council of Learned Societies, in cooperation with the School of Education, Hebrew University, Jerusalem.

Landberg, Carlo de. 1940. *Glossaire de la Langue des Bedouins 'Anazeh.* Uppsala-Leipzig: K.V. Zetterstéen.

Lane, Edward William. 1863–93. *Arabic-English Lexicon,* 8 vols. London. Also published in New York by Frederick Ungar, 1955. Reprinted in Germany and Beirut.

Madina, Maan Z. 1973. *Arabic-English Dictionary.* New York.

Massignon, Louis. 1922. *Essai sur les origines du Lexique technique de la Mystique Musalmane.* Paris.

The Middle East Centre for Arab Studies. 1959. *A Selected Word List of Modern Literary Arabic.* Beirut: Khayats. Reprinted, 1969.

Moinfar, Mohammad Djafar. 1970. *Le Vocabulaire Arabe dans le Livre des Rois de Firdausi. Étude Philologique et de Statistique Linguistique.* Wiesbaden: Otto Harrassowitz.

Muslih, Omar T. 1970. *Glossary of Petroleum Terms. English-Arabic.* Beirut: Dār al-Nahār.

Oweida, Ali Mahmoud. 1970. *The New Medical Pharmaceutical Dictionary. English–Arabic. With three appendices on clinical data, incompatibilities of drugs and chemicals, and posological tables.* Cairo: Dār al-Fikr al-'Arabī.

Pellegrini, Giovan Battista. 1972. *Gli Arabismi nelle Lingue Neolatine. Con Speciale Reguardo all'Italia,* 2 vols. Brescia: Paideia Edtitrice.

Penrice, J. 1971. *A Dictionary and Glossary of the Koran.* New York.

Petroleum Translation Publishing Services. 1972. *Dictionary of Petroleum. English-French-Arabic.* Publications of PTPS, Beirut, P.O. Box 5079. Beirut: al-Dār al-Sharqiyya Press.

Sabek, Jerwn. 1970. *Dictionary of Economics: Commerce, Industry, Finance, Law, with explanations and examples. English-Arabic.* Beirut: Imprimerie Joseph S. Saikali.

Al-Saran (Assaran), Hassan. 1967. *Al-Mustalah. English-Arabic Dictionary of Basic Scientific and Technical Terms.* Beirut. Reprinted. Taipei, 1977.

Schaller, Anton. 1967. *Dictionary of Surgical Terms. Latin-German-Arabic.* Vienna.

Siddiqi, Abdussattar. 1919. *Studien über die Persischen Fremdwörter im Klassischen Arabisch.* Göttingen: Vandenhoeck & Ruprecht.

Steingass, F. 1969. *A Learner's English-Arabic Dictionary.* Beirut: Librairie du Liban.

Taylor, Walt. 1933. *Arabic Words in English.* S.P.E., Tract no. 38. Oxford: The Clarendon Press.

———. 1934. *Etymological List of Arabic Words in English.* The Egyptian University Publication. Cairo: Noury Press.

Al-Wahab, Ibrahim I. 1963. *Law Dictionary: English-Arabic.* Baghdad. Revised edn., 1972.

Wahba, Magdi. 1968. *An English-Arabic Vocabulary of Scientific Technical and Culture Terms.* Cairo: Immobilia Building.

———. 1974. *A Dictionary of Literary Terms. English-French-Arabic.* Beirut: Librairie du Liban.

Wehr, Hans. 1961. *A Dictionary of Modern Written Arabic.* Edited by J. Milton Cowan. Ithaca, New York: Cornell University Press. Reprinted, Wiesbaden: Otto Harrassowitz. 3rd printing 1971. 2nd revised edn. 1980.

Yamulky, Perihan. 1966. *A Select Glossary of English Literary Terms (with Arabic translation): English-Arabic & Arabic-English.* Baghdad: University of Baghdad.

3.0 ARABIC LITERATURE

3.1 General

Abd-el-Jalil, J.-M. 1947. *Brève Histoire de la Littérature Arabe.* Paris.

Blachère, Régis. 1964. *Historie de la Littérature arabe des origines à la fin du XVe siècle de J.-C.* Paris: Adrien-Maisonneuve.

Boustany, Salahiddine. 1954. *The Press during the French Expedition in Egypt, 1798–1801*. Cairo.

Brockelmann, Carl. 1898–1902. *Geschichte der Arabischen Litteratur*, 2 vols. Weimar. Reprinted, Leiden: E.J. Brill, 2 vols. & 3 supplement vols., 1937–49.

Browne, E.G. 1902–24. *A Literary History of Persia*, 4 vols. 2nd edn., 1930. Cambridge: Cambridge University Press.

Cerulli, E. 1949. *Il "Libro della Scala" e la questione delle fonti arabo-spagnole della Divina Commedia*. Vatican City.

Conant, Martha P. 1908. *The Oriental Tale in England in the Eighteenth Century*. Reprinted, New York: Octagon Books, 1967.

Daghīr, Yūsuf As'ad. 1955. *Maṣādir al-Dirāsāt al-Adabiyyah* (sources of Arabic literature, in Arabic). Beirut.

Dozy, Reinhart P.A. 1881. *Recherches sur l'histoire et la litterature de l'Espagne pendant le moyen age*. 2 vols. 3rd edn. Leiden: E.J. Brill.

Gabrieli, Francesco. 1956. *Storia della lettereratura araba*. 2nd edn. Rome.

Gibb, H.A.R. 1974. *Arabic Literature: An Introduction*. Reprint of 1963 edn. London, Oxford & New York: Oxford University Press.

Hammer-Purgstall, J. von. 1850–56. *Litteraturgeschichte der Araber bis zum Ende des 12. Jahrhunderts der Hidschret*, 7 vols. Vienna.

Hartmann, M. 1899. *The Arabic Press of Egypt*. London.

Huart, Clément. 1903. *A History of Arabic Literature*. London.

Ibn Qutaiba. 1947. *Introduction au Livre de la Poésie et des Poètes*. Edited and translated into French by Gaudefroy-Demombynes. Paris.

Kokan, Muhammad Yusuf. 1971. *"India's contribution to Arabic literature"*, in *Dr. V. Raghavan Shashtyabdapurti Felicitation Volume*, 296–303. The Kuppuswami Research Institute, Mylapore, Madras. Madras: G.S. Press.

Kuryłowicz, Jerzy. 1973. *Studies in Semitic Grammar and Metrics*. Polska Akademia Nauk, Komitet Jezykoznawcze. Prace Jezykoznawcze, 67. London: Curzon Press.

Levy, R. 1923. *Persian Literature*. London.

Meester, Marie E. de. 1915. *Oriental Influences in the English Literature of the Nineteenth Century*, in *Anglistische Forschungen* (Heidelberg), no. 46.

Nallino, Carl A. 1950. *La littérature arabe*. Paris.

Nicholson, Reynold A. 1921. *Studies in Islamic Poetry*. Cambridge.

———. 1922. *Translations of Eastern Poetry and Prose*. Cambridge.

———. 1977. *A Literary History of the Arabs*. Reprint of 1930 edn. Cambridge, London, New York & Melbourne: Cambridge University Press.

Reiske, J.J. 1765. *Proben der arabischen Dichtkunst*. Leipzig. 2nd revised edn., Hoogly, 1841.

Schack, A.F. von. 1877. *Poesie und Kunst der Araber in Spanien und Sicilien*, 2 vols. 2nd edn. Stuttgart.

Smith, Byron Porter. 1939. *Islam in English Literature*. Beirut: American Press.

Stetkevych, Jaroslav. 1970. *The Modern Arabic Literary Language: Lexical and Stylistic Developments*. A Publication of the Center for Middle Eastern Studies, no. 6. Chicago & London: The University of Chicago Press.

3.2 Ancient Literature

Ahlwardt, W. 1870. *The Dīwāns of the Six Ancient Arabic Poets*. London.

Arberry, Arthur J. 1957. *The Seven Odes*. London: Cambridge University Press.

El-Ashmāwī, Mohammed Zaki Mohammed. 1954. *Arabic Literary Criticism until the Fifth Century of Hijra with Special Reference to Abdul Qāhir's Theory of Construction*. Ph.D. diss., University of London.

Bateson, Mary Catherine. 1970. *Structural Continuity in Poetry: A Linguistic Study in Five Pre-Islamic Arabic Odes*. The Hague & Paris: Mouton.

Blachère, Régis. 1935. *Un Poète arabe du IVe siècle de l'Hégire*. Paris.

Bloch, Alfred. 1946. *Vers und Sprache im Altarabischen. Metrische und Syntaktische Untersuchungen*. Basel: Verlag für Recht und Gesellschaft.

Blunt, Lady Anne. 1903. *The Seven Golden Odes of Pagan Arabia*, translated from the original Arabic by Lady Ann Blunt and done into English Verse by Wilfrid Scawen Blunt. London.

Bohlen, P. von. 1824. *Commentatio de Motenabbio.* Bonn.

Bonebakker, S.A. 1966. *Some Early Definitions of the Tawriya and Ṣafadi's Faḍḍ al-Khitām.* Publications in Near and Middle East Studies, Columbia University, Series A, 8. The Hague: Mouton.

Al-Būṣīrī. 1894. *La Bordah du Cheik el-Bousiri.* Arabic poem translated into French by René Basset. Paris: Leroux. English translations by J.W. Redhouse in *W.A. Clouston's Arabian Poetry for English Readers,* Glasgow, 1881. Also by Arthur Jeffery in *Reader on Islam,* The Hague, 1962.

Clouston, W.A. 1881. *Arabian Poetry for English Readers.* Glasgow.

Compton, Linda Fish. 1972. *Andalusian Muwashshaḥs with Mozarabic and Arabic Kharjas: Towards a Better Understanding of the Oldest Known Lyrical Poetry in Romance Vernacular.* Ph.D. diss., Princeton University.

Cour, A. 1920. *Ibn Zaidūn. Un poète arabe d'Andalousie.* Constantine.

Dermenghem, E. 1931. *Al-Khamrīya* (a mystic poem by Ibn al-Fāriḍ). Paris.

Dieterici, F. 1847. *Mutanabbi und Seifuddaula.* Leipzig.

Al-Ghazālī (al-Ghazzali). 1933. *O Youth.* Translated by G.H. Scherer. Beirut.

Al-Ḥallāj, Husain Mansour. 1955. *Dīwān* (anthology of his poems). Edited and translated into French by Louis Massignon. Paris: Cahiers du Sud.

Al-Hamadhānī, Badī' al-Zamān. 1915. *The Maqamāt* (the Assemblies). Translated by W. Prendergast. Madras.

Hamilton, T., translator. 1820. *Romance of 'Antar.* London.

Hammar-Purgstall, J.von. 1824. *Al-Motenabbi, der grösste arabische Dichter.* Vienna.

Al-Ḥarīrī. 1844. *Die Vewandlungen des Abu Seid von Serug* (translation of al-Hariri's *Assemblies*). Translated by F. Rückert. 2 vols. Stuttgart and Tübingen.

———. 1867–98. *The Assemblies, 2 vols.* Translated by T. Chenery, and continued by P. Steingass, London.

Haywood, John A. 1974. *'Thousand and One Nights",* in *Encyclopaedia Britannica,* 15th edn.

Heinrichs, Wolfhart. 1969. *Arabische Dichtung und Griechische Poetik. Ḥāzim al-Qarṭajannis Grundlegung der Poetik mit Hilfe Aristotelischer*

Begriffe. Wiesbaden: Franz Steiner.

Hirschberg, J.W. 1931. *Der Dīwān des al-Samaw'al ibn 'Ādiyā'*. Cracow.

Ibn Abī Ṭālib, 'Alī. 1907. *La Kaṣīda ez-Zainabiyya* (a poem attributed to 'Ali). Translated by A. Raux. Paris.

Ibn Bajja (Avempace). 1946. *Tadbīr al-Mutawaḥḥid* (El régimen del solitario). Edited by M. Asín Palacios. Madrid. Also edited in Beirut, 1978.

Ibn Ḥazm. 1953. *The Ring of the Dove*. Translated by A.J. Arberry. London.

Ibn Ṭufail. 1900. *Ḥayy Ibn Yaqẓān*. Translated into French by Leon Gaithier. Algiers.

———. 1904. *The Awakening of the Soul*. Translated by P. Bronle. Wisdom of the East Series. London.

Ikhwān al-Ṣafā'. 1869. *Dispute between Man and the Animals*. Translated into English by J. Platts. London: W.H. Allen & Co.

Jacobi, Renate. 1971. *Studien zur Poetic der Altarabischen Qaṣīda*. Akademie der Wissenschaften und der Literature (Mainz). Wiesbaden: Franz Steiner.

Al-Jāḥiẓ. 1915. *"The merits of the Turks"* Translated by Harley Walker. In the *Journal of the Royal Asiatic Society*. London.

———. 1922. *Kitāb al-Maḥāsin wal-Aḍdād*, 2 vols. Translated into German by O Rescher. Stuttgart.

———. 1951. *Le Livre des Avares*. Translated by Charles Pellat. Paris.

Lasater, Alice Elizabeth. 1971. *Hispano-Arabic Relationships to the Works of the Gawain-Poet*. Ph.D. diss., University of Tennessee.

Lewin, B., editor. 1950. *Der Dīwān des Abdallah ibn al-Mu'tazz*. Istanbul.

Linker, Susan Mott. 1973. *Los Arabismos en la Poesia Castellana, Aragonesa y Leonesa del Siglo XIV* (Spanish text). Ph.D. diss., University of North Carolina at Chapel Hill.

Lyall, Sir Charles James. 1885. *Translations of Ancient Arabian Poetry, Chiefly Pre-Islamic*. London.

———. 1930. *Ancient Arabian Poetry*. London.

Al-Ma'arrī, Abū al-'Alā'. 1898. *The Letters of Abū al-'Alā'*. Translated into English by D.S. Margoliouth. Oxford.

———. 1947. *The Epistle of Forgiveness*. Edited by Kāmil Kīlānī. Translated by G. Brackenbury. Cairo.

Mandoza, Nancy. 1973. *Arabian Daze and Bedouin Knights: Arabic Rhetorical Theory to 1492.* Ph.D. diss., Washington State University.

Mehren, A.F.M. von. 1853. *Die Rhetorik der Araber. Nach den Wichtigsten Quellen Dargestellt und mit Angefugten Textauszugen nebst einem Literatur-Geschichtlichen Anhang Versehen.* Kopenhagen und Wien. Reprinted, 1970.

Miquel, Andre, translator. 1957. *Kalīla wa Dimna.* French translation. Paris.

Nöldeke, Theodor. 1864. *Beitrage zur Kenntniss der Poesie der alten Araber.* Hannover.

———. 1899–1901. *Fünf Mu'allaqāt übersetzt und erklärt.* 2 vols. Vienna.

Nykl, A.R. 1933. *El Cancionero de Aben Guzmān* (Ibn Quzmān). Madrid.

———. 1946. *Hispano-Arabic Poetry.* Baltimore.

Palmer, E.H. 1976. *The Poetical Works of Bahā al-Dīn Zuhair.* Cambridge.

Potter, G.R. 1929. *The Autobiography of Ousāma.* Broadway Medieval Literatures. London.

Prendergast, J. 1915. *The Maqāmāt (Assemblies) of Badī' al-Zamān al–Hamadhānī.* London.

Ramli, Bashir Mohamed. 1969. *Philology, Rhetoric and Literary Criticism in the Study I'jāz during the Fourth Century A.H.* Ph.D. thesis, University of London.

Al-Rāzī, Fakhruddīn. 1924–5. *Al-Mabāḥith al-Mashriqiyya,* 4 vols. Hyderabad.

———. 1939–40. *Majma' al-Rasā'il,* 2 vols. Hyderabad: Deccan.

Schmidt, Werner. 1971. *Die Natur in der Dichtung der Andalus-Araber. Versuch einer Strukturanalysis Arabischer Dichtung.* Ph.D. diss., Christian-Universitat zu Kiel.

Al-Ṭughrā'ī. 1881. *Lāmiyyat al-'Ajam* (a poem). Translated by J.W. Redhouse in W.A. Clouston's *Arabian Poetry for English Readers,* Glasgow.

Ullmann, Manfred. 1966. *Untersuchungen zur Rajazpoesie. Ein Beitrag zur Arabischen Sprach- und Literaturwissenschaft.* Wiesbaden: Otto Harrassowitz.

Wagner, Ewald. 1965. *Abū Nuwās. Eine Studie zur Arabischen Literatur der Frühen 'Abbasidenzeit.* Akademie der Wissenschaften und der Literatur, Veröffentlichungen der Orientalischen Kommission, 17. Wiesbaden.

Weil, Gotthold. 1958. *Grundriss und System der altarabischen Metren.* Wiesbaden: Otto Harrassowitz.

Zaidān, Jurjī. n.d. *Al-Abbassa ou la soer du Calife.* Translated by M.Y. Bitar and Charles Moulié. Edited by C. Farrière. Paris.

Zimmermann, Samuel A. 1969. *Arabic Influence in the Tales of El-Conde Lucanor.* Ph.D. diss., University of Florida.

3.3 Modern Literature

Abdel Meduid, Abdel Aziz. 1950. *The Modern Arabic Short Story: Its Emergence, Development, and Form.* Cairo.

Arberry, Arthur John. 1952. *"Fresh light on Aḥmad Fāris al-Shidyāq",* in *Islamic Culture* (Hyderabad) 26. 155–64.

———. 1975. *Modern Arabic Poetry: An Anthology with English Verse Translations.* Reprint of 1950 edn. London: Cambridge University Press.

Aziz, Yowell Yousef. 1968. *The Influence of English Grammar, Syntax, Idiom and Style upon Contemporary Literary Arabic.* Ph.D. diss., University of St. Andrews, Scotland.

El-Azma, Nazeer Fowzi. 1969. *Free Verse in Modern Arabic Literature.* Ph.D. diss., Indiana University at Bloomington.

Cachia, Pierre. 1956. *Ṭāha Husayn, His Place in the Egyptian Literary Renaissance.* London: Luzac & Co.

Edham, I.A. 1936. *Abū Shādī the Poet.* Leipzig.

Al-Ḥakīm, Tawfīq. 1950. *Théâtre arabe.* Paris.

Haywood, John A. 1971. *Modern Arabic Literature, 1800–1970: An Introduction, with Extract in Translation.* London: Lund Humphries.

Husain, Ṭāha. 1932. *An Egyptian Childhood.* Translated into English by E.H. Paxton. London.

———. 1948. *The Stream of Days.* Translated by Hilary Wayment. London.

Izzedien, Yousuf. 1962. *Poetry and Iraqi Society, 1900–1945.* Baghdad.

Jayyūsī, Salma Khadra. 1977. *Trends and Movements in Modern Arabic Poetry*, 2 vols. Leiden: E.J. Brill.

Jibran (Gibran), Jibran Khalil. 1926. *The Prophet.* London: Heinemann.

Khouri, Mounah A. 1971. *Poetry and the Making of Modern Egypt, 1882–1922.* Leiden: E.J. Brill.

Landau, J. 1958. *Studies in the Arab Theater and Cinema.* Philadelphia.

Lecerf, J. & G. Wiet. translators. 1947. *Le livre des jours.* Paris.

Moreh, S. 1966. *"Blank verse in modern Arabic literature"*, in *Bulletin of the School of Oriental and African Studies* (London) 29.483 ff.

———. 1966. *Strophic, Blank and Free Verse in Modern Arabic Literature.* Ph.D. thesis, University of London.

———. 1968. *"Free verse in modern Arabic literature: Abū Shādī and his school, 1926–46"*, in *Bulletin of the School of Oriental and African Studies* (London) 31.28–51.

Naimy, Mikhail. 1964. *Khalil Gibran: His Life and Work.* Beirut.

Roth-Laly, Arlette. 1967. *Le Théâtre Algérien de Langue Dialectale, 1926–1954.* Paris: François Maspero.

Selim, George Dimitri. 1970. *The Poetic Vocabulary of Iliya Abu Madi (1889–1957): A Computational Linguistic Study of 47, 766 Words.* Ph.D. diss., Georgetown University.

Serjeant, R.B. 1951. *Prose and Poetry from Ḥaḍramawt.* Oxford: Taylor's Foreign Press.

Stetkewych, Jaroslav. 1962. *Modern Arabic Poetic and Prose Language.* Ph.D. diss., Harvard University.

Subhi, Hasan Abbas. 1969. *The Influence of Modern English Writers on Arab Poets from 1939–1960.* Ph.D. diss., University of Edinburgh.

Al-Zubaidi, Abd Al-Mun'im K. 1967. *Al-Akkād's Critical Theories with Special Reference to his Relationship with the Dīwān School and to the Influence of European Writers upon him.* Ph.D. diss., University of Edinburgh.

3.4 Folklore

Bauer, Leonhard. 1903. *Volksleben im Lande der Bibel.* Leipzig: Kommissionsverlag von H.G. Wallmann.

Burckhardt, John Lewis. 1980. *Arabic Proverbs: The Manners and Customs of the Modern Egyptians,* translated and explained by J.L.

Burckhardt. Introduction by C.E. Bosworth. Reprint of 1972 edn. London: Curzon Press.

Al-Dhubaib, Ahmad M. 1966. *A Critical and Comparative Study of the Ancient Arabic Proverbs contained in al-Maidani's Collecion.* Ph.D. diss., University of Leeds.

Freytag, G.W. 1838–43. *Arabum Proverbia.* Arabic text with Latin translation, 3 vols. Bonn.

Ghanem, Mohamed Abdu. 1969. *Verse Used in Ṣan'ānī Songs.* Ph.D. diss., University of London.

Goitein, S.D.F. 1934. *Jemenica: Sprichwörter und Redensarten aus Zentral-Jemen. Mit Zahlreichen Sach- und Worterlauterngen.* Leiden: E.J. Brill. Reprinted, 1970.

Hurgronje, Christian Snouck. 1886. *"Mekkanische Sprichwörter und Redensarten",* in *Bijdragen tot de Taal- land- en Volkenkunde van Nederlandsch Indie* 5/1. 433–576. Also in *Verspreide Geschriften, Deel* 5.1–112 (1925).

Jargy, Simon. 1970. *La Poésie Populaire Traditionelle Chantée au Proche-Orient Arabe.* Paris & The Hague: Mouton.

Al-Jawharī, Muḥammad. 1975. *Maṣādir Dirāsat al-Fulkulūr al-'Arabī* (sources of the Arabic folklore, in Arabic). Cairo.

Johnson-Davies, Denys. 1946. *Tales from Egyptian Life.* Cairo.

Littmann, Enno. 1902. *Neuarabische Volkspoesie.* Berlin.

———. 1902. *Neuarabische Volkspoesie gesammelt und ūbersetzt.* Berlin.

———. 1937. *Kairener Sprichwörter und Rastel.* Abhandlungen für die Kunde des Morgenlandes, 22. 5. Wiesbaden: Franz Steiner. Reprinted, Leipzig, 1966.

———. 1944. *Kairener Volksleben. Arabische Texte Hausgegeben und Ubersetzt.* Abhandlungen für die Kunde des Morgenlandes, 26. 2. Wiesbaden: Franz Steiner. Reprinted, Nendeln, Liechtenstein: Kraus Reprint Ltd., 1966.

Al-Marzūqī, Muḥammad. 1967. *Folk Literature in Tunisia* (in Arabic). Tunis: The Tunisian Publishing House.

Massou, I.S. 1963. *Religious Folklore of the Bethlehem District in Jordan.* Ph.D. diss., University of London.

Vinnikov, I.N. 1941. *Araby v SSSR (Etnografija, folklor i jazyk).* Ph.D. diss., University of Leningrad.

3.5 Novels & Short Stories

Ebied, R.Y. & M.J.L. Young, translators. 1977. *Arab Stories: East and West.* Leeds: Monograph and Occasional Series, no. 11., Leeds University Oriental Society.

Al-Ḥakīm, Tawfīq. 1939. *La caverne des songes.* Translated by Khédri. Paris.

———. 1947. *The Maze of Justice.* Translated by A. Eban. London.

———. 1965. *Quei della Caverna.* Translated by R. Rubinacci. Naples.

———. 1966. *The Tree Climber.* Translated by Denys Johnson-Davies. London.

Idris, Yusuf. 1978. *The Cheapest Nights: Short Stories.* Translated by Wadida Wassef. African Writers Series. London: Heinemann, Washington, D.C.: Three Continents Press.

Jibran, Jibran Khalil. 1947. *Rebellious Spirits.* London.

———. 1948. *Nymphs of the Valley.* London.

Johnson-Davies, Denys. 1978. *Modern Arabic Short Stories.* Selected and translated by Johnson-Davies. Reprint of 1967 edn. Arab Authors Series. London: Heinemann Educational Books Ltd.

Mahfouz, Naguib. 1967. *Mirmar.* Translated by Fatma Moussa-Mahmoud. Edited by Maged el Kommos and John Rodebbeck. Introduction by John Fowles. African Writers Series. London: Heinemann Educational Books Ltd. Reprinted, 1978.

———. 1970. *Midaq Alley.* African Writers Series, 151. London: Heinemann Educational Books.

Rouger, Gustave, translator. 1923. *Le roman d'Antar.* Paris.

Salih, Tayeb. 1969. *Season of Migration to the North.* Translated from the Arabic by Denys Johnson-Davies. Arab Authors Series. London: Heinemann Educational Books. Reprinted, 1980.

———. 1969. *The Wedding of Zein, and other Stories.* Translated by Denys Johnson-Davies. African Writers Series, 47. London: Heinemann Educational Books Ltd. Reprinted, 1980 (Arab Authors Series).

Taimūr, Maḥmūd. 1950. *Le courtier de la mort.* Paris.

———. 1952. *La belle aux lèvres charnues.* Paris.

———. 1953. *La fleur au cabaret.* Paris.
———. 1954. *Bonne fête.* Paris.

3.6 Anthologies

Abdel-Malek, Anouar. 1965. *Anthologie de la littérature arabe contemporaine, II: les essais.* Paris.

Abū Nuwās. 1855. *Dīwān* (Anthology of his poems). Translated into German by W. von Kremer. Vienna.

Arberry, Arthur John. 1965. *Arabic Poetry: A Primer for Students.* Cambridge: The University Press.

———. 1967. *Poems of al-Mutanabbī: A Selection with Introduction, Translations and Notes.* Cambridge: The University Press.

Badawi, M.M. 1970. *An Anthology of Modern Arabic Verse.* Reprinted, 1975. Oxford University Press.

Boullata, Issa J., translator & ed. 1976. *Modern Arab Poets.* Arab Authors Series. London: Heinemann Educational Books.

Farazdaq. 1870–5. *Dīwān* (anthology of his poems). Translated into French by R. Boucher. Paris.

Howarth, Herbert & Ibrahim Shakrullah. 1944. *Images from the Arab World.* London: Pilot Press.

Ibn al-Abraṣ, 'Abīd. *Dīwān* (anthology of the poems by Ibn al-Abraṣ). Translated into English by Sir Charles Lyall, Leiden: E.J. Brill.

Imru'al-Qais. 1837. *Dīwān d'Amro'lkais.* Translated into French by MacGuckin de Slane. Paris.

Jarīr & Farazdaq. 1905. *The Naqā'iḍ of Jarīr and al-Farazdaq.* Edited by Anthony Ashley Bevan. Leiden: E.J. Brill.

Al-Khansā'. 1944. *Dīwān: I tempi . . . e il canzoniere della poetessa araba al-Khansā'.* Translated into Italian by G. Gabrieli. Rome.

Khemiri, T. & G. Kampffmeyer. 1930. *Leaders in Contemporary Arabic Literature.* Berlin.

Labīd. 1891. *Dīwān: Die Gedichte des Lebīd.* Übers. A. Hüber. Leiden.

Lyall, Sir Charles James. 1918. *Al-Mufaḍḍaliyyāt* (anthology of Arabic poetry). Oxford.

Makarius, R. & L. 1964. *Anthologie de la littérature arabe contemporaine, I: le roman et la nouvelle.* Paris.

Monteil. Vincent. 1961. *Anthologie bilingue de la littérature arabe.* Beirut.

Al-Mutanabbī, Abū al-Ṭayyib. 1964. *Dīwān* (Anthology). Edited by Nāṣif al-Yāzijī. Beirut.

Al-Nābigha. 1869. *Dīwān* (anthology of his poems). Translated into French by Hartwig Derenbourg. Paris.

Rückert, Friedrich, translator. 1846. *Hamāsa oder die älteste arabischen Volkslieder übersetzt und erläutert,* 2 vols. Stuttgart.

Wightman, George & Abdullah Y. al-Udhari, translators. 1975. *Birds Through a Ceiling of Alabaster: Three Abbasid Poets. Arab Poetry of the Abbasid Period.* Harmondsworth, Middlesex, England: Penguin Books Ltd.

4.0 JOURNALS RELATED TO ARABIC AND ISLAMIC STUDIES

Abr-Nahrain
An Annual under the auspices of the Department of Semitic Studies, University of Melbourne. Leiden: E.J. Brill.

Al-Andalus
Revista de las Escuelas de estudios árabes de Madrid y Granada. Madrid & Granada.

American Journal of Arabic Studies, The
Leiden: E.J. Brill.

Arabica
Revue d'études arabes. Leiden: E.J. Brill.

Al-'Arabiyya
Journal of the American Association of Teachers of Arabic, University of Chicago.

Asian and African Studies
Department of Oriental Studies of the Slavonic Academy of Sciences, Bratislava. London: Curzon Press.

Atlal
Publication of the Directorate General of Antiquities, Riyadh, Saudi Arabia.

Bibliotheca Orientalis
Leiden: Nederlands Instituut voor het Nabije Oosten.

Bulletin d'Études Orientales
Damas.
Bulletin of the School of Oriental and African Studies.
S.O.A.S., University of London.
Bustan
Hammar-Purgstall-Gesellschaft-Österreichische Zeitschrift für Kultur, Politik und Wirtschaft der Islamischen Länder.
Central Asiatic Journal
International periodical for the languages, literature, history and archaeology of Central Asia. The Hague & Wiesbaden.
Comptes rendus du Groupe Linguistique d'Études Chamito-Sémitique.
Paris.
Der Islam
Zeitschrift für Geschichte und Kultur des Islamischen Orients. Berlin.
Die Welt des Islams
Leiden: E.J. Brill.
Die Welt des Orients
Wissenschaftliche Beiträge zur Kunde des Morgenlandes. Vandehoeck & Ruprecht in Göttingen.
Folia Orientalia
Revue des études orientales. Kraków.
International Journal of Middle East Studies
Middle East Studies Association of North America. Cambridge: Cambridge University Press.
Islamic Culture
An English Quarterly. Hyderabad, India.
Islamic Literature, The
Lahore, Pakistan.
Islamic Quarterly, The
A review of Islamic Culture. London: The Islamic Cultural Centre.
Islamica
Leipzig
Journal of Arabic Literature
Leiden: E.J. Brill.
Journal of Maltese Studies
Valetta, Malta.

Journal of Near Eastern Studies
Chicago.
Journal of Semitic Studies
Department of Semitic Studies, University of Manchester.
Manchester: The University Press.
Journal of the American Oriental Society
The American Oriental Society, New Haven, Conn.
Journal of the Faculty of Arts
University of Malta, Msida, Malta.
Journal of the Faculty of Arts
University of Riyadh, Riyadh, Saudi Arabia.
Journal of the Royal Asiatic Society of Great Britain and Ireland.
London.
Levante
Revista Trimestrale de Centro per la Relazione Italo-Arabe. Rome.
Al-Lisān al-'Arabī (The Arabic Tongue)
Publication of the Bureau for Coordination of Arabization of the Arab League, Rabat.
Al-Lisāniyyāt (Linguistics)
Revue Algérienne de Linguistique. Alger: Institut de Linguistique et phonétique. Université d'Alger.
Mélanges de l'Institut Dominican d'Études Orientales.
Cairo.
Mélanges de l'Université Saint-Joseph
Beirut, Lebanon.
Middle East Journal
A quarterly publication of the Middle East Institute, Washington, D.C.
Middle East Studies Association Bulletin
New York.
Middle Eastern Affairs
Elmont, New York.
Middle Eastern Studies
London: Frank Cass.
Muslim World, The
Hartford, Connecticut.

Oriens
Milletlerarasi Sark Tetkikleri Cemiyeti Mecmuasi/Journal of the International Society for Oriental Research. Leiden.
Orientalia
Commentarii periodici Pontificii Instituti Biblici. Nova Series. Roma.
Orientalia Gandensia
Jaarboek van het Hoger Instituut voor Oosterse, Oosteuropese en Afrikaanse taalkunde en geschiedenis bij de Rijksuniversiteit te Gent Leiden-Leuven.
Orientalia Pragensia
Praha.
Orientalia Suecana
Uppsala-Stockholm, Sweden.
Revue de l'École Nationale des Langues Orientales
Paris.
Revue de l'Institut des Manuscrits Arabe Le Caire.
Cairo, Egypt.
Revue de l'Occident Musulman et de la Méditerranée, Centre National de la Scientifique et de Universités d'Aux-Marseille.
Aix-en-Provence.
Revue des Études Islamiques
Paris.
Revue du Monde Musulman.
Paris.
Rivista degli Studi Orientali
Roma.
Rocznik Orientalistyczny
Polska Akademia Nauk, Komitet Nauk Orientalistyeznych.
Warszawa, Poland.
Sefarad
Revista del Instituto Arias Montano Estudios Hebraicos y Oriente Proximo.
Studia et Acta Orientalia
Association d'Études Orientales de la Republique Socialiste de Roumainie. Bucarest.
Studia Islamica
Paris.
Studia Orientalia
Societas Orientalis Fennica. Helsinki, Finland.

Studies in Islam
New Delhi.
Sumer
A journal of archaeology and history in Iraq. Directorate General of Antiques. Baghdad, Iraq.
Al-Turāth al-Sha'bī (Folklore)
A monthly journal issued by the Ministry of Culture and Information, Baghdad, Iraq.
Voice of Islam
Karachi, Pakistan.
Zeitschrift der Deutschen Morgenländischen Gesellschaft.
Wiesbaden.
Zeitschrift für arabische Linguistik
Journal of Arabic Linguistics/Journal de Linguistique Arabe.
Wiesbaden: Otto Harrassowitz.

5.0 ENCYCLOPAEDIAS OF RELEVANCE TO THE SUBJECT

A Dictionary of Islam. 1885. Edited by T.P. Hughes. London Reprinted, 1935.
Encyclopaedia Britannica. 1974. 15th edn. Also other edns.
Encyclopaedia of Islam. 1908–38. 1st complete edn.
Leiden: Luzac & Leiden: E.J. Brill.
Encyclopaedia of Islam. 1957–(in progress). New edn.
Leiden: E.J. Brill & London: Luzac.
Encyclopaedia of Religion and Ethics. 1922. Edited by James Hastings.
New York: Charles Scribner's Sons.
Encyclopaedia of the Persian Gulf. 1980. Baltimore: Johns Hopkins University Press.
Shorter Encyclopaedia of Islam. 1953. Edited by Hamilton A.R. Gibb and J.K. Kramers. London: Luzac.

INDEX

بسم الله الرحمن الرحيم

إهداء

إلى مقام حضرة صاحب الجلالة

الملك فهد بن عبد العزيز المفدى

وولي عهده الأمين صاحب السمو الملكي

الأمير عبد الله بن عبد العزيز

والنائب الثاني صاحب السمو الملكي

الأمير سلطان بن عبد العزيز

لما يولونه للغة العربية والدراسات الإسلامية

من الاهتمام الكبير والتشجيع المتزايد

والله ولي التوفيق

أعد هذا الكتاب خصيصاً للاحتفال بالذكرى الخامسة والعشرين
(العيد الفضي) لميلاد جامعة الملك سعود
مع أطيب التمنّيات والوفاء لجامعتي الفتيّة .

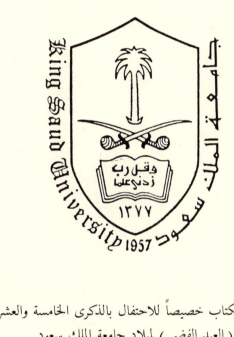

الثقافة العربية الإسلامية

من خلال اللغة والأدب

تأليف

الدكتور محمد حسن باكلا

أستاذ اللسانيات والصوتيات

كلية الآداب - معهد اللغة العربية

جامعة الملك سعود - الرياض - المملكة العربية السعودية

مؤسسة كيغان پول العالمية

لندن - بوسطن - ملبورن - هنلي

١٤٠٤ هـ / ١٩٨٤ م

مُقدِّمة

من حقّ اللغة العربيّة على العرب والمسلمين المحافظة عليها بالمداولة والاستعمال الصحيحين الدقيقين؛ فأساس اللغة الاستعمال، وحياتها في التداول بها على الألسنة والأقلام. ومن حقّ العربيّة على أبنائها العرب أن يسعوا لنشرها والتعريف بها في كلّ زمان ومكان. ولا يتوقّع من اللغة – أيّ لغة – أن تنتشر بنفسها أو أن يكون لها القدرة على الانتشار الذاتيّ، لأنّ هذا ليس طبيعيّاً في سنن اللغات. والواقع أنّ العربيّة – لغة وحضارة – لم يكن لها لتنتشر لولا جهود السلف المخلصة وأعمالهم الخالدة الّتي حقّقت لها الانتشار والاتساع – عموديّاً وأفقيّاً – في كثير من بقاع العالم القديم والجديد. وليس كعصرنا هذا عصر تجد العربية فيه منافسة شديدة على البقاء والانتشار (حتّى في عقر دارها). فلغة الضاد في عصرنا الحديث في أمسّ الحاجة من أيّ عصر مضى إلى تخطيط علمي دقيق وعمل دائب مستمرّ ومسئوليّة ضخمة جسيمة على الأفراد والجماعات والحكومات للحفاظ عليها ودفعها إلى الأمام كي تنال مكانتها اللائقة بها والملائمة لها. والمسئولية تقع على عاتق كلّ عربيّ جنساً أو لغة، داخل الوطن العربي أو خارجه. إن أساليب نشر العربية بالطرق التقليدية في هذا العصر قد تؤدّي أحياناً إلى العزوف عن تعلّمها إلى لغات وآداب أخرى. ونجد بالفعل هذا الاتجاه بين الطلّاب من العرب وغيرهم. وعندما يترجم هذا الميل أو العزوف إلى أرقام فإنّ العربية – لغة وأدباً وحضارة وثقافة – تنتابها خسائر لا تقدّر بثمن ولا تقيّم (أو تقوّم إن شئت) بمال.

وعلى الرغم من أنّ المكتبة العربيّة تكتظّ بالكتب العربيّة المتداولة بين أبناء العرب على مختلف مستوياتهم وطبقاتهم الأدبيّة والثقافية فإنّها تعدّ - إذا ما قيست بأخواتها من اللغات العالمية الأخرى - فقيرة جداً كمّاً ونوعاً، وبخاصّة فيما يتعلّق بتعريف العربيّة وآدابها للناطقين باللغات الأخرى. بل إنّ من المخجل حقّاً أن يقال إنّ ما يكتبه غير العرب والمسلمين - وبخاصة من الغربيّين - عن العروبة والإسلام أكثر فيضاً وأعمق تأثيراً وأسرع انتشاراً. ويظلّ هذا المشكل قائماً ما لم يتّجه البحث العلميّ لدينا إلى حلّ سليم وسريع له. ويزداد المشكل عمقاً واتّساعاً في عصرنا عندما نرى الأنظار ترنو إلى العربيّة وآدابها دون أن تجد ما يبلّ الصدى ويروي الغليل. أذكر أنّني في زياراتي المتكرّرة لمكتبات شرقيّة وغربيّة كثيراً ما ألاحظ عدم توفّر أو توافر الكتب المناسبة للمستويات المختلفة من القرّاء، وبخاصّة ممّن يرغبون في معرفة أو تحصيل معلومات عن العرب ولغتهم وآدابهم. وعندما يقارن الوضع بلغات حديثة ليست لها عراقة العربيّة وانتشارها وأهمّيّتها نجد أنّ بعض هذه اللغات في وضع أحسن ومركز أقوى. ويزيد الأمر سوءاً وتعقيداً عندما يحس العربيّ منّا بأنّ من أبناء جلدته - حتّى من بين المثقّفين منهم - من يقلّل من أهمّيّة وضع كتب أو موادّ تثقيفيّة بلغات حديثة غير غربيّة عن العربيّة وآدابها وحضارتها. أذكر أنّني فوجئت في إحدى المناسبات من زميل عربيّ من كلّيّة علميّة وصل به الحدّ إلى السخرية منّي لأنّني ألقيت بحثاً باللغة الإنجليزيّة عن اللسان العربيّ مبيّناً فيه مساهمة العرب والمسلمين في ميدان الدراسات اللغويّة. ولا أشكّ في صدق نيّة زميلي الفاضل وحرصه على لغتنا الجميلة. ولكن... لم يشعر زميلي الفاضل بأهمّيّة العمل الّذي قمت

به في محفل عالميّ، وكأنّ زميلي الفاضل كان يشعر بأنّني لو استخدمت العربيّة لفهمني جميع الحاضرين في قاعة المحاضرات. قلت في نفسي: جزاك الله يا زميلي الفاضل عن العربيّة وأبنائها خير الجزاء، لأنّني كنت أعرف حقّ اليقين أنّ من بين عشرات الحاضرين لم يكن عدد من يفهم العربيّة منهم يتجاوز عدد أصابع اليد الواحدة.. بله اليدين. زد على ذلك أنّ من بينهم من ليس لديه كبير اهتمام بالعربيّة إلاّ أنّه يرغب في معرفة شيء عنها لأغراض علميّة بحتة أو غيرها. وربّما كان منهم من ليس عنده الاهتمام أو الرغبة. ولو عنّ لي التفكير في إلقاء البحث بالعربية على هذا الجمع من الناس لكان عليّ أن أنتظر مدّة طويلة من الزمن قد تبلغ عدة سنوات حتّى يتمكّنوا من تعلّم العربية وبالأخص فهم اللغة العلميّة منها إذ تمتلىء كتب التراث العربيّ وحتّى الكتب العصريّة بالمصطلحات العلميّة والفنيّة الّتي يتعذّر فهمها حتّى على العرب الفصحاء منّا إلاّ إذا شرحت لهم. ونسي زميلي الفاضل في زحمة تفكيره العاطفيّ أقوال السلف الصالح وأفعالهم في الحثّ على إفهام الناس على قدر عقولهم ومداركهم ومخاطبتهم بألسنتهم ولغاتهم. كما نسي زميلي الفاضل أنّ السماء لا تمطر ذهباً ولا فضّة ولا كتباً ولا لغات. واقتنعت في قرارة نفسي بأنّ الوعي اللغويّ من أضعف جوانب المعرفة لدينا نحن العرب المحدثين.

إنّ اللغة - بمختلف أشكالها الصوتيّة والكتابيّة والإشاريّة - أداة للاتصال بين البشر. واستعمال العربيّة أو غيرها من اللغات إنّما هو باعتبار أنّها وسيلة من وسائل نقل المعرفة والأفكار والعلم والحضارة.

وفي دائرة كلّ لغة يستطيع مستخدمها التعبير عن أفكاره ومشاعره بكلّ صدق ودقة ووضوح. وعلى هذا فإنّ اللغات في حدّ ذاتها إنّما هي وسائل وليست غايات. ولقد سبقنا الغرب في هذا العصر إلى هذا التفكير السليم. وظلّت اللغة العربيّة وآدابها خارج الوطن العربي محصورة في نطاق ضيّق وكتب محدودة عدداً ونفعاً دبّجتها أقلام غير عربية في أكثر الأحيان. وسارع الغرب إلى نشر لغاته وآدابه ومن ثمّ حضارته بشتّى الوسائل والطرق العلميّة الحديثة ملتزماً في ذلك التجديد والتحسين كلّما تطلّب الأمر على أساس علميّ مدروس.

وإذا ما قام أبناء العربيّة اليوم بالتعريف بلغتهم وآدابهم وثقافتهم وحضارتهم العريقة لغير الناطقين باللسان العربيّ على المستوى الدوليّ فانّ هذا العمل في حقيقة الأمر يعتبر واجباً وجزءاً أساسيّاً من مسئوليّات كلّ فرد منّا. وإذا التزمنا جميعاً بهذه المسئوليّة فإنّ في هذا كسباً كبيراً للعربيّة لغة وثقافة وحضارة. ولو أخذ كلّ عربي منّا على عاتقه مسئوليّة نشر العربيّة بين مائة فرد فقط من غير العرب لشملت العربيّة كافّة بقاع هذا الكون.

وكتاب «اللغة العربيّة وآدابها: مقدّمة للناطقين باللغات الأخرى» لبنة متواضعة في هذا الاتّجاه. والهدف الأساسي من هذا الكتاب هو التعريف بالعربيّة لغة وأدباً قديماً وحديثاً للقارىء غير الملمّ بلغتنا أو الطارق الجديد لأبوابها، حيث يضع هذا الكتاب أمامه شذرات من أفكار متنوّعة وباقات من أزهار متفرّقة ليتزوّد منها قبل التعمّق في اللغة العربيّة وآدابها وثقافتها وحضارتها، أو لتجتذبه إلى هذا الميدان كوافد

أو ضيف جديد. كما يعدّ هذا الكتاب مفتاحاً للثقافة العربيّة الإسلاميّة حيث تتوفّر في نهاية الكتاب ببليوغرافيّة تشمل عدداً كبيراً من مصادر الدراسات العربيّة بلغات مختلفة وتغطّي ميادين متعدّدة يمكن للقارىء أن يرجع إليها لمزيد من المعلومات والتفاصيل من موضوعات طرقت أو لم تطرق في هذا الكتاب.

يتكوّن متن هذا الكتاب من سبعة وثلاثين فصلاً ، حاولت فيها التزام الاختصار والقِصر في الكمّ والبساطة في الكيف ما أمكن حتى لا يشعر القارىء بالملل من الطول المفزع أو كثرة المعلومات والمعالجات الأكاديمية الّتي لا تفيد غير المتخصّصين. ووزّعت الفصول بحسب الموضوعات إلى قسمين رئيسين. أحدهما يتناول الجانب اللغويّ عن العربية ، والآخر يعالج الجانب الأدبي والثقافيّ منها.

ويحتوي القسم الأوّل على أربعة عشر (١٤) فصلاً تتناول موضوعات متنوّعة متفرّقة حرصت فيها على إعطاء صورة عامّة عن وضع اللغة العربيّة في عالمنا المعاصر، وكذلك محاولة الإجابة على بعض التساؤلات الّتي وجّهت إليّ في مناسبات كثيرة.

يعالج الفصل الأوّل أصل العربيّة والعائلة اللغويّة الّتي تنتمي إليها ، مع عقد بعض المقارنات اللفظيّة بينها وبين بعض أخواتها من اللغات الساميّة. ويتحدّث الفصل الثاني باختصار عن مكانة العربيّة بين اللغات وبين اللغات العالميّة بالذات ، وكيف أنّ العربيّة أصبحت لغة عالميّة مرتين في التاريخ بفضل الحضارة العربيّة الإسلاميّة ، وهذا

ممّا لم يتحقّق لأيّ لغة أخرى. وفي الفصل الثالث «تحديث العربيّة» استعراض لبعض جوانب التطوّر اللغويّ وبخاصة اكتساب المفردات للتعبير عن مستحدثات العصر سواء في العصور الإسلاميّة الأولى أو العصر الحديث. والفصل الرابع يضفي رؤية جديدة على مكانة العربيّة في أفريقيا، وكيف أنّ العربيّة – لغة وحضارة – لها جذور عريقة في هذه القارّة – قارّة المستقبل – مع إلقاء بصيص من الضوء على الوضع اللغويّ الراهن في بعض البلدان الأفريقيّة. وقصرت الحديث في الفصول الثلاثة التالية على الدراسات اللغويّة العربيّة. فبيّنت في الفصل الخامس جهود العرب والمسلمين الأوائل في الحقل اللغويّ وبعض الدراسات الميدانيّة القديمة كصناعة المعاجم وإصلاح الكتابة العربيّة وصناعة النحو العربيّ. أمّا الفصلان السادس والسابع فينحصر الكلام فيهما على جهودهم الرائدة في ميدان الدراسات الصوتيّة ويشتمل الفصل السابع على بعض النتائج المعمليّة الّتي تدعم وتسند أقوال علماء الصوتيّات القدامى من العرب والمسلمين. ويشمل الفصل الثامن الحديث عن تأثير العربيّة في غيرها من اللغات وأسبابه. وينحصر الكلام هنا على الألفاظ المستعارة من العربية في لغات مختلفة. والفصل التاسع يتناول تأثيرات اللغات في العربيّة قديماً وحديثاً مع إلماعات سريعة إلى بعض قضايا التعريب والترجمة والنقل في العصر الحديث. ويحتوي الفصل العاشر على بعض المعلومات عن الوضع اللغويّ في البلدان العربيّة مع تلميحات إلى بعض القضايا الراهنة كقضيّة الفصحى واللهجات (أو ما يسمّى عند البعض بالعامّيّات). ويتناول الفصل الحادي عشر قضيّة الازدواجيّة اللغوية (أو الثنائيّة اللغوية كما يطلق عليها أحياناً) في الوطن العربيّ.

والفصلان التاليان – الثاني عشر والثالث عشر – يعالجان التوزيع اللهجي في المغرب العربيّ وفي منطقة الخليج كأنموذجين للاختلافات اللهجيّة في الوطن العربيّ، مع إعطاء بعض الأمثلة على الاختلافات اللفظيّة والدلاليّة في بعض اللهجات في هاتين المنطقتين. ويتناول الفصل الرابع عشر – وهو الفصل الأخير من القسم الأوّل – أصل الكتابة العربيّة وتطوّرها داخل الوطن العربيّ وخارجه. ويضمّ القسم الثاني من هذا الكتاب بعض أبواب الأدب العربيّ بمفهومه الواسع. فيستعرض الفصل الخامس عشر أهم الأدوار التاريخية للأدب العربيّ. وتتخصّص الفصول الثلاثة التالية في استعراض سريع لأدباء العصر الجاهلي وشعرائه، مع تحليل بعض النصوص الأدبيّة لهذا العصر. ويعالج الفصل التاسع عشر أدب العصر الاسلاميّ ابتداء بظهور الاسلام حتّى نهاية العصر الأمويّ. ويتناول الفصل العشرون بعض خصائص الأدب في العصر العبّاسيّ، وبخاصّة إبّان الفترة الذهبيّة. أما الفصلان الحادي والعشرون والثاني والعشرون فيقتصران على المتنبّي: حياته وأدبه وشعره. ويتناول الفصل الثالث والعشرون أدب أبي العلاء المعرّي وبشّار بن برد. والفصلان اللذان يليانه يدرسان باختصار الأدب في العصر الفضّيّ وفي عصر المماليك على التوالي. ويشمل الفصل السادس والعشرون أدب عصر النهضة. والفصل السابع والعشرون يستعرض بعض خصائص الأدب الحديث. والفصول الثلاثة التالية استعراض لأدب المرأة العربيّة. فيعالج الفصل الثامن والعشرون أدب المرأة في العصور القديمة، أمّا الفصلان التاسع والعشرون والثلاثون فهما عن أدب المرأة العربيّة المعاصر. ويتناول الفصل الحادي والثلاثون القصّة القصيرة في الأدب العربيّ، بينما يعالج الفصل الثاني

والثلاثون الأدب العربيّ الشعبيّ. أمّا الفصل الثالث والثلاثون فيقدّم لمحة خاطفة عن مكانة قصص «ألف ليلة وليلة» في التراث الشعبيّ العربيّ وفي الآداب العالميّة. وتتمّة للحديث عن أدب الفولكلور العربي يتناول الفصل الرابع والثلاثون الأمثال العربية وأهمّيّتها الثقافية والحضاريّة. وبينما يعالج الفصل الخامس والثلاثون بعض قضايا الأسلوب في الأدب العربي ويستعرض وجهات نظر الأدباء واللغويّين المحدثين في هذا الموضوع، يلقي الفصل السادس والثلاثون بعض الضوء على النقد العربيّ في القديم والحديث. ويتناول الفصل الأخير في هذا القسم الحديث باختصار عن أدب الرحلات ومكانته في الأدب العربيّ. وقد اخترت نصّاً من كتاب رحلات ابن بطّوطة يحكي فيه مشاهداته وانطباعاته عن بلاد الصين عندما زارها خلال حكم المغول. ولقد وجدت أنّ بعض ما جاء في وصف ابن بطّوطة لعالم الصين قبل أكثر من ستّة قرون لا يزال ينطبق ويصدق حتّى في عصرنا الحاضر، وبخاصة فيما يتعلق بجمالها وفنونها وفواكهها وعادات أهلها، على الرغم من التقدّم السريع والتطوّر الصناعي الكبير الّذي تمرّ به الصين في أجزائها المختلفة.

ومن الطبيعي أنّ الموضوعات الّتي طرقها هذا الكتاب لا تغطّي جميع جوانب اللغة العربيّة وآدابها كما أنّها لا تفي بحاجة القارىء النهم ولا تبلّ صداه. إلاّ أنّني أعتقد بأن هذه بداية متواضعة آمل أن تليها دراسات وأبحاث أخرى لتكمل هذا النقص الذريع والفجوة الكبيرة في المكتبة العربيّة.

وفي رأيي أنّنا إذا أردنا من غير الناطقين بالعربيّة فهم تاريخنا وحضارتنا ولغتنا وثقافتنا وتراثنا فهما صحيحاً فإنّه يتحتّم علينا أن نعمل جاهدين مخلصين في سدّ هذا الفراغ بأنفسنا وبأيدينا لا بأيدي غيرنا. ولا أشكّ في أنّ العالم الخارجيّ سيزيد اهتمامه بقضايا الوطن العربيّ وثقافته وحضارته العريقة متى ما وجد المادّة الموضوعيّة المتنوّعة والملائمة لفهمه وإدراكه.

وفي الختام، أسأل الله أن يوفّقنا ويسدّد خطانا لكلّ ما فيه خير ومصلحة لوطننا العربي ولأمتنا العربية الإسلامية. إنّه سميع مجيب. وآخر دعوانا أن الحمد للّه ربّ العالمين، وصلّى الله وسلّم على أفصح من نطق بالضاد إلى يوم الدين.

المؤلّف

لندن ١٤٠١ هـ/١٩٨١ م — محمّد حسن باكَلاّ